THE CAMBRIDGE
PRAGMATISM

Pragmatism established a philosophical presence over a century ago through the work of Charles Peirce, William James and John Dewey, and has enjoyed an unprecedented revival in recent years owing to the pioneering efforts of Richard Rorty and Hilary Putnam. The essays in this volume explore the history and themes of classic pragmatism, discuss the revival of pragmatism, and show how it engages with a range of areas of inquiry including politics, law, education, aesthetics, religion and feminism. Together they provide readers with an overview of the richness and vitality of pragmatist thinking and the influence that it continues to exert both in philosophy and in other disciplines. The volume will be of interest to students and scholars of pragmatism, American philosophy and political theory.

ALAN MALACHOWSKI is a fellow of the Centre for Applied Ethics at the University of Stellenbosch. He is author of *Richard Rorty* (2002) and *The New Pragmatism* (2010). He is the editor of *Reading Rorty* (1990), *Business Ethics: Critical Perspectives on Business and Management* (2002), *Richard Rorty* (2002) and *Pragmatism* (2004).

OTHER VOLUMES IN THE SERIES OF CAMBRIDGE COMPANIONS

ABELARD Edited by JEFFREY E. BROWER and KEVIN GUILFOY
ADORNO Edited by THOMAS HUHN
ANCIENT SCEPTICISM Edited by RICHARD BETT
ANSELM Edited by BRIAN DAVIES and BRIAN LEFTOW
AQUINAS Edited by NORMAN KRETZMANN and ELEONORE STUMP
ARABIC PHILOSOPHY Edited by PETER ADAMSON and RICHARD C. TAYLOR
HANNAH ARENDT Edited by DANA VILLA
ARISTOTLE Edited by JONATHAN BARNES
ATHEISM Edited by MICHAEL MARTIN
AUGUSTINE Edited by ELEONORE STUMP and NORMAN KRETZMANN
BACON Edited by MARKKU PELTONEN
BERKELEY Edited by KENNETH P. WINKLER
BOETHIUS Edited by JOHN MARENBON
BRENTANO Edited by DALE JACQUETTE
CARNAP Edited by MICHAEL FRIEDMAN
CONSTANT Edited by HELENA ROSENBLATT
CRITICAL THEORY Edited by FRED RUSH
DARWIN 2nd edition Edited by JONATHAN HODGE and GREGORY RADICK
SIMONE DE BEAUVOIR Edited by CLAUDIA CARD
DESCARTES Edited by JOHN COTTINGHAM
DEWEY Edited by MOLLY COCHRAN
DUNS SCOTUS Edited by THOMAS WILLIAMS
EARLY GREEK PHILOSOPHY Edited by A. A. LONG
EARLY MODERN PHILOSOPHY Edited by MICHAEL RUTHERFORD
EPICUREANISM Edited by JAMES WARREN
EXISTENTIALISM Edited by STEVEN CROWELL
FEMINISM IN PHILOSOPHY Edited by MIRANDA FRICKER and JENNIFER HORNSBY

FOUCAULT 2nd edition Edited by GARY GUTTING
FREGE Edited by MICHAEL POTTER and TOM RICKETTS
FREUD Edited by JEROME NEU
GADAMER Edited by ROBERT J. DOSTAL
GALEN Edited by R. J. HANKINSON
GALILEO Edited by PETER MACHAMER
GERMAN IDEALISM Edited by KARL AMERIKS
GREEK AND ROMAN PHILOSOPHY Edited by DAVID SEDLEY
HABERMAS Edited by STEPHEN K. WHITE
HAYEK Edited by EDWARD FESER
HEGEL Edited by FREDERICK C. BEISER
HEGEL AND NINETEENTH-CENTURY PHILOSOPHY Edited by FREDERICK C. BEISER
HEIDEGGER 2nd edition Edited by CHARLES GUIGNON
HOBBES Edited by TOM SORELL
HOBBES'S 'LEVIATHAN' Edited by PATRICIA SPRINGBORG
HUME 2nd edition Edited by DAVID FATE NORTON and JACQUELINE TAYLOR
HUSSERL Edited by BARRY SMITH and DAVID WOODRUFF SMITH
WILLIAM JAMES Edited by RUTH ANNA PUTNAM
KANT Edited by PAUL GUYER
KANT AND MODERN PHILOSOPHY Edited by PAUL GUYER
KANT'S CRITIQUE OF PURE REASON Edited by PAUL GUYER
KEYNES Edited by ROGER E. BACKHOUSE and BRADLEY W. BATEMAN
KIERKEGAARD Edited by ALASTAIR HANNAY and GORDON DANIEL MARINO
LEIBNIZ Edited by NICHOLAS JOLLEY
LEVINAS Edited by SIMON CRITCHLEY and ROBERT BERNASCONI
LOCKE Edited by VERE CHAPPELL

LOCKE'S 'ESSAY CONCERNING HUMAN UNDERSTANDING'   Edited by LEX NEWMAN
LOGICAL EMPIRICISM   Edited by ALAN RICHARDSON and THOMAS UEBEL
MAIMONIDES   Edited by KENNETH SEESKIN
MALEBRANCHE   Edited by STEVEN NADLER
MARX   Edited by TERRELL CARVER
MEDIEVAL JEWISH PHILOSOPHY   Edited by DANIEL H. FRANK and OLIVER LEAMAN
MEDIEVAL PHILOSOPHY   Edited by A. S. MCGRADE
MERLEAU-PONTY   Edited by TAYLOR CARMAN and MARK B. N. HANSEN
MILL   Edited by JOHN SKORUPSKI
MONTAIGNE   Edited by ULLRICH LANGER
NEWTON   Edited by I. BERNARD COHEN and GEORGE E. SMITH
NIETZSCHE   Edited by BERND MAGNUS and KATHLEEN HIGGINS
NOZICK'S 'ANARCHY, STATE AND UTOPIA'   Edited by RALF BADER and JOHN MEADOWCROFT
OCKHAM   Edited by PAUL VINCENT SPADE
THE 'ORIGIN OF SPECIES'   Edited by MICHAEL RUSE and ROBERT J. RICHARDS
PASCAL   Edited by NICHOLAS HAMMOND
PEIRCE   Edited by CHERYL MISAK
PHILO   Edited by ADAM KAMESAR
THE PHILOSOPHY OF BIOLOGY   Edited by DAVID L. HULL and MICHAEL RUSE
PIAGET   Edited by ULRICH MÜLLER, JEREMY I. M. CARPENDALE and LESLIE SMITH
PLATO   Edited by RICHARD KRAUT
PLATO'S 'REPUBLIC'   Edited by G. R. F. FERRARI
PLOTINUS   Edited by LLOYD P. GERSON
PRAGMATISM   Edited by ALAN MALACHOWSKI
QUINE   Edited by ROGER F. GIBSON JR.

RAWLS *Edited by* SAMUEL FREEMAN
RENAISSANCE PHILOSOPHY *Edited by* JAMES HANKINS
THOMAS REID *Edited by* TERENCE CUNEO *and* RENÉ VAN WOUDENBERG
ROUSSEAU *Edited by* PATRICK RILEY
BERTRAND RUSSELL *Edited by* NICHOLAS GRIFFIN
SARTRE *Edited by* CHRISTINA HOWELLS
SCHOPENHAUER *Edited by* CHRISTOPHER JANAWAY
THE SCOTTISH ENLIGHTENMENT *Edited by* ALEXANDER BROADIE
ADAM SMITH *Edited by* KNUD HAAKONSSEN
SOCRATES *Edited by* DONALD MORRISON
SPINOZA *Edited by* DON GARRETT
SPINOZA'S 'ETHICS' *Edited by* OLLI KOISTINEN
THE STOICS *Edited by* BRAD INWOOD
LEO STRAUSS *Edited by* STEVEN B. SMITH
TOCQUEVILLE *Edited by* CHERYL B. WELCH
WITTGENSTEIN *Edited by* HANS SLUGA *and* DAVID STERN

The Cambridge Companion to
PRAGMATISM

Edited by Alan Malachowski

CAMBRIDGE
UNIVERSITY PRESS

University Printing House, Cambridge CB2 8BS, United Kingdom

Published in the United States of America by Cambridge University Press, New York

Cambridge University Press is part of the University of Cambridge.

It furthers the University's mission by disseminating knowledge in the pursuit of education, learning and research at the highest international levels of excellence.

www.cambridge.org
Information on this title: www.cambridge.org/9780521110877

© Cambridge University Press 2013

This publication is in copyright. Subject to statutory exception and to the provisions of relevant collective licensing agreements, no reproduction of any part may take place without the written permission of Cambridge University Press.

First published 2013

Printed in the United Kingdom by CPI Group Ltd, Croydon CR0 4YY

A catalogue record for this publication is available from the British Library

Library of Congress Cataloguing in Publication data
The Cambridge companion to pragmatism / edited by Alan Malachowski.
   p. cm. – (Cambridge companions to philosophy)
ISBN 978-0-521-11087-7 (Hardback) – ISBN 978-0-521-12580-2 (Paperback)
1. Pragmatism. I. Malachowski, Alan R.
B832.C36 2012
144'.3–dc23   2012016336

ISBN 978-0-521-11087-7 Hardback
ISBN 978-0-521-12580-2 Paperback

Cambridge University Press has no responsibility for the persistence or accuracy of URLs for external or third-party internet websites referred to in this publication, and does not guarantee that any content on such websites is, or will remain, accurate or appropriate.

CONTENTS

List of contributors	page xi
Preface	xiii
Introduction: the pragmatist orientation ALAN MALACHOWSKI	1

I Classic pragmatism

1. 'The principle of Peirce' and the origins of pragmatism — 17
   CHRISTOPHER HOOKWAY

2. James's holism: the human continuum — 36
   ALAN MALACHOWSKI

3. Dewey's pragmatism: instrumentalism and meliorism — 55
   DAVID HILDEBRAND

II Pragmatism revived

4. W. V. O. Quine: pragmatism within the limits of empiricism alone — 83
   ISAAC NEVO

5. Hegel and pragmatism — 105
   RICHARD BERNSTEIN

6. Heidegger's pragmatism redux — 124
   MARK OKRENT

7   Practising *pragmatist–Wittgensteinianism*   159
    PHIL HUTCHINSON AND RUPERT READ

8   *Putnam, pragmatism and the fate of metaphysics*   189
    DAVID MACARTHUR

9   *Imagination over truth: Rorty's contribution to pragmatism*   207
    ALAN MALACHOWSKI

III Pragmatism at work

10 *Pragmatism and feminism*   231
    MARJORIE C. MILLER

11 *Education and the pragmatic temperament*   249
    CAROL NICHOLSON

12 *Dewey's pragmatic aesthetics: the contours of experience*   272
    GARRY L. HAGBERG

13 *Pragmatism and religion*   300
    ANTON A. VAN NIEKERK

14 *Radical pragmatism*   324
    MICHAEL SULLIVAN AND DANIEL J. SOLOVE

    Bibliography   345
    Index   367

CONTRIBUTORS

RICHARD BERNSTEIN is Vera List Professor of Philosophy at the New School of Social Research. His most recent book is *The Pragmatic Turn* (2010).

GARRY L. HAGBERG is James H. Ottaway Professor of Aesthetics, Philosophy, Bard College. He recently published *Describing Ourselves: Wittgenstein and Autobiographical Consciousness* (2008).

DAVID HILDEBRAND is Associate Professor of Philosophy, University of Colorado, Denver. He is the author of *Beyond Realism and Antirealism: John Dewey and the Neopragmatists* (2003).

CHRISTOPHER HOOKWAY is Professor of Philosophy, University of Sheffield. His books include *Peirce* (1992) and he contributed to *The Cambridge Companion to Peirce* (Cambridge, 2004).

PHIL HUTCHINSON is Faculty Member, Department of Interdisciplinary Studies, Manchester Metropolitan University. He is the author of *Shame and Philosophy: An Investigation in the Philosophy of Emotions and Ethics* (2008).

DAVID MACARTHUR is Senior Lecturer in the Department of Philosophy, University of Sydney. He is co-editor of *Naturalism and Normativity* (2010).

ALAN MALACHOWSKI is Fellow of the Centre for Applied Ethics, University of Stellenbosch. His books include *Richard Rorty* (2002) and *The New Pragmatism* (2010).

MARJORIE C. MILLER is Professor of Philosophy, Purchase College, SUNY. She is co-editor of *Pragmatism and Feminism* (1996).

ISAAC NEVO is Associate Professor in the Department of Philosophy, Ben-Gurion University. His published articles include 'Linguistic Epiphenominalism: Davidson and Chomsky on the Status of Public Languages' (*Journal of the History of Philosophy*).

CAROL NICHOLSON is Professor of Philosophy, Rider University. Her publications include 'Postmodernism, Feminism, and Education: The Need for Solidarity' (*Educational Theory*).

MARK OKRENT is Professor of Philosophy, Bates College. He is the author of *Heidegger's Pragmatism: Understanding, Being, and the Critique of Metaphysics* (1991).

RUPERT READ is Reader in the Department of Philosophy, University of East Anglia. He is co-editor (with Alice Crary) of *The New Wittgenstein* (2000) and, with Matthew A. Lavery, *Beyond the Tractatus Wars: The New Wittgenstein Debate* (2011).

DANIEL J. SOLOVE is John Marshall Harlan Research Professor of Law, George Washington Law School. He has recently published *Nothing to Hide: The False Tradeoff between Privacy and Security* (2011).

MICHAEL SULLIVAN is Associate Professor, Department of Philosophy, Emory University. He is the author of *Legal Pragmatism: Community, Rights, and Democracy* (2007).

ANTON A. VAN NIEKERK is Professor of Philosophy and Chair of the Philosophy Department, Stellenbosch University. His published articles include 'Contingency and Universality in the Habermas–Rorty Debate' (*Acta Academica Supplementum*).

PREFACE

The publication of this collection of essays is timely. Since its inception, pragmatism has always had a noteworthy philosophical presence, but its revival in recent years has greatly increased both its historical interest and its contemporary worth. In the latter case, although pragmatism still faces stern opposition, it has once more become, to use William James's famous phrase, 'a live option'. But with timeliness comes editorial responsibility.

Pragmatism has a rich history that inspires different, and even opposing, developments and interpretations of its legacy, along with correspondingly different assessments of its prospects. Some pragmatists want to align themselves with the empiricist tradition as they see it feeding into the natural sciences. In their eyes the triangle of founding figures – Charles Sanders Peirce, William James and John Dewey – has Peirce presiding at the apex. Others wish to divorce themselves from this approach, though usually on amicable terms. Their triangular image is upside down by comparison, with Peirce at the bottom and James and Dewey at level-pegging, but firmly on top. Some who prefer this ranking also want to rock the motif a bit by elevating either James or Dewey. Add the more radical inclination, encouraged by Richard Rorty, to push pragmatism to virtually autonomous limits at a point of perceived innovation, and clearly there is much scope for variation in editorial policy.

Although the strategy adopted here is outlined in the introduction, the main aim behind it is probably worth stating now. This is to provide a relatively neutral overview of pragmatism in historical terms – taking the reader from its inception through to its recent revival while, at the same time, introducing its main ideas. 'Neutral' means without taking a stand on issues concerning the respective merits of different forms of pragmatism. This, it must be added, is editorial neutrality. The contributors are not strictly bound by it, and some have taken such a stand.

When first looking over my proposed table of contents, I had misgivings as to whether it would compromise even this kind of distanced editorial neutrality. For on the face of it, only the first three chapters, less than a third of the book, would give classic pragmatism its due. The dilemma, if it was one, could not easily be resolved. There were two practical obstacles. First, allocating more space to the founding figures would inevitably encroach on the territory covered by the *Cambridge Companions* already devoted to them. I was prepared to do that. But the second obstacle gave me pause. Since its revival, the prospects for pragmatism are very different from what they were, say, thirty years ago. This remains true even when the robustness that pragmatism manifested during its fallow period is properly acknowledged (the significance of this qualification will become clear in the introduction). Such changes in circumstances need to be catered for. Readers should be able to appreciate how pragmatism has changed and what, as a result, it has, and might, become.

Part II was therefore designed to deal with the first requirement and part III with the second. This apparently left no extra space to address my initial misgivings. However, as the project forged ahead, the dilemma was resolved in ways that I should probably have anticipated.

When pragmatism was described 'at work' in part III by the authors of the chapters on feminism, education, aesthetics, religion and law, my concerns about 'lack of balance' proved to be unfounded. In those chapters, resources from different forms of pragmatism are called upon as befits the tasks in hand. A happy pragmatic outcome. The revivalists are never ignored, but their influence is not overbearing. In this sense the reader is, after all, given a picture of pragmatism in the round.

A great many philosophers have worked hard and creatively over many years to preserve the historical integrity of pragmatist studies, develop pragmatist thought and put pragmatist ideas into practice. Though the vast majority go unrecognized here through limitations of space, I would like to dedicate this volume to their endeavours.

Interested readers should be able to track most of them down through the references, bibliography and net resources.

I am grateful to Richard Bernstein for allowing us to use his article 'Hegel and Pragmatism' for which he has copyright. This was previously published in his collection of essays entitled *The Pragmatic Turn* (Polity, 2010). I would also like to thank all the contributors for their friendly cooperation and the thoughtful work they have put into their essays. I hope readers learn as much as I did from their diverse approaches to pragmatism. I should thank Hilary Gaskin and Anna Lowe of Cambridge University Press for their courtesy, patience and professionalism in guiding this project through to completion. On a more personal note, Glen von Malachowski, my brother, has been a bastion of support over the years. His family home has provided a philosophically inspiring, safe haven on many occasions.

Finally I must thank my own family, Lesley, Jannie and Sophie, for their encouragement and love at all times. My debt to them continues to mount. I hope I will one day figure out how to repay them.

ALAN MALACHOWSKI

Introduction: the pragmatist orientation

When in effect launching pragmatism in the public realm, William James claimed that it did not involve 'particular results, but only an attitude of orientation' – this, he said, 'is what the pragmatist method means'. James further claimed that the method was 'primarily' one 'of settling metaphysical disputes that otherwise might be interminable'.[1]

The orientation he referred to leads 'away from first things, principles, "categories", supposed necessities' and 'towards last things, fruits, consequences, facts'.[2] In another take, James informed readers that pragmatists turn their 'back resolutely and once for all upon a lot of inveterate habits dear to professional philosophers'. These include 'abstraction and insufficiency, verbal solutions, bad *a priori* reasons, fixed principles, closed systems and pretended absolutes and origins'. For the inclination of pragmatists is, instead, he urged, 'towards concreteness and adequacy, facts, actions and power', leading to 'the open air and possibilities of nature, as against dogma, artificiality, and the pretence of finality in truth'.[3] Now, more than a century later, James's bold characterizations still ring true. Despite the variations that have evolved during that period, they capture much of what is so attractive, interesting and intellectually vibrant about pragmatism today.

The term 'pragmatism' was baptised on 26 August 1898 when James addressed the Philosophical Union of the University of California at Berkeley. His talk was aptly entitled 'Philosophical Conceptions and Practical Results'. In it, James inaugurated the first popular tale of pragmatism's origins by attributing his own renewed sense of philosophical direction to the guidance he had received some twenty years earlier from his friend Charles Sanders Peirce and his 'principle of practicalism – or pragmatism' in particular. Peirce had expressed this principle in the following terms:

> Consider what effects, which might conceivably have practical bearings, you conceive the object of your conception to have. Then your conception of these effects is the whole of your conception of the object.[4]

James's narrative lures us towards Peirce's famous paper 'How to Make our Ideas Clear' (1878) in which this formulation was hatched. But it also harks back to discussions that James and Peirce had with members of an informal group calling itself, 'half-ironically, half-defiantly', the Metaphysical Club, which met in Cambridge in the early 1870s.[5] The work of one of the thinkers talked about there, the Scottish philosopher Alexander Bain, was the inspiration for Peirce's pragmatic conception of beliefs as habits of action. Further development of this particular storyline would need to uncover affinities between pragmatism and some of America's earlier philosophers as well as its ambivalent relationship to idealism and hence to thinkers further afield. This would involve some serious historical investigation.

A comprehensive, rich and authoritative history of pragmatism has yet to be written.[6] But any adequate account must acknowledge, as we have just begun to, that it has been consituted by what Richard Bernstein calls 'contested narratives'.[7] Though he is talking specifically about logical positivism, Gustav Bergmann captures the general characteristics that justify thinking of pragmatism as a philosophical movement in spite of this:

> A philosophical movement is a group of philosophers, active over at least one or two generations, who more or less share a style, or an intellectual origin, and who have learned more from each other than they have from others, though they may, and often do, quite vigorously disagree among themselves.[8]

On the last feature, encapsulated by the Bernstein notion of contested narratives, Robert Westbrook's recent description, though over dramatic, is to the point:

> Pragmatism is best conceived less as a well defined, tightly knit school of thought than as a loose, contentious family of thinkers who have always squabbled, and have sometimes been moved to disown one another.[9]

For even the trio of founding figures, Peirce, James and Dewey, who are discussed individually here in part 1, did not generally conceive

Introduction

or speak of pragmatism in unison. Indeed, both Peirce and Dewey were wary of the very name 'pragmatism'. Provoked by James's liberal interpretation and what he perceived as 'merciless abuse' in literary journals, Peirce famously went so far as to replace it with the deliberately, and successfully, off-putting term 'pragmaticism'. Meanwhile, Dewey often preferred to operate under the banner of 'instrumentalism' and variants thereof. At times, even James himself seemed on the verge of ditching 'pragmatism' for either 'humanism' or 'radical empiricism'. However, among the narratives that Bernstein alludes to, one, especially, has been dominant until recently. This holds that regardless of its internal differences, pragmatism was quickly, and deservedly, relegated to the sidelines by the emergence of analytic philosophy.

Pragmatism was supposedly unable to avoid being pushed aside in this way because it failed to find satsfactory answers to the fierce criticisms levelled by some of its early critics, most notably, Bertrand Russell and G. E. Moore. It is certainly true that in confronting such criticisms, pragmatism lost ground. For James and Dewey unwittingly conceded the terms of debate, thereby failing to develop their own pragmatist outlook at the very moment when analytic philosophy was creating an enticing alternative agenda. But, this latter point is supplanted in the dominant narrative by the more damaging view that when the analytic agenda started to catch on, pragmatism was left stranded simply because its intellectual inferiority had been amply demonstrated. A less plausible variant occasionally finds a receptive audience. This dismisses the effect of analytic philosophy's early success and puts a later date on pragmatism's decline. Dewey's death in 1952 is usually the pivotal point here. But we can ignore this narrow version. It has all the defects, and none of the explanatory advantages, of its more comprehensive rival.

On that broader understanding, pragmatism fizzled out after burning briefly with some bright promise. Eclipsed by analytic philosophy, it became a historical curiosity, residing as a dim relic in the museum of ideas, and showing little sign of vitality even when gestured towards by such commanding figures as Rudolf Carnap and W. V. O. Quine.[10]

If that was the whole story, then the main motivation for this collection of essays would have to be put down to historical curiosity. However, there is more to it. In the first place, the dominant narrative has lost its grip. It served well enough in the short term, if only as a surreptitious vehicle of academic politics, smoothing the way for its own ascendency even as it celebrated and rationalized the global, institutional success of analytic philosophy. But it was never going to stand up to serious scrutiny. The story carries *some* conviction in partly explaining why pragmatism largely dropped off the academy's official reading lists and out of its sanctioned research projects for a lengthy period. Nevertheless, inadequacy on other matters of detail only compounds its larger predictive failure. For pragmatism is back and is now perhaps more visible and more active than ever. The circumstances in which this has come about are unusual, perhaps unique.

The dominant narrative fails under close examination in two areas. First, its claim that pragmatism was manifestly unable to answer the objections of its early analytic critics is too swift and dogmatic. When these criticisms and the replies to them are investigated, it is clear that the circumstances often involved opposing sides talking past one another rather than one side defeating the other by sheer force of argument on neutral territory.[11] Furthermore, when the development of analytic philosophy itself is examined more carefully, it also becomes clear that rather than remaining dormant, or being discarded, in the face of that development, pragmatist ideas exerted a good deal of influence. That this may not have been obvious is due to the fact that much that pragmatism had to offer was silently and smoothly absorbed rather than ignored or refuted. Talisse and Aiken, who deplore the eclipse narrative, are emphatic on this point. They claim that twentieth-century philosophers constantly engaged the views of pragmatist opponents and that explicit discussion of Dewey's ideas, for example, only seemed scarce because those ideas had already been inextricably woven into much of the prevailing discourse.[12] In a separate lively and insightful discussion of pragmatism's fate during the cold war, Talisse makes a forceful case for rejecting the dominant narrative completely:

If we examine the work of the most influential figures in mainstream philosophy from the past sixty years – Ludwig Wittgenstein, Nelson Goodman, C. I. Lewis, Ernest Nagel, W. V. O. Quine, Donald Davidson, Wilfred Sellars, Hilary Putnam, John Rawls, John Searle, Daniel Dennett, Crispin Wright, Michael Dummett, David Wiggins, Jurgen Habermas, and Robert Nozick – we find that they either explicitly acknowledge a distinctively pragmatist inheritance or take themselves to be responding critically to identifiably pragmatist arguments. Judged by the centrality of distinctively pragmatist theses concerning meaning, truth, knowledge, and action to ongoing debates in philosophy, pragmatism is easily among the most successful philosophical trends of the past two centuries. It seems, then, that the eclipse narrative is demonstrably false; pragmatism was alive and well throughout the Cold War, and continues to be a major force on the philosophical scene.[13]

Placed alongside the previous considerations, such remarks appear to provide ample support for a myth-destroying account, one of greater complexity and historical verisimilitude, in which pragmatism's fate is characterized in more favourable terms. But events that the dominant narrative was unable to foresee have led to a situation in which this is just one of a host of intriguing possibilities. For two famous American thinkers, who won their analytic spurs early on in their careers, shook the kaleidoscope of received history to separate out important features of the pragmatist orientation that offer, or so they argued, a fresh sense of direction to philosophy in general. The thinkers in question, Hilary Putnam and Richard Rorty, are discussed in separate chapters in part II. Their approach differs. Putnam is concerned to highlight the value of certain classic pragmatist ideas, as set out in the writings of the founding figures, by both digging beneath the kind of hasty, hostile rhetoric that obscured them and explaining how they can be used to tackle contemporary problems. His contribution to pragmatism can be summed up as follows:

1. He has returned to the texts of classic pragmatism to show, in detail, how they have been misread, especially by the early critics.
2. He has helped to show how some of the problematic views of the classic pragmatists, can be modified so that they are relevant now and/or can hold their own against or improve upon more recent alternatives.
3. He has developed a form of holism that derives from James, but embraces what he finds convincing in the relevant writings of later thinkers such as W. V. O. Quine.
4. Relying mainly on Dewey's work, he has explored ways in which pragmatism can help resolve current difficulties in

ethics, education and politics. In doing this, he has helped set back on track the ambitious pragmatist agenda for social improvement that was stalled by the early criticisms.

In his chapter on Putnam, David Macarthur acknowledges the debt Putnam owes to classic pragmatism even though Putnam has reservations about its views on truth and verification. Then Macarthur develops a related theme that, despite its importance, tends to be ignored. This involves Putnam's 'ambivalence towards metaphysics' (p. 189). In tackling this theme, Macarthur shows that Putnam's position – 'somewhere between James and Dewey' (p. 192) – is more nuanced than prevalent readings allow.

By continually touching base with classic pragmatist texts and ensuring that those texts are properly interpreted, Putnam is more conservative than Rorty. For Rorty is less interested in classic pragmatism's original or inherent value than the possibilities of its inspirational force and utility once it has been modernized on his terms. The modernization he has in mind involves:

1 divesting pragmatism of its dependence on empiricism, a dependence that he regards as having been ruptured in any case by the work of Wittgenstein, Wilfrid Sellars, W. V. O. Quine and Donald Davidson;
2 relinquishing what he sees as an unfortunate tendency towards science worship, one that looks to scientific method as a model for all modes of inquiry.

When updated in this way, Rorty believes that pragmatism will be well placed to take advantage of the innovations hatched by post-linguistic turn thinkers without having to heed the aims and ideology of the analytic tradition that many of those thinkers are taken to represent.

By drawing greater attention to pragmatism as an independent source of ideas and themes, Putnam and Rorty interrupted such progress as it had been making by stealth within mainstream philosophy. Vigorous responses to their attempts to bring pragmatism out into the open created the complex situation in which it now finds itself, one that has generated a multitude of opportunities for further competing narratives.

Some philosophers who have been encouraged to take a second, or even just a first, look at pragmatism, are still convinced that the dominant narrative was correct in its main substantive claim: pragmatist views have little merit because they are vulnerable to obvious objections. These philosophers believe the narrative deserves to be reinstated on those terms and that for non-pragmatist philosophers, it should be business as usual. Others are unimpressed by, or hostile to, Rorty's interpretations and his reformist ambitions. Pushing a conservatism that exceeds Putnam's own, they wish to resurrect a form of classic pragmatism. Of these, different advocates favour different points of emphasis, ranging from a focus on one or other founding figure or theme to a combination thereof (though considerably higher estimations of both Peirce and science are common themes).

In general, the glare of publicity that Putnam and Rorty attracted to pragmatism had a double effect with regard to conservatism about its prospects. Some new conservatives were created: those who, when their attention was drawn to it, realized that classic pragmatism had something to offer them. In addition, especially in Rorty's case, the extra publicity stiffened the resolve of many who already had sympathy with classic pragmatism. They felt that its integrity now needed to be defended, if only on grounds of historical accuracy.

Despite the evident backlash, Rorty also acquired enthusiastic supporters who began to spin tales about what can best be called the New Pragmatism.[14] In these, empiricism and scientism are indeed likely to be shed like stale skin so that a fresh orientation, better adapted to contemporary circumstances, emerges. But even here, things are complicated. Rorty's stripped down conception of pragmatism has solid supporters, though probably more from outside the philosophical establishment than within. There are also those within the fold who recognize the force of many of Rorty's suggestions, but want to hitch them up to constraints that will engender a more straightforward and robust form of objectivity than his notorious 'conversational', 'peer group pressure' and 'solidarity' models seem to allow for. They are convinced that such models cannot cater for an obvious social need for us to get things right about the world.[15] Off to one side, but still important and influential, there is Robert Brandom who appears to have been immaculately retracing Rorty's footsteps in order to figure out how pragmatism and analytic philosophy can be reconciled.[16] Another thinker having impact from the wings is Huw Price. In a series of imaginative, insightful and good-humoured papers that ingeniously weave pragmatist and analytic themes together, he has added detail and subtlety to the anti-representationalism of Dewey and Rorty.[17] David Macarthur, author of the Putnam chapter in this volume, as described earlier, is one of his collaborators.

In the middle of these large-scale narrative projects, some fruitful micro-historical research has also been undertaken, provoked and stimulated, no doubt, by pragmatism's greater visibility and vitality. A quick example of this is Richard Bernstein's subtle adjustment to the origins of pragmatism story. This is one in which he moves the Peircian starting point back to a series of papers published in 1868–9,[18] thereby displacing the standard account, as introduced above, that homes in on the later, more widely known, 'The Fixation of Belief' and 'How to Make our Ideas Clear'.

How can a project such as this *Companion* cater for the historical complexities we have described? One way to simplify things would be to set aside matters of historical origins and concentrate on the views of thinkers who have uncontroversially sailed under a pragmatist flag. But this would be a strange way to tackle a philosophical approach that often challenges the very distinction between historical context and intellectual content and favours trying on ideas for size: a form of fallible experimentation that it should be happy to apply, as it is surely obliged, to its own identity and origins. There is, moreover, little point in going to the other extreme of tracking down and assessing the accuracy of every historical wrinkle in the various faces that pragmatism has presented so far. The results would be overwhelming. To steer a more sensible course, this collection sets out to achieve the following.

First, it attempts to give the reader a historically sensitive overview of classic pragmatism by discussing the contributions of Peirce, James and Dewey. This is the motivation for part I. There is no agenda, hidden or otherwise, that seeks to elevate or denigrate these contributions in comparison to either other forms of philosophy or even the kinds of pragmatism that developed later. The reader should therefore get an unbiased feel for the ways in which these founding figures approach philosophy and hence for what they consider to be important and how they want to go about things, philosophically speaking. Space does not allow for detailed attention to other major figures such as F. C. S. Schiller, George Herbert Mead and Clarence Irving Lewis, who helped launch pragmatism and made contributions to its core ideas. However, the three opening chapters should provide the kind of grounding in basic pragmatist thought that will make their work more accessible and intriguing. This grounding should also prepare readers to tackle their own version of the dilemma of choice identified by Nicholas Rescher: 'It is clearer than ever that pragmatism as a whole comprises a collection of rather different doctrines and that if one is to be a pragmatist one must choose among them'.[19]

Part II deals with pragmatism's recent revival, one that cannot be denied even though the dominant narrative is badly mistaken. Questions of 'how?' and 'why?' are addressed indirectly: by invoking a complexity of contextual detail comensurate with that of pragmatism's origins and the contested tales of its ongoing identity.

First-off, chapter 4, deals with an important transitional figure, W. V. O. Quine, who, despite distancing himself from it, made substantial contributions to pragmatism of his own, contributions that, as Isaac Nevo points out, 'no student of that school can safely ignore' (p. 83). In chapters 5 to 7, the possible connections between pragmatism and thinkers of an ostensibly different orientation are examined, the key examples being Hegel, Heidegger and Wittgenstein. It is an important feature of how pragmatism has spread its wings during, and since, its revival that such connections have been explored (though, some critics would say exploited). Again, limitations of space prevent discussion of other figures, the most notable, perhaps, being Nietzsche.[20]

In chapter 5, Richard Bernstein provides a synoptic view of three periods in American philosophical history when Hegel's ideas have come to the fore. In doing so, he shows how these are related to pragmatism. Bernstein's wide-ranging discussion deals with the attitude of the classic pragmatists towards Hegel before moving on to consider the views of Wilfrid Sellars, Robert Brandom and John McDowell, emphasizing pragmatist themes in each case. Mark Okrent's *Heidegger's Pragmatism: Understanding, Being and the Critique of Metaphysics*[21] is a seminal text for those who wish to understand how, and why, pragmatism has recently begun to spread its wings. In that book, Okrent argued that the early Heidegger exhibited a kinship with the classic pragmatists in the sense that he, too, was a pragmatic verificationist regarding linguistic meaning and conceptual content. In chapter 6 Okrent discusses what he sees as a deeper and more important affinity that accounts for this. It concerns 'what it is for an agent to be intentionally engaged with a world' (p. 126).

Apart from scattered remarks on James, Wittgenstein did not engage with classic pragmatists. Nevertheless, he was coopted as a chief ally of pragmatism by Richard Rorty. As early as 'Pragmatism, Categories and Language' (1961), Rorty tried to show that 'the closer one brings pragmatism to the writings of the later Wiggenstein and those influenced by him, the more light they shed on each other'.[22] And, in *Philosophy and the Mirror of Nature*,[23] Wittgenstein is one of the three heroes (the others being Heidegger and Dewey) who show us how to shake off the dead hand of the epistemological tradition that culminated in the analytic approach to philosophy. Furthermore, Hilary Putnam takes the possibility of a significant connection between pragmatism and Wittgenstein seriously enough to devote a chapter of his *Pragmatism*[24] to the very issue as to whether Wittgenstein was a pragmatist.

In chapter 7, Phil Hutchinson and Rupert Read survey the usual motivation for exploring this issue, but then they push the associated debates into new territory. They do this by demonstrating their own solution to a problem precipitated by these. The problem is that of finding a way to write 'authentically' on what they call 'the Wittgenstein-pragmatism nexus'. And the solution is to 'write authentically *as* a Pragmatist-Wittgensteinian'.[25] The authors try to show how this pans out in the field of environmentalism. Here, their foil is the claim by Williams and Parkman that '[e]ffective solutions to environmental problems must be framed in very pragmatic ways – in terms of consequences and actions' (p. 173).

The chapters just discussed present a minor organizational puzzle. In trying to forge connections with the philosophers concerned, pragmatist thinkers are obliged to dip into the past. For this reason the corresponding chapters have been given a conventional historical ordering. However, much of their significance stems from the impetus given to historical explorations by the two contemporary philosophers most responsible for pragmatism's revival: Richard Rorty and Hilary Putnam.[26] In this sense, these philosophers merit chronological priority. However, the present ordering has been chosen in the interests of neutrality. It enables readers to get a feel

Introduction

for possible connections and historical interpretations *before* they encounter those who mainly inspired the search for them. Of course, this will work best for those who have little knowledge of recent developments in pragmatist studies. For others who may feel uncomfortable with this somewhat topsy-turvy approach, it will do no harm to read part II in reverse order after tackling Quine in chapter 4.

Pragmatism's key feature is the primacy it gives to practice. The final selection of articles, entitled 'Pragmatism at work', is devoted to showing how this feature comes into play in five broad areas of inquiry: feminism, education, aesthetics, religion and law. Indeed, the claim that Majorie Miller makes in her discussion of the first of these, 'Feminism and Pragmatism' (chapter 10), can be generalized to cover all five areas and more besides: 'One of the features of pragmatism which makes it so useful for feminist analysis is the intimate relation between theory and practice' (p. 235). In her contribution on education, Carol Nicholson argues that pragmatism is best thought of as an 'international, multicultural and interdisciplinary movement of thought and social practice which has had a profound cultural impact' (p. 250). However, she points out that 'in spite of a brief period in the early twentieth century during which Dewey's ideas were popular', it has had minimal success 'in making lasting changes in education' (p. 250). To remedy this, she suggests a shift away from the narrow interpretation of 'pragmatism as a movement within philosophy departments of the United States' to the widespread encouragement of the teaching of pragmatism as 'flexible habit of mind'. This form of teaching can inculcate what she calls 'the pragmatic temperament', one that is 'open to uncertainty, change and different point of view' (p. 250).

In his discussion of pragmatist approaches to aesthetics, Garry Hagberg introduces a subtle twist to the theme of 'practice' by exploring what he claims Dewey regards as 'the central aim of aesthetic theory': 'the full elucidation of what the product does with and in experience' (p. 272). This elucidation has to cover 'the human conditions and contexts from which' a work of art 'emerged as well as "the human consequences it engenders in actual life-experience"' (p. 272). Such an approach has the interesting twofold effect of discouraging the crass reification of the physical embodiment of a work of art while, at the same time, revealing 'truths of practice behind the cloak of theory' (p. 272). In chapter 13, Anton van Niekerk provides an informative discussion of the pragmatist approach to religion. He takes us from James's examination of the nature and utility of religious belief to Dewey's exploration of the connections between religion, experience and human action, rounding off with a critical assessment of Rorty's surprising late adoption of a reconciliatory attitude towards religious beliefs and social practices. In chapter 14, Michael Sullivan and Daniel J. Solove argue that thin and self-consciously banal pragmatist accounts of law, as advocated by Richard Posner and endorsed by Richard Rorty, are normatively inadequate. They should give way to a much thicker legal pragmatism that 'has political valence, substantive values and far from being banal, is radical at its core' (p. 325).

These examples of pragmatism at work show how the terminological, doctrinal and methodological differences referred to at the outset are often washed away in practice. Even though classic pragmatism and its offshoots remain in vigorous competition with new pragmatism and its friends and acquaintances, while the analytic appropriation of pragmatism threatens both groups on the flanks, the task of actually applying pragmatist thought brings out the practical imperative to use whatever will work. Thus we find historical and doctrinal borders between the old and the new being perpetually crossed or even broken down.

Pragmatism is rapidly increasing its geographical reach with interest in it growing in many countries including Brazil, Argentina, India, China, Hungary and Poland. All this makes it harder to predict the exact forms in which pragmatism will survive in the years to come, but more likely that it will survive and, indeed, flourish.

NOTES

1 James, 1998, pp. 32 and 28.
2 James, 1998, p. 32.
3 James, 1998, p. 31.
4 Peirce, 1972, p. 281. Peirce is quoting from his earlier article in *Popular Science Monthly* 12, January 1878.
5 See Peirce, 1955, p. 269.
6 For an attempt, see Malachowski (2014a).
7 Bernstein, 1955a.

8 Bergmann, 1992, p. 63.
9 Westbrook, 2010, p. 185.
10 Carnap's contribution to pragmatism has yet to be properly evaluated. For a promising start, see Richardson, 2007. Quine's contribution has also been neglected, though not to the same extent. Isaac Nevo makes amends in this volume (ch. 4).
11 Even Russell had some intimation of this. Witness his remarks at the end of his critical review of Dewey's *Logic: The Theory of Inquiry*: 'Ultimately, the controversy between those who base logic upon "truth" and those who base it upon "inquiry" arises from a question of values, and cannot be argued without, at some point, begging the question': Russell, 2004, p. 62. For more details on reinterpretations of the early criticisms of pragmatism, see Malachowski, 2004b. And, for a recent assessment that generally ignores counter evidence and hence tends to perpetuate the myth, see Misak, 2010b.
12 Talisse and Aiken, 2008.
13 Talisse, 2010, p. 257.
14 For arguments in favour of now using 'New Pragmatism' instead of the more common 'neo-pragmatism', see Malachowski, 2010.
15 See, for example, Stout, 2009.
16 See Brandom, 2010.
17 Price, 2011.
18 Bernstein, 2010b.
19 Rescher, 2000, p. 41. Rescher rightly continues: 'But of course it constitutes no valid objection to any particular version of pragmatism that there exist alternatives to it!'
20 Despite Rorty's advocacy, Nietzsche's affinity with pragmatism has probably been exaggerated. See Malachowski, 2014b.
21 Okrent, 1988.
22 Rorty, 1961.
23 Rorty, 1980.
24 Putnam, 1995.
25 The authors qualify this immediately with 'at least seeking to do so, and to understand what it really means to do so'.
26 To be more precise: Rorty was more responsible for reaching out to philosophers outside the received comfort zone, whereas Putnam helped create a richer conception of philosophy that motivated such attempts.

PART I

Classic pragmatism

1 'The principle of Peirce' and the origins of pragmatism

I PEIRCE: THE ORIGINATOR OF PRAGMATISM

Charles Sanders Peirce (1839–1914) has been recognized as the originator of pragmatism by many of his fellow pragmatists, most notably by William James (1842–1910) and John Dewey (1859–1952). When James announced that he was a pragmatist in 1898, he identified the doctrine with 'the principle of Peirce' to be found in the latter's paper 'How to Make our Ideas Clear' (1878).[1] Indeed, he explained the content of pragmatism by writing that 'Mr Peirce, after pointing out that our beliefs are really habits of action, said that, to develop a thought's meaning, we need only determine what conduct it is fitted to produce: that conduct is, for us, its sole significance' (James, 1975b, p. 28). He described Peirce as holding that 'the tangible fact at the root of all our thought-distinctions, however subtle, is that there is no one of them so fine as to consist in anything but a possible difference of practice' (James, 1975b, p. 29). James and Peirce had been fellow members of a 'Metaphysical Club' in Harvard in 1872 at which many of the ideas characteristic of pragmatism were argued out by a group of young philosophers and lawyers including the Darwinian philosopher Chauncey Wright and Oliver Wendell Holmes.[2]

In his article on 'The Development of American Pragmatism' (1925), Dewey acknowledged that Peirce was the originator of pragmatism and he was happy to endorse Peirce's claim that 'the rational purport of a word or any other expression lies exclusively in its conceivable bearing upon the conduct of life' (LW2: 3). However, this agreement on the nature of pragmatism should not prevent our recognizing that the three philosophers brought different backgrounds to pragmatism and that this led to their versions of the doctrine having very different characters. Peirce was a talented mathematician whose aim was to bring 'mathematical exactitude' to philosophy and who was happy to describe himself as a logician and to describe pragmatism as a logical rule, part of the method of science. He thought that neither James nor Dewey had much aptitude for logic, as he understood it.[3] Peirce was influenced by Kant and had a taste for systems of categories and for philosophical architectonic. James dedicated his lectures on pragmatism to John Stuart Mill and identified pragmatism with a readiness to turn away from categories and systems and he was interested in applying pragmatism to religion. And Dewey's work is often described as having a Hegelian character and links pragmatism to social and political concerns.

When subsequent pragmatists acknowledge their debts to Peirce, they usually refer to the two canonical papers, published in 1877 and 1878, 'The Fixation of Belief' and 'How to Make our Ideas Clear'. They were the first two of a series of six papers published in the *Popular Science Monthly* under the title *Illustrations of the Logic of Science* (W3: 242–338, EP1: 109–99). Each paper contributed one of the two ideas that, together, were characteristic marks of pragmatism. 'The Fixation of Belief' defended a strongly fallibilist and anti-Cartesian approach to epistemology and the logic of science. It defended the 'method of science' as the only defensible method for the conduct of inquiry, emphasizing the need to test our theories and beliefs by reference to experience, and taking a realist standpoint. 'How to Make our Ideas Clear' contributed a rule for clarifying hypotheses and concepts, James's 'principle of Peirce' or, in Peirce's phrase, the pragmatist maxim. One use of such a rule is to identify words and sentences which are empty and of no cognitive value, apparent concepts which can be obstacles to philosophical and scientific progress. In this usage, the maxim is a tool which reveals that 'almost every proposition of ontological metaphysics is either meaningless gibberish ... or else is downright absurd' (CP4: 423, EP2: 338). As well as criticizing a priorism in metaphysics, the maxim has a positive role. It can be used to clarify important and philosophically challenging concepts such as *truth*, *reality* and *probability*.

Peirce himself restricted the scope of pragmatism to this rule or maxim for clarifying concepts, and this is reflected in James's usage much of the time and Dewey's in the passages cited above. The fallibilist epistemology provides part of the intellectual background to the maxim and is thus inseparable from pragmatism more strictly defined. Others use the word pragmatism more broadly to refer to some broader frameworks of ideas which incorporate something like the pragmatist rule for clarifying ideas into a broader philosophical framework of ideas.

As James acknowledged in his 1898 lecture celebrating pragmatism, Peirce's 1878 paper was largely ignored after it was published. James wrote that it 'lay entirely unnoticed by anyone for twenty years until [James] ... brought it forward again and made a special application of it to religion' (James, 1975b, p. 29). In 1898, 'the times seemed ripe for its reception'. Unsurprisingly, this stirred Peirce to action. By 1905, he complained at the misuse of the word 'pragmatism', claiming that 'it gets abused in the merciless way that words have to expect when they fall into literary clutches' (CP5: 414, EP2: 334). He then proposed to use the word 'pragmaticism' to serve the important role of 'expressing the original definition', while being 'ugly enough to be safe from kidnappers' (CP5: 414, EP2: 335). In 1903 he delivered a series of lectures on pragmatism at Harvard; in 1905–6 he published three papers on his pragmaticism in *The Monist* which furthered his ambition to prove the correctness of his version of doctrine; and his late manuscripts contain a mass of fascinating material on pragmatism and our reasons for accepting it.

Although these writings have had only a limited impact, they are important for at least three reasons. First, Peirce attempted to arrive at a more careful and detailed characterization of his form of the pragmatist maxim. Second, he identified the supplementary doctrines on which pragmaticism relied but which were not accepted by other pragmatists. And third, he attempted to explain why we should accept it. If the pragmatist maxim was correct, then we should be able to demonstrate that this was the case and, in writings from 1905 and later, he promised to provide a rigorous 'mathematical' or 'strict' proof of the pragmatist maxim (CP5: 415, EP2: 335, CP6: 485, EP2: 445).

We shall begin with the non-Cartesian epistemological framework of 'The Fixation of Belief' which was accepted by most, if not all, pragmatists. Then, in *Section three*, we turn to the pragmatist maxim as presented in Peirce's 1878 paper, 'How to Make our Ideas

Clear'. After examining the application of the pragmatist maxim to the clarification of the concepts of *truth* and reality (section IV), we turn to Peirce's writings on pragmatism from 1903 and later. This will involve reviewing his attempts to provide a much more rigorous and careful formulation of the principle (section V) and introducing the strategies he adopted for demonstrating the correctness of pragmatism (section VI). The chapter concludes with a discussion of another feature that distinguished Peirce's pragmaticism from some other versions of pragmatism: his insistence that pragmatism was inseparable from realism.

II 'THE FIXATION OF BELIEF': DOUBT, INQUIRY AND THE METHOD OF SCIENCE

'The Fixation of Belief' (1877), the paper which prepared the ground for Peirce's defence of pragmatism, was an investigation of the normative standards, the 'guiding principles' and methods, which should govern our reasoning and inquiries. The aim of the paper was to identify the most 'essential' or important of these normative principles. The essential principles are those which can be derived from facts 'which are already taken for granted in asking whether a certain conclusion follows from certain premises' (W3: 246, EP1: 113). They are derived from the presuppositions of the logical question. These include the fact that inquirers have states of *belief* which combine with their desires in order to guide action and the fact that there are states of *doubt* which motivate us to action designed, if possible, to eliminate the doubt, replacing it by belief. It is in harmony with this that *inquiry* is initially identified as an activity ('a struggle') which is motivated by the 'irritation of doubt' and which seeks to 'attain a state of belief' (W3: 247, EP1: 114). The paper investigates what methods we should adopt for responsible inquiry that will enable us to replace doubt by stable belief.

For reasons similar to Richard Rorty's (Rorty, 2000 p. 4), Peirce does not begin from the idea that our aim in inquiry is *truth*. Once we arrive at a belief we will automatically *think* it to be true, whether it is really true or not. In that case, we will believe we have achieved our goal even if we haven't. This means that we need a different, more informative, specification of our goal (W3: 248, EP1: 115). But the search for the methods that will genuinely lead to 'settled' belief takes us to a more substantive conception of what our goals should be. In this chapter I shall not examine Peirce's detailed argument for this which consists in the examination of alternative methods which, on examination, have a tendency to unsettle belief rather than settling it. Peirce endorses the method of science as the only one which is in harmony with the assumptions of the logical questions. This method employs a distinctive 'hypothesis':

> There are real things, whose characters are entirely independent of our opinions about them; those realities affect our senses according to regular laws, and, although our sensations are as different as our relations to the objects, yet, by taking advantage of the laws of perception, we can ascertain by reasoning how things really are, and any man, if he have sufficient experience and reason enough about it, will be led to the one true conclusion.
>
> (W3: 254, EP1: 120)

As Peirce observes, this method employs the concept of a mind-independent *reality*. Unlike the methods he rejects, which allow our choice of what to believe to be influenced by subjective or accidental matters such as the will, the decisions of a figure of authority, or our sense of what it feels natural or appropriate to believe, the method of science ensures that what we believe is determined 'by nothing human, but by some external permanency', or 'by nothing extraneous to the facts' (W3: 253, EP1: 120).[4]

The epistemological framework that Peirce has outlined has two features which are characteristically pragmatist: it is anti-sceptical and it is fallibilist.[5] The anti-scepticism was prefigured in a paper from 1868, 'Some Consequences of Four Incapacities', which attacked the Cartesian method of doubt (W3: 211–13, EP1: 28–9 and see Hookway, 2008). Announcing that 'we cannot begin with complete doubt', Peirce observes that '[w]e must begin with all the prejudices we actually have when we enter upon the study of philosophy'. He denies that we can simply doubt these things with the aid of 'a maxim', for the many certainties that we reply upon 'are things which it does not occur to us *can* be questioned'. The same idea is expressed in 'The Fixation of Belief': we cannot doubt something simply by formulating the question of whether it is true or by questioning whether we are dreaming or victims of evil demons. Inquiry has to begin with 'real and living doubt' (W3: 248, EP1: 115).

Peirce's emphasis upon 'real doubt' reflects the fact that our normal practice requires us to come to doubt propositions only when we have a positive reason to do so; it is not sufficient reason for doubting something that we cannot provide positive grounds for believing it. In most cases we only need to produce a reason for belief when there are already reasons for doubt whose force must be resisted or when we are changing our corpus of beliefs (Levi, 1999, pp. 178; Hookway, 2008, pp. 314–18). The Cartesian method, by contrast, assumes that the fact that we do not possess a strong reason to believe a proposition provides us with a reason to doubt it, and Peirce objects that we need reasons to change our everyday practice.

Peirce expressed his fallibilism by writing that 'I will not ... admit that we know anything whatever with *absolute certainty*' (CP7: 108). It is compatible with his response to scepticism that someone might 'find reason to doubt what he began by believing, but in that case he doubts because he has a positive reason for it, and not on account of the Cartesian maxim' (W2: 212, EP1: 29). This fallibilism is reflected in how Peirce understands the virtues of the method of science. It is not accepted because it will lead us to true, or highly probably, beliefs in the short run. Rather the use of inductive reasoning is self-correcting: it may take us to beliefs that are false; but, as is exemplified by methods of statistical sampling, further inductive testing will, eventually, reveal the error and provide guidance in coming up with something better. As Peirce puts it, the structure of our reasoning 'should not form a chain which is no stronger than its weakest link, but a cable whose fibres may be ever so slender, provided they are sufficiently numerous and intimately connected' (W2: 213, EP1: 29). Our fallibility provides no grounds for sceptical despair.

III 'HOW TO MAKE OUR IDEAS CLEAR': THE PRAGMATIST MAXIM

Early in 'How to Make our Ideas Clear', Peirce reminds the reader that 'the very first reason we have a right to demand that logic shall teach us is how to make our ideas clear' (W3: 260, EP1: 126). This is necessary for us to become masters of our own thought and possession of such mastery is required for 'great and weighty thought'. Most logic books of the time deal with this issue, but they make no advance upon the traditional approach which exploits the Cartesian distinctions between ideas that are *clear* and those that are *obscure* and between ideas that are *distinct* and those which are *confused*. The benefits that Peirce and other logicians see in such clarity become evident when we recall that our grasp of many concepts and ideas is tacit and habitual. Until we have an explicit grasp of a concept's content, we will be limited in our capacity to reflect upon how we are using it and how we ought to use it. The search for clarity is the search to make what is, at best, implicit explicit. Peirce claims that 'The principles set forth in ['The Fixation of Belief'] lead, at once, to a method of reaching a clearness of thought of a far higher grade than the "distinctness" of the logicians' (W3: 261, EP1: 127). This method involves use of the 'pragmatist maxim', although, of course, this phrase is not used in writings from the 1870s.

Why should a method for clarifying ideas be so important in the context of Peirce's account of inquiry and the method of science? Before answering this question directly, we should identify how Peirce describes the kinds of clarification offered by the traditional Cartesian distinctions. In Peirce's terms these provide two 'grades of clarity' which are not without value but which cannot meet our most important needs. The first grade, probably of 'little merit' and corresponding to the Cartesian notion of 'clarity', consists in no more than 'acquaintance with the idea so as to have become familiar with it, and to have lost all hesitancy in recognizing it in ordinary cases' (W3: 258, EP1: 124–5). This need not involve the explicit awareness of how the idea works which we need in order to be 'masters' of our meanings. The second grade of clarity, corresponding to Cartesian 'distinctness', is obtained when we can give a precise definition of the concept, perhaps by giving a set of necessary and sufficient conditions, often using an abstract vocabulary (W3: 258, EP1: 125).

It is easy to see why Peirce should hope for a greater degree of clarity about the contents of our ideas and concepts than is provided by such a definition. First, the clarification provided by a verbal definition of a concept can only be conditional. If we do not already possess a sufficiently clear grasp of the concepts that are employed in the definition, then the definition will not give us all we need: '[n]othing new can ever be learned by analyzing definitions' (W3: 260, EP1: 126).[6] This reminds us of what a clarification should ideally do for us. It should enable us to have a fully explicit grasp of the content of a concept or hypothesis, one which makes it wholly clear how the concept can be used. A complete clarification must leave us with a complete understanding of how we can legitimately use the concept in our reasoning and inquiries. The pragmatist clarification is intended to provide just that.

Now we can see what this pragmatist clarification is supposed to offer, we can identify three uses for which the pragmatist clarification is important for Peirce's project. First, there are concepts which have an important role in Peirce's logic which are philosophically problematic. For example, the related concepts of *reality* and of mind-independence have a very important role in Peirce's account of the method of science, and until we are clear about just what their contents are, the nature of the method of science itself is unclear. Other concepts, such as *probability*, which is discussed in the third of the papers, 'The Doctrine of Chances', are also fundamental to Peirce's logic of science (W3: ch. 62, EP1: ch. 9). Philosophers who are unsympathetic to Peirce's project will use these concepts in their own ways, and it is important to clarify what is distinctive about their use in the pragmatist project.

A second use consists in demonstrating that some alleged 'concepts' are empty, that they have no legitimate role in reasoning and inquiry. In writings from the late 1860s and early 1870s, we see something akin to a pragmatic argument against a flawed understanding of *reality* and against the Kantian idea of a thing in itself. The third use is internal to the exercise of the method of science. If we are to inquire well, exercising rational self-control as we do so, we need a reflective grasp of the contents of our concepts and hypotheses which will guide us in deciding what methods to use in testing them.[7]

So what is the content of the pragmatist maxim? How is it supposed to provide us with such a high grade of clarity about our concepts? According to Peirce, the clue to how we can obtain a higher grade of clarity lies in the fact that inquiry is an activity that begins in a state of *doubt* and ends when the doubt is replaced by settled *belief*. We can clarify a hypothesis or proposition by giving an explicit account of what is involved in believing it. And we clarify concepts by identifying what is involved in believing propositions of which those concepts are constituents. Peirce asks the question 'what, then, is a belief?', and the most important part of his answer is that 'it involves the establishing in our nature of a rule of action, or, say for short, a *habit*' (W3: 263, EP1: 129)[8]

> The essence of belief is the establishment of a habit, and different beliefs are distinguished by the different modes of action to which they give rise. If beliefs do not differ in this respect, if they appease the same doubt by producing the same rule of action, then no mere differences in the manner of consciousness of them can make them different beliefs.
> (W3: 263–4, EP1: 129–30)

We clarify a concept or hypothesis by identifying the habits that it produces (W3: 265, EP1: 131), and, since 'every stimulus to action is derived from perception' and 'every purpose of action is to produce some sensible result', we are led to the conclusion that 'every real distinction of thought' is a matter of what is 'tangible and practical', a matter of 'a possible difference in practice' (W3: 265, EP1: 131).

At this point, Peirce feels able to state what he later called the maxim of pragmatism, the rule that leads to the third, and highest, grade of clarity:

> Consider what effects, which might conceivably have practical bearings, we conceive the object of our conception to have. Then, our conception of these effects is the whole of our conception of the object.
> (W3: 266, EP1: 132)

He remained satisfied with this formulation, repeating it in his 1903 *Lectures on Pragmatism* and in a paper published in 1905, 'Issues of Pragmaticism' (CP5: 19, 5.438, EP2: 135, 346).

In 'How to Make our Ideas Clear', the maxim is supported by (rather casual) examples: what we mean by saying that something is hard is 'that it will not be scratched by many other substances' (W3: 266, EP1: 132); and when we say that something is heavy, we mean that 'in the absence of opposing force it will fall'. Another example employs the concept of transubstantiation. For Protestants, Peirce suggests, the wine and wafer become flesh and blood 'only in the tropical sense' that they nourish our souls as flesh would nourish our bodies (W3: 265, EP1: 131). But, he continues, Catholics understand the sacrament literally: the wafer and wine are literally flesh and blood 'although they possess all the sensible qualities of wafer-cake and diluted wine'. He then reminds us of 'how impossible it is that we should have an idea in our minds which relates to anything but conceived sensible effects of things'. The moral he wants us to draw is clear, and, indeed, it may be part of the recommendation for the maxim that it has this consequence.

Two features of Peirce's 1878 account of the pragmatist maxim are likely to cause concern. First, the standard formulation of the maxim uses the concepts of 'practical consequences' and 'consequences which have practical bearings' without explaining what these terms mean with much clarity. Some of the differences between Peirce, James and other pragmatists are manifested in their different ways of interpreting this concept. This means that Peirce's formulation of the maxim of pragmatism can be endorsed by thinkers whose versions of pragmatism are quite different. Peirce later came to see this as a strength of his original formulation, although he also tried to arrive at a more precise one. Secondly, Peirce's argument for his maxim rests on some controversial assumptions. The first is that a belief is a habit of action: anyone who wishes to adhere to a priori metaphysics and thus reject the pragmatist account of the content of concepts would insist that there are roles for beliefs other than those involved in guiding our practical reasoning. The second controversial assumption here is the more general one that once we have clarified what is involved in *believing* a proposition or applying a concept to something in a *belief*, we have a complete clarification of all the uses of that proposition or concept. Perhaps there is more to having mastery of a proposition than knowing what is involved in believing it. These are topics to which we shall return in sections v and vi.

IV PEIRCE ON TRUTH AND REALITY

The final section of 'How to Make our Ideas Clear' turns to an application of the pragmatist maxim in logic, namely to the concept of *reality*. This is not surprising. The method of science requires that our beliefs be fixed by some 'external permanency – something on which our thinking has no effect' (W3: 253, EP1: 120). It assumes that 'there are real things whose characters are entirely independent of our opinions about them' (*ibid.*). Moreover, in an 1871 review of a new edition of Berkeley's writings, Peirce engaged in a debate between two conceptions of reality, nominalist and realist (EP1: 87ff.). The former leads to scepticism and many other philosophical ills, while the latter, according to Peirce, was fully adequate to our needs. As we shall see, the pragmatist maxim helps to show that the nominalist conception of reality is empty while the realist conception passes muster as the conception of reality required for the method of science. In this section, we shall consider what is at issue in the 1871 discussion, examine how Peirce accounts for truth and reality in 'How to Make our Ideas Clear' and consider some of the problems that this conception of reality faces.

Interested in whether universals are real, Peirce asks what is meant by the word *real*. He observes that real things 'have an existence independent of your mind or mine or that of any number of persons. The real is that which is not whatever we happen to think it, but is unaffected by what we may think of it (W2: 467, EP1: 88). Whether universals will count as real depends upon 'two widely separated points of view, from which *reality* ... may be regarded' (*ibid.*). The nominalist perspective argues as follows:

Where is the real, the thing independent of how we think it, to be found? There must be such a thing, for we find our opinions constrained; there is something somewhere, therefore, which influences our thoughts, as is not created by them. We have, it is true, nothing immediately present to us but thoughts. These thoughts, however, have been caused by sensations, and those sensations are constrained by something out of mind. This thing out of mind, which directly influences sensation, and through sensation thought. Because it *is* out of the mind, is independent of how we think it, and is, in short, the real.

(EP1: 88)

This leads to nominalism and other forms of anti-realism because we can think of the real only as the unknown cause of our sensations and thoughts. The real constrains our opinions but we are somehow cut off from it.

The 'realist conception of reality' which Peirce favours has a different starting point. Although our beliefs always have 'an arbitrary accidental element', due to our different locations, background knowledge and so on, it 'universally tends in the long run to a definite form, which is the truth' (EP1: 89). Although agreement may be delayed, 'there is then, to every question, a true answer, a final conclusion, to which the opinion of every man is constantly gravitating' (EP1: 89). Since the final opinion is independent of 'all that is arbitrary and individual in thought', Peirce concludes that 'everything ... which will be thought to exist in the final opinion is real, and nothing else' (*ibid.*).

The conception of reality which Peirce defended in his 1871 review is very similar to the pragmatist account of that concept that we find defended in 'How to Make our Ideas Clear'. He begins by observing that if we are concerned with the first grade, interpreting clarity as familiarity, the concept of *reality* is as clear as anything can be. However, he quickly moves to grade two, offering the abstract definition of the real as 'that whose characters are independent of what anybody may think them to be' (W3: 271, EP1: 137). Seeking to reach the third grade of clarity, applying the pragmatist maxim, Peirce reminds us that 'all the followers of science are fully persuaded that the processes of investigation, if only pushed far enough, will give one certain answer to every question to which they can be applied' (W3: 273, EP1: 138). This gives the practical outcome of truth and Peirce concludes:

The opinion which is fated to be ultimately agreed to by all who investigate, is what we mean by the truth, and the object of a true proposition is the real. That is the way that I would explain reality.

(W3: 273, EP1: 139)

The 1878 discussion differs from that of 1871 in two important ways: Peirce reaches his account of *reality* via an account of *truth* while there is nothing about truth in the earlier review;[9] and the later paper makes no reference to the nominalist conception of reality. The latter is not surprising because we would expect that application of the pragmatist maxim would find no coherent meaning in *reality* as it is described from the nominalist standpoint. In dealing with the nominalist conception, the earlier discussion is trying to say things that cannot, according to Peirce's pragmatism, be intelligibly expressed.

These views about truth and reality have a number of echoes in the writings of other pragmatists. Although most of what William James wrote about truth lacks the close connections with *science* that mark Peirce's work, although his account of truth as whatever is expedient in the way of belief is very different from Peirce's claims, still James defended a conception of 'absolute truth' which is close to Peirce's view: a belief is absolutely true when it will never be shaken by further experience. James describes it 'that ideal vanishing point towards which we image that all our temporary truths will some day converge' (James, 1975a, pp. 106–7). John Dewey's writings on logic make little use of the concept of *truth*. However, in *Logic: The Theory of Inquiry*, he identifies Peirce's account of truth in 'How to Make our Ideas Clear' as 'the best definition of *truth* from the logical standpoint' that he is aware of (Dewey, 1938, p. 346n). Finally, Peirce's rejection of the nominalist conception of reality lays the foundations for Dewey's rejection of the copy theory of truth.

V   LATER FORMULATIONS OF THE PRAGMATIST MAXIM

In 1903 William James arranged for Peirce to give a series of lectures on pragmatism at Harvard. This gave him the opportunity to demonstrate how his version of pragmatism was superior to the versions that were achieving fame and notoriety for James and others. The lectures were hard going, being produced at a time when Peirce was working out the architectonic structure which led to the elaboration of a system of categories grounded in phenomenological investigations and to the attempt to show that logic should be grounded in aesthetics and ethics. But they also contain rewarding material. In section III, we commented upon the vagueness of the 1878 formulation of the pragmatism maxim:

Consider what effects, which might conceivably have practical bearings, we conceive the object of our conception to have. Then, our conception of these effects is the whole of our conceptions of the object.

How we should understand these conceivable practical bearings is unclear, and this formulation leaves us with little idea of how the maxim should be applied in practice.

A recurring feature of Peirce's writings on pragmatism after 1903 was that his version of the pragmatist maxim, unlike James's, was a logical principle which could be *proved*. We shall examine the proof he offered in the 1903 lectures in the following section. It was in this connection that he acknowledged that he could not yet provide the precise clarification of 'practical bearings' that he required. He proposed to begin his search for a demonstration of the correctness of pragmatism using the unclear 1878 formulation that we have discussed. But he proposed that a better formulation of the pragmatist maxim would emerge as the argument for the correctness of pragmatism was worked out in detail. In this section, we shall describe some of the versions of the maxim that resulted from this process.

The first is taken from the 1903 *Lectures on Pragmatism*:

> Pragmatism is the principle that every theoretical judgment expressible in a sentence in the indicative mood is a confused form of thought whose meaning, if any, lies in its tendency to enforce a corresponding practical maxim expressible as a conditional sentence having its apodosis in the imperative mood.
>
> (CP5: 18, EP2: 134–5)

Suppose I make the judgement that the petrol tank of my car is empty. Relying on background knowledge, I may infer from this:

> If I want to drive to Manchester today and the nearest petrol station is at the supermarket, then: Go to the supermarket and fill the car!

The truth of my judgement makes a difference to what it is rational for me to do, and studying what kind of difference the truth of the judgement can make to what I should do is a way of becoming clear about the content of the judgement. And if the truth of the judgement could not make any difference to what I should do, then the judgement is empty. This makes explicit how the truth of the judgement can have practical bearings.

A passage from a published paper from 1905 clarifies this further:

> The entire intellectual purport of any symbol consists in the total of all general modes of rational conduct which, conditionally upon all the possible circumstances and desires, would ensue upon the acceptance of the symbol.
>
> (CP5: 438, EP2: 346)

This shows that the imperatival element should be general, not just the command of a particular act, and it also emphasizes that we are concerned not with a single practical maxim that can be derived from the proposition but 'the total' of such maxims. Peirce may not have been fully satisfied even in these formulations but at least they attempt to replace the familiar vague formulations of the pragmatist maxim with something more precise that shows what is involved in the talk of practical bearings.

VI ARGUING FOR THE PRAGMATIST MAXIM

'How to Make our Ideas Clear' argues for the pragmatist maxim by reference to an account of the nature of belief. This rests upon an assumption: if we have an explicit grasp of what would be involved in believing some proposition, then we have all the information we need in order to use that proposition for cognitive purposes. This argument rests on the additional assumption that a belief is a habit of action. The conclusion to be drawn from these premises is that we have a maximally clear grasp of the content of a proposition when we know what habit of action would be involved in believing it.

Peirce's manuscripts from 1903 and later explore a number of different routes for demonstrating the correctness of pragmatism. This work is fascinating for the strategies that it suggests, for the new arguments for the maxim that Peirce was working towards, and it displays an awareness of the problems that we have identified with the original argument. The argument employed in the 1903 *lectures on pragmatism* employs a very different strategy.[10] The strategy is to provide a complete classification of all the sorts of things we do with concepts in the course of our cognitive activities, and then to ask whether a pragmatist clarification provides all the information we need for using our concepts in these ways through exercising logical self-control. Peirce thus recognizes that we do more with hypotheses than believing them, more with concepts than form beliefs in which they are applied to things. The 1903 argument begins with the observation that all of our cognitive activities involve, or are composed of, inference and argument; perhaps we can identify belief and judgement as legitimate when identified as conclusions of sound arguments. Peirce then tries to argue that there are just three kinds of argument: deduction, induction and abduction. If he can show that the pragmatist maxim provides all the clarification that is required for responsible use of arguments of each of these three kinds, then he has shown that it provides all we need to be able to employ any of our concepts in any aspect of reasoning and inquiry. There is evidence that Peirce had some doubts that his classification of arguments was complete, which may explain why he was not fully satisfied with his use of this strategy.[11]

A further strategy he employed resembled the original 1878 argument in 'How to Make our Ideas Clear' in associating habits of action with concepts and hypotheses, but it did not do so by using the premises that *beliefs* are habits of action (W3: 263–5, EP1: 129–30). Instead, it focused on what can count as *understanding* a concept or proposition. Peirce's theory of signs and representation, his *semiotic*, held that a sign (a word, concept, a thought, etc.) has a particular object only because it can be interpreted or understood as a sign of that object. The thoughts, expectations, inferences, etc. that constitute this understanding serve as an *interpretant* for the sign. A verbal interpretation provides only a conditional kind of understanding: it is conditional upon our already having a grasp of the words used in the interpretant. Peirce tries to argue that the only thing that can serve as an *unconditional* interpretant, in Peirce's terminology an ultimate logical interpretant, is the acquisition of a habit of action or the change in an existing habit of action. If this is correct and application of the pragmatist maxim provides a description of this habit, then perhaps we can construct an argument within the theory of representation and interpretation. But this is very unclear and controversial.

VII PRAGMATICISM AND REALISM

In his 1905 paper 'Issues of Pragmaticism', Peirce announced that one of the 'essential consequences' of pragmaticism was 'the scholastic doctrine of realism' (CP5: 453, EP2: 354); in a manuscript he described himself as a realist of 'a somewhat extreme stripe' (CP5: 470). Realism about generals (about laws and universals) distinguished Peirce's pragmaticism from the inferior pragmatisms of James, the British pragmatist F. C. S. Schiller and others.

There is a passage in 'How to Make our Ideas Clear' which shows why pragmatism is widely supposed to lead to anti-realist doctrines such as nominalism. Having explained that when we call something 'hard' we mean that 'it will not be scratched by many other substances' (W3: 266, EP1: 132), Peirce says that 'there is absolutely no difference between a hard and a soft thing so long as they are not brought to the test'. He continues:

Suppose, then, that a diamond could be crystallized in the midst of a cushion of soft cotton, and should remain there until it was finally burned up. Would it be false to say that the diamond was soft?

His conclusion is that it would not be false, and the utterance would involve 'not a matter of fact, but only of the arrangement of facts' (W3: 266–7, EP1: 133). This looks like nominalism. But twenty-seven years later, in 'Issues of Pragmaticism', he wrote that to say that the diamond was not hard would be 'a monstrous perversion of the word and concept *hard*' (CP5: 457, EP2: 356–7). This is because the diamond's being hard is not an isolated fact. We know that diamonds are made of carbon and we know many things about the structure and properties of carbon in different circumstances which are inseparable from hardness. In thinking of something as a diamond, we already think of it as subject to all the laws that govern the behaviour of carbon and diamonds (CP5: 457, EP2: 356–7). We can accept general conditional propositions about, for example, how the diamond would have reacted if we had been in a position to try to scratch it. Peirce's pragmaticism is thus only plausible because we can appeal to 'would-be's and 'would-do's. Much of his work in logic and metaphysics after 1900 was concerned with explaining how this form of realism can be true.

A similar problem arises for Peirce's claims about truth. We assume that there are hidden secrets, truths that we will never discover. This seems to be inconsistent with Peirce's claim that, if a proposition is true, then we are destined or fated to arrive at a stable belief in it. Peirce's observation that we can't rule out the possibility that relevant evidence will come to light is not a strong response to the problem. One possible response, which exploits Peirce's realism, would be that, given our knowledge of the laws that govern the fact which is of issue, and given what is known about our capacities as inquirers, we can come to recognize how we could have, or have had, knowledge of these truths had we inquired into the matter in other circumstances.[12]

The pragmatist maxim has a verificationist flavour, but Peirce's realism shows that his position is very different from the verificationism of the logical positivists. Like other pragmatists, he takes experience to be much richer than, for example, Hume or the logical positivists would allow. We have experience of necessary connections, and of external things as instantiating and governed by laws. Indeed, in 'Issues of Pragmaticism', he emphasizes that pragmatism requires the conditional propositions which express pragmatist clarifications must express something *true* (EP2: 354). If we can establish truths about what *would* happen were we to try to scratch some object, then we are committed to the conclusion that 'a possibility can be a real kind' (*ibid.*). There are real *objective* modalities which are manifested in our experience of necessity, chance, time and other phenomena.

NOTES

1. There is a correspondence between Peirce and James in 1893 about the origins of 'pragmatism'. Peirce asked James 'Who originated the word "pragmatism"?' and James responded that Peirce 'invented "pragmatism"' (CP8: 253 and n.8). (For conventions in citing Peirce's works see the bibliography.) Peirce claimed that the word was taken from Kant's concept of a 'pragmatic belief', a belief with a role in the anticipation of experience (EP2: 331–2).
2. For an illuminating account of the activities and importance of the Metaphysical Club, see Louis Menand's book on the topic (Menand, 2001).
3. Dewey had no contact with the Metaphysical Club, and, although he studied for his doctorate at Johns Hopkins University while Peirce was a lecturer in logic there, he did not come to appreciate Peirce's writings until later. Peirce was very critical of the kind of logic advocated in books like *Studies in Logical Theory* (1903, MW2) and *Logic: The Theory of Inquiry* (1938, LW12) (CP8: 180–4). (For conventions on citing Dewey's works again see the bibliography.)
4. Wiggins (2004) is a valuable discussion of these arguments and shows how the idea of belief being determined by 'nothing extraneous to the facts' can be applied in unpromising cases such as moral beliefs and mathematical *beliefs*.
5. These are two of the four features which Hilary Putnam has employed in an attempt to identify what is distinctive about pragmatism. The other two are the rejection of a dichotomy between fact and value, and 'the primacy of practice' (Putnam, 1994b, p. 152).
6. Peirce accused Descartes of reverting to 'the old formalities of logic, and, above all, abstract definitions played a great part in his philosophy' (EP1: 126).
7. This third use of the pragmatist maxim is most evident in Peirce's writings from after 1900, especially in 'What Pragmatism Is' and 'Issues of Pragmaticism', two papers published in *The Monist* in 1905 (EP2: chs. 24 and 25).
8. The concept of *habit* has an important place in Peirce's pragmatism. As Peirce's manuscripts from 1907 make clear, it does not involve a

commitment to Skinnerian behaviourism. Peirce insists that reflection enables us to change our habits and treats them as tools for rational self-control (see EP2: 413).

9 Peirce's account of *truth* is one of the doctrines for which he is best known. It is surprising that his published work contains very little on this topic, and, on the few occasions when he does discuss it, it is treated simply as a tool for thinking about *reality*.

10 For more detailed discussion of Peirce's strategies for defending pragmatism see Fitzgerald (1966) and Hookway (2004a, 2008).

11 See Hookway, 2004a, 2008 for discussion of how this argument is supposed to work and of why Peirce came to have doubts about its efficacy. Fitzgerald provides further discussion of it and of the doctrines upon which it depends (Fitzgerald, 1966, pp. 106–35), as does Turrisi, 1997.

12 I doubt that this is a wholly satisfactory solution to the problem of hidden secrets. Some other suggestions are defended in Hookway 2000, ch. 2 and Misak 2004.

ALAN MALACHOWSKI

2 James's holism: the human continuum

Of pragmatism's three most renowned founders, Charles Peirce, William James and John Dewey, it is James who is usually regarded as the popularizing figure. This is understandable, given the great verve with which his *Pragmatism* (1907) and much of its sequel *The Meaning of Truth* (1909) were written.[1] Those books, the first especially, put pragmatism on the intellectual map. There was, however, a downside. By taking pragmatism out of the protective, somewhat scientistic, wrapping that Peirce had placed it in, and by broadening it out and emphasizing its more accessible, humanistic side, James drew the fire of some harshly vocal critics. Even Peirce was aggrieved, and to the extent of distancing himself from the very term pragmatism.[2]

However, the fiercest critics were external: those immersed in the creation of a wave of technical, logico-linguistic innovations that they believed would at last carry philosophy towards quasi-scientific maturity. I am alluding primarily, of course, to G. E. Moore and Bertrand Russell.[3] The British duo stressed that in trying to reduce philosophy to mere matters of practical human concern, and, in particular, in tying his account of *truth* down in this way, James was advocating an absurd pragmatist position, one that provokes rather obvious, but nevertheless insuperable, objections. On this jaundiced view, James might be obliged, for example, to believe that 'X exists' is true on grounds of mere convenience, regardless of whether X actually exists. Furthermore, or so Russell insisted, James's pragmatism allows, if not actively encourages, a sort of philosophical gunboat mentality: were pragmatism to reign, key issues would inevitably get to be decided by force.

There is an interesting, and no doubt important, historical tale to be told about the early criticisms of James's pragmatism. A mythical version has long been in circulation. It holds that these criticisms were fatally damaging to pragmatism and hence rightly relegated it to the sidelines of intellectual history. Like many myths, this one lingered on without attracting much critical attention.[4] But, over the past few decades, a number of philosophers have begun to undermine its credibility. Hilary Putnam, for example, shows that Russell was cavalier, to say the least, in his treatment of James's texts, and failed to pay sufficient attention to the complexities of the account of truth they embed.[5] Timothy Sprigge also raises some potent doubts about whether Moore and Russell grasped the full import of some of James's views and the motivation behind them. He further suggests that in their haste to condemn him, these godfathers of analytic philosophy failed to fathom the extent and signficance of James's understanding of 'absolute idealism', an influential philosophical position that, like them, he was eager to depose.[6] Similarly, several other philosophers reviewing the situation find additional myth-busting evidence, ranging from textual irresponsibility to sheer failure to comprehend what James was trying to achieve.[7] In this chapter, however, we will be concerned with neither the myth in question, nor, indeed, the status of the criticisms it enshrines.

Instead, we will explore something that the myth undoubtedly diverts attention away from: the intriguing and, in many ways prescient, holism. For this, as Hilary Putnam persuasively argues,[8] pervades James's pragmatism and, as Isaac Nevo also astutely claims, 'grounds and qualifies [his] pragmatic account of knowledge and truth'.[9] By focusing on holism, we can obtain a more perspicuous view of James's overall contribution to both pragmatism and philosophy in general. This view finds him dignified well above the popularizing level and, at the same time, enables us to see why, for all their apparent obstructive force, the early criticisms of James's pragmatism turn out to have little relevance to much of the substance of that contribution. Furthermore, James's pluralism, based on the assumption that 'there is no possible point of view from which the world can appear as an absolutely single fact',[10] assumes a more robust complexion when viewed against the sturdy backcloth of his holism.

In *Pragmatism*,[11] James substitutes a subtle and complex holistic picture, one in which tentacles of practically verifiable connections entwine themselves inextricably after reaching out to one another from multiple directions, for a more traditional, but much simpler, philosophical depiction wherein things James typically regards as interwoven are not only kept separate, but duly conceptualized in a dichotomous manner, one that renders them highly problematic – perhaps for all time to come. Whereas in James's own delineation, knowledge and reality, fact and value, and experience and the world are radically interdependent, in the simpler image they necessarily stand on opposite sides of chasms, both real and conceptual, that, by threatening to generate scepticism along with other forms of intellectual instability, motivate grand bridge-building ventures such as foundationalism in epistemology or absolutist moral theory in ethics. Moreover, it has often been difficult for many philosophers to see the whole of James's own picture precisely because they can only look at it through a philosophical lens that has long embedded such focal points of separation. This encourages them to seek out easy targets according to entrenched divisions on their own philosophical map. It gives them the general impression that by resorting to tentacles of practical interdependence James was making no more than a feeble effort to span preexisting fissures. In short, they ignore the big holistic picture and tend to regard James as someone who was trying to use *ad hoc* holistic theories to do roughly what they themselves want to do (i.e. counter epistemological scepticism and so on), but in a rather hamfisted way.

To view other thinkers as, at best, ineffectively engaged in their own projects, is a common failing of too many analytic philosophers, caused, in the main, by a habitual neglect of history and the correlative tendency to issue precipitate verdicts of logico-linguistic incompetence.[12] Since he disputes extensively with Moore and Russell on their own territory, James is prone to encouraging this misconception.[13] However, his agenda is different from theirs. And, as should become clear, it is somewhat different, as well, from that of later philosophers whose enthusiastic embrace of holism appears to be congruent with, if not inspired by, James's own. Of these, the most notable exponents are Quine, Davidson, Putnam and Rorty.

THE HOLISTIC PICTURE

> Holism is the pragmatist alternative to the dichotomous tendencies of traditional metaphysics.
>
> (Nevo, in this volume, p. 91)

Pragmatism starts from an abiding premise of 'practical difference'. If a view makes no such difference, then it can be of no great philosophical importance. James famously takes the premise from Peirce and immediately tries to show how it can be used to resolve traditional problems, confronting first 'what is driest', which he considers to be 'the problem of *Substance*', and then such perennials as *'the question of design in nature'* and *'the free will problem'*.[14] In this connection, he also begins to talk about pragmatism as method: 'The *pragmatic method* is primarily a method of settling metaphysical disputes that otherwise might be interminable.'[15] The key to success here is the Peircean focus on 'practical consequences':[16]

> What difference would it practically make to anyone, if this notion rather than that notion were true? If no practical difference whatever can be traced, then the alternatives mean practically the same thing, and all dispute is idle.[17]

James insists this method can be highly successful: 'It is astonishing to see how many philosophical disputes collapse into insignificance the moment you subject them to this simple test of tracing concrete consequences.'[18] However, for philosophical purposes, no matter how effective it is, method alone is never enough. It has to come with salient explanations as to *how it does*, and, more importantly, *why it should*, succeed. Moreover, it needs to hook up in some fashion, if only by way of rejection, with philosophy's discourse, history and traditions. A self-professed clairvoyant who achieves spectacular, but rationally inexplicable, empirical results on a consistent basis over the long term may be said to have, or at least be capable of exhibiting, a method for discovering truths. But it is not a philosophical method. This is where James's holistic picture comes in. And this is also where a key source of his motivation for sketching that picture differentiates him from later holists.

James's holistic picture is all encompassing. But, it is a picture, not a theory. This is often overlooked, if only because, as we intimated, the picture embraces areas that are commonly hived off and then treated as subjects of separate pragmatist theories – of truth, meaning, knowledge, sensation and so forth. In James's overall scheme of things, explanation comes largely prepacked. It is apparent, for example, that the pragmatic method can be applied to traditional problems concerning human beings and their relationships to each other and the world because those relationships are themselves holistically underpinned. Or, to put it in what, at first, may seem to be uninformatively circular and thoroughly unpragmatic terms: method matches reality.[19] Notice, however, that this convenience of 'fit' is not simply a put up job. James's holism is genuinely all pervasive. But it constrains with its own standards of epistemic rigour what, when pictured, it depicts. Even though it operates with criteria of convenience, it does not allow for invention of philosophically convenient realities willynilly.[20]

The dualistic representations of human beings that James rejects gain traction from long-established ideas and social practices that assume, or can apparently make it seem, that such representations cater for what people (and the world) are actually like. It can be difficult to shake off the idea that minds and bodies are radically, and hence problematically, different in their very nature, for example, when the surrounding culture is replete with artefacts, beliefs and images that make such an idea seem apposite. Religious notions of the soul and its independence from the body are a case in point.[21] This kind of all-pervasive, cultural verisimilitude cannot simply be argued away in the absence of a viable alternative way of looking at things. Ratiocination will soon blunt its teeth if tries to consume all the prevailing props of social and intellectual life. But, James *has* an alternative portrait, the viability of which he wishes to demonstrate pragmatically. Far from being epistemologically alienated from the world around them and shut off, psychologically, from their own bodies, human beings are holistically embedded creatures: their mind–world and mind–body relations form a continuum. The obvious question then is: 'Why go for that when cultural orthodoxy suggests otherwise?'

It is in furnishing general resources for an answer to this question that James's holistic picture becomes truly interesting. In this picture, a number of traditional, problem-mongering dualities are swiftly erased. Since human creatures are, in certain practical respects, *creators* of knowledge and truth, there is no need, moreover it makes no sense, for them to entertain the fantasy of global doubt that Peirce berated in his famous attacks on Cartesian scepticism:

> We cannot begin with complete doubt. We must begin with all the prejudices that we actually have when we enter upon the study of philosophy. These prejudices are not to be dispelled by a maxim, for they are things that it does not occur to us *can* be questioned. Hence this initial scepticism will be mere self-deception, and not real doubt; and no one who follows the Cartesian method will ever be satisfied until he has formally recovered all those beliefs that in form he has given up.[22]

Although James retains some residual attachment to philosophy's ubiquitous 'idea' idea, he tends to work with an account of mind–world relations in which such intermediaries play a low key role. This in turn deflects some associated epistemological worries.[23] And, when he portrays the workings of the mind that no longer has to burden itself with such worries, he depicts it in correspondingly holistic terms: sensations, for example, are interlinked – as conveyed by James's use of the images of a mosaic and also a web.[24] Such images obviate the need for troublesome dualistic specifications. So characterized, sensations are not atomistic elements that get mechanically shuffled and configured in isolation in mental space by operations of the mind, as assumed by earlier empiricists of human psychology such as Locke and Hume. Epistemological problems generated by that kind of psychology fall by the wayside.

HOLISM WITHOUT IDEALISM

As he develops his pragmatism, James still displays some sympathy with absolute idealism: the view that there is a single, unified world consciousness which embodies everything that exists. And he takes some time to extract himself from its influence – not least because of the attractions that its philosophical fruits, primarily a coherence theory of truth and an holistic account of knowledge, have for a thinker as opposed as James is to older rationalist and empiricist approaches to truth and knowledge.[25] Moreover, as Rorty observes, the 'idealist metaphysics' that generated those fruits 'seemed both true and demonstrable to some of the best minds of the nineteenth century'.[26] Indeed, James's pragmatism should be regarded as at least partly an attempt to preserve what is valuable in idealism by divesting it of it's a priori trappings and incorporating it within a robust and more up to date philosophical outlook. For what singularly fails to engage James's sympathy is the idealist notion that the existence and functioning of individual minds can only be made sense of by assuming that they are somehow contained within, or subsumed by, one superior, all-embracing mind, and that human experiences are thereby rendered part of the affective life of that mind. None of this sits well with his 'evidential holism'[27] which, in supplying some of the rigour we referred to above, demands experiential justification rather than rational supposition or conjecture. The all-embracing mind and its absolute nature do not figure within facets of ordinary experience or the belief systems derived therefrom.

Furthermore, as Sprigge reminds us, James finds absolute idealism *morally* repugnant.[28] That the misery and suffering commonly endured by human beings should be construed as a 'condition of the perfection of the eternal order', as Royce, for instance, once held,[29] was not something that James can, or would want to, stomach. Moreover, his basic pragmatist instincts also come into play here, as when, in his famous and heart-wrenching example of the poverty-stricken working man who commits suicide because he is unable to feed his family, it is made quite clear that the hypothesis of the moral perfection of the world, central to absolute idealism, makes no discernible difference at ground level.[30] The example graphically illustrates James's conviction that absolute idealism 'has small sympathy with facts' in general and 'remains supremely indifferent to what the particular facts in our world actually are'.[31] It is for this reason that he generally considers it to be, as Suckiel rather nicely puts it, 'so abstract as to vaporize into insignificance when it [comes] to dealing with concrete issues'.[32] Although James sets aside the all-embracing mind of absolute idealism, he is, at times, somewhat ambiguous as to just how distant from the latter some of his views are or need to be. His pragmatism evidently leaves it far behind, barely visible on the horizon of feasible thought. But, his radical empiricism, the locus of the holistic account of the internal workings of the mind that we referred to towards the end of section two above, remains close enough to provoke concerns as to whether it is simply a brand of idealism deceptively dressed in empiricist clothing.

James expounds his key ideas on radical empiricism during the last decade of his life. Two things make this form of empiricism radical. First, it puts 'direct experience' in the driving seat of philosophy: 'it must neither admit into its constructions any element that is not directly experienced, nor exclude from them any element that is directly experienced'.[33] And, the second radical feature follows from this: 'relations that connect experiences must themselves be experienced relations, and any kind of relation experienced must be accounted as "real" as anything else in its system'.[34] In asserting the requirement that 'conjunctive relations' should be held to be 'as real as the terms united by them',[35] James believes he is not only doing away with global atomism, as it were (i.e. both within and without the mind), but also taking some of the mystery out of relations: as items of experience, their existence neither demands the support of transcendental arguments nor invites scepticism in the absence of such arguments.[36] A philosophical position that aims this high certainly appears to be radical.[37] But, the question as to whether James's thoroughgoing empiricism adds any value to, or rather detracts from, his pragmatism is best considered against the backcloth of the holism that characterizes the latter.

PRAGMATISM

When James makes the notion of 'practical difference' central to pragmatism,[38] it seems to many commentators that he is merely provoking a hard question: 'How can practical consequences serve as the touchstone for philosophical significance?' The chief concern behind this question, made much of by the early critics, and still frequently raised when pragmatism is critically assessed, is that dependence on practical upshots has to involve desires and interests and hence leads to relativism, subjectivism and other forms of irrationalism. But, this worry is fuelled by precisely the kind of philosophical thinking that James wishes to overcome. Moreover, it cloaks a prior question, one that has greater claim to being a natural reasonable response to the emphasis on the practical, as opposed to the knee jerk philosophical reaction that sees only dire epistemic outcomes: 'If belief in some claim (e.g. "That eagles are efficient raptors") has entirely satisfactory practical consequences that spin out holistically across the relevant community, what right have philosophers, as such, to raise objections to it?' James, with what Dewey so aptly calls 'his never-failing instinct for the concrete',[39] insists that when the significance of this latter question is fully appreciated, the need for a change 'in the seat of authority' will also be recognized: 'The centre of gravity of philosophy must alter its place. The earth of things long thrown into shadow by the glories of the upper ether, must resume its rights.'[40]

James's holistic picture is both complex and all-embracing, as we have said, and when it is restricted to his pragmatism, three main features indicate why his call for a shift in philosophy's 'centre of gravity' is well motivated, and on the basis of precisely the sort of prior issue about practical consequences just described. The first feature, involves its manifestation of the epistemic rigour we have also already referred to, but only in rather general terms. The second, offers reassurance that 'the glories of the upper ether' are illusory and hence best forgotten. And, the third rescues pragmatism from the world-eclipsing pitfalls of idealism.

Pragmatism is frequently accused of allowing, or even encouraging, intellectual standards to fall to a level that courts irrationalism. Such accusations begin with the early reproaches to James. They overlook the multifarious qualifications and constraints that are so conspicuously packed into the pages of *Pragmatism* and generally assumed to still be in place by many later pragmatists including, most notoriously, Rorty.[41] In their blindness in this respect, critics flatly ignore the robust epistemic position that the pragmatist commonly occupies on account of these restrictions, a position graphically depicted by James:

> Pent in, as the pragmatist more than anyone else sees himself to be, between the whole body of funded truths squeezed from the past and the coercions of the world of sense about him, who so well as he feels the immense pressure of objective control under which our minds perform their operations?
>
> (James, 1998, pp. 111–12)

Futhermore, allegations of irrationalism tend to float straight past James's own contention that the shoe of intellectual irresponsibility is actually firmly ensconced on the other foot.

When describing the details of the holistic character of belief acquisition, James invokes the constraints of both conservatism – 'in this matter of belief, we are all conservatives' (1998, p. 35) – and what we might best call 'tangible benefits'. An intention to adopt the belief that p is true, for example, must "run the gauntlet of all other beliefs" (1998, p. 43) which themselves will have already been put to trial in that way. This helps ensure that successful candidates for belief exhibit at least the epistemic virtues of the network of beliefs they are joining.[42] So there will be no empirical or logical wildcards: nothing that is clearly recognised to be evidentially suspect and nothing that either exhibits gross inconsistency in its own right or would create such were it to be adopted.[43] More generally, and here the conservatism really kicks in: nothing is to be accepted that will cause too much upset, where this means nothing that will deform the working network:

> An *outrée* explanation, violating all our preconceptions would never pass for a true account of a novelty. We should scratch around industriously til we found something less eccentric. The most violent revolutions in an individual's beliefs leave most of his old order left standing. Time and space, cause and effect, nature and history, and one's own biography remain untouched. New truth is always a go-between, a smoother-over of transitions. It marries old opinion to new fact so as to ever show a minimum of jolt, a maximum of continuity.
>
> (James, 1998, p. 35)

The whole process, as James describes it, involves holistic trade-offs with the consistency and practical efficacy of other beliefs; at the limit: all of them. Such trading is predominant in the case of the second constraint we mentioned. The amount of disruption that our belief systems can and should tolerate is proportionate to the amount of tangible benefit to be gained from adopting a new belief. But, it is important to recognize what work 'tangible' is doing here. We should not think of benefits as being subjective, as being anything like, or having any strong connection with, units of personal satisfaction. It is precisely this kind of interpretation that misleads critics into thinking that there is a direct and slippery slope from practical consequences to a crazy life of epistemic abandon. James is not saying that we should be prepared to ditch a whole host of our beliefs to make room for an otherwise challenging belief if it simply makes us feel sufficiently good. Benefits have to fit in with the belief and behavioural system in total and the benefits, as a working system, that it already yields. Only those beliefs that, when distributed throughout the human–world continuum, make the whole set up function in tangibly better ways, or do not damage it appreciably, should be up for adoption. Revolutions are not ruled out. But they are not going to occur, and nor should they, on the back of feel good factors.

Notice that the word 'should' has more than once sneaked into our exposition. A common philosophical reaction to descriptions of putative practices is to retort: 'Well even if things are as you say, that doesn't mean this is how they *should* be. For normative force we need something more than mere description.' James's insistence that the glories of the upper ether are illusory comes into play here. He points out that when we are seeking guarantees that our belief-acquiring practices are sound, there is nowhere better to look than the practices themselves. Indeed, there is nowhere else to look. Appeals to a practice-transcendent reality, a place from which or against which our belief acquisition accomplishments can be judged, are empty. They fail the test of practical difference. Moreover:

When we talk of reality 'independent' of human thinking, then, it seems a thing very hard to find. It reduces to the notion of what is just entering into experience, and yet to be named, or else to some aboriginal presence in experience, before any belief about the presence had arisen, before any human conception had been applied. It is what is absolutely dumb and evanescent, the merely ideal limit of our minds. We may glimpse it, but we never grasp it; what we grasp is always some substitute for it which previous human thinking has peptonized and cooked for our consumption. If so vulgar an expression were allowed, we might say that wherever we find it, it has already been *faked*.

(James, 1998, pp. 119–20)

James's overriding epistemic moral is clear: appeals to an elusive practice-superior reality add nothing useful to our explanations as to how belief systems function and, thus lacking, they can provide no real guidance as to how they *should* function. Moreover, by distracting us from the details of the practical constraints on such systems, they are liable to subtract value. Since the practice-superior dimension is explanatorily inert, normative concerns must be grounded elsewhere. And where better to look than the consequences of the practices in question? This line of argument also supports James's view that, ironically, it is the rationalist, the advocate of practice-superior realism, who, though an unwitting dabbler in unfathomable mysteries, more deservedly incurs the charge of 'irrationalism'. Pragmatists take care to spell out the complexities of how our belief-knowledge systems work to our benefit in practice. And in doing so, their approach to what 'agreement with reality' amounts to contrasts with the 'rationalists' or 'intellectualists' who James claims are 'more off hand and irreflective'. Pragmatists, he further points out, 'are more analytic and painstaking' (James, 1998, p. 96).[44]

A Jamesian pragmatist holds that our knowledge practices can only be reformed from within. The boundaries of these practices stretch beyond parochial concerns, making 'within' seem less obviously objectionable. Even so, doesn't this still commit the cardinal idealist sin of leaving out the world itself? It is difficult, perhaps currently impossible, to state what is at issue here in neutral terms.

From James's point of view it is a banal fact that the world plays its part in our knowledge practices. What gets left out in the pragmatist account is only the ideal, rarefied version of it conjured up by certain philosophers. For such philosophers, however, the Jamesian holistic picture is ontologically lightweight. Lacking attachments to their normatively constrained conception of the real world, it is liable to drift into oblivion, taking its exponents with it. To this, James's first, but wholly adequate, reponse is to ask, in line with the principle of practical difference, for a clear indication as to just where, and how, in our knowledge practices the posited practice-independent world is able to exert an influence that keeps them from so drifting. It is a potent response, and one that has yet to be adequately addressed.

THE UPSHOT

We have shown some of the ways in which James's holism generates accounts of belief acquisition and knowledge that are far removed from the intemperate 'irrational' or 'relativistic' accounts that hostile critics have saddled them with. But what should we make of this? Some commentators seem to think that when we establish just how interesting, reliable and sensible many of James's views on mind, belief and knowledge are, we are also elevating his status with the philosophical tradition. For we are thereby showing that he makes an hitherto underrecognized or undervalued contribution to the empiricist tradition. This latter claim can perhaps be cemented by weaving historical connections between James and earlier empiricists such as Locke and Hume and then, on the substantive side, demonstrating how he improved upon some of their efforts. Such an interpretation is conservative. But, it has innovative possibilities. It can show, for example, how James's work also looks forward to the coming of the post-Humean empiricism of Quine and even the post-empiricist approach of Davidson. In the former case, James's views chime with Quine's global revisability conjecture and holism of confirmation. Although beliefs systems are dominated by 'older truths' – James says that 'their influence is absolutely controlling' (1998, p. 35) – they are subject to even wholesale revision in the right circumstances. On the subject of confirmation, James is more radical than Quine at his most radical. At one stage, Quine went so far as to hold that because scientific theories can only call upon evidence holistically conceived, the relevant item of empirical significance is the whole of science rather than any individual claims or the sentences that express them.[45] James goes further.

For him, the vehicle of confirmation is *the whole of life*. As for Davidson, his ingenious holistic argument to the effect that beliefs are inherently veridical[46] finds a potential ally in James. Indeed, both sides can benefit. The Davidsonian view that the widespread existence of falsehoods would disrupt meaning to the extent that such a situation, were it to obtain, could not even be described (e.g. the existence of a preponderance of falsehoods in my beliefs about trees threatens to undermine the claim that they are about *trees* and even, at the limit, whether they are *beliefs*) adds weight to James's contention that in depicting truth-acquisition practices that rely on coherence with existing beliefs (subject to trade-offs) and multiple criteria of practical convenience and utility, nothing substantial is left out. And James's detailed portrait of the complexity of the holistic assimilation, verification and validation of beliefs adds some flesh to the skeleton of Davidson's line of argument, reinforcing Davidson's claim that nothing important is left out of his account.

Two things are going on here that have not been clearly distinguished. First, we gesture towards the 'conservative' project of finding James's rightful place in the history of philosophy. And in doing so, we allude to a possible upgrading that makes him a key figure in the empiricist tradition. This already has a radical element in that it involves a rethinking of how this tradition pans out: one that perhaps gives James parity with, or even some priority over, other figures that eclipsed him in the past (this might include Russell and Ayer, for example). Then, in discussing how James's pragmatism looks forward, we start to raise the issue as to what use can be made of it. The pairing of James and Davidson takes his pragmatism out of the historical context proper by putting the emphasis on what can be done with his views rather than on how they fit into the philosophical tradition. This is suggestive of an even more radical option, made much of by Rorty:[47] we do best by James when we set aside the project of getting a rearview mirror historical fix on his ideas and treat his views entirely pragmatically. For Rorty, this means identifying how James's views can now make a difference to philosophy. And he recommends concentrating on the elements in James's pragmatism that encourage us to pursue philosophical agendas that do not concern themselves with the clutch of problems that define the tradition within which the conservative historical project seeks to resituate James. We can, for instance, lean on James's holistic ways of talking about belief acquisition in order to create an account of human life that does not get bogged down in difficulties caused by the dualities – as between, for example, mind and world or appearance and reality– that characterize the Western epistemological tradition. In claiming that we should aim for just such an account, Rorty also suggests an answer to our earlier question as to whether James's radical empiricism adds value to his pragmatism. James seeks to characterize experience in ways that free it from both atomistic interpretations and experience-world difficulties. Like Dewey,[48] he wants to create a world-inclusive conception of experience. But Rorty argues that when the social aspects of James's holism are given proper weight, experience drops out of the picture. Radical empiricism's holistic attempt to embed the world within experience can only drag pragmatism back into the kind of problems it should strive to leave behind.

Rorty has been much criticized for neglecting the historical context of James's texts and for trying to lift his views out of that context on a piecemeal basis. But such criticism tends to overlook the differences between wilfully distorting the historical picture and selectively extracting constituents from that picture in order to put them to fresh use under different socio-intellectual conditions. In attempting to do the latter, Rorty is not necessarily guilty of tampering with the past. There need be no inconsistency between viewing James as both an important contributor to the empiricist tradition and the provider of some raw materials for constructing a philosophical position that renders that tradition superfluous.

NOTES

1. Anderson, 2009a, p. 508. Ellen Kappy Suckiel captures exactly why James's writing had, and still has, such appeal: 'His philosophical style is emotionally engaging and direct. He used metaphorical and pictorial language to bring home complex and subtle philosophical points, and he reached out to accommodate, as well as influence, the aesthetic and emotional sensibilities of his audience.' Suckiel, 2009, p. 30.
2. Peirce famously opted for 'pragmaticism': a replacement that he correctly judged to be 'ugly enough to be safe from kidnappers'; Peirce, 2004, vol. 1, p.80.
3. 'The idea that Russell and his followers put our discipline on the secure path of science is very dear to many analytic philosophers': Rorty, 2007b, p. 281.
4. The myth has two dimensions. One holds that the early criticisms were causally instrumental in relegating pragmatism to the sidelines of intellectual culture. The other regards the criticisms in question as unanswerable.
5. See *Pragmatism: An Open Question* (Putnam, 1995), esp. pp. 8–26 and Putnam, 2004a.
6. See Sprigge, 2004 and 2009.
7. See Baldwin, 1990, pp. 167–8; Hertz, 1971; and Phillips, 1984. For a detailed defence of Dewey against Russell's similar attacks on him, see Burke, 1994.
8. 'One of the chief characteristics of James's philosophy is its *holism*: there is an obvious, if implicit, rejection of many familiar dualisms: fact, value, and theory are all seen by James as interpenetrating and interdependent': Putnam, 1995, p. 7.
9. Nevo, 1995b, p. 155.
10. James, 1897, pp. viii–ix.
11. James, 1998. All page references in the main body of the text are to this edition.
12. Anderson suggests that those who try 'to logicize James' work' proceed on the premise that 'James was simply inept at logic and needs to have his argumentation properly explicated and amended'. He then

makes an astute observation: 'It does not seem to occur to them that James might simply have had philosophical reasons for *not* logicizing.' Anderson, 2009a, p. 510.

13   The same can be said of Dewey. It is not until Rorty comes along that pragmatists are clearly shown how to pursue their own path without getting caught up in past battles. Nevertheless, many critics have failed to accept, or even see, what Rorty is encouraging in this respect and they continue to pick fights with pragmatists over issues that have little pragmatic value. For more on this, see Malachowski, 2002a.

14   James, 1998, pp. 45, 56 and 59. Italics in the original.

15   James, 1998, p. 28. In his contribution to this volume (pp. 189–206), David Macarthur rightly points out that pragmatism's approach to metaphysics has been neglected for reasons connected with the rise of positivism (for details, see p. 191). He then goes on to suggest that James's 'method' actually has 'very little anti-metaphysical bite' (p. 193). Metaphysical options for the traditional problems James discussed were left open and empiricist metaphysics, for example, remained unscathed. But James can also be read in the relaxed way Rorty reads him: as providing useful ways of talking about topics traditionally of metaphysical interest in purely practical terms without bringing metaphysics as such into the picture. It begs two big questions to assert that such talk presupposes, for instance, an empiricist metaphysics. The first is the question of whether James is best interpreted as belonging to the empiricist tradition. And the second is whether there is any need to posit a metaphysical component, one that deals with what Dewey calls 'absolute finalities', to his pragmatist discourse.

16   James, 1998.

17   James, 1998.

18   James, 1998, p. 30.

19   James fully accepts that the notion of correspondence to reality has a *practical* role to play *within* our belief and knowledge practices, but objects when this notion is worked up into theoretical explanations of those practices. Once the reality side of things is taken out of its live practical context, it runs out of explanatory steam: there is, he claims, nothing useful we can then say about it.

20   James stresses that the creator of 'philosophical realities' faces two stiff constraints: the tribunal of existing truths and the provision of sufficiently worthwhile benefits. In the latter case, the benefits can only reign supreme if they justify overruling the tribunal and readjusting the network of existing beliefs accordingly. The 'anything goes' relativism that James, and pragmatism in general, is so often accused of cannot possibly flourish in the face of such constraints.

21 Though these presumably found a warmer reception when introduced by philosophers on account of prior notions dating back as far as the ancient Greeks.
22 'Question concerning Certain Faculties', *Charles S. Peirce: The Essential Writings*, p. 86. It is worth noting that Peirce appreciated some aspects of Cartesianism. For an enlightening exposition of what this amounted to, see Anderson, 2009b. James took on board Peirce's anti-Cartesianism as displayed in the quotation, but by extracting the epistemic value of what Peirce calls 'prejudices' gave it a more positive spin. In doing this, he is a precursor of Wittgenstein and Davidson – and, through them, Rorty.
23 Sceptical concerns about the very possibility of knowledge are much to the point here.
24 Here, for example, is James's gloss on his 'mosaic philosophy': 'In actual mosaics the pieces are held together by their bedding, for which bedding the Substances, transcendental egos, or Absolutes of other philosophies may be taken to stand. In radical empiricism, there is no bedding; it is as if the pieces clung together by their edges, the transitions between them forming their cement ... the metaphor serves to symbolize the fact that Experience itself, taken at large, can grow by its edges.' James, 1996c, pp. 86–7.
25 Donovan, 1995, p. 219. The idealist roots of pragmatism are often ignored even when it is accused of idealist tendencies: 'Traditional pragmatism, in its own day, was nourished by the holistic account of knowledge offered by Royce, Green, and Morris. In fact, the influence of idealism on pragmatism can be summarized in terms of the decisive role that the coherence theory of truth played in undermining versions of the correspondence theory common to the older empiricist and rationalist traditions' (Donovan, 1995, p. 217).
26 Rorty, 2007c, p. 96.
27 The phrase is Nevo's. See Nevo, 1995b, p. 156.
28 Sprigge, 2009.
29 The phrase is Royce's (Royce, 1959, vol. II, p. 345). Interestingly, Royce classed James, along with Schiller, as a 'pure pragmatist' and described himself as an 'absolute pragmatist'. Peirce also considered Royce to be a pragmatist, as does Putnam.
30 James, 1998, pp. 49–51
31 James, 1998, pp. 39 and 40.
32 Suckiel, 2009, p. 31.
33 James, 1996c, p. 42.
34 James, 1996c, p. 42.
35 James, 1996b, p. 107.

36 On the possibility of experiencing relations, Peirce went even further than James. For, as Short reminds us, 'unlike both Kant and the empiricists, Peirce held that the content of experience, prior to analysis, is continuous' (Short, 2007, p. 81). The upshot of this, as Anderson succinctly points out, is that 'If Peirce is right, we can directly experience possibles and laws'; Anderson, 2009a, p. 506.
37 We defer discussion of the problematic aspects of James's empiricist ambitions.
38 James, 2004a, p. 203. For an interesting discussion of how, in emphasizing the practical, James underestimated the rational import of Peirce's approach to pragmatism, see ch. 5 of Murphy, 1990, pp. 39–57.
39 James, 2004a, p. 181.
40 James, 1998, p. 35.
41 When Rorty makes one of his throwaway philosophical remarks that tend to provoke incredulity, if not hostility, he is often assuming a background of naturalistic epistemic rigour that can be found in the work of both James and Dewey. A more historically sophisticated audience would pick up on these allusions. Though even sophisticated commentators can be wrong about this because they do not actually see the rigour in James's account. Sleeper raises an interesting case in point because he shows that even Dewey, exhibited this failure: 'Robert Frost used to complain about poets who wrote blank verse. It was, he said, like playing tennis with the net down ... For James, of course, pragmatism *was* something like blank verse; a feature that caused Dewey to complain about it. Not only had James let the "net" down, Dewey believed, but he had established no base-lines either.' Sleeper, 2004, p. 155.
42 James claims that beliefs run on a credit system, where epistemic trust is nevertheless justified because there are verification points where knowledge is put directly into the communal belief bank. This does not, however, commit him to a realist metaphysics for philosophical back-up. It is worth remembering, too, that for James, coherence does not simply involve an appropriate fit as between beliefs. It also covers the requirement of comporting with experience and life. The latter point is made very explicit in Putnam 1995, p. 26, n. 26.
43 James describes the epistemic phenomenology of belief acquisition as follows: 'The process is always the same. The individual has a stock of old opinions already, but he meets a new experience that puts them to a strain. Somebody contradicts them; or in a reflective moment he discovers that they contradict each other; or he hears of facts with which they are incompatible; or desires arise in him which they cease to satisfy. The result is an inward trouble to which his mind till then

had been a stranger, and from which he seeks to escape by modifying his previous mass of opinions. He saves as much of it as he can, for in this matter of belief we are all conservatives. So he tries to change first this opinion, and then that (for they resist change very variously), until at last some new idea comes up which he can graft upon the ancient stock with a minimum of disturbance of the latter, some idea that mediates between the stock and the new experience and runs them into one another most felicitously and expediently' (James, 1998, pp. 34–5).

44 The pragmatist is more rationalist than the rationalist in the sense in having a richer repertoire of reasons to explain the practical nature and efficacy of belief and knowledge acquisition. Knowledge occupies what Sellars memorably calls 'the logical space of reasons' (Sellars, 1963, p. 169). By contrast, the rationalist jumps out of this space pretty quickly to invoke notions of correspondence or confrontation with reality about which there is little of rational substance to be said. By staying within a richer explanatory environment James can be seen as preparing the ground for Robert Brandom's 'rationalist pragmatism' – though it is not yet clear whether Brandom is as keen as James is to divest the term 'rationalist' of its traditional connotations (see Brandom, 1994).

45 The canonical text for Quine is 'Two Dogmas of Empiricism', 2004c.

46 'A Coherence Theory of Truth', reprinted with 'Afterthoughts, 1987' in Malachowski, 1990.

47 For further discussion of Rorty's approach to James, see Malachowski, 2011.

48 For more on Dewey's 'inclusive' conception of experience, see Malachowski, 2010, pp. 24–5.

DAVID HILDEBRAND

3 Dewey's pragmatism: instrumentalism and meliorism

Of all the classic pragmatists, perhaps John Dewey best epitomizes how full and varied an intellectual's life could be.[1] An enormously productive scholar and prominent public intellectual whose career spanned over sixty years, Dewey significantly contributed to a wide range of subjects, including aesthetics, education, epistemology, ethics, logic, metaphysics, politics, psychology and religion. Lecturing extensively at home and abroad, Dewey addressed serious moral issues such as war and peace, economic and political freedom, equality for women and minorities, freedom of speech and educational change. Active in political organizing, Dewey played crucial and germinative roles in influential organizations: the American Association of University Professors, the American Civil Liberties Unions and the National Association for the Advancement of Colored People, to list just a few.

Born in 1859 to Lucina and Archibald Dewey, a grocer, Dewey spent his childhood and college years in Burlington, Vermont. After two years of teaching high school, Dewey did his graduate studies in philosophy at the Johns Hopkins University. Taught by Charles S. Peirce, George Sylvester Morris and George Stanley Hall (a pragmatist, Hegelian and experimental psychologist respectively), he completed graduate school in 1884 after two years with a dissertation criticizing Kant's psychology. Reflecting years later, Dewey credited his study of Hegelianism with liberating him from philosophical and personal difficulties, and initiating lifelong attempts to integrate a plurality of experiences (psychical, bodily, imaginative, practical) into dynamic wholes. Dewey and his first wife, Alice Chipman Dewey, had six children and adopted another. Two boys died tragically young (at two and eight). After Alice died,

Dewey married Roberta Lowitz Grant and they adopted two children. John Dewey died at home in New York City on 1 June 1952 of pneumonia.

Dewey's professional career suffered few setbacks. He held numerous posts (including department chairmanships) at the Universities of Michigan, Minnesota and Chicago, concluding his career at Columbia University (retiring in 1930). Continuously productive, he published 32 books, 605 articles or essays, 126 reviews and 233 other miscellanea (including published radio addresses, prefaces, introductions, forewords, interviews, pamphlets, book chapters, published letters, memorials, work reports, syllabuses, letters to the editor, etc.).[2] Notably, many of his most renowned works were published well after he reached sixty years old.

An enormous number of cultural, personal and intellectual sources shaped Dewey's philosophical views. While space prevents discussion of even a short list of influences (which would include Kant, Hegel, G. S. Morris, G. H. Mead, Jane Addams, F. J. E. Woodbridge and Albert Barnes), something must be said about Charles Darwin and William James. In different ways, their work made *experience* the source and telos of Dewey's naturalistic pragmatism. Darwin's work provided a robust portrait of experience as an organic and transactional process of change. As Dewey remarked in 1909 (the fiftieth anniversary of *Origin of Species*), Darwin's impact upon the course of philosophy's history was revolutionary:

> The conceptions that had reigned in the philosophy of nature and knowledge for two thousand years, the conceptions that had become the familiar furniture of the mind, rested on the assumption of the superiority of the fixed and final; they rested upon treating change and origin as signs of defect and unreality. In laying hands upon the sacred ark of absolute permanency, in treating the forms that had been regarded as types of fixity and perfection as originating and passing away, the *Origin of Species* introduced a mode of thinking that in the end was bound to transform the logic of knowledge, and hence the treatment of morals, politics and religion.
>
> (MW4: 3)[3]

Throughout his career, Dewey undertook to spell out those logical transformations. He began by challenging existing epistemologists' investigations into knowledge (as, for example, the search for static correspondences between names and things) and proposed, instead, that philosophers focus upon *knowing* as the active, strategic management of dynamic *transitions*:

> The influence of Darwin upon philosophy resides in his having conquered the phenomena of life for the principle of transition, and thereby freed the new logic for application to mind and morals and life. When he said of species what Galileo had said of the earth, *e pur si muove*, he emancipated, once for all, genetic and experimental ideas as an organon of asking questions and looking for explanations.
>
> (MW4: 7–8)[4]

William James's work also gave Dewey a conception of experience which fused, dynamically, both percepts–concepts and relations–relata.[5] More significant, perhaps, was James's lesson that experience was of *moral* moment – experience is what it is because it *matters* to some unique *someone*. Ultimately James teaches Dewey as much about *how* to philosophize (experience *as method*) as about philosophy's subject matter (experience *as stuff*). James drives home Peirce's anti-Cartesian message that philosophical progress can only be made if pragmatism abandons traditional efforts to transcend a human perspective; in this sense, pragmatism must be a humanism. As much as anyone, James showed Dewey how a philosopher might also live his philosophy: James's sense of life was itself vital. He had a profound sense, in origin artistic and moral, perhaps, rather than 'scientific', of the difference between the categories of the living and of the mechanical:

> Some time, I think, someone may write an essay that will show how the most distinctive factors in his general philosophic view, pluralism, novelty, freedom, individuality, are all connected with his feeling for the qualities and traits of that which lives. Many philosophers have had much to say about the idea of organism; but they have taken it structurally and hence statically. It was reserved for James to think of life in terms of life in action.
>
> (LW5: 157–8)

James and Darwin, then, were especially noteworthy contributors to what eventually became Dewey's unique view of experience and nature: a living, changing, transactional drama of organisms-in-environments using the tools of nature, body, mind, and language to accommodate and create personal and cultural change.

DEWEY AS 'PRAGMATIST'

Though famous as an exponent of 'pragmatism', Dewey exhibited relatively little allegiance towards this label, referring variously to his approach as 'radical empiricism', 'humanism', 'naturalism', 'instrumentalism', 'experimentalism', and late in life, 'operationalism'. What really mattered to Dewey was that he make clear that the meanings of terms, concepts or propositions should be judged by their experimental *consequences* (broadly considered) in 'inquiry'. Inquiries may take various forms (scientific, philosophic or, typically, quotidian) but are always conducted from some perspective, draw upon particular histories (such as preceding events, inquiries), to serve particular purposes or ideals. An inquiry's success depends on how well it works – that is, whether or not its fruits (conclusions, judgements, solutions) produce satisfactory experiences. The practical (or non-transcendent) nature of inquiry is central to pragmatism, a philosophy which Dewey emphasized 'takes its stand with daily life' (MW10: 39) and remains committed to the 'actual crises of life' (MW10: 43). Because pragmatism commits to linking meaning-criteria with present and future experience, it is perhaps just as fair to label pragmatism a metaphilosophical *attitude* or *stance* as a doctrine (or theory) of meaning. (By 'stance' I mean that it is more than an academic philosophical position; it is *vision*, a way of approaching philosophy *ab extra*.) Pragmatism's status *qua* stance derives from its acute self-consciousness of the fact that a term's meaning cannot be explicated innocently, that is, without implying specific and future practical consequences. And *those* implications – if one is completely forthright – evince some position about what *will and should* happen. As formulated and asserted, facts imply values; they are entangled. 'The trail of the human serpent is thus over everything', as James put it. From this stance, knowing cannot be spectatorship but is rather a tool (or tactic) of dynamic agency. 'Knowing', Dewey writes, 'is literally something which we do; that analysis is ultimately physical and active; that meanings in their logical quality are standpoints, attitudes, and methods of behaving toward fact, and that active experimentation is essential to verification' (MW10: 367).[6] And because knowing, as a tactic of agency, is present in all areas of life, pragmatism 'should be applied as widely as possible; and to things as diverse as controversies, beliefs, truths, ideas, and objects' (MW4: 101).

MELIORISM AND THE PRACTICAL STARTING POINT

One term that encapsulates pragmatism's fundamental continuities (knowing and doing, fact and value) is 'meliorism', and most, if not all, of Dewey's work can be profitably understood as guided by a 'melioristic motive'. Meliorism is the view that it is both a logical and moral error to declare that life – presently or ultimately – is either perfectly good or bad; life should be understood as *improvable*, primarily through intelligent, human effort. As applied to philosophy, meliorism suggests that no philosophical questions (even regarding truth and knowledge) can ever be fully isolated from endeavours to preserve and create value; more generally, it means that philosophy's *raison d'être* is to make life *better*. Meliorism is no sentimental faith, but a working hypothesis whose plausibility rests upon observation and experience. Trying out this hypothesis obliges the philosopher (any intellectual, really) to keep alive a dynamic interaction between theory and practice so that results continue to address the problems rooted in daily life. A second key to grasping Dewey's pragmatism is something which may be called a 'practical starting point'. While many take the epitome of Dewey's philosophy to be his instrumentalist epistemology or experiential approach to aesthetics, a more general and revelatory approach might focus instead upon where Dewey believes philosophical activity *starts*. As Douglas Browning puts it:

Understanding John Dewey's comprehensive and, in its details, dauntingly complex philosophy requires taking account of his view of the three essential phases of experience, namely, (1) the starting point in everyday experience of all of our attempts to enhance the meaning of our lives, (2) the process of the experiential transformation of such experience, and (3) the experience of consummatory achievement. Though much has been written about the last two phases and many scholars have centered their interpretations of Dewey on one or both of them, the first phase has been too often neglected. This is unfortunate, since Dewey's notion of experience, which is the key to grasping the import of each of these phases, is initially shaped at the starting point and carried forward from it.[7]

In works like *Reconstruction in Philosophy* (1920) and *The Quest for Certainty* (1929) Dewey challenges the near universal tendency of successive generations of philosophers to start with dualistic, theoretical and certainty-seeking assumptions. Not only were such prejudicial frameworks unfounded, they diverted philosophy towards insoluble puzzles and from practical problems. Instead, Dewey argues, philosophy should start from lived experience and pay the kind of careful attention necessary to avoiding such assumptions in the first place.

This chapter cannot, of course, cover the full range of Dewey's thought; instead, it seeks to convey the gist of Dewey's philosophy by presenting four facets of his thought: *mind, inquiry, growth* and *wisdom*. 'Mind' examines Dewey's *functionalism* and his naturalistic (i.e. interactional–ecological) model of mind. 'Inquiry' follows how a functioning mind moves, *instrumentally*, from doubt to belief. 'Growth' then traces two ways instrumental inquiry is elaborated when applied as a cultural tool: (1) for the growth of children (as *education*); and (2) for solving public problems (as *democracy*). 'Wisdom', finally, examines Dewey's general view of philosophy: as a cultural and moral enterprise which should eschew contemporary predilections for technical definition or clinical exactitude and return to the pursuit of wisdom. Such a pursuit, Dewey believed, could progress via the criticism of meaning *if* the point of such criticism became consciously ameliorative – anchored, that is, by a *moral* relation to ordinary experience. While philosophy, in Dewey's view, can take forms both technical and abstract, it must not hide beneath these qualities but ultimately prove its worth as equipment for living.

MIND: FUNCTIONAL PSYCHOLOGY

We begin with Dewey's interest in and reconstruction of psychology's elements because this early work initiated lifelong efforts to define and redefine 'experience', a notion that became central to every area of his philosophy.[8] Initially, Dewey hoped psychology could answer the most profound human questions, but he grew to believe that the nature of experience was too rich for the constraints imposed by this (or any single) science. Influenced by study of physiological and experimental psychology (especially of Wilhelm Wundt and G. Stanley Hall, a graduate school professor in whose laboratory Dewey conducted experiments on attention) Dewey published his first book, *Psychology* (EW2) in 1887.

Psychology steered between two prevailing schools: the newer physiological psychology and introspectionism, which arose from eighteenth-century associationism (*à la* Hume and Locke). It was psychology's turn towards evolutionary biology that had the defining impact upon Dewey's outlook. In 'The New Psychology' he wrote:

> The influence of [evolutionary] biological science in general upon psychology has been very great ... To biology is due the conception of organism ... In psychology this conception has led to the recognition of mental life as an organic unitary process developing according to the laws of all life, and not a theatre for the exhibition of independent autonomous faculties, or a rendezvous in which isolated, atomic sensations and ideas may gather, hold external converse, and then forever part.
>
> (EW1: 56)

This new way of seeing the world – as organisms-in-environments – opened doors for Dewey, empowering his attacks on traditional dualisms not only between mind/body and concept/percept, but those affecting ethics and democracy, such as individual/society. Still, while Dewey clearly preferred physiological psychology to introspectionism, he also criticized its uncritical acceptance of modern-period accounts of experience, viz. as amalgamations of atomized sensations, operating mechanically in cause–effect sequences. A careful student of both Hegel and Darwin, Dewey surmised that such a psychology could never successfully explain a dynamic and living world filled with experienced meaning.

> The idea of environment is a necessity to the idea of organism, and with the conception of environment comes the impossibility of considering psychical life as an individual, isolated thing developing in a vacuum ... I refer to the growth of those vast and as yet undefined topics of inquiry which may be vaguely designated as the social and historical sciences, – the sciences of the origin and development of the various spheres of man's activity.
>
> ('The New Psychology', EW1: 56–7)

In retrospect, these writings make clear why Dewey felt compelled to reconstruct psychology. For to fully understand experience, it was necessary to look beyond methods focusing only on the biological and mechanical towards approaches incorporating contextual elements of experience provided by culture and language. Dewey's recognition of this was aided, in no small part, by William James.

While there is not space to present many details of Dewey's efforts to reconstruct psychology, four things are worth considering: the impact of William James; Dewey's critique of the reflex arc concept; his consequent development of an organic, functionalist (or 'ecological') model; and that model's implications for the realist theory of perception.

WILLIAM JAMES AND THE 'REFLEX ARC'

It is impossible to overstate James's influence on Dewey, particularly his *The Principles of Psychology* (1950). Dewey taught the *Principles* to graduate students just after publication, and James's general approach, 'radical empiricism', taught Dewey that appeals to infinite absolutes never instruct us what to do next; indeed, such pragmatic guidance only comes from 'study of the deficiencies, irregularities and possibilities of the actual situation' (MW14: 199). In other words, psychology *could* give an account of intelligent selves with unified consciousnesses *without* appealing to anything transcendent (e.g. the Hegelian Absolute).[9] Dewey singles out the importance of James's *Psychology* in giving his thinking 'a new direction and quality'. It was James's substitution of a 'stream of consciousness' (for discrete elementary psychological states) as well as James's emphatically biological conception of the mind which, Dewey says, 'worked its way more and more into all my ideas and acted as a ferment to transform old beliefs' (LW5: 157).

Dewey's 'The Reflex Arc Concept in Psychology' (1896) was seminal both for Dewey's own development (advancing his conception of experience) and the history of psychology (marking the end of introspectionism and the birth of functionalism). It celebrates how the 'reflex arc' model offered psychologists a more empirical and experimental mode of explanation than did introspectionism's mysterious and unobservable 'psychic entities'. However, it also criticizes the reflex arc for artificially separating events into discrete (and analysable) sequences. 'As a result', Dewey wrote, 'the reflex arc is not a comprehensive, or organic unity, but a patchwork of disjointed parts, a mechanical conjunction of unallied processes' ('The Reflex Arc Concept', EW5: 97). In lieu of the reflex arc's stimulus–response model, Dewey suggested understanding behaviour as embedded in wider 'sensori-motor coordinations', continual circuits in which organism and environment effect both adjustment and reconstitution. As Thomas Alexander put it, 'What Dewey proposes ... is to *start* with the idea of the organism already dynamically involved with the world and aiming toward unified activity' (Alexander, 1987, p. 129). This defend-then-critique strategy toward the reflex arc concept allowed Dewey to show why a new account of experience was needed. After all, an event description premised on a (supposedly ultimate) disjunction promulgated an erroneous picture of experience. Organisms do *not* passively receive a stimulus and only later become active responders; rather, Dewey argued, organisms are already active transactors with environments. Indeed, psychologists themselves are transactors, and once this is recognized, even definitions of 'stimulus' and 'response' can be seen to pivot on whatever pragmatic purposes are guiding the experimental situation as arranged. Psychologists, Dewey said, are seeking to discover 'what stimulus or sensation, what movement and response mean' and such terms 'mean distinctions of flexible function only, not of fixed existence' (EW5: 102).

Several long-term implications of Dewey's paper should be mentioned. First, by applying the holism found in James's psychology, Dewey formulated a model of organic interaction which served every area of his later philosophy. Second, by insisting on functional interpretations of scientific terms (e.g. 'stimulus', 'response'), he laid the groundwork for epistemological instrumentalism – roughly, the view that meaning determination for abstract terms (whether commonsensical, scientific or logical) requires assessing them within an environment which includes the inquirer (including specific purposes, historical circumstances and potential consequences). Psychology and philosophy must *start* amid the flow (or stream) of lived experience and, from that stance, create pragmatic standards of clarity and validity for abstract concepts.

PERCEPTION AND PSYCHOPHYSICAL DUALISM

The implications of the organic and interactional model nascent in the 'Reflex Arc' paper for philosophers concerned with issues of perception and realism were profound. Realists, with whom Dewey argued vigorously in the early twentieth century, argued that perception is primarily a process of passive reception; the function of cognition is primarily selective, not constitutive. Extending the critique of 'Reflex Arc', Dewey argued that their picture derived from psychophysical dualist assumptions, such as the notion that erroneously pictures the perceiving mind (inner, subjective) as radically separated from a causal world (outer, objective). This 'spectator model of knowing', as Dewey called it (see LW4, MW12), falsifies actual instances of perception which, after all, *start* with an engaged and purposeful creature in an environment constituted by ongoing processes. Perception is always agential; percepts are *taken*, selectively and purposefully, from a perspective. To fully acknowledge this, however, would require philosophers and psychologists to abandon subjectivism as a starting point and the concomitant notion that perceptual episodes are just 'presented' to a waiting, isolated self. Instead, Dewey argued, perceptual experience should be understood as one among many empirically available and natural events in which we are engaged. 'It would be much more correct to say', Dewey writes, 'that the self is contained in a perception than that a perception is presented to a self...[T]he organism is involved in the occurrence of the perception in the same sort of way that hydrogen in involved in the happening – producing – of water' (MW6: 119).

By rejecting an 'inner/outer' model of perception, Dewey also advances a naturalistic metaphysical picture of qualities. Traditional approaches isolated qualities with discrete labels (as 'hard' or 'red' or 'sweet', etc.) and then puzzled over *where* they were! (Are qualities in us? In nature? etc.) Dewey's model argues that qualities are interacting processes taking place *between* organism and environment: a quality is a *transactional event*, not a sensory impingement by some 'raw' external datum.[10]

In sum, a perception is never instantaneous, passive or simply locatable in an individual consciousness; nor is it a case of knowledge. Rather, it is an embodied relation of adjustment between an already-functioning organism and an environment. (Indeed, mind itself is an event – one constituted by a system of meanings and purposes).[11] While a perceptual event (such as flash of light) may be incorporated as an ingredient of *inquiry* (and result in a knowing judgement), it is fallacious to transpose the results of inquiry back upon the initial perceptual event and announce that it is 'original'.[12]

INQUIRY: INSTRUMENTALISM

The organic and interactional (hence 'ecological') model Dewey develops in his psychology proved innovative for subsequent theories of knowledge and learning. For once this ecological picture of things was worked out, a host of traditional epistemological conceptions (premised upon metaphysical dualisms such as mind/world, appearance/reality) became untenable, even nonsensical. 'So far as the question of the relation of the self to known objects is concerned', Dewey writes, 'knowing is but one special case of the agent–patient, of the behaver–enjoyer–sufferer situation' (MW6: 120). This wholesale repudiation of the metaphysics propping up traditional epistemologies required that Dewey invent a new psychology, logic and philosophy of education; over the course of his career, he does.

The overarching approach Dewey devised came to be widely known as 'instrumentalism' or 'pragmatism'. Like his earlier (functionalist) reconstructions in psychology, instrumentalism sought to criticize and mediate traditional divisions entrenched in various areas and move philosophy beyond divisions such as science/religion, empiricism/rationalism and realism/idealism. Dewey's 1912 summary in 'Contributions to *A Cyclopedia of Education*' is worth quoting at length:

'[Pragmatism] falls in line with the growing influence of the theory of evolution, asserting that reality itself is inherently and not merely accidentally and externally in process of continuous transition and transformation, and it connects the theory of knowledge and of logic with this basic fact. It connects with historic spiritual philosophies in its emphasis upon life, and upon biological and dynamic conceptions as more fundamental than purely physical and mathematical ideas. While claiming to be strictly empirical in method, it gives to thought and thought relations (universals) a primary and constructive function which sensational empiricism denied them, and thus claims to have included and explained the factor that historic rationalisms have stood for. In somewhat similar fashion, it claims to mediate between realistic and idealistic theories of knowledge. It holds to reality, prior to cognitive operations and not constructed by these operations, to which knowing, in order to be successful, must adapt itself.'

(MW7: 328)

Important, earlier statements of Dewey's instrumentalism (and definitive breaks with Hegelian logic) are made in 'Some Stages of Logical Thought' (1900) which follows Peirce's well-known 1877–8 papers by celebrating science's method of thinking, naming it the 'doubt–inquiry process' (MW1: 173).[13] This account is soon developed in *Studies in Logical Theory* (MW2: 1903), where, along with his Chicago collaborators, Dewey acknowledges a 'preeminent obligation' to James.[14]

In *Studies*, Dewey criticizes transcendentalist logic in detail, and concludes that logic ought *not* assume the existence of either thought or reality *in general* but should content itself with the use or function of ideas in experience. 'The test of validity of [an] idea is its functional or instrumental use in effecting the transition from a relatively conflicting experience to a relatively integrated one' (MW2: 359). Thus, Dewey's instrumentalist position, in effect, abandons any and all psychophysical dualisms as well as any correspondentist theories of knowledge. 'In the logical process', he writes,

> the datum is not just external existence, and the idea mere psychical existence. Both are modes of existence – one of *given* existence, the other of *possible*, of inferred existence ... In other words, datum and ideatum are divisions of labor, cooperative instrumentalities, for economical dealing with the problem of the maintenance of the integrity of experience.
> (MW2: 339–40)

BEYOND EMPIRICISM, RATIONALISM AND KANT

Though Dewey did not see his instrumentalism as just another move in epistemological debates, it may help readers to see, briefly, how it responds to tensions between rationalism and classical empiricism, and to Immanuel Kant's response to these. Classical empiricists typically insisted that knowledge originates in sensory experience, e.g. the 'blank slate' of the mind receives the external world's replicas as ideas, associates them, and, with luck, comes to reflect nature's structure. Rationalists, in contrast, argued that because knowledge had to be both abstract and deductively certain, it could not originate with the senses but rather from an immaterial faculty, the mind, which could reason unmolested by the vagaries of the senses. Kant's response to this tension was to refuse to assign an originary place to either concepts or percepts, arguing instead that mind and world are together necessary for the creation of knowledge. More important, Kant argued that understanding mind's product (knowledge) requires an account of what the mind itself contributes as an active and systematic structurer of incoming representations. Dewey's response to this situation in epistemology was to acknowledge the cogency of Kant's criticisms of empiricism and rationalism, while going on to severely criticize his retention of several crucial but unjustified assumptions. Chief among them were Kant's assumptions that knowledge must be certain; that intellect and nature were categorically distinct; and that a noumenal realm of things-in-themselves could be posited. Moreover, Kant claimed that the sensations necessary to knowledge are initially inchoate yet can never be observed as such because they are first structured by mental categories (which render them experience-able). Dewey's response is that Kant never actually offers an argument justifying this fundamental claim.

Significantly, Dewey does more than critique Kant's system; taking his cue from James he insists upon a complete change of standpoint, that of lived experience or 'radical empiricism'. From this standpoint, one may accept as real – as meaningful – that which comes to us as comprehensible, as related, as anticipated, as felt. If you, dear reader, examine your own experience as you read these words you will see that you do not *begin* with atoms of impressions (or ideas) and then associate them together to make meaning out of meaninglessness. Moreover, it seems needlessly baroque to require some vast machinery of categories as a prerequisite for meaning. Perhaps it is most important that your experience's meaning derives, for the most part, *not* from past sensation or inborn structure but from your *prospects* – your future goals, purposes and projected meanings. This idea – that meaning emerges from the co-penetration of future and present – is perhaps the *key* advance pragmatism makes over Kant and earlier modern epistemology. Ideas have significance based upon their power to control, predict or guide the course of future action, not upon their static reflecting of 'reality' (be it sensory or conceptual). Dewey writes, 'When experience is aligned with the life-process and sensations are seen to be points of readjustment, the alleged atomism of sensations totally disappears. With this disappearance is abolished the need for a synthetic faculty of super-empirical reason to connect them'(MW12: 131–2). As a theory of meaning-for-action, pragmatism, like the living philosopher who wields it, *leans forward*. Thus, Dewey's instrumentalism rejects modern epistemology and, by replacing Kant's mind-centred system with a decentred, dynamic and ecological one, effects 'a reversal comparable to a Copernican revolution'.[15] No longer just a product of evolution, intelligence stands now as a tool or instrument actively guiding evolving creatures. As an epistemology, instrumentalism is completely at home within naturalism.

Given this repudiation of these fundamental pillars of epistemology, one might wonder what becomes of logic and epistemology. For Dewey, these inquiries persist but become more empirical:

> We are trying to know knowledge ... The procedure which I have tried to follow, no matter with what obscurity and confusion, is to begin with cases of knowledge and to analyze them to discover why and how they are knowledges. Why not take the best authenticated cases of faithful reports which are available, compare them with the sufficiently numerous cases of reports ascertained to be unfaithful and doubtful, and see what we find?
> (MW13: 60)

This 'inquiry into inquiry', as Dewey defines logic in 1938, amounts to the systematic collection, organization and description of empirical discoveries about the conditions of genuine inquiry; the pragmatic aim of this new logic is fundamentally ameliorative: to provide a general and 'important aid in proper guidance of further attempts at knowing' (MW10: 23).

INQUIRY, KNOWLEDGE AND TRUTH

In many works, Dewey details the elements and processes of active thinking and problem solving. I shall briefly mention three key elements: the pattern of inquiry, knowledge and truth. Regarding inquiry, if one examines how people actually solve problems, a pattern of inquiry is manifest and prevalent. Dewey details a five-phase pattern in 'Analysis of Reflective Thinking' (LW8) and the *Logic* (LW12). Explicitly disavowing the traditional opposition between reason and emotion, Dewey argues that inquiry initiates with a phase in which there is (1) a *feeling* that something is amiss. This feeling is unique, a *particular* doubtfulness whose singular and pervasive quality helps direct subsequent stages of inquiry. Next, because what is initially present is indeterminate, (2) a *problem* must be carefully formulated; problems do not preexist inquiry, as frequently assumed.[16] Next (3) a *hypothesis* is constructed, imaginatively utilizing both perceptual facts and theoretical ideas to forecast possibilities consequent on the execution of various operations. Then, (4) one *reasons* about the meanings involved in the hypothesis' central ideas, ferreting out unnoticed conflicts and consequences that might require revision of the hypothesis or even the problem's formulation. Finally, (5) one takes *action*, actually evaluating and testing the hypothesis to reveal whether the proposal satisfactorily converts an indeterminate situation into a determinate one which may prompt the inquiry to conclusion.

This 'pattern', Dewey was careful to note, is descriptively schematic and one should not expect most *actual* inquiries to present phases in ways so discrete and straightforwardly sequential. Moreover, he cautioned that his pattern was not meant to describe how people *always* think but rather how they would think if they followed more exemplary kinds of inquiry, like those found in the empirical sciences.

Given this account of inquiry's process and function in helping organisms adjust to their environment, it is not surprising that Dewey shunned philosophers' typical idol-worship of terms like 'knowledge' and 'truth'. 'Knowledge, as an abstract term, is a name for the product of competent inquiries. Apart from this relation, its meaning is so empty that any content or filling may be arbitrarily poured in' (LW12: 16). As for 'truth', Dewey defined it mainly as a way of coaxing interlocutors to pay some sympathetic attention to his theory of inquiry. 'Like knowledge itself', Dewey writes, 'truth is an experienced relation of things, and it has no meaning outside of such relation' (MW3: 118).[17] Here, Dewey directs attention back to the *process* of inquiry; within that process, 'truth' is a label describing what *that* inquiry has accomplished for *those* purposes. Indeed, logic and epistemology might remain cognizant of this 'if', Dewey quips, 'we were always to translate the noun "truth" back into the adjective "true," and this back into the adverb "truly"' (MW3: 118). For instrumentalism, then, truth and knowledge are adjectival not nominative terms, because as Peirce told us, inquiry goes on indefinitely. 'There is no belief', Dewey writes, 'so settled as not to be exposed to further inquiry' (LW12: 16). In other words, following Dewey, a better way to explain the honour which has been attached to 'truth' and 'knowledge' is to see these concepts in the same light as a tool or piece of equipment: they have proved useful or reliable enough to be counted upon as resources for further inquiries.

A SOCIOCULTURAL MATRIX

Consistent with Peirce and James before him, Dewey conceives of logic and inquiry – indeed, philosophy – as emerging from and returning to lives which, for creatures like us, includes a sociocultural matrix. 'Logic is a social discipline [and] every inquiry grows out of a background of culture and takes effect in greater or less modification of the conditions out of which it arises' (LW12: 27).[18] Accordingly, epistemologies must be formulated much less narrowly, that is, in ways sympathetic to and ameliorative of the social and political realm in which every epistemologist lives. Epistemology, no less than philosophy itself, performs a cultural-critical function: 'The life of all thought is to effect a junction at some point of the new and the old, of deep-sunk customs and unconscious dispositions, that are brought to the light of attention by some conflict with newly emerging directions of activity' (LW3: 6). As he turned his attention to the conflicts around him (in education, ethics, politics, art, and religion), Dewey's functionalist view of mind and his instrumentalist approach to knowing provided him with the transactional tools he needed to help effect such junctions.

GROWTH: EDUCATION AND DEMOCRACY

It is perhaps still fair to say that Dewey is better known as an educator than as a philosopher. Yet if one reflects upon his career, it is clearly a mistake to categorically separate these two roles. In 1916 Dewey reflected that *Democracy and Education* (MW9) 'was for many years that [work] in which my philosophy, such as it is, was most fully expounded' (LW5: 156). In *Democracy*, Dewey went so far as to place *all* of philosophy within the sphere of education. Such a claim, Dewey knew, would sound odd to many, but it reflected his conviction that philosophy was rapidly being appropriated by a specialized class using increasingly technical language. A recovery of the philosopher's role as engaged and critical citizen could be aided, Dewey thought, if philosophers tried to see their subject matter from the perspective of education. Education offers a vantage ground from which to penetrate to the human, as distinct from the technical, significance of philosophic discussions ... The educational point of view enables one to envisage philosophic problems where they arise and thrive, where they are at home and where acceptance or rejection makes a difference in practice. If we are willing to conceive education as the process of forming fundamental dispositions, intellectual and emotional, toward nature and fellow-men, philosophy may even be defined *as the general theory of education* (MW9: 338).

Throughout his career, Dewey was active in education: devising curricula, reviewing and administering schools, running departments, participating in collective organizing and lecturing on many aspects of education. Moreover, his creation of the University of Chicago's Department of Pedagogy and Laboratory School gave Dewey the chance to experiment with nascent theories of psychological functionalism and instrumental logic. These schools also became sites of democratic expression by the local community.

SOCIETY, THE CHILD AND CONTINUOUS LEARNING

Application of functionalism to education can be traced back to Dewey's 'Reflex Arc' paper. That critique demonstrated that psychology had misinterpreted human experience as a sequence of fits and starts, rather than a circuit of continuous activity. Since learning is a specific kind of experience it should be understood analogously: learning does not occur in fits and starts but as a progressive and cumulative process where inquirers can move beyond the dissatisfaction of doubt toward the satisfaction attending the resolution of problems. The paper had also shown that the subject of a stimulus (analogously: the pupil) is never a passive recipient of sensation, but an active agent inhabiting a larger environmental field. Such fundamental facts demanded, Dewey argued, that educators abandon pedagogies that pictured blank slates awaiting inscription-by-curriculum. 'The question of education', Dewey writes, 'is the question of taking hold of [children's] activities, of giving them direction' (MW1: 25).[19]

Dewey's philosophy of education emerged in the 1890s amid a fierce debate between educational 'traditionalists' and 'romantics'. In numerous articles and books such as *My Pedagogic Creed* (1897),

The School and Society (1899), *Democracy and Education* (1916), and *Experience and Education* (1938) he advanced an interactional model that sought to bypass the debate by assigning privilege to *neither* society nor child. While he agreed with the romantics' emphasis upon the child as indispensable starting point for pedagogy – and maintained that education must attend carefully to children's habits, powers, instincts and personal histories when designing curricula – Dewey also insisted that the child could not be the *only* starting point.[20] The needs, values and interests of extant groups (family, community, nation) were also indispensable – but *not* singularly authoritative – starting points.

Dewey's opposition to traditionalists' authoritarian discipline and the pedagogy of memorization was more fully-fledged. While he agreed that there was a need to pass along content (facts and values), he argued strenuously that schooling should not indoctrinate the child but rather serve to *incorporate* a unique individual into a changing society which also belonged to that child. Following lifelong friend and colleague G. H. Mead, Dewey argued that the child's 'self' was, in large measure, an emerging construct of both personal and social experience; no child's words, deeds or interests could be understood as existing in isolation from their social context. To reflect these facts of social psychology, schools needed to become communities in their own right which could reflect and shape the needs and interests of children and their society: 'The school cannot be a preparation for social life excepting as it reproduces, within itself, the typical conditions of social life' (EW5: 61–62).[21]

DEMOCRACY THROUGH EDUCATION

I hope that I have made clear the continuities between Dewey's functionalism, instrumentalism and educational philosophy and may now expand upon a further continuity between these views and his view of democracy. As intimated above, Dewey's efforts to connect school with society were motivated by more than just his desire for better pedagogy. Because individual ethical responsibilities arise from and return to the social realm, such responsibilities can only be developed in schools which enact the structures of social and democratic life. Democratic life consists not only of vocations and economic self-sufficiency, but of compassionate problem solving, creative expression, and civic self-governance. The full panoply of roles a child will assume in life is vast; once this fact is appreciated, it becomes incumbent upon society to make education its highest political and economic priority:

> There will be almost a revolution in school education when study and learning are treated not as acquisition of what others know but as development of capital to be invested in eager alertness in observing and judging the conditions under which one lives. Yet until this happens, we shall be ill-prepared to deal with a world whose outstanding trait is change.
> (LW17: 463)

Democracy, in Dewey's view, went much deeper than a form of government. 'Democracy', Dewey writes, 'is not an alternative to other principles of associated life [but] the idea of community life itself' (LW2: 328). As the lives of individuals-in-communities change, conflicts and needs arise which require intelligent administration; we need to make sense out of new experience. Education is our means. Education 'is that reconstruction or reorganization of experience which adds to the meaning of experience, and which increases ability to direct the course of subsequent experience' (MW9: 82). Put otherwise, creative experimentation was germinative of America's political identity. Thus, to fulfil their roles as citizens and participate fully in the development of American democracy, students needed training in the habits (empirical, imaginative and fallibilistic) which had made experimental science so successful. Dewey called these habits and attitudes 'intelligence'.[22]

Regnant in all three spheres just mentioned – science, education, and democratic life – is Dewey's philosophical naturalism (the ecological model discovered via radical empiricism); such a naturalism places its hope not in immutable laws (of logic, nature or God) or ultimate ends, but in the capacity of human beings to learn from life and reinvest in it. In 'Creative Democracy: The Task before Us' (1939) Dewey writes:

> Democracy is the faith that the process of experience is more important than any special result attained, so that special results achieved are of ultimate value only as they are used to enrich and order the ongoing process. Since the process of experience is capable of being educative, faith in democracy is all one with faith in experience and education. All ends and values that are cut off from the ongoing process become arrests, fixations. They strive to fixate

what has been gained instead of using it to open the road and point the way to new and better experiences.

(LW14: 229)

COMMUNICATION AND DEMOCRACY

Dewey's vision of democracy-as-process makes no transcendent appeals for explanation or justification; because experience is the source of both method and value, the educational process is pivotal for eventual success or failure. Developing abilities to communicate – critically, empathetically, imaginatively – lies at the heart of the educational mission. Our age is, depending one's standpoint, either blessed or cursed with rapid and torrential volumes of information. This places, arguably, a new magnitude of strain on the formation of knowledge and wisdom. Dewey's life spanned the rise of the telegraph, penny newspaper, radio and television, and he was alert to the epistemic and political misuses to which such media could be put. In works like *The Public and its Problems* (LW2) he expressed concern with the general American tendency to fix belief by preferring authority over critical debate and inquiry. Such anti-inquirential habits could be traced, as we have seen, to authoritarian pedagogical methods; they could also be linked to popular communicative practices such as advertising or corporate and political propaganda. Of course, these practices have mushroomed since Dewey's day. Pursuit of a genuine democracy, then, relies even more upon educators and journalists – indeed upon anyone with a critical education – to reveal and debunk deceptive or authoritarian methods of persuasion and demand sceptical and independent thinking. Only culture-wide vigilance, starting in the schools and spreading outward, can ensure the kind of free and open communication which makes inquiry productive and mitigates the persistent threat of social and economic factionalization.

WISDOM: PHILOSOPHY AS EQUIPMENT FOR LIVING

Dewey's late period saw no slackening in intellectual output. Works of startling range, freshness and systematic depth – such as *Experience and Nature* (1925), *The Quest for Certainty* (1929), *Art as Experience* (1934), and *Logic: The Theory of Inquiry* (1938) – were all written after Dewey's sixtieth birthday. What is worth highlighting about this period is how Dewey reformulated his conception of experience to make explicit the connection between philosophy and the search for wisdom. He desired to show why and how philosophy (including metaphysics) was, in function, a kind of *criticism*. And, while such criticism did its work at inordinately general levels of abstraction, it could nevertheless be motivated and oriented by the human need to create value in natural and cultural arenas.

To show how philosophy based in experience could constitute wisdom, he sought to explain how philosophical abstractions could emerge from and return to a world already replete with values. The key, discussed earlier in connection with perception, involved a correction of philosophy's starting point. Dewey singled out as especially pernicious the tendency of philosophers to initiate their inquiries with terms and concepts imbued with the results of previous inquiries. They assume what we may call a 'theoretical starting point', and the result, Dewey complains, 'is invariably the desiccation and atomizing of the world in which we live or of ourselves' (LW6: 7).

In *Experience and Nature* Dewey confronts this starting point anew, developing his own starting point which he calls, alternately, the 'experiential', 'empirical' and 'denotative' method. This involved preliminary critical work to deracinate long-standing associations of 'experience' with various traditional starting points, each initially assuming a variety of entities (e.g. 'impressions', 'ideas', 'minds', 'virtues', etc.). In response to this critical survey of previous views, he calls for philosophers to 'go behind the refinements and elaborations of reflective experience *to the gross and compulsory things of our doings, enjoyments and sufferings* – to the things that force us to labor, that satisfy needs, that surprise us with beauty, that compel obedience under penalty' (LW1: 375–6, my emphasis). Dewey's call does more than reiterate his concord with James's 'radical empiricism'. He makes, in effect, a fundamental announcement of the preferred method and purpose for philosophy. He stresses philosophy's essentially *melioristic* role by pointing directly at the *problematic* nature of the starting point: 'A philosophy which accepts the denotative or empirical method ... points to the contextual situation in which thinking occurs. It notes that the starting point is the actually *problematic*, and that the problematic phase resides in some actual and specifiable situation' (LW1: 61). In other words, philosophy arises in *our* world, *our* world needs healing, and so philosophy must be conducted with conscious intent to return its products to the stream of common life. This continuity – of philosophy and everyday life – is *the gist* of the denotative method: 'As a method', Dewey writes, 'denotation comes first and last' (LW1: 371).

It is worth noting that *Experience and Nature* is arguably Dewey's most 'metaphysical' work, one which offers an account of 'generic traits of existence' as part of an extended theory of experience-and-nature. Despite many critics' prima facie assumptions about such a project – e.g. that it must be foundational, essentialist, and so it must contradict pragmatism's basic creed, etc. – careful reading shows that it was intended and expressed as an empirical enterprise, open to experimental test, emerging from a value-laden world, and aiming to 'render goods more coherent, more secure and more significant in appreciation' (LW1: 305).[23] Philosophy is criticism, and metaphysics, as Dewey put it, is the 'ground map of the province of criticism' (LW1: 309).[24] But metaphysical mapmaking (as Dewey conceives it) is a form of inquiry; to have any value as inquiry it must remain connected to the exigencies present in ordinary experience. It must serve a philosophy conceived as criticism-for-wisdom.

CONCLUSION

At this writing, a three-decade trend of reinvigorated interest in Dewey's philosophical work continues. Critical interest takes various forms (monographs, critical editions, articles, conference presentations) across multiple disciplines. One benefit has been a renewed attention to the classical pragmatists' original writings. This has helped limit the damage that heterodox interpretations (such as those of Richard Rorty) have had upon those encountering Dewey for the first time. As Richard Bernstein put it, 'There are still many thinkers who take Rorty's idiosyncratic version of pragmatism as canonical – and what is worse, they accept his tendentious readings of the classical pragmatists as authoritative' (Bernstein, 2010a, p. 127). While the jury is still out as to whether the consequences of Rorty's integration of the 'linguistic turn' with pragmatism (sometimes called 'neo-pragmatism') will succeed in displacing pragmatism, one may safely say that a rough consensus exists that Rorty's creative interpretations of classical pragmatism have been judged, on the whole, as misleading.[25]

Beyond such internecine debates, interest in Dewey's writings may stem from the example he set to concertedly apply theory to practice while insisting that practice can also modify theory. This mutual and dialectical influence of theory and practice were hallmarks of both experimental science and instrumentalism–pragmatism. It is unsurprising that in today's more technocratic academic milieu, Dewey's approach – open to dialogue, open to correction – seems exciting, fresh and applicable beyond academic contexts. Dewey's scholarly work consistently reached beyond the problems of philosophers to practical affairs calling for amelioration, many of which persist today.[26] This can be seen in the application of Deweyan pragmatism to issues involving animals and the environment, health care, psychiatry, public administration, political theory, aesthetic and literary criticism, communication theory, education and technology. If pragmatism is correct to suggest that the test of an idea's meaning and value lies in action, then it is more than likely that the twenty-first century will continue to look to John Dewey's pragmatism as philosophical equipment for living.

NOTES

1 Some of the ideas in this essay draw upon works by Hildebrand 1999, 2003 and 2008. Biographical material is gleaned primarily from Dykhuizen, 1973.
2 Figures tabulated from *The Collected Works* and the Supplementary Volume 1 and reported to me by The Center for Dewey Studies, Southern Illinois University Carbondale, Carbondale IL 62901. The Center's catalogues also include over 23,415 items of correspondence.
3 Abbreviations EW, MW and LW indicate volumes from the *Early*, *Middle* and *Later Works* in the critical edition of Dewey's works (Southern Illinois University Press). As abbreviated here, the series (EW, MW or LW) is followed by volume then page number.
4 See Browning, 2007.
5 Particularly James's 1890 *Principles of Psychology* (James, 1950).
6 Defending his right to dismiss certain traditional philosophical problems because of pragmatism's practical emphasis, Dewey took pains to clarify that this did not mean that all knowledge was therefore crudely practical – driven by immediate, mean, or pecuniary aims. He writes, 'my pragmatism affirms that action is involved in *knowledge*, not that knowledge is subordinated to action or "practice"' (LW14: 13).

7 Browning, 1999, p. 2. See also Browning, 1998, Myers and Pappas, 2004, Myers, 2001, Pappas, 2008, and Hildebrand, 1999, 2003 and 2008.
8 Early formulations of 'experience' enabled Dewey to pivot from existing conceptions of mind-as-container (or substance) toward mind as process, in transaction with both social, linguistic, and natural environments.
9 Dewey expressed dissatisfaction with idealism's formalistic presumption in the essential unity and perfection of Reality. Such a presumption, Dewey complained, obstructs our capacity to conduct moral inquiry in a genuinely empirical and experimental way. Thus, it obstructs truly actionable conviction and results in pessimism. See e.g. 'Anti-Naturalism in Extremis' (LW15: 46–63).
10 See LW1: 198–9 and LW2: 51.
11 Mind, Dewey argues, *emerges* as sentient beings evolve and symbolize experience. Mind is 'minding', the habitation and use of a system of meaningful signs, 'an agency of novel reconstruction of a pre-existing order' (LW1: 168). This 'process' view of mind is advanced in *Art as Experience*: 'Mind is primarily a verb. It denotes all the ways in which we deal consciously and expressly with the situations in which we find ourselves ... [In] its non-technical use, "mind" denotes every mode and variety of interest in, and concern for, things: practical, intellectual, and emotional. It never denotes anything self-contained, isolated from the world of persons and things, but is always used with respect to situations, events, objects, persons and groups' (LW10: 268, 267). Consciousness, too, is a verb – the rapid transitioning of qualitatively felt events. If we understand mind as a vocabulary of meanings, then consciousness can be pictured as the reconstruction and realization of those meanings for the purpose of the direction and reorganization of experience. Consciousness is 'that phase of a system of meanings which at a given time is undergoing redirection, transitive transformation' (LW1: 233).
12 James had referred to this illegitimate transposition as 'vicious abstractionism' and Alfred North Whitehead named it the 'Fallacy of Misplaced Concreteness'. See Dewey, MW6: 110, James, 1975a and Whitehead, 1997.
13 See Peirce, EP1: 109–23. Peirce's 'Fixation' paper sets the quest to know into a natural and biological explanatory framework and argues that reflective inquiry (a more expansive phrase than the traditional 'reasoning') arises from demands faced by organisms. Experience of those demands is named 'doubt', their satisfactory resolution, 'belief'.
14 James was extremely pleased with the Chicago School, which in turn pleased Dewey greatly. In a 1903 letter to James, Dewey gives him the

credit, commenting, 'I have simply been rendering back in logical vocabulary what was already your own' (Perry, 1935, p. 526).

15 See *The Quest for Certainty*: 'The old centre was mind knowing by means of an equipment of powers complete within itself, and merely exercised upon an antecedent external material equally complete in itself. The new centre is indefinite interactions taking place within a course of nature which is not fixed and complete, but which is capable of direction to new and different results through the mediation of intentional operations' (LW4: 232).

16 'The way in which the problem is conceived', Dewey notes, 'decides what specific suggestions are entertained and which are dismissed; what data are selected and which rejected; it is the criterion for relevancy and irrelevancy of hypotheses and conceptual structures' (LW12: 112).

17 This relation (or function) is valuable for inquiry, of course; Dewey retains this sense by using 'warranted assertibility' or 'warrant' in lieu of 'truth'.

18 Cf. Peirce: 'Logic is rooted in the social principle ... We must not stop at our own fate, but must embrace the whole community. This community, again, must not be limited, but must extend to all races of beings with whom we can come into immediate or mediate intellectual relation' (Peirce W3: ch. 62, EP1: 149).

19 Dewey wrote *How We Think* (1910, MW6: 105–352) primarily to show teachers how to apply instrumentalism to education. The book argues that because the process of learning is akin to the process of thinking, education's intellectual side can be most effectively accomplished by equipping children with scientist-like habits. 'The native and unspoiled attitude of childhood', Dewey writes, 'marked by ardent curiosity, fertile imagination, and love of experimental inquiry, is near, very near, to the attitude of the scientific mind' (MW6: 179).

20 Even today, many conflate Dewey's position with the romantic or 'progressive' view, despite Dewey's consistent resistance to the romantic/progressive's overweening emphasis on the child's interests/desires.

21 One proposal Dewey had for integrating society and school (in 'Democracy in Education' (ME3: 229–339)) involved organizing pedagogy around community-based 'occupational projects' (such as the creation of a meal, from the growth of ingredients on up). Such projects, not to be conflated with rigid vocational education, gave the student a direct involvement with experimental inquiry and impressed the need to 'take an active share in the personal building up of his own problems and to participate in methods of solving them' (MW3: 237).

22 As Richard Bernstein points out, Dewey preferred to talk about 'intelligence' rather than 'reason', not least because of the philosophical

propensity to set reason apart from emotion, desire and passion. 'He preferred to speak about intelligence and intelligent action. Intelligence is not the name of a special faculty. Rather, it designates a cluster of habits and dispositions that includes attentiveness to details, imagination, and passionate commitment. What is most essential for Dewey is the *embodiment* of intelligence in everyday practices' (Bernstein 2010a, p. 85).

23 Richard Rorty's criticism of Dewey for his metaphysical efforts are the most prominent, though they are heterodox for many respected scholars of the American philosophical tradition. See, e.g. Rorty, 1998b; see also Hildebrand, 2003.

24 In 'Context and Thought' Dewey adds, 'Philosophy is criticism; criticism of the influential beliefs that underlie culture; a criticism which traces the beliefs to their generating conditions as far as may be, which tracks them to their results, which considers the mutual compatibility of the elements of the total structure of beliefs. Such an examination terminates, whether so intended or not, in a projection of them into a new perspective which leads to new surveys of possibilities' (LW6: 19). On the issue of Dewey's metaphysics as 'ground map' see Sleeper, 1986 and Sleeper, 1992, p. 184. See also Ortega y Gasset, 1969, p. 121: 'Metaphysics is not a science; it is a construction of the world, and this making a world out of what surrounds you is human life. The world, the universe, is not given to man; what is given to him is his circumstances, his surroundings, with their numberless contents.'

25 A good sampling of this consensus can be found in Saatkamp, 1995.

26 To list just a few problems which have endured from Dewey's time until ours, consider: the competition between religious and secular forces to shape laws and define cultural identity; the struggle by individuals to live meaningfully and beautifully in roles designed by an increasingly industrial and corporate world; the challenge to democratic communication amidst torrents of fragmented information streams; obstacles to fairness and social justice faced by minorities; last, but not least, an increasingly urgent need to apply broadly experimental and scientific thinking to social problems – along with the need of familiarizing populations with those methods.

PART II

Pragmatism revived

4 W. V. O. Quine: pragmatism within the limits of empiricism alone

The term 'pragmatism' is used thematically and historically. Most commonly, its use is to refer to a nineteenth- and twentieth-century American school of philosophy, whose main protagonists were C. S. Peirce, W. James and J. Dewey.[1] Alternatively, its use is to characterize a broad family of philosophical views, held by many philosophers of various periods and persuasions. W. V. O. Quine, a prominent twentieth-century analytic philosopher, is known to have kept a careful distance from the historical school in question.[2] While readily admitting to certain affinities between pragmatism and his own thinking, Quine turned his back on American pragmatism, and criticized some important pragmatist tenets.[3] On the other hand, he utilized pragmatist themes for his own theoretical purposes. In doing so, he made contributions to pragmatism that no student of that school can safely ignore.

In 'Two Dogmas of Empiricism', Quine described the conclusion of his arguments against analyticity and reductionism as 'a shift to pragmatism', and as constituting a more 'thorough' pragmatism than that admitted to by R. Carnap and C. I. Lewis.[4] Whereas these earlier masters accepted a restricted form of pragmatism with respect to the choice between languages, or conceptual schemes, but not with respect to theory-choice in the empirical sciences, Quine focused his critical attention on the latter. Finding the conceptual/empirical distinction lacking in point of empirical support, he moved to extend pragmatism to questions of empirical fact as well. In doing so, Quine brought tools from the pragmatist toolkit, e.g. holism, to bear on the problems of logical positivism and logical analysis. At the same time, he brought analytic rigour to these pragmatist tools and arguments, raising them to the attention of contemporary philosophers.

For Quine, however, these contributions were secondary to a physicalist version of empiricism (some would say 'scientism') that most pragmatists would not accept. Quine had complained that the pragmatism of Lewis and Carnap leaves off at the imagined boundary between the analytic and the synthetic. Utilizing his own image, it could be said that Quine's pragmatism leaves off at the equally imagined boundaries between theory and observation and between facts and values. These limits, so it has been argued, leave Quine's pragmatism in a state of philosophical disorder. In this paper, I shall accept Quine's word regarding his distance from the historical school of American pragmatism. My focus will rather be on Quine's kinship with pragmatism as a general philosophical outlook, and on the uses he makes of pragmatist themes for his own non-pragmatist purposes. This combination, so I shall argue, is not always successful. Arguing from pragmatist principles, Quine may have created philosophical expectations that his more comprehensive views could not fulfil.

THE NATURE OF PRAGMATISM

In what follows, I shall take pragmatism to consist of the view that human cognition is a matter of practice, rather than mere contemplation, and that it is inseparable from the subject's overall engagement with the world she cognizes. Whereas traditional philosophers had sought a vantagepoint so general that it could capture reality as a whole in a single unified grasp, and whereas the cognizing subject had consequently been understood as a mere observer at the outer limits of that reality, pragmatism renounces the view that such a vantagepoint is either possible or necessary for any theoretical purpose. On this account, the cognizing subject is not merely a 'spectator' but rather an agent, constructing the objects of her cognition, rather than receiving them passively from the 'outside'. Consequently, the products of cognitive processes – perceptions, memories, inferences, beliefs – are not mere representations, 'corresponding' to some independent reality, but rather creations, or constructions, to be evaluated in the light of human purposes. There is no pure contemplative viewpoint from which the practical role of the cognitive agent could somehow be cancelled, and upon which a more general perspective can be attained; nor is such a viewpoint necessary for any theoretical purpose in philosophy.

In James's words, 'the knower is not simply a mirror floating with no foot-hold anywhere, and passively reflecting an order that he comes upon and finds simply existing. The knower is an actor, and coefficient of the truth on one side, whilst on the other registers the truth which he helps to create.'[5] A similar view is expressed by Dewey. For him, philosophy 'becomes not a contemplative survey of existence nor an analysis of what is past and done with, but an outlook upon future possibilities with reference to attaining the better and averting the worse'. Furthermore, 'philosophy will have to surrender all pretension to be peculiarly concerned with ultimate reality. Or with reality as a complete (i.e. completed) whole: with the real object.'[6] Quine echoes this fundamental pragmatist perspective at the beginning of 'Ontological Relativity': 'With Dewey I hold that knowledge, mind, and meaning are part of the same world that they have to do with, and that they are to be studied in the same empirical spirit that animates natural science. There is no place for a prior philosophy.'[7]

Thus pragmatism constitutes a philosophical response to some of the most enduring claims of traditional philosophy. From Plato onwards, the contemplative tradition in philosophy saw human cognition as having to transcend its immersion in particularity and achieve a perspective on reality as a whole. Whether as prisoners in Plato's cave, moving from shadows to forms, or as a 'cogito' in Descartes's dream, moving from cogitations to God and extended substances, cognitive subjects were thought of as rising to an observation of reality 'as such'. Consequently, these cognitive subjects, as well as their representations, were thought of as separated from the reality reflected by them. The ambiguous role of appearances *vis-à-vis* reality, of the *res cogitans vis-à-vis* the *res extensa*, speaks to the impossibility of this metaphysical project, but the concepts of epistemology: representation, correspondence, etc., by which the subjective was thought to be certified as objective, were all fashioned in this light. The dignity of the metaphysical aspiration traditionally overshadowed the epistemological impracticality of achieving it.

Pragmatism sharply reverses these priorities. It holds that cognition is inseparable from practice, and that consequently there is no humanly attainable viewpoint from which reality could be viewed in its totality. From this, various consequences follow that pragmatists have developed. First, if there is no pure contemplative viewpoint, philosophy, too, must begin *in media res*, that is, from within the world which constitutes its object. Philosophy must be continuous with other activities and branches of knowledge, rather than a distinct a priori discipline. Secondly, the concept of truth cannot be accounted for in terms of 'correspondence' to a world existing independently of all human conceptions. It is not necessary to compare human conceptions with a pre-conceptualized world existing independently of all of them. The concept of truth stands in need of some other account.

Thirdly, it follows that traditional philosophical dichotomies, e.g. the dichotomies of subject/object, appearance/reality, a priori, a posteriori, value/fact, theory/experience, and others that depend on them, cannot be justified. While these distinctions can have unobjectionable uses, they do not form the unbridgeable dualities that traditional metaphysicians had taken them to be. As dualities, they rest on the untenable assumption that reality must, as a whole, be separated from the subject, in relation to which it is to be represented in cognition; otherwise, there would be no ground for the supposition that what appears on one side of any such duality necessarily does not appear on the other. Logical positivists, for example, have placed great emphasis on the assumption that if any proposition is synthetic, it must be empirical, and if non-empirical, it must be analytic (if cognitively significant at all); pragmatists like Morton White (1950), and indeed, Quine (2004c), undermined that move by questioning the analytic/synthetic dichotomy.

Fourthly, it follows that epistemological foundationalism, the view that there must be an ultimate, self-justifying basis upon which all knowledge must rest, cannot be sustained. Similarly, the traditional quest for certainty, that is to say, for an indubitable basis that will render knowledge claims absolute and non-negotiable, cannot be accepted. Fallibilism, rather than the quest for certainty, is the proper epistemological attitude when beginning *in media res*; knowledge forms a holistic system of inter-dependencies, and within it no knowledge claim is immune to revision. On the other hand, scepticism, too, must be dismissed, since the very possibility of philosophical scepticism rests on the necessity of the vantagepoint that has been rejected. The sceptic supposes that appearances could be exactly as they are while the reality 'beyond' them is radically different. For the pragmatist, this is merely an abstract and barely coherent possibility that constitutes no real ground for doubt.

Finally, it follows that facts and values cannot be completely separated. Cognition is part and parcel of an evaluative viewpoint, while evaluative judgements are no blind acts of volition but rather a matter of rational deliberation. Non-cognitivist ethics becomes as untenable and superfluous as transcendent metaphysics and foundational epistemology were also found to be. Ethics can no more be reduced to subjective expression than science can be reduced to empirical observation. In both, cognition and practical engagement are inseparably intertwined.

Clearly, these vague characterizations are not unique to American pragmatism. They have their root in Kant's understanding of the role of spontaneity, along with receptivity, in the construction of human knowledge, though Kant, of course, had not abandoned all noumenal notions. They can also be detected, differences notwithstanding, in the writings of many other philosophers, e.g. Wittgenstein on meaning as use, or Goodman on worldmaking, who are not counted among the pragmatists.

It should, however, be stressed that pragmatist philosophers argue not just against the *possibility* of a prior metaphysical vantagepoint, but also against its *necessity* for the validation of cognitive products. There is, thus, a constructive aspect to pragmatism which suggests an alternative account of cognition, and does not rest content with nihilism. Pragmatism does not do away with cognition, reason or logic on the ground that they are found to depend on human contingencies. It does not seek to escape from philosophy (or metaphysics) altogether. It does not fall into the trap of continuing to assume that a metaphysical vantage point is necessary, even though it is impossible to attain. The latter move is richly exemplified by competing philosophical movements, e.g. Bergson's philosophy in Dewey's time, or post-structuralism in our own. The only major exception to this understanding of pragmatism is Richard Rorty's attempts to nudge pragmatism into a postmodern hostility to any constraints on inquiry that are not 'conversational' constraints.[8] But Rorty's views are not typical of pragmatism. Indeed, Dewey's critique of Bergson on this point, as quoted below, is equally applicable to Rorty:

The pervasiveness of the tradition is shown by the fact that so vitally a contemporary thinker as Bergson, who finds a philosophic revolution involved in abandonment of the traditional identification of the truly real with the fixed (an identification inherited from Greek thought), does not find it in his heart to abandon the counterpart identification of philosophy with search for the truly Real; and hence finds it necessary to substitute an ultimate and absolute flux for an ultimate and absolute permanence.[9]

Much the same could be said about Rorty. While abandoning notions of correspondence and essence, he, too, does not abandon the view that epistemology requires such notions. Like Bergson, he ends up substituting an absolute conversational flux for an absolute epistemological constraint. But in this move the pragmatist middle ground is lost. Rather than celebrating, with Rorty and Bergson, the absence of external, or fixed, constraints, pragmatists are likely to accept, with Dewey, that nothing constitutes a conversation, let alone an inquiry, unless it is already suffused with standards of intelligence and objectivity, though these cannot be understood independently of human practices.[10]

Further debates arise within pragmatism on more specific issues. I shall here mention three such debates that will become relevant for our appraisal of Quine's pragmatism. First, it is a matter of internal pragmatist debate whether or not any spontaneity/receptivity distinction survives the removal of representations as the immediate objects of cognition, and whether or not a holistic and pragmatic conception of cognition leaves room for any notion of the 'given'. Secondly, pragmatists debate whether or not the concept of truth can survive its severance from the concept of correspondence, or may have to be replaced by more modest terms of cognitive appraisal such as 'warranted assertibility'. A third debate concerns the fact/value distinction. Here, too, controversy rages between those who consider values to be as objective as facts, though perhaps in a different way, and those who seek to maintain the dualism in one form or another.

This framework of internal pragmatist debate makes it possible to assess Quine's relation to pragmatism as a philosophical view. Whereas other pragmatists appealed to a broad, non-contemplative notion of experience, Quine argues for pragmatism on the basis of empiricist principles, and appeals to practice only within limits that are determined by these principles, i.e. only in relation to theory.

Hence, Quine exempts empiricism from the scope of his pragmatism, and preserves a notion of givenness that other pragmatists would view as no less mythical than the notion of analyticity. The resulting tension is resolved only by a resolute turn on Quine's part to a physicalist form of naturalism that few pragmatists would accept. In relation to truth, Quine brings together a 'semantic' definition of truth (Tarski's), a holistic account of confirmation and a fallibilist account of knowledge to create an account of what it is to judge truth 'earnestly' and 'absolutely'. Here Quine could be seen as resolving, through logical and semantic analysis, problems that the traditional pragmatists have left open. Regarding the place of values, Quine retains an empiricist perspective according to which the gulf between science and ethics cannot be overcome.[11] On this picture, Quine's pragmatism is selective, confined to the philosophy of science, and subordinate to what is for him a more basic perspective, namely a naturalist form of empiricism.

There is, indeed, a fundamental level, besides the exemption of empiricism, at which Quine is certainly not a pragmatist. While having no investment in the contemplative view of human cognition, and no commitment to representations of any kind, Quine shows little faith in any concept of human practice that goes beyond 'the physical constitution and behavior of organisms'.[12] Quine is a 'confirmed extensionalist'[13] who firmly believes in the cognitive status of extensional contexts only, to the exclusion of any intensional ones, including intentional contexts such as those required in the description of practice (where extensional contexts depend (for truth-value) exclusively on the denotations of terms, while intensional contexts are sensitive to connotations as well). What this means is that for Quine, intentional claims, being non-extensional, cannot be taken at face value, i.e. as objectively true or false, and since practice cannot be understood apart from such intentional concepts as 'belief' and 'desire', pragmatist claims regarding cognition as a form of practice cannot be taken at face value either. Quine's 'flight from intension'[14] is clearly incompatible with the spirit of pragmatism, as is his doctrine of the 'special' indeterminacy of translation. One cannot advocate a practice-oriented view of cognition unless one possesses a concept of practice, but a non-cognitivist view of intentionality does not yield the requisite concept of practice. A merely 'practical' conception of practice, suitable for daily purposes but not for the scientific 'limning' of 'the true and ultimate nature of reality',[15] is not a conception upon which human cognition can be made to rest. So in this important respect, Quine cannot be understood as a pragmatist, and whatever themes he does take over from the pragmatist tradition, he must be understood as employing them against their grain. Quine is a non-cognitivist regarding practice, not a pragmatist regarding cognition, though his arguments along the road, particularly his arguments for holism and against the analytic/synthetic distinction, were couched in pragmatist terms, i.e. in terms of the options that are open for the practising scientist. The tension between these two viewpoints runs through the entirety of Quine's work.

Let me clarify the point by looking more closely into Quine's celebrated argument for the flight from intension. The irreducibility of intentional language to physical language is, so Quine claims, 'of a piece' with the indeterminacy of translation. Whereas the followers of Brentano would take the irreducibility in question as proof of the objectivity of the intentional, assuming that if intentions cannot be reduced to physical magnitudes, then they must have an independent existence, Quine argues that since the physical alone is real, physically irreducible intentions are not part of reality. In this eliminative respect, irreducibility can be made compatible with indeterminacy. It follows that intentional claims, claims about belief, desire, action, thought, meaning and so on, cannot be taken as determinately true or false. Quine would not 'forswear' daily use of such concepts, and unlike other behaviourists would not seek to reform the intentional 'vernacular', but he does warn that intentional language cannot be used when scientists 'limn the true and ultimate structure of reality'.[16] That purpose can only be served by a 'canonical notation' that contains no intensional devices. However, Quine's dichotomous view that extensional language represents ('limns') reality, accurately or inaccurately, but that non-extensional language merely expresses our purposes, is tantamount to saying that the practical is insufficient for a full accounting of our cognition, contrary to pragmatist perspectives. It is also tantamount to saying that there is an accurate or inaccurate perspective to be had on 'ultimate reality', once we take leave of our daily purposes and our ordinary idioms of belief and desire. This is precisely what a pragmatist would deny. Indeed, if the intentional idiom is, as Quine admits, practically indispensable, what more would it need to acquire cognitive status?

And yet, Quine makes important contributions to pragmatism, and the 'shift' he proposes from an atomistic, word by word empiricism to a fully holistic view of empirical confirmation, while not entirely unanticipated in earlier pragmatist literature, constitutes a decisive argument in favour of such pragmatism. Hence, a question arises as to the overall consistency of Quine's views, and whether his kind of pragmatism, namely, a pragmatism subordinated to an extensionalist, behaviourist and physicalist form of empiricism, is a sustainable package.

HOLISM

Holism is the pragmatist alternative to the dichotomous tendencies of traditional metaphysics. As noted, these tendencies reflect traditional aspirations for a point of view so general as to encompass the totality of the real in a single view. Generality pushes the viewer and her viewpoint outside the totality they aspire to encompass (while also demanding that they be included), and this translates into a subject/object dichotomy, from which other such dichotomies can be derived. By contrast, holism claims that the subjective and the objective cannot be neatly separated and that consequently both the higher vantage point aspired to, and the totality it is supposed to encompass, are illusory.

Quine's version of these ideas is very well known. While 'truth in general' depends on both language and extra-linguistic fact, it is not the case that the truth of any particular sentence is analysable into separable linguistic and factual components, while in the case of analytic statements the factual component is empty. The boundary between the analytic and the synthetic has not been adequately drawn by empiricist standards, and so the notion that there is a line to be drawn is a 'metaphysical article of faith'. Science can only be tested as a collective body, not sentence by sentence. No statement is immune to revision, and any statement can be held 'come what may'. The whole fabric of science is 'man-made'. Even logical truth is revisable, and even the simplest existential claims are merely posited.[17]

Two issues arise on which Quine's holism remains problematic. First, an epistemological role for extra-linguistic fact is not rejected out of hand. The distinction between language and fact remains operative in the form of a distinction between the man-made fabric, on the one hand, and experience, on the other. The distinction, however, involves a notion of the empirical 'given' that seems to elude any holistic contextualization. Critics have responded either by demanding a more comprehensive holism, incorporating any distinction between the theoretical and the given, or else by pointing out that if Quine's holism is not to sacrifice the 'world', it stands in need of a stronger and more substantive notion of truth, and so a greater distance from pragmatism on this issue.

Famously, Rorty has argued that the analytic/synthetic distinction and the theory/given distinction must stand and fall together, and that one cannot consistently remove the one without the other. If the world is lost as an objective constraint on discourse, it is, in Rorty's language, 'well lost'.[18] Elsewhere, Rorty takes both Quine and Sellars to task for not following their respective arguments wherever they lead; Quine does not renounce the distinction between the given and the postulated, despite having renounced the analytic/synthetic distinction and its derivatives, on the basis of a comprehensive holistic argument, while the writings of Sellars remain permeated with notions of analysis and necessity, despite the holistic arguments by which he undermines the 'given'.[19] A consistent holism, or what Rorty calls 'epistemological behaviorism', would equally undermine both kinds of privileged representations, the analytic and the given. As Rorty puts it, 'if assertions are justified by society rather than by the character of the inner representations they express, then there is no point in attempting to isolate *privileged* representations'.[20]

Indeed, if all privileged representations are to be rejected, then any epistemological justification can only be conventional, and conversely. Matters are more complicated, however, if this broad version of holism, along with its relativist consequences, is resisted.[21] A more trenchant argument has been advanced by Davidson. Davidson has argued that by retaining the distinction between conceptual scheme and empirical content, Quine was guilty of maintaining a 'third dogma' of empiricism.[22] The latter dogma, so Davidson argues, leads to the incoherence of 'alternative conceptual schemes', or of languages that are untranslatable to a given language, and since there are no such languages or schemes, there is also no non-conceptual content, and nothing that remains worthy of the title of empiricism once the three dogmas are removed. Unlike Rorty, Davidson does not celebrate the loss of the world, but tries to retain it by retaining a non-immanent notion of truth. Davidson's criticism of Quine can be understood as making the point that Quine has not gone far enough in one direction (namely, the post-empiricist direction), while going too far in another direction (namely, the pragmatist direction regarding the concept of truth).

Quine has responded to that by claiming that removing empiricism as a theory of truth is not anything he opposes, but that empiricism remains in force as a theory of evidence, and that Davidson, by removing it altogether, runs the risk of conflating truth and belief.[23] Indeed, Davidson removes the third dogma and concludes that 'nothing ... no thing, makes sentences and theories true: not experiences, not surface irritations, not the world',[24] but that conclusion does not suffice for the removal of empiricism as a theory of evidence, which does not make sentences true, but does make them more or less justified, or better and worse confirmed. Davidson retorts that justification, being a logical relation, can only take place between items with propositional or conceptual content, and so not between 'surface irritations' and theoretical statements. So again empiricism gives way to a coherence theory of truth and knowledge.[25] For Quine, however, one moves 'from stimulus to science' and ultimately the move is causal, not rational or logical. For him, empiricism remains evidentiary only, rather than a theory of truth, but he must couch evidentiary relations in causal terms, that is, in terms of his naturalized epistemology, and this, while possible, takes us away from pragmatism. Quine's pragmatism is revealed here, again, as subordinate to his empiricist naturalism and physicalism.

So Quine has to choose. Retaining empiricism as a theory of evidence, indeed, retaining the very notion of evidence, requires coherence-type standards of justification that cast a shadow of doubt on the very notion of the given. On the other hand, retaining the given as mere 'surface irritation' takes it out of the realm of evidence and justification and gives it a merely causal role. Quine is happy with the latter move, which makes epistemology a component part of empirical psychology, but he also insists on a shadow of traditional evidentiary relations in the form of his doctrine of double containment. While epistemology is contained in science, it also contains science in a way reminiscent of traditional foundationalism, since it describes, in general terms, the relation of science to its stimulatory evidence. Rather than getting lost in this seeming loop of double containment, one should simply note Quine's dual perspective: the naturalist-extensionalist perspective, on the one hand, and the pragmatist-holist perspective, on the other.[26] Quine can retain both his holism and his empiricism only by moving to a naturalized, causal account of epistemology, and that account takes him away from the pragmatism that animated his holism in the first place.

The second issue that arises from Quine's holism has to do with the status of logic. Here too Quine seems to be of two minds. In 'Two Dogmas of Empiricism', Quine excludes logical truth from the category of analytic statements that he eschews, confining his argument to statements that can be obtained from logical truths by substitution of synonyms. This seems to imply that logical truths are not quite as revisable as synonymy-based analyticities. A 'change of logic', he says elsewhere, is a 'change of subject', and when someone offers to revise the law of non-contradiction, she cannot retain the meaning of the logical particles, e.g. that of negation, for the duration of the argument.[27] This goes back to an even older argument of Quine's against conventionalism in logic: one cannot base logic on conventions, since one would need logic to derive the infinitude of logical truths from finitely many human conventions.[28] On the other hand, the holism he ends up advocating grants logic no special status in terms of being open to revision. No statement is immune to revision in the light of recalcitrant observations, including such logical laws as the excluded middle that has been considered for revision in light of developments in theoretical physics. It seems that Quine faces a dilemma. If logical statements are revisable, then logic does seem to rest on arbitrary conventions; if not, then it is in some sense analytic.

The dilemma can be exemplified in terms of the status of the principle of non-contradiction. Is this principle revisable in light of recalcitrant experiences, or is it not so revisable? Clearly, if no statement is immune to revision, then neither is the principle in question. So Quine would seem to favour the positive horn of the dilemma. However, the idea of revision in the light of recalcitrant experiences makes no sense unless the term 'revision' is understood to incorporate a standard of logical consistency. Otherwise, the point of such revision is moot. On this line of reasoning it would appear that logical consistency is constitutive of the very idea of a holistic web of sentences, and cannot be rationally, or even meaningfully, revised. But if that is correct then not every statement is open to revision, and some statements, contradictions, for example, cannot be held come what may. Indeed, they cannot be held at all.[29]

For Quine, the unit of empirical significance is the whole of science. But what kind of 'whole' is it? Quine speaks metaphorically about a man-made fabric with experiential edges and about a field of force with experiential boundary conditions. These metaphors are not equivalent. If science is merely a field of force, its operations, given changes in the boundary conditions, can only be constrained by other forces, and reason has nothing to do with it. On this picture, logic itself is merely one of the (blind) forces at play. If, on the other hand, science is like a man-made fabric, namely, an artefact of purposive activity, then some form of rationality is built into it. Indeed, one may ask, what is a web of belief, or for that matter, even a single belief? Nothing, it seems, can be such a web, or such an item, unless already informed by logic, that is to say, by standards of reasoning that are acquired along with language and belief formation. And while these standards need not be completely fixed and unchanging, there must be a kernel that is fixed.

So, again, Quine seems to be of two minds. The tough-minded behaviourist picture is of the whole cognitive system as a field of force, leaving no room for any standards that are not merely further forces in the equation. This, of course, is not a pragmatist picture. Here cognition is not viewed as a human activity, but rather as the operation of a machine. This picture goes well with Quine's extensionality thesis, the aspect of his account that knows 'no propositional attitudes, but only the physical constitution and behavior of organisms'.[30] The tender-minded picture is of the cognitive system as a web of intentional elements such as beliefs, statements or activities that are inherently amenable to rational standards and logical criticism. But this picture is not easy to integrate with the doctrines of extensionalism and physicalism. You can't have standards in a world populated by physical and set-theoretic entities alone.

TRUTH

Holism suggests the empirical underdetermination of scientific theory. The point of holism is that only a large body of theory predicts observation sentences, and that consequently a failed prediction does not, of itself, determine which component of that large body is to be revised. It follows that more than one way of revising scientific theory so as to fit the sensory input are possible, and that theories could be conceived that are empirically equivalent but logically non-equivalent.

Indeed, Quine inflates the doctrine of empirical underdetermination to cover not just ordinary cases, but also idealized ones. Underdetermination is claimed to arise not just between empirically equivalent theories relative to all available evidence, but also between theories that are empirically equivalent relative to all possible evidence: past, present and future. In both its forms, the thesis raises serious difficulties regarding the notion of truth. If empirical justification relative to all possible evidence is as strong a standard of confirmation as can be imagined, and if two conflicting theories can meet the standard, it would seem that contradictory statements would have to be accepted as true (or confirmed to be true). Over the years, Quine has gradually withdrawn from the stronger thesis of empirical underdetermination, suggesting that any two such ideally justified but competing theories might really just be notational variants of one another. But even the weaker thesis raises an issue regarding the relation between confirmation and truth. Empirical justification relative to all available evidence, or even just a large chunk of it, is a good-enough standard of confirmation, and so, again, contradiction is threatened.

Quine has addressed this difficulty with his so-called immanence doctrine of truth. The latter doctrine shares with pragmatism the rejection of correspondence theories of truth, and with it any notion of theory as a 'mirror' of reality. Quine, however, advocates a Tarski-type 'semantic definition of truth', according to which 'truth' is merely a meta-linguistic predicate, defined for a specific object language, whose function is described in terms of semantic ascent. To say of a sentence p that it is true is merely to reassert p. It does not add any further information. Thus, "'p' is true if and only if 'p'" captures the whole content – the logical role – of the concept of truth, where the sentence p used on the right-hand side of the equivalence is a translation into the meta-language of the object-language sentence quoted on its left-hand side. Tarski has shown how to construct a derivation of such T-sentences, for all sentences of a formal language of a certain type, and that the resulting predicate has all the true sentences of the object language in its extension. For Quine, this extensional definition of 'true in L' is as much a definition of truth as need ever be given.

Quine worries that this position might be understood as relativism. His answer is to join the theory-immanence of truth with fallibilism – another pragmatist doctrine – regarding the acceptance of theories. Fallibilism is the view that any theory, no matter how well confirmed, might still be false, or revisable, but that does not preclude accepting it as (absolutely) true. Thus, equal confirmation of two conflicting theories need not require acceptance of both as equally true, with contradictory or relativistic consequences; rather one theory could be accepted with the understanding that acceptance is risky, i.e. subject to possible revision. On this view, relativism is thwarted despite the immanence of truth. Quine puts all this as follows:

Have we now so lowered our sights as to settle for a relativistic doctrine of truth – rating the statements of each theory as true for that theory, and brooking no higher criticism? Not so. The saving consideration is that we continue to take seriously our own particular aggregate science ... Unlike Descartes, we own and use our beliefs of the moment, even in the midst of philosophizing, until by what is vaguely called scientific method we change them here and there for the better. Within our own total evolving doctrine, we can judge truth as earnestly and absolutely as can be; subject to correction, but that goes without saying.[31]

The first sentence of this remarkable passage expresses the worry about relativism. If different and incompatible theories, T_1 and T_2, are equally confirmed, we would apparently have to accept that both are true, but this cannot be done consistently unless truth is relative to theory, i.e. unless a different truth predicate, 'True-in-T_1' vs. 'True-in-T_2' is taken to apply to each. But then the immanence of truth would seem to preclude 'higher criticism', since there would be no telling which of the theories was ultimately true. There would be no theory-transcendent truth-predicate by which such a judgement could be made. But Quine does not fall into this relativistic trap. His argument is the following. Though the two (incompatible) theories in question are equally confirmed, we do not have to accept both as true, and so we are under no pressure to relativize the truth-predicate. Rather we continue to accept our own theory in full seriousness, namely, with a non-relativist claim to truth, and we acknowledge other possibilities not by accepting them as 'equally true', but rather by allowing our own theory to be correctible by the standards of our own scientific method. Acceptance is always provisional and subject to correction by scientifically evolved standards. *Pace* Descartes, it does not require any firmer foundation.

In short Quine deals with the problem of relativism by invoking two pragmatically flavoured doctrines: first, the semantic doctrine of truth, according to which truth is immanent and does not involve any positing of extra-theoretical 'facts'; secondly, the doctrine of fallibilism, according to which equally confirmed theories need not be equally accepted, for acceptance of theories is always provisional, risky and subject to revision. Elsewhere, Quine calls this position 'sectarianism' (as distinguished from 'ecumenicism'), but it is worth noting that the term 'pragmatism' fits this position as well.[32] Clearly, the acceptance of theories is a cognitive matter that within this argument Quine treats in practical rather than contemplative terms.

Quine's position on the immanence of truth has been criticized as deflationist. In particular, Putnam has argued that Quine's doctrine amounts to the claim that the concept of truth is an empty concept. Recall that the doctrine of immanence rests on accepting Tarski's definition of truth as an exhaustive account, though Tarski's definition applies, on pain of semantic paradoxes, only to language-immanent truth predicates, one at a time, and not to any concept that might be common to all of them. Taking such a definition to exhaust all we can say about truth amounts to dismissing the universal concept (of truth) altogether. Quine is happy to do just that, resting his case on the paradoxical consequences of the alternative, but that, so Putnam argues, leaves him with no account of what truth, in general, is, and such an account would be needed if anything philosophical were to be said about the relation of language to the world. According to Putnam:

On this interpretation to say, as Quine does, that there is only 'immanent truth' is – as close as makes no difference – to say *il n'y a pas de hors texte*.[33]

Clearly, Putnam's reference to Derrida's phrase is critical. Leaving nothing outside the text leaves one without any language/world relation to describe. Putnam presents Quine as accepting this position along with Rorty and Derrida, but sees this as a *reductio ad absurdum* of the position. In effect, he takes this view as consonant with a form of relativism, namely, with the inference that if truth is merely immanent, then there are no objective constraints on theory acceptance – nothing outside the text – and that, consequently, anything goes. Putnam further dismisses all attempts to replace external constraints by internal ones, claiming that the same problem would arise regarding them, namely, that either those internal constraints would incorporate an independent standard of precisely the kind rejected earlier, or else they would be quite empty as constraints.

In other places, Putnam speaks more favourably of pragmatism, but this argument is a classical argument against pragmatism, and in particular against the idea that in the absence of external standards, internal or 'evolving' standards will have to do. For the anti-pragmatist, this merely pushes the problem a step further. So the question really is: can there be any 'integrity' to the immanent standards that a pragmatist must invoke, if his rejection of correspondence is not to be reduced to nihilism? Derrida's phrase regarding the *hors texte* does suggest a nihilism of that sort, and Putnam takes the nihilism by *reductio* to argue for transcendence. But pragmatists take this position, in either form, to be much too pessimistic, and in this regard Quine, too, though clearly not in favour of expediency definitions of truth, exhibits a pragmatist orientation.

THE FACT/VALUE DISTINCTION

Another consequence of the pragmatist approach is the undermining of the fact/value distinction. If cognition is inseparable from practice, it must also be soaked in values, since practice is simply inconceivable apart from evaluative contexts. The point has been emphasized by a number of contemporary pragmatists. Rorty, for example, insists that 'there is no epistemological difference between truth about what ought to be and truth about what is, nor any metaphysical difference between facts and values'.[34] Similarly, Putnam argues that facts and values are deeply entangled, and that knowledge of facts presupposes knowledge of values.[35]

Both these philosophers argue to that effect by extending an argument from holism – essentially Quine's argument – as it applies to other dichotomies. If science is such a tightly knit system that it does not leave room for a separation of meaning from fact at the level of individual sentences, and which depends, rather, on the practically rational decisions of its practitioners, then it is also too tightly knit to leave room for a separation of facts from values at that basic level, and is similarly dependent on the evaluative preferences of these same practitioners. Putnam, in particular, emphasizes that this is not a mere analogy of arguments, but the logical extension of a single argument. The very notion of a fact – the objective correlate of a synthetic statement – stands in ruin, once the analytic/synthetic distinction is eliminated. There simply is no such objective correlate. Consequently, it is also not available as a foil against which the notion of a value can be understood.

Quine, himself, however, does not take this line. For him, the fact/value distinction retains much of its dichotomous flavour, both epistemologically and metaphysically. On the metaphysical level, Quine traces valuation to a primitive, but relatively autonomous psychological mechanism – the reward/penalty axis. The operation of this mechanism is deemed unconnected to another primitive mechanism of habit formation – an innate quality space, on which learning by induction depends. Quine sees the two mechanisms as operating together. The conditioning of responses depends on spotting similarities between rewarding or punishing stimulants. But he does not consider the evolutionary possibility that the qualities in the quality space have been selected precisely for these purposes, and that consequently even the simplest habit formation does not exhibit a full dualism of belief and valuation. For him the dualism is basic: 'such is the bipartite nature of motivation: belief and valuation intertwined. It is the deep old duality of thought and feeling, of the head and the heart, the cortex and the thalamus, the words and the music'.[36] Though clearly intertwined in behaviour, belief and valuation work separately at every step.

Just as induction develops into the hypothetico-deductive method, so primitive valuation develops into ethics through a process by which means are transmuted to ends. Thus, 'We come to relish the sport of fishing as much as we relish the fresh trout to which it was a means.'[37] The different ways in which values can shift and transmute generate a diversity of values, some moral, some prudential, some cultural, some almost universal, and with diversity, disagreement arises. However the duality noted earlier – the bipartite nature of valuation – precludes any objective resolution of differences. The epistemology of ethics bears witness to the fundamental division between belief and valuation that is not mitigated by any form of holism. In Quine's words:

> Disagreement on Moral matters can arise at home, and even within oneself. When they do, one regrets the methodological infirmity of ethics as compared with science. The empirical foothold of scientific theory is in the predicted observable event; that of a moral code is in the observable moral act. But whereas we can test a prediction against the independent course of observable nature, we can judge the morality of an act only by our moral standards themselves. Science, thanks to its link with observation, retains some title to a correspondence theory of truth; but a coherence theory is evidently the lot of ethics.[38]

Clearly, these are not the words of a pragmatist. Quine's holism, we saw, retains a distinction between the theoretical and the observational, and that distinction serves him in creating the epistemological space for the fact/value distinction. The notion of observation retained by Quine's holism is the notion of fact against which values are kept in their secondary place of infirmity. The belief/valuation duality becomes a science/ethics distinction that Quine's system does not seek to overcome. Notice, however, that this notion of observable fact also brings back a little of the correspondence theory of truth, as Quine explicitly acknowledges. But can he have it both ways? Can truth be immanent in one context, i.e. the context of theory choice, where Quine is making a genuine contribution to pragmatism, and non-immanent in another context, namely the context of evaluation, where Quine's pragmatism wears off? Quine's moves in this context exhibit the very same duality that was pointed to earlier between his naturalistic outlook and the pragmatist arguments he employs along the road.

By denying that the morality of an observable moral act can itself be observed, Quine traces the fact/value distinction within the act itself, as if the observable and the evaluative could always be separated. This, however, presupposes that we can observe and describe moral acts but when we come to the morality in them we have to resort to non-observable values. We can, for example, describe and observe cruel acts, but their cruelty is a matter of our own moral standards. But can we do so? Do we have a non-evaluative, purely descriptive language, in which we can capture which acts are cruel, prior to normatively judging them in these terms? Putnam has argued that we cannot do that. We cannot describe cruel acts in any language that does not itself employ normative concepts and considerations (without losing the point of grouping them together). Hence, we cannot factorize 'thick moral concepts' into separate descriptive and normative components. Putnam goes on to conclude that the factual and the normative are deeply interdependent, not merely intertwined in producing behaviour. In effect, he extends the argument Quine himself employed with respect to the meaning/fact distinction, namely, that the difference between these terms cannot be traced within any component statement, to the case of the fact/value distinction. Quine, however, balks at this analogy.

In doing so Quine reveals the limitedness of his pragmatism. His holism is too restricted. He debunks the fact/meaning distinction which underlies the analytic/synthetic dichotomy, while retaining the fact/value and correspondence/coherence distinctions. Among other things, this presupposes a 'purely' descriptive viewpoint on the world of fact in its totality, a viewpoint which keeps the world separate from values, and undermines the pragmatist intuition, culled from Dewey, that mind and language are part of the world they serve to describe. Separating values from that world, viewing the world as shorn of values, which are, then, to be located in the mind and seen as projections, or 'transmutations', is a relapse to a rather traditional dualism. It requires precisely the viewpoint that pragmatists have denied, a viewpoint which is itself, somehow, outside that world, but from which an evaluative stance can be expressed.

As noted, Quine separates values from facts on a (reformed) empiricist basis that retains a pre-theoretical notion of observation. But his point is not unconnected to his thesis of extensionalism. Clearly, if statements of belief and desire, like all non-extensional statements, can only be accepted on a non-cognitive basis, but not as cognitively true or false, value judgements can fare no better. So the modified empiricist argument for the 'infirmity' of value judgements gives epistemological support to the metaphysical argument of extensionalism. But these are dimensions in which Quine's pragmatism has receded far to the background, and more traditional viewpoints have been allowed to take over.

NOTES

1. Other figures include F. C. S. Schiller, George Herbert Mead, Morton White, as well as contemporary figures such as Richard Rorty and Hilary Putnam.
2. For a relatively detailed review of Quine's references to the pragmatist tradition, see Koskinen and Pihlström, 2006, pp. 309–46.
3. For Quine's affinity with Dewey, see Quine's statement in 'Ontological Relativity'. Quine 1969c, p. 27. An affinity with Peirce is recorded in Quine's 'Epistemology Naturalized', Quine, 1969b, p. 80, where Peirce is cited as a source for the claim that 'the meaning of a sentence turns purely on what would count as evidence for its truth'. Regarding James, Quine is quoted as 'departing radically' from him on both his 'pragmatic theory of truth' and his 'Will to believe': Bergström and Føllesdal, 2000, p. 66. On being identified with the pragmatists, Quine says: 'it was not clear to me what it took to be a pragmatist' and that examining the 'card-carrying pragmatists' on their tenets does not yield a unified picture (Quine, 1985, p. 415).
4. See Quine, 2004c, esp. pp. 20 and 46.
5. James, 1971, p. 23.
6. Dewey, 1993, p. 1.
7. Quine, 1969a, p. 26.
8. Rorty 1982c, p. 165. See also Rorty, 1980, 1989a.
9. Dewey, 1993, p. 1.
10. Rorty himself coins the distinction between deconstruction and circumvention to describe the difference here noted, claiming his own view to be circumventive rather than deconstructive. Most commentators, however, take him to be closer in spirit to the deconstructive side, and certainly there is plenty of textual evidence to support this view. See Rorty 1991b, pp. 85–106).
11. See Quine, 1981a, pp. 55–66.
12. Quine, 1960, p. 221.
13. For this phrase, see Quine, 2004a, pp. 329–37.
14. Quine, 1960, pp. 191–232.
15. Quine, 1960, p. 221.
16. Quine, 1960, p. 221.

17 Quine, 2004c, pp. 36, 37, 43, 42.
18 Rorty, 1982a, p. 3.
19 Sellars, 1963.
20 Rorty, 1980, p. 174.
21 Rorty has denied that epistemological behaviourism, or what he later called 'ironism', implied relativism, but few have been persuaded. His denial is based on defining 'relativism' in narrow terms as the view that all claims are as good as all others in every respect, but relativism with respect to truth survives the rejection of 'relativism' so defined. See Rorty, 1982a, pp. 160–75.
22 Davidson, 1984, p. 189.
23 See 'On the Very Idea of a Third Dogma', Quine, 1981c, pp. 38–42.
24 Davidson, 1984, p. 194.
25 See Davidson, 2001, pp. 137–53.
26 The loop is merely apparent, since 'containment' is used in two different senses: epistemology is contained in science in one sense of the term, while science is contained in epistemology's subject matter in another. But the dual perspective of Quine's epistemology, the pragmatist and the naturalist, is real enough.
27 Quine, 1970, pp. 80–1.
28 See Quine, 2004b, esp. pp. 26–9.
29 In fact, Quine has conceded the analyticity of logic in the Bergstrom–Føllesdal interview. Consider the following: 'I think of the truths of logic as analytic in the traditional sense of the word, that is to say, by virtue of the meanings of the words.' Bergström and Føllesdal, 2000, p. 71. The problem with Carnap was that he extended the term to apply across the board, and particularly to mathematical truths, which on Quine's view remain non-analytic. In this context, Quine explains the revisability of some logical truths as purpose-relative and restricted in scope.
30 Quine, 1960, p. 221.
31 Quine, 1960, pp. 24–5.
32 See Quine, 1990: ch. 5, esp. p. 98.
33 Putnam, 1994b, p. 341.
34 See Rorty 1982c, p. 163.
35 Putnam 1995, 2002.
36 See 'On the Nature of Moral Values', Quine, 1981b, p. 55.
37 Quine, 1981b, p. 57.
38 Quine, 1981b, p. 63.

RICHARD BERNSTEIN

5 Hegel and pragmatism

I want to consider three moments in the history of philosophy in the United States when Hegel became a source of philosophical inspiration and discussion: the latter part of the nineteenth century, the mid-twentieth century and the present time. Each of these moments is directly or indirectly related to pragmatism. The second half of the nineteenth century in America witnessed a strong interest in German philosophy, especially in Kant, Hegel and, more generally, the tradition of German idealism. The early issues of the *Journal of Speculative Philosophy* (founded in 1867) were filled with articles about, and translations of, Fichte, Schelling and Hegel. In the opening article of the first issue, W. T. Harris declared: 'He, then, who would ascend into the thought of the best thinkers the world has seen, must spare no pains to elevate his thinking to pure thought. The completest discipline for this may be found in Hegel's *Logic*' (Harris, 1867, p. 6). In Great Britain too, a version of idealism was flourishing. T. H. Green, F. H. Bradley and Bernard Bosanquet were among the most prominent of the British idealists who advocated a form of absolutism – a single coherent system in which everything is internally related.[1] They were all sharp critics of traditional British empiricism. We sometimes forget that both Bertrand Russell and G. E. Moore, considered to be two of the most important founders of analytic philosophy, were originally defenders of idealism. In America the great proponent of absolute idealism was the charismatic Harvard philosopher Josiah Royce. Absolute idealism flourished in both the United States and Britain. The influence of absolute idealism had been so strong at the turn of the twentieth century that when William James was invited to give the Hibbert Lectures at Oxford in 1907, he declared in the following passage:

> Fortunately, our age seems to be growing philosophical again – still in the ashes live the wonted fires. Oxford, long the seed-bed, for the English world, of the idealism inspired by Kant and Hegel, has recently become the nursery of a very different way of thinking. Even non-philosophers have begun to take an interest in a controversy over what is known as pluralism or humanism. It looks a little as if the ancient English empiricism, so long put out of fashion here by nobler sounding Germanic formulas, might be re-pluming itself and getting ready for a stronger flight than ever.
>
> (James, 1977, p. 7)

I will briefly describe the significance of Hegel for Dewey, Peirce and James. I begin with Dewey because Hegel had the greatest influence on his thinking.

DEWEY'S EARLY HEGELIANISM

In his autobiographical sketch (1930), Dewey tells us that as an undergraduate at the University of Vermont, he was "subconsciously ... led to desire a world and life that would have the same properties as had the human organism" (Dewey, 1981, p. 2). At that time Dewey had not yet discovered Hegel.[2] But when he entered the graduate programme in philosophy at Johns Hopkins, he came under the dominant influence of G. S. Morris – an enthusiast for Hegel and idealism:

> While it was impossible that a young and impressionable student unacquainted with any system of thought that satisfied his head and heart, should not have been deeply affected, to the point of at least a temporary conversion, by the enthusiastic and scholarly devotion of Mr. Morris, this effect was far from being the only source of my own "Hegelianism". The 'eighties and 'nineties were a time of new ferment in English thought; the reaction against atomic individualism and sensationalistic empiricism was in full swing. It was the time of Thomas Hill Green, of the two Cairds, of Wallace, of the appearance of the *Essays in Philosophical Criticism*, co-operatively produced by a younger group under the leadership of the late Lord Haldane. This movement was at the time the vital and constructive one in philosophy.
>
> (Dewey, 1981, p. 6)

What did the young Dewey find so attractive in Hegel? It was not Hegel's claims about the Absolute, or the unfolding of the categories in the *Logic*, or the grand sweep of Hegel's narrative of the West, or even the technical details of Hegel's dialectic. It was the sense of life, the dynamism and especially the vision of organic interrelated reality that Dewey found so appealing. What Dewey wrote about his teacher, G. H. Morris, might just as well have been said about himself:

> I should say that he was at once strangely indifferent to and strangely preoccupied with the dialectic of Hegel. Its purely technical aspects did not interest him. But he derived from it an abiding sense of what he was wont to term the organic relationship of subject and object, intelligence and the world ... His adherence to Hegel (I feel quite sure) was because Hegel had demonstrated to him, in a great variety of fields of experience, the supreme reality of this principle of living unity maintaining itself through the medium of differences and distinctions.
>
> (Cited in Wenley, 1917, pp. 136–7)

But Dewey's most revealing remark about Hegel's inspiration is the following:

> There were, however, also "subjective" reasons for the appeal that Hegel's thought made to me; it supplied a demand for unification that was doubtless an intense emotional craving, and yet was a hunger that only an intellectualized subject-matter could satisfy. It is more than difficult, it is impossible, to recover that early mood. But the sense of divisions and separations that were, I suppose, borne in upon me as a consequence of a heritage of New England culture, divisions by way of isolation of self from the world, of soul from body, of nature from God, brought a painful oppression – or, rather, they were an inward laceration. My earlier philosophic study [prior to his discovery of Hegel] – had been intellectual gymnastic. Hegel's synthesis of subject and object, matter and spirit, the divine and the human, was, however, no mere intellectual formula; it operated as an immense release, a liberation. Hegel's treatment of human culture, of institutions and the arts, involved the same dissolution of hard-and-fast dividing walls, and had a special attraction for me.
>
> (Dewey, 1981, p. 7)

Despite these heady attractions, Dewey gradually drifted away from Hegel. Darwin replaced Hegel as a source of inspiration for the organic, dynamic, changing character of life. But the 'subjective' factors that originally attracted Dewey to Hegel stayed with him throughout his life and deeply marked his own experimentalist version of pragmatism. Dewey, in effect, naturalized Hegel. Dewey's concept of experience as a transaction that spans space and time, involving both undergoing and activity, shows the Hegelian influence. Subject and object are understood as *functional* distinctions within the dynamics of a unified developing experience. Like Hegel, Dewey is critical of all dualisms and the fixed dichotomies that have plagued philosophy, including mind and body as well as nature and experience. Dewey's hostility to the merely formal and static was inspired by Hegel. Dewey, like Hegel, was alert to the role of conflicts in experience: how they are to be overcome in the course of experience and how new conflicts break out. Typically he approaches philosophical problems in a Hegelian manner by delineating opposing extremes, showing what is *false* about them, indicating how we can preserve the *truth* implicit in them, and passing beyond these extremes to a more comprehensive resolution. Like Hegel, Dewey believed that philosophy must be approached in its historical context.

PEIRCE'S AMBIVALENCE TOWARD HEGEL

Peirce's original philosophical source of inspiration was Kant – and not Kant as interpreted through Hegelian spectacles. Peirce detested what Hegel and the Hegelians took to be the character of logic. He even criticized Dewey severely for the pernicious influence of Hegelianism on his early 'logical' studies. The latter are better characterized as 'natural history' than normative logic.[3] But eventually Peirce came to recognize the affinity between his pragmaticism and Hegelian absolute idealism:

> The truth is that pragmaticism is closely allied to Hegelian absolute idealism, from which it is sundered by its vigorous denial that the third category (which Hegel degrades to a mere stage of thinking) suffices to make the world, or even so much as self-sufficient. Had Hegel, instead of regarding the first two stages with his smile of contempt, held on to them as independent or distinct elements of a triune Reality, pragmaticists might have looked upon him as the great vindicator of their truth.
>
> (CP5: 436)

Peirce is referring to his categorial scheme of Firstness, Secondness and Thirdness, which he takes to be basic for any adequate philosophical understanding of phenomena, logic, signification, experience and reality. Writing to Lady Welby in 1904, Peirce declares:

I was long ago (1867) led, after only three or four years' study, to throw all ideas into the three classes of Firstness, of Secondness, and of Thirdness. This sort of notion is as distasteful to me as to anybody; and for years, I endeavored to pooh-pooh and refute it; but it long ago conquered me completely. Disagreeable as it is to attribute such meaning to numbers, and to a triad above all, it is true as it is disagreeable.

(CP8: 328)

Peirce, of course, recognizes the affinity between his threefold categorical scheme and Hegel's penchant for triads. But he claims that Hegel viewed these categories as mere stages of *thinking*. He failed to appreciate that the categories designate elements that have an independence that is *not* reducible to thinking. Peirce's critique of intuitionism – the core of the Cartesianism that he sought to displace – complements Hegel's critique of the very idea of pure (unmediated) immediacy.

JAMES: HEGEL'S 'ABOMINABLE HABITS OF SPEECH'

James, the great popularizer of 'pragmatism', had a deep aversion to German philosophy, and rarely resisted an opportunity to ridicule what he took to be its misguided pretentiousness. James's real enemy was not so much Hegel, but rather the version of idealism advocated by British idealists and by his Harvard colleague Josiah Royce. Unfortunately, Royce is scarcely read today – except by specialists. Yet Royce is the American philosopher who exhibited the most sensitive understanding of Hegel and German idealism. In this late work, Royce also noted the convergence of Hegelian and pragmatic themes developed by Peirce.

James spent two chapters of *A Pluralistic Universe* explaining what is wrong with 'monistic idealism', and lamenting the pernicious influence of Hegel. Pluralism, as James understood it, is a radical alternative to any form of Hegelianism. James deplored Hegel's 'abominable habits of speech', 'his passion for the slipshod in the way of sentences, his unprincipled playing fast and loose with terms; his dreadful vocabulary'. 'All these things make his present-day readers wish to tear their hair – or his – out of desperation' (James, 1977, p. 44). 'The only thing that is certain is that whatever you may say of [Hegel's] procedure, someone will accuse you of misunderstanding it.' In short, Hegel epitomized precisely what philosophers should avoid: vicious intellectualism, abstract monism, cultivated obscurity and long grandiloquent pretentious sentences that sound profound but are really quite vacuous. Summing up his criticism of monistic idealism, James declares:

> The prestige of the absolute has rather crumbled in our hands. The logical proofs of it miss fire: the portraits which its best court-painters show of it are featureless and foggy in the extreme; and, apart from the cold comfort of assuring us that with *it* all is well, and that to see that all is well with us also we need only rise to its eternal point of view, it yields us no relief whatever. It introduces, on the contrary, into philosophy and theology certain poisonous difficulties of which but for its intrusion we never should have heard.
>
> (James, 1977, p. 63)

Yet, for all his disdain of Hegel and absolute idealism, James tells us that Hegel was 'a naively observant man' who 'plants himself in the empirical flux of things and gets the impression of what happens' (James, 1977, p. 44). He extols Hegel for his keen awareness of the quality of the world as alive, and as involving a dialectic movement in things. He singles out Hegel's revolutionary achievement: 'Concepts were not in his eyes the static self-contained things that previous logicians had supposed, but were germinative, and passed beyond themselves into each other by what he called their immanent dialectic' (p. 46). The category of negation is Hegel's most original stroke: 'Merely as a reporter of certain empirical aspects of the actual, Hegel is great and true' (p. 49). James displays a rare ability to understand sympathetically those whom he most bitterly opposes. His portrait is based on Hegel's *Logic*, a primary Hegelian text for the British idealists. If James had discussed Hegel's *Phenomenology of Spirit* he might have found even more direct support for the aspects of Hegel's thinking that he singles out for praise – the dynamic living quality of experience and reality.

Nevertheless, James's devastating caricature of Hegel helped to suppress any serious interest in him. Many Anglo-American philosophers today would still endorse James's portrait of Hegel. Ironically, Hegel, who had been a source of inspiration for Dewey, was killed off by James's popular version of pragmatism. It is too mild to say that serious interest in Hegel in the United States waned during the next fifty years. It was completely moribund – and this is just the way that most philosophers in America thought it should be.

THE REVIVAL OF INTEREST IN HEGEL

Beginning in the 1950s, and in subsequent decades, the situation slowly changed. When I was a graduate student in the 1950s, the question was frequently asked, 'Do you do philosophy? Or do you do the history of philosophy?' The presumption was that there was little of genuine philosophical interest to be found in turning to the history of philosophy – except to show how confused and misguided past philosophers had been. At best, we might recast some of the occasional insights of past philosophers in the new way of words. By this criterion, Hegel was not even worthy of being read. For many analytic philosophers, Hegel was an exemplar of the type of vacuous speculation that every respectable analytic thinker should avoid. But gradually – at least among a marginal group – there were signs of a growing interest in Hegel. There were three primary reasons for this. The first was clearly political. With the emergence of the New Left there was a search for an intellectual basis that could serve to motivate and legitimate the call for social justice and radical democratic action. The early 'humanistic' Marx was being rediscovered. And it soon became evident that Marx led one back to Hegel. This was the time when left-wing students in America were discovering the rich Marxist tradition of Lukács, Gramsci and the Frankfurt School. Initially, Hegel was read through the spectacles of Western Marxism, Hegel seen through the eyes of Adorno and Marcuse. When I wrote *Praxis and Action* during the late 1960s (Bemstein, 1971) and argued that Marxism, existentialism, pragmatism and analytic philosophy were movements that arose out of, or in reaction to, Hegel, there were scarcely any philosophers in the United States who took Hegel seriously. Although the New Left stimulated commentaries and new translations of Marx and Hegel, it still did not influence the mainstream academic philosophy taught in graduate schools.

There was a second source of the interest in Hegel. No respectable philosopher of the time could completely ignore the analytic orientations that were emerging during the 1950s and 1960s. But there was a group that found the limited scope of analytic philosophy stifling. They were searching for an alternative, a way in which one could take on board the new insights and achievements of the linguistic turn, but also broaden philosophical discourse – to show how philosophy could still deal with the range of human culture and experience instead of focusing exclusively on a narrow set of technical issues. I would place Charles Taylor, Alasdair MacIntyre, Richard Rorty and myself in this group. One of the consequences of the growing interest in Hegel at mid-century was the production of new translations, commentaries and serious discussions of Hegel's work. I do not think it is an exaggeration to say that, in the 1950s, one could count on one hand the number of books published in America that dealt with Hegel – and these were of uneven quality. But today, fifty years later, there are good reasons to say that the Hegelian *Geist* has moved to America, where we find some of the most creative and thought-provoking Hegelian scholarship.

A third source of the renewed interest in Hegel that also had its origins in the 1950s was so subterranean as to be almost totally neglected. Nevertheless, it is this underground current that has come to shape some of the most original philosophical inquiry today. I am thinking here of the work of Wilfrid Sellars.

SELLARS: 'INCIPIENT *MEDITATIONS HEGELIÈNNES*'

A philosopher comes alive and speaks to us from the past when his work becomes a fertile source for dealing with current philosophical problems, when his work can be engaged in novel ways. Otherwise, paying homage to the tradition is a way of embalming it. This is what I see happening in the United States today with regard to Hegel. To demonstrate this, I shall return to Sellars, who leads us *back* to Peirce and *forward* to the recent contributions of John McDowell and Robert Brandom. I shall also take a side-glance at Richard Rorty, who was also influenced by Sellars and was Brandom's teacher. Rorty was also one of the first to take note of this Hegelian turn.

Initially, the German philosopher who comes to mind when we think of Sellars is Kant, not Hegel. Like that of Peirce, Sellars's philosophy can be understood as variations on Kantian themes. But a careful reading of his work, especially his classic monograph *Empiricism and the Philosophy of Mind* (Sellars, 1997), reveals how close his orientation is to the opening sections of Hegel's *Phenomenology*. Sellars's critique of the Myth of the Given reads as if it were a translation of the opening sections of the *Phenomenology* into what Sellars called the 'new way of words'. Sellars, who has a sophisticated knowledge of the history of philosophy, introduces his critique of the Given with an allusion to Hegel's critique of immediacy. If we translate Sellars back into Hegel's idiom, we can say that the critique of the Given rejects the claim that there is immediate knowledge that doesn't involve any conceptual mediation – a type of direct intuitive knowledge that *allegedly* serves as the foundation for all inferential knowledge. Put this way, Sellars's monograph calls to mind those early articles of Peirce that appeared in the *Journal of Speculative Philosophy*. Peirce anticipates many of the arguments developed by Sellars.[4] Peirce, like Sellars, argues that once we give up the Myth of the Given, we are led to a non-foundational, fallibilistic, intersubjective understanding of concept formation and inference. This also entails a rejection of representationalist semantics and requires a more holistic understanding of meaning and inference. The appropriation and critique of Kant by Peirce and Sellars reflect the very spirit of Hegel. Richard Rorty was one of the first to suggest that Sellars was leading us from Kant to Hegel.

Let me be a bit more specific. I am not suggesting that Hegel directly influenced either Peirce or Sellars in their critiques of the Myth of the Given. Rather, I am claiming something that is more important and interesting. Just as Hegel detected a dialectical instability in the key Kantian dichotomies and distinctions – for example, between sensibility and understanding, receptivity and spontaneity – so both Sellars and Peirce were alert to this dialectical instability – and the need to pass beyond it. If we think of Hegel as introducing a philosophical line of argument that has its own integrity, then we can say that both Peirce and Sellars share this critical mode of thinking.[5] Without denying the 'truth' of empiricism – that in our empirical and scientific knowledge, we are subject to a brute compulsion – Peirce and Sellars challenge the very idea that there is (or can be) any knowledge 'below' the level of concepts, 'below' what Kant and Hegel call *Verstand* (understanding). There is no 'pure' receptive knowledge that does not *always already* involve what Kant calls spontaneity. There is no immediate knowledge or knowledge by acquaintance when this is understood to be a type of immediate *self-authenticating* episode that can presumably serve as an epistemic foundation for inferential knowledge. Both argue that a major confusion in the classical empiricist tradition was to confuse brute compulsion (Peirce's Secondness) with epistemic justification (Peirce's Thirdness). Russell's understanding of 'knowledge by acquaintance', one of the targets of Sellars's critique of the Given, exemplifies what Hegel had already criticized in the opening dialectical critique of 'Sense Certainty' in his *Phenomenology*. Both Peirce and Sellars swerve away from some of the excesses of Hegel. Both seek to develop a fallibilistic communal understanding of inquiry that is compatible with the 'truth' implicit in the empiricist tradition – where experience serves to check the validity of our knowledge claims.

During his creative years at the University of Minnesota, Yale and the University of Pittsburgh, Sellars had his dedicated admirers. But his philosophical contributions were overshadowed by those of Quine and Davidson. In the past few decades, primarily as a result of the publications of John McDowell and Robert Brandom, there has been a much greater appreciation of the fecundity of Sellars's work. McDowell and Brandom, known as the 'Pittsburgh Hegelians', have acknowledged the influence of Sellars on their own philosophical investigations, and they have also been explicit about this Hegelian turn. I suspect that many of John McDowell's former Oxford colleagues thought it was a joke when he declared, in the preface to *Mind and World*, 'one way that I would like to conceive this work is as a prolegomenon to the reading of [Hegel's *Phenomenology of Spirit*]'. (McDowell, 1996). But it is no joke, and McDowell is extremely insightful about Hegel. In the same preface (written before the publication of Brandom's *Making It Explicit* (1994), he also acknowledges 'the substantial marks of Brandom's influence' – and especially his 'eye-opening seminar on Hegel's *Phenomenology of Spirit*' which McDowell attended in 1990 (McDowell, 1996, p. ix). In *Articulating Reasons*, Brandom affirms that his philosophical work represents a continuation of this Hegelian line of thinking. He tells us, 'My teacher Richard Rorty has described the enterprise to which this volume is a contribution as an extension of Sellars's; to make possible a further transition from a *kantian* to a *hegelian* approach to thought and action' (Brandom, 2000a, p. 32).

Brandom explains what he means:

> First, I am interested in the divide between *nature* and *culture*. In this context we can identify the realm of the cultural with activities that either consist in the application of concepts in judgment and action or that presuppose such capacities. The *Geisteswissenschaften* have as their proper aim the study of concept use and things made possible by it – activities of which only concept users are capable. One of my principal goals is to present and explore the consequences of a particular sort of principle of demarcation for the realm of culture, so understood. Although of course cultural activities arise within the framework of a natural world, I am most concerned with what is made possible by the emergence of the peculiar constellation of conceptually articulated comportments that Hegel called 'Geist.' Cultural products and activities become explicit as such only by the use of normative vocabulary that is in principle not reducible to the vocabulary of the natural sciences. ... The study of natures itself has a history, and its own nature, if any, must be approached through the study of that history. This is a picture and an aspiration that we owe to Hegel.
>
> (Brandom 2000a, p. 33)

Brandom also stresses a second dimension of Hegelian influence – what he calls Hegel's *'pragmatism* about conceptual norms'. I will shortly explain what Brandom means by this and how it brings us back to the pragmatism of Peirce.

THE 'PITTSBURGH HEGELIANS': MCDOWELL AND BRANDOM

McDowell's references to Hegel are sparse, but they are revealing. At a crucial stage in the development of his argument in *Mind and World* he writes:

> It is central to Absolute Idealism to reject that the conceptual realm has an outer boundary, and we have arrived at a point from which we could start to domesticate the rhetoric of that philosophy. Consider, for instance, this remark of Hegel's: "In thinking, I *am free*, because I am not in an *other*." This expresses exactly the image I have been using, in which the conceptual is unbounded; there is nothing outside it. The point is the same as the point of that remark of Wittgenstein's ... We – and our meaning – do not stop anywhere short of the fact.
>
> (McDowell, 1996, p. 44)

This is a central thesis of *Mind and World*. In his attempt to escape from the oscillating seesaw such that we *either* fall victim to some form of the Myth of the Given *or* slip into an unsatisfying 'frictionless' coherentism, McDowell argues that the conceptual realm is unbounded and that the world imposes *rational* constraints upon us. At first glance (and some would say, even after a second or third glance), many of his critics fail to see what is the difference that makes a difference between what he is advocating and the coherentism that he criticizes and rejects.[6] McDowell seeks to show – in his Wittgensteinian mode of therapeutic reflection – that the philosophical anxiety resulting from this oscillating seesaw is alleviated once we realize that the conceptual realm is unbounded and does not cut us off from reality. On the contrary, it is precisely *because* of this unboundedness that we can achieve knowledge and access to a reality that is independent of us. Reality is not located 'outside' the conceptual realm. McDowell succinctly states his main point thus:

> In a particular experience in which one is not misled, what one takes in is *that things are thus and so. That things are thus and so* is the content of the experience and it can also be the content of a judgement if the subject decides to take the experience at face value. So it is a conceptual content. But *that things are thus and so* is also, if one is not misled, an aspect of the layout of the world: it is how things are.
>
> (McDowell, 1996, p. 26)

McDowell takes this to be a gloss on the Wittgensteinian remark: "When we say, and *mean*, that such-and-such is the case, we – and our meaning – do not stop anywhere short of the fact; but we mean: this – is – so" (cited in McDowell, 1996, p. 27).

When we unpack McDowell's meaning, it sheds light on his project as well as on Hegel's. McDowell is aware of the popular view that Hegelian idealism, with its emphasis on mind (*Geist*), thought (*Denken*) and concept (*Begriff*), fails to do justice to a reality and a world that is 'outside of' and independent of mind and thought. This caricature of Hegel is based on the presupposition that the distinction between what is 'inside the mind' and 'outside the mind', or what is 'inside' the conceptual realm and 'outside' this realm, is itself unproblematic. Presumably idealism is the philosophical position that tells us that there is nothing that is 'outside the mind'.

McDowell correctly realizes that this is a caricature; Hegel's idealism involves a total rejection of this entrenched dichotomy of what is 'inside' and 'outside' the conceptual realm. Hegel (like McDowell) categorically rejects this misleading picture. McDowell's Hegelian claim is that a proper understanding of what it means to affirm the unboundedness of the conceptual shows us that it is precisely *because of* this unboundedness that we can come to know of a reality that is independent of us. What McDowell says about Wittgenstein is just as true of Hegel:

[T]here is no ontological gap between the sort of thing one can mean, or generally the sort of thing one can think, and the sort of thing that can be the case. When one thinks truly, what one thinks *is* what is the case. So since the world is everything that is the case ... there is no gap between thought, as such, and the world. Of course thought can be distanced from the world by being false, but there is no distance from the world implicit in the very idea of thought.

(McDowell, 1996, p. 27)

A second, related feature of McDowell's philosophical investigations that bears a strong affinity with Hegel is his critique of what he calls the 'disenchanted' conception of nature, which has dominated so much of modern philosophy. He seeks to recover the idea of 'second nature'. McDowell draws upon Aristotle's ethical writings rather than Hegel to explain what he means. But we should not forget how much Hegel himself is indebted to Aristotle. Furthermore, Hegel also argued that the 'truth' of nature is spirit. McDowell's basic point is that as long as we operate with a conception of nature that is completely disenchanted, and a conception of naturalism that is essentially reductionist, we cannot avoid the philosophical anxieties and aporias of a bifurcation of nature and freedom. We need to rethink the concept of nature in a manner that is compatible with the idea of a human *second nature*. In this way we avoid both reductionism and dualism, both of which McDowell takes to be philosophically unacceptable. We open the way to a more adequate conception of nature that is compatible with the *sui generis* character of spontaneity. McDowell gives an eloquent description of the type of integration that he envisions when he writes:

We need to recapture the Aristotelian idea that a normal mature human being is a rational animal, but without losing the Kantian idea that rationality operates freely in its own sphere. The Kantian idea is reflected in the contrast between the organization of the space of reasons and the structure of the realm of natural law. Modern naturalism is forgetful of second nature; if we try to preserve the Kantian thought that reason is autonomous within the framework of that kind of naturalism, we disconnect our rationality from our animal being, which is what gives us a foothold in nature ... If we want to combine avoiding the problems with a more substantial acknowledgement of them, we need to see ourselves as animals whose natural being is permeated with rationality, even though rationality is appropriately conceived in Kantian terms.[7]

We should not forget that Hegel himself sought to integrate Aristotle with Kant in a manner that is very similar to the way in which McDowell characterizes this need for a genuine synthesis.

McDowell merely sketches what this rethinking of the concept of nature requires. There are many hurdles that need to be overcome to carry this out successfully.[8] In this context, I shall limit myself to the observation that this project bears a strong affinity with post-Kantian idealism. Fichte, Schelling and Hegel all felt that Kant had left us in an intolerable position insofar as he introduced what seemed to be a categorical dichotomy between the realm of nature and the realm of freedom. They all felt, as the later Kant came to realize in the *Critique of Judgment* (Kant, 1987), that this chasm had to be bridged. They all rejected what McDowell calls 'bald naturalism', which in their vocabularies was identical with 'naturalism'. They would all agree with McDowell when he affirms that spontaneity is *sui generis* (McDowell, 1996, p. 76). And each, in his distinctive manner, sought to rethink the concept of nature in a way that shows how it is continuous with the higher reaches of rationality and thought. I do not want to suggest that the German idealists were successful in carrying out this project, just as I do not think that McDowell thus far has provided more than hints about how this is to be done. Actually, the type of naturalism that McDowell proposes has an even closer affinity with the non-reductive emergent naturalism of Peirce, James and Dewey.

I cannot explore the rich and multifarious ways in which we see the traces of Hegel in Brandom – or the differences between him and McDowell. But I do want to pick up one major strand in his appropriation of Hegel – what Brandom calls 'Hegel's pragmatism'. Like

Peirce, Sellars and McDowell, Brandom's starting point is Kant. His philosophical reflections begin with Kant's insights about normativity and rationality. He tells us:

> One of Kant's great insights is that judgments and actions are to be distinguished from the responses of merely natural creatures by their distinctive *normative* status, as things we are in a distinctive sense *responsible* for. He understood *concepts* as the norms that determine just what we have made ourselves responsible for, what we have committed ourselves to and what would entitle us to it, by the particular acts of judging and acting.
>
> (Brandom, 2000a, p. 33)

This is Brandom's starting point, but he thinks that there are many hard questions about normativity that are not adequately accounted for by Kant. He goes on to tell us:

> Kant, however, punted many hard questions about the nature and origins of this normativity, of the bindingness of concepts, out of the familiar phenomenal realm of experience into the noumenal realm. Hegel brought these issues back to earth by understanding *normative* statuses as *social* statuses – by developing a view according to which ... *all transcendental constitution is social institution*. The background against which the conceptual activity of making things explicit is intelligible is taken to be implicitly normative essentially *social* practice.[9]

This is a succinct statement of Brandom's philosophical project – one that he pursues with analytic finesse and systematic thoroughness. Carrying it out requires the development of a concept of discursive social practices that enables us to do full justice to the normativity implicit in these social practices. Brandom characterizes Hegel's pragmatism as 'a *rationalist* pragmatism' (Brandom, 2000a, p. 34). He thinks that Hegel's pragmatism is richer and more fertile than the pragmatism that one finds in Peirce, James and Dewey, or even the 'pragmatism' of the early Heidegger and the later Wittgenstein. I strongly disagree with Brandom's assessment of the American pragmatic tradition.[10] He fails to recognize that Peirce's pragmaticism is a normative pragmatism that is based upon an inferential semantics. We also find in Peirce an anticipation of Brandom's inferential semantics, and his all-important distinction between what is implicit and what is explicit in social practices. For example, Peirce tells us that all reasoning involves inferential 'leading' or 'guiding' principles:

That which determines us, from given premises, to draw one inference rather than another, is some habit of mind ... The particular habit of mind which governs this or that inference may be formulated in a proposition whose truth depends on the validity of the inferences which the habit determines; and such a formula is called a *guiding principle* of inference.

(CP5: 367)

I am not suggesting that everything of importance in Brandom is already to be found in Peirce. But I do want to affirm that being sensitive to anticipations, similar dialectical moves and closely related argumentative strategies enables us to detect continuities in the pragmatic tradition. Specifically, it enables us to become more reflective about the Hegelian motifs in a pragmatic tradition that reaches back to Peirce and encompasses the philosophical contributions of Dewey, Sellars, McDowell and Brandom. It opens us to a rethinking of the course of philosophy in the United States during the past 150 years. Sellars, McDowell and Brandom are solidly grounded in analytic philosophy, but their philosophical investigations cut across the divide between Anglo-American and continental philosophy.

I agree with Richard Rorty when he writes, in his introduction to Sellars's *Empiricism and the Philosophy of Mind*, that the 'pro-Hegelianism' of Sellars and Brandom 'suggest that the Sellars–Brandom "social practice" approach to the traditional topics of analytic philosophy might help reconnect that philosophical tradition with the so-called "Continental" tradition' (Rorty, 1997a, p. 11):

Philosophers in non-anglophone countries typically think quite hard about Hegel, whereas the rather skimpy training in the history of philosophy which most analytic philosophers receive often tempts them to skip straight from Kant to Frege. It is agreeable to imagine a future in which the tiresome 'analytic-Continental split' is looked back upon as an unfortunate, temporary breakdown of communication – a future in which Sellars and Habermas, Davidson and Gadamer, Putnam and Derrida, Rawls and Foucault, are seen as fellow-travelers on the same journey, fellow-citizens of what Michael Oakeshott called a *civitas pelegrina*.

Rorty's suggestion about the future of philosophy is consistent with the thesis that I have been advocating in this chapter. If we concentrate on the vital and varied development of pragmatic themes during the past 150 years, if we are sensitive to the ways in which pragmatic thinkers have detranscendentalized Kant and incorporated Hegelian motifs, then those standard 'tiresome' classifications – 'analytic–continental' – actually *obscure* the pragmatic sea change that has been taking place in philosophy.

NOTES

1   British idealism bears a strange and strained relation to Hegel. Themes such as the Absolute, internal relations and the concrete universal are appropriated from Hegel. But there is little of the passion of Hegel's *Phenomenology* or of Hegel's sweeping vision of historical conflict and political struggle.
2   Dewey writes that his earliest philosophical interest was stimulated by a course in physiology that used a text by T. H. Huxley: 'It is difficult to speak with exactitude about what happened to me intellectually so many years ago, but I have an impression that there was derived from that study a sense of the interdependence and interrelated unity that gave form to intellectual stirrings that had previously been inchoate, and created a kind of model of a view of things to which material in any field ought to conform' (Dewey 1981, p. 2).
3   See Peirce's review of Dewey's *Studies in Logical Theory* (CP8: 188–90).
4   I explore the similarities between Peirce and Sellars in Bernstein 1964.
5   In *Praxis and Action* (1971), I wrote: 'The opening section of the *Phenomenology*, "Consciousness," which deals with "sense certainty," "perception," and "understanding," is rarely read and discussed by contemporary philosophers. This is a pity because these sections can be read as a perceptive and incisive commentary and critique of a dialectical development in epistemology which has been repeated in contemporary analytic philosophy. The stages in contemporary epistemological investigations which have moved from phenomenalism with its foundation in "sense data" to the emphasis on a "thing language" as an epistemological foundation, to the realization of the importance of "theoretical constructs" and finally the "new" concern with total "conceptual frameworks" or "language games" closely parallels the development that Hegel sketches for us in the opening sections of the *Phenomenology*. One can find analogues in the development of epistemology during the past fifty years for the difficulties that Hegel locates at each dialectical stage. I do not mean to suggest that Hegel was

prophetic, but rather that he had a genuine insight into a dialectical progression of epistemological positions, which has repeated itself in a linguistic mode during our time' (p. 24).

6 In his original lectures, McDowell takes Davidson as the primary representative of this coherentism, and he accuses Davidson of having a 'blind spot'. McDowell has been criticized for taking Davidson as a foil and for distorting him. Consequently, in the published version of the lectures, McDowell adds an afterword, 'Davidson in Context', in order to show why he counts 'Davidson as an ally rather than an opponent' (McDowell, 1996, pp. 130–61).

7 McDowell, 1996, p. 85. Robert Pippin develops this Hegelian conception of nature in Pippin, 2008. See especially ch. 2, 'Naturalness and Mindedness: Hegel's Compatibilism'.

8 For a discussion of these hurdles, and the problems that McDowell still needs to confront, see Bernstein, 1995b.

9 Brandom, 2000a, pp. 33–4. For a fuller account of the contribution of Kant to the understanding of normativity, as well as the problems with Kant's account, see ch. 1, 'Toward a Normative Pragmatics', in Brandom, 1994, pp. 3–66.

10 I can illustrate what I mean, and why I disagree with Brandom's characterization of the American pragmatic tradition, with reference to a distinction he makes in *Articulating Reasons* (2000a). He distinguishes the 'rationalist pragmatism' of Hegel, which 'gives pride of place to reasoning in understanding what it is to say or do something' (2000a, p. 34), from 'conceptual assimilationism', where the emphasis is placed on the continuities between discursive and non-discursive creatures. But there is no reason why one cannot be *both* a rationalist pragmatist and a conceptual assimilationist. This is precisely the position that Peirce advocates. The following passage illustrates how Peirce understands the continuities and the differences between different grades of self-control, including those that Brandom takes to be characteristic of human rationality:

> There are inhibitions and coordinations that entirely escape consciousness. These are, in the next place, modes of self-control which seem quite instinctive. Next, there is a kind of self-control which results from training. Next, a man can be his own training-master and thus control his self-control. When this point is reached much or all the training may be conducted in the imagination. When a man trains himself, thus controlling control, he must have some moral rule in view, however special and irrational it may be. But next he may undertake to improve this rule; that is, to exercise a control over his control of control. To do this he must have in view something higher than an irrational rule. He must have some sort of

moral principle. This, in turn, may be controlled by reference to an esthetic ideal of what is fine. There are certainly more grades than I have enumerated. Perhaps their number is indefinite. The brutes are certainly capable of more than one grade of control; but it seems to me that our superiority to them is more due to our greater number of grades of self-control than it is to our versatility.

(CP5.533)

6 Heidegger's pragmatism redux

Consider what effects, which might conceivably have practical bearings, we conceive the object of our conception to have. Then, our conception of those effects is the whole of our conception of the object.[1]

From all these sophisms we shall be perfectly safe so long as we reflect that the whole function of thought is to produce habits of action; and that whatever there is connected with a thought, but irrelevant to its purpose, is an accretion to it, but no part of it.[2]

The circumspective question as to what this particular thing that is ready to hand may be, receives the circumspectively interpretive answer that it is for such and such a purpose. If we tell what it is for, we are not simply designating something; but that which is designated is understood *as* that *as* which we are to take the thing in question.[3]

In the projecting of the understanding, entities are disclosed in their possibility. The character of the possibility corresponds, on each occasion, with the kind of Being of the entity understood. Entities within the world generally are projected on the world – that is, upon a whole of significance, to whose reference-relations concern, as Being-in-the-world, has been tied up in advance. When entities within-the-world generally are discovered along with the Being of Dasein – that is, when they have come to be understood – we say that they have *meaning*.[4]

We also come here to the further question whether, in general, anything is given *as a being* to animals ... On closer consideration we see that, speaking cautiously, since we ourselves are not mere animals, we basically do not have an understanding of the 'world' of the animals. But since we nevertheless live as existents – which is itself a special problem – the possibility is available to us, by going back from what is given to us as existents, to make out reductively what could be given to an animal that merely lives but does not exist.[5]

INTRODUCTION

As with every other philosophical tradition, pragmatism has been characterized in a wide variety of ways. Probably the most pervasive of those characterizations turns on the distinctive way in which pragmatists have tended to understand the content of concepts, or determine the meanings of sentences or words. This pragmatic direction in semantics is well exemplified by the first quote above from Peirce. Peirce prescribes a technique for determining an agent's conception of an object, or understanding the meaning of a term. On this view the content of the conception of the object is fixed by the answer to the following question: if the conception of the entity was accurate or if it were the case that the term really applied appropriately to the object, then, under various circumstances, which effects would the entity have that would make a difference to us? If we want to know what it is for some object, say a slab of granite in my kitchen, to be harder than another object, say a knife blade, then we should ask what would happen, that would matter to us, were it really the case that the granite was harder and, for example, the blade was drawn along the granite. And the answer to that question tells us what we mean when we say that the granite is harder than the knife and what is involved in our conception of the granite as harder than the knife blade.

This pragmatic attitude towards linguistic meaning and conceptual content has two sides. First, pragmatists have a distinct tendency towards verificationism. Meaning turns on the conditions under which we would be warranted in asserting or believing that some sentence was true, or that some attribution was appropriate, rather than depending directly on the conditions under which the sentence was true. But this emphasis on assertibility conditions for a specification of meaning or conceptual content is not the primary aspect of the pragmatic view of meaning. It in turn arises out of the distinctively 'pragmatic' stance of the pragmatists. In general, pragmatists don't much care about how things 'really and truly' are 'in-themselves', if how they truly are makes no difference to our ability to cope with the world in ways that matter to us. And, in general, a difference between two possible ways in which something might be can make a difference to our ability to cope with things in ways that matter to us only if, now or in the future, we could *tell* that those two ways in which the thing might be *are* different. So, given the pragmatism expressed in the maxim I cited from Peirce, the content of a concept of an object is something like a prediction of what we would be able to detect, that would matter to our projects, regarding the effects of placing the object in various circumstances.

Pragmatist verificationism is thus distinguished from its positivist cousin by its distinctive kind of empiricism concerning evidence and warrant. For the positivist, the meaning of a term or the content of a concept is fixed by the conditions under which we would be warranted in ascribing the term or attributing the concept, just as it is for the pragmatist. But for the positivist, as heir of the classic British empiricists, those conditions ultimately are cashed out in terms of a set of possible sensations. For pragmatists, on the other hand, a different set of possibilities, the possible practical effects of operations with and on objects, fix the contents of our conceptions and the meanings of our words.

Stylistically and substantively there are a great many differences between the classical American pragmatists and the Heidegger of *Being and Time*; Heidegger was a phenomenologist, the pragmatists were not. The pragmatists were empiricists who were suspicious of a priori investigations; Heidegger was neither an empiricist nor suspicious, in general, of the a priori. There is an important respect in which Heidegger was an anti-naturalist; the pragmatists could never be accused of that particular sin against modernity. Nevertheless, in my 1988 book, *Heidegger's Pragmatism*,[6] I argued that there was a very real sense in which the early Heidegger was indeed a close kin of the American pragmatists. In particular I argued that, regarding linguistic meaning and conceptual content, Heidegger was a pragmatic verificationist. And I stand by that claim.

There is, however, a deeper and more important agreement between the Heidegger of *Being and Time* and the pragmatists, an agreement that accounts for the similarity of their views regarding linguistic meaning and the contents of concepts. This agreement concerns what it is for an agent to be intentionally engaged with a world, or, in more overtly Heideggerean terms, the basic constitution of the Being of Dasein. In this chapter I would like to focus on this deeper similarity, as well as on the significant respects in which Heidegger's brand of pragmatism concerning the structure of intentionality differs from his American cousins.

I TWO VIEWS OF THE AS STRUCTURE OF ENGAGEMENT

Over the last several centuries it has become a philosophical commonplace that when we humans engage with objects, or events, or properties we engage with them *as* this or that. I see the entity that is sitting on my bird feeder as a goldfinch. I can infer certain things about my daughter's behaviour because I believe her to be a teenager, and I can be depressed about some of that behaviour when I feel it to be rude. My granddaughter takes this object back to the kitchen because she recognizes it as a pot; my dog fails to recognize it as a pot and thus fails to do so. The structure of our language reflects this fact about our engagement with the world. Aside from the problematic case of our use of proper names, when we designate an entity linguistically we do so at least in part by specifying it as belonging to a certain class of entities. And when we want to say something about such an entity, which has already been designated as this or that, we further specify that it can also be taken *as* that or this; the pot as well designed, for example.

To say that our engagement has an *as* structure is at least to say that we can stand in certain types of 'relations' with an entity when that entity is taken to be in one way, while we fail to stand in those 'relations' when it is taken differently.[7] That is, we seem to engage with things not directly but rather in so far as those things are engaged *as* something or other.[8] I want to drink the liquid, but not the poison, even though the liquid is the poison. I believe that the beaver is not a pest, although I also believe that all rodents are pests, even though the beaver is a rodent. Indeed, there is a strong tradition in twentieth-century philosophy that takes this intensional dimension of our engagement with things as the defining mark of intentionality, which in turn is often seen as the defining mark of mentality itself.[9] This view, which identifies the mental with intentional directedness, and which treats the *as* structure as the defining feature of the intentional, is extremely wide spread in contemporary philosophical thought. A remarkably diverse group of philosophers, including phenomenologists and analysts, pragmatists and cognitivists, all share this basic conception of mentality.

This very breadth of agreement, however, hides a crucial disagreement. This disagreement concerns the basic nature of the *as* structure that all agree is the essential feature of human engagement with the world. At bottom, this disagreement turns on whether or not it is a necessary condition for an agent to be able to treat something *as* some kind of entity that that agent be able to *represent* that thing to itself as being of that kind. Let me illustrate the different views that I want to highlight.

The division in question is especially clear in the differing attitudes of the two camps of philosophers towards a certain traditional model of the nature and role of explicit judgements in the constitution of the *as* structure. One of the ways in which we are capable of treating something *as* something is by forming an explicit discursive judgement concerning that thing. For example, when I see a hammer I might assert, or at least judge, that that thing over there that I perceive is a hammer, and thereby intend it *as* a hammer. Since judgements are essentially acts that can and ought to be supported by evidence, when I form the judgement my judging ideally occurs for a reason, and, it might be thought, that reason counts as a reason only in virtue of the fact that I believe that any entity that satisfies some set of conditions counts as a hammer, and I believe that this entity satisfies those conditions. Kant attempted to elucidate this structure of judgement by introducing the technical notion of a 'concept'. For Kant, concepts are a particularly important species of the genus 'representation'. As far as I know, Kant never explicitly tells us what it is to be a representation.[10] From how he employs the term, however, it is obvious that for Kant a representation is a mental *entity*, a *something* placed *before* the mind (which might or might not be conscious), that stands in the special relation of 'making present again' something other than itself. Part of what distinguishes concepts from other kinds of representations is that concepts are *rules*, and that they represent their objects in virtue of their being the rules that they are. Thus, Kant tells us that a concept 'is always something general, and something that serves as a rule'.[11] In another of his dicta, Kant clarifies the sense in which concepts are always rules. A concept, he says, is 'a mark, that can be common to several things'.[12] So on this Kantian conception of a concept, a concept is a mark, or standard or criterion that can be used as a rule (which for Kant is always associated with the major premise of an argument) in a decision procedure used to determine which of a group of things satisfies that standard. When we use such a concept to cognize an entity we *apply* that concept to the entity, and when we do so we treat that entity *as* an entity of the kind picked out by that concept or standard.[13] On this Kantian view, to take some S as a P is always literally to form a representation, or mental *something*, in which S is represented to satisfy the rule that is the concept P. This new representation is the judgement, and on this view without forming a judgement no agent can take anything as anything at all.

Similarly, the Fregean notion of *Sinn*, or sense or meaning, originally arose out of reflection on this same discursive variety of the *as* structure of human language and engagement with the world. It can be informative to me to find out that the morning star is the evening star because I think of that celestial object *as* this or that, as the morning star or the evening star, and when I do so my thoughts, and the language that is used to express those thoughts, have different senses, or meanings, or modes in which the object is presented, even though the object that is presented is the same for both of those modes. On this Fregean view, meanings are ways in which we engage with entities; if I refer to Venus with an expression that has the meaning 'the morning star', then I am engaging with Venus *as* the morning star. And, in determining which thing is the morning star, I use the sense embedded in 'the morning star' as a criterion or standard that supplies the premise in an argument that concludes with the judgement that *that* thing *is* the morning star.

Occupying one side of the divide regarding the *as* structure of human engagement are those who hold that the primary way in which an agent engages with an entity as something is in an act of judgement that involves a recognition of an entity as falling under a concept. For those in this camp, other ways in which we engage with things or properties in the world *as* this or that, such as perceiving something as, or using something as, depend upon and are derivative from this basic capacity to judge. Unless we had the concept of *bird* available to us, unless we could 'make present' to ourselves the rule that must be followed or the standard that must be met for something to count as a bird, we could not see the goldfinch *as* a bird, and unless we possessed the concept of a hammer, we could not take this thing *as* a hammer in hammering with it. Or so the story goes. On this view, no agent is capable of engaging with something as something unless she is capable of judging that that thing is of a certain type. But since on this view such an act of judgement intrinsically involves treating the concept that one is applying in the judgement *as* a concept, that is, as a mark or criterion that serves as a rule for judgement, no agent who is incapable of treating her own principles for judging as principles for judging, that is as concepts, is capable of treating any entity *as* anything at all. For those who adhere to this view, the realm of those who are capable of intentionality is coextensive with the realm of those who engage with the world intensionally, and both are coextensive with the realm of those who judge by means of the application of a concept treated as a concept. I will call such thinkers 'representationalists'.

On the other side of the divide are those who are suspicious of the judgemental model of the *as* structure of engagement because they believe that there is another way in which an agent can engage with the entities within the world that is independent of, prior to, and necessary for judgement. Consider the case of my two-year-old granddaughter, Betsy, who is a wiz at sorting blocks according to their shapes. She routinely places triangular blocks in triangular holes, spherical and cylindrical blocks in round holes, and cubical blocks in square holes. On the other hand, Betsy is quite shaky at linguistically identifying the shapes involved, and entirely hopeless at the task of specifying what it is about the blocks she handles that qualifies them to be put in their appropriate holes. Does Betsy engage with the sides of the various blocks *as* square or triangular or round? On the one hand, Betsy's lack of linguistic competence, and her inability to either articulate the conceptual inferential linkages among these concepts and other concepts or act on those links in her behaviour drive us towards the view that she lacks the concepts involved. On the other hand, in her behaviour Betsy surely seems to *treat* the blocks *as* round, etc., and this pushes us in the direction of accepting that Betsy is capable of engaging with shapes *as* shapes.

The answer to the question regarding whether or not Betsy engages with shapes as shapes turns on what is required for treating an entity *as* this or that, of course, and the answer to that question would seem to turn on whether or not for an agent to treat an entity as an x it is necessary that that agent be able to treat the concept of x *as* a concept, that is, as something that is general and can serve as a rule for judgement. We have good evidence that Betsy is incapable of treating her ability to sort things into round and non-round as facilitated by a concept, as enabled by something general that serves as a rule. She can neither say what it is that qualifies this block, but not that one, to fit into that hole, nor can she even *designate* that qualifying characteristic. So we have no reason to think that Betsy specifically uses some characterization of that quality as a mark that supplies the rule for deciding between cases of round and cases of non-round. Her act of placing a block in the right hole is simply an expression of her generalized motor-perceptual ability. And, if the ability to treat some rule that is descriptively accurate of cases of a pattern of behaviour *as* a rule for deciding those cases (by articulating the content of the rule or representing the rule as such), is a necessary condition for possessing the corresponding concept, then Betsy lacks shape concepts. On the other hand, Betsy does in fact respond perceptually and in action to the roundness and squareness of things. Regardless of colour and composition, she places all the cubical blocks in square holes and all the spherical blocks in round holes; Betsy seems to engage with the blocks *as* round and square.

Now, as the proponents of the necessity of the capacity to judge for the possibility of an intensional engagement with things are quick to point out, entities that are not intentional agents are quite as capable of differential responsiveness as is Betsy. Iron bars respond differentially to the presence and absence of water vapour, after all. It is even possible for non-intentional agents to respond differentially to features such as shape, independently of color and composition, just as Betsy does. So what distinguishes Betsy's shape sorting from the mere differential responsiveness of the iron bar or the record changer, if it is not the capacity to judge?[14]

The implicit answer proposed to this question by anti-representationalists is that Betsy's shape sorting behaviour is embedded in a purposive or teleological context – Betsy responds as she does to the blocks *in order to* sort them so that they can fit through the slots. On this alternative understanding of the *as* structure, the necessary and sufficient condition for an agent treating something *as* something is that the agent acts purposively in order to bring about ends. Such agents have practical interests, their activities are evaluable in light of those interests, and, when they respond to the properties of things *as* they ought to respond in order to facilitate the achievement of those ends, they engage with those things *as* belonging to various types. On this view Betsy differs from record changers insofar as she has ends of her own, and in light of those ends, she has interests of her own.[15] And in light of those interests, things are revealed *as* they are relevant to those interests. Let me illustrate how this is supposed to work.

When an intensional agent engages with an entity, she is responsive to some feature, property or relation of that thing, and, crucially, she is responsive to that aspect *because* it is that aspect. When I form the judgement that that thing over there is a hammer, I form that judgement in response to the supposed fact that it satisfies the conditions that qualify the thing as a hammer. In addition to my relation to the hammer itself, my judgement depends upon my ability to sort things according to the principle embedded in the concept of a hammer, which supplies the norm for judging. On any given occasion the agent can misapply the concept of course, and judge a piece of wet pasta to be a hammer. But unless the agent were in general responsive to the hammerness of things (and equally responsive to many other such properties) it would be wrong to say that she was treating something as something, at all. Similarly, when an agent uses an entity as an entity of a certain type, or avoids some entity as detrimental to the achievement of her goals, she needs to be responsive to the features, properties or relations of the thing that qualify it as potentially instrumental or detrimental to her ends. If she *is* responsive to those properties in the appropriate way, the agent takes the thing *as* a hammer, or whatever. And, just as in the case of judgement, there is a norm associated with the type against which the agent's action is evaluable. The agent's act is correct in treating an entity as of some type just in case she can succeed in using the thing *as* it is taken to be. And, just as in the case of judgment, the agent can make mistakes when her acts are measured against their corresponding norm, but when she makes too many mistakes she no longer counts as acting for ends and no longer counts as taking anything *as* anything. In effect, in cases of purposive action, what is to be accomplished in the act provides a norm against which the act is evaluable. And, since to act for an end implies that the agent has taken things *as* instrumental or detrimental in definite ways, this same end prescribes a norm against which those ways of taking things is also evaluable.

On this view, all that is required for an agent to treat a square block *as* square is that the agent be capable of responding differentially to the shape of the block in order to achieve some end of that agent. Whether or not the agent possesses any 'representation' of the block is strictly irrelevant to the issue of whether or not the agent in fact engages with the block as square. So whatever conditions are necessary and sufficient for an agent to count as acting in order to achieve some end are also necessary and sufficient for that agent to engage with entities *as* something. And, for those who hold this view of the *as* structure, the types *as* which the agent engages with things are *primarily practical*. Such types are *practical* both in the sense that they reveal entities as they are relevant to the interests of the agent, that is, relevant to the achievement of the agent's ends, and in the sense that agents engage with things as this or that by actually overtly acting on and with those things. Such types are seen to be *primarily* practical in the sense that it is held that nothing could engage with entities *as* anything at all unless they also engaged with them *as* practically relevant. That is, it is held that engaging with things *as* they are revealed to be in and by the practical interests and actions of the agent is a necessary condition for an agent engaging with things in any way *as* anything at all.

As I am using the term, anyone who adopts this basic view of the as structure is a 'pragmatist'. Using this standard, philosophers as diverse as Peirce, Dewey, the late Wittgenstein, the early Heidegger, Merleau-Ponty, Hubert Dreyfus, Daniel Dennett and Alva Noe all count as pragmatists. And using that same standard philosophers as diverse as Kant, Descartes, Frege, Russell, Husserl, Fodor and Searle all count as representationalists. On this usage, pragmatic verificationism regarding linguistic meaning and conceptual content is not the defining characteristic of pragmatism. This semantic theory is merely a widely shared inference from the fundamental point of similarity among pragmatists.[16] Rather, the defining feature of pragmatism is its peculiar variety of *anti-representationalism*. For the pragmatist, whether or not an agent engages with things as this or that is not a matter of how or whether it represents those things. It is a matter of whether or not the agent interacts with its surroundings as an environment in which it acts to achieve its ends and in which it responds to things as illuminated by its interests.

As it turns out, there are two main kinds of pragmatism. These kinds are delineated by their differing analyses of the necessary conditions on an agent genuinely acting in light of their interests in order to achieve an end. There are those, such as Merleau-Ponty, Alva Noe and Dewey, who hold that both the teleology of action and the *as* structure are fundamental features of the perceptual-motor abilities that underlie normal human, and indeed, animal agency, where those abilities are defined in terms of the organic instrumental practical interests of the agent. There is another camp, however, including the early Heidegger, who hold that only agents that are capable of adhering to socially articulated ends, means and proprieties, such as humans, are, in the crucial sense, capable of acting for the sake of some goal, and only such agents engage with the entities within the world as this or that. In the next section of this chapter I will articulate the central structure of the biological-naturalistic style of pragmatism. Then, in the following section, I will go on to illuminate the distinctive character of the early Heidegger's pragmatism by contrasting it with the naturalistic form.

II NATURALISTIC PRAGMATISM

The intuition behind the naturalistic form of pragmatism is that the notion of an organic agent itself only makes sense in terms of something like an intensional engagement of that agent in its environment. An organism is essentially something that literally must make a living. That is, to be an organism is to interact with an environment in such a way as to continue the processes that constitute the life of the organism. For this to happen, certain features of the environment must be utilized in very specific ways to achieve very specific ends. That is, the organism, as such, mines its environment for necessary resources, and only counts as an individual when it does so successfully. So to view a heap of structures as an individual organism is to view it as engaged in the process of utilizing various features of the environment to achieve various ends, all of which are part of or conducive to the achievement of the single integrated end of the agent maintaining its integrity as an individual, by keeping it alive. The organism has an 'interest' in features of the environment only in so far as those features are conducive or detrimental to its continuance. In so far as the organism continues it must successfully treat those features of the environment that are in some particular way potentially useful to the achievement of the necessary tasks involved in its survival *as* potentially serviceable in this way; it engages these features in their *serviceability*. The organism needs to avoid other features of the environment if it is to survive; in so far as they are avoided they are engaged as detrimental, in their detrimentality. As Kathleen Akins nicely puts it, the features that animals sense in their environment are 'narcissistic'.[17] And this is not an accident. For what distinguishes the sensation of an organism from a mere differential responsiveness is precisely this narcissistic standpoint.

Alva Noe (among others, including myself)[18] has recently argued that this narcissistic *as* structure is a necessary concomitant of life as such, as opposed to a sophisticated add-on. Consider the lowly bacterium.

> The bacterium is geared into the world not merely in the sense that the presence of sugar causes a certain bacteriumlike congeries of atoms to migrate in the direction of greater intensity of sugar; the bacterial mesh with its surroundings are of a different quality than that. The bacterium needs sugar to live and is adapted to its surroundings, and that's why it is impelled toward the sugar. The bacterium is not merely a process, it is an agent, however simple; it has interests ... The basic fact is that the bacterium comes into focus for biology as an organism, as a living being, once we appreciate its integrity as an individual agent, as a bearer of interests and needs. With the bacterium we find a subject and an environment, an organism and a world. The animal, crucially, has a world; that is to say, it has a relationship with its surroundings.[19]

Noe's suggestion is the naturalistic, organic, pragmatic suggestion. The suggestion has a number of aspects. First, the biological description of the bacterium's behaviour appeals to the bacterium as an individual that responds to its environment in the light of its interests and needs as a kind of organic agent. Second, treating the organism as a unit that has interests has *explanatory* power, and for that reason such understanding of the organism as agent is indispensable. The biological understanding of the bacterium's behaviour appeals to the bacterium as an individual agent that responds to its environment as it does *because* of its needs and interests as the kind of organic agent that it is. But, third, for the organism to be a unit that has interests is the very same thing as for the organism to be a unit that, through its *actions*, unveils the things in its world *as* needed and to be avoided in specific ways and for specific purposes. Organisms are, essentially, agents that act on their environment in order to realize ends that are intrinsic to and necessary for their continuance. And, in so far as organisms act, that action *itself* amounts to the organism taking features of its environment *as* serviceable or detrimental to its interests. When the organic agent succeeds in using and avoiding things as they ought to be used if they are to serve its interests, the agent also successfully *reveals* the things in its world *as* really being serviceable and detrimental in the ways that, in its action, it takes them to be. This is the cash value, in this context, of the claim that the organism 'has a world'.

The biological basis of this kind of pragmatism explains certain of the characteristic tendencies of the pragmatic tradition of philosophy. In particular, in addition to being anti-representationalist, biologically based pragmatists have distinctive views of the way in which knowledge is integrated with and dependent upon action and tend to be semantic holists and pragmatic verificationists. And, while none of these positions is strictly implied by the basic, stripped down biologically based interpretation of the *as* structure I have presented, they are all suggested by that model. I will briefly discuss these linkages.

Because organisms are integrated units involving a variety of interlocking processes, and organisms engage through their actions with features of their environments as they are relevant to the continuance of those processes, biological pragmatists characteristically think that the 'world' of the organism has a holistic structure. If some organism takes some entity *as* of some particular type, this can only be because that type is salient and relevant for the organism's interests. But since those interests are relative to the ongoing life of the organism, and that life consists of continuing processes, in which each stage of the process is both dependent on the successful completion of earlier stages and necessary for the inauguration and completion of succeeding stages, the interests of the organism are defined holistically. From this holism of interests it is natural to infer a holism of the types revealed by those interests. A tiger needs a source of energy, and in the light of that interest reveals aspects of its world to be *food*. But since some of the sources of that energy are too large to be consumed at a time given the metabolic resources of the tiger, and the tiger will also need food tomorrow, its interests could be served if it could preserve some of that food for later use. But the world of the tiger also includes other animals that could use that food, and who are thereby potentially detrimental to the interests of the tiger. That is, they are revealed by the interests of the tiger *as competitors*; that is, as poachers of *food*. On the other hand, if competitors could be kept from discovering the food, the tiger's interests could be served, and this interest in concealment from others reveals features of the world of the tiger to be *camouflage*, that is, potential instruments for hiding *food*. And so it goes. It is the *things* in the world of the tiger that have meanings, and since those meanings are revealed only in light of the context of significance established by the interlocking interests of the organic agent, each of those meanings is defined only in relation to the meanings of the other things in the world of the agent. The world of the organism is not a collection of independent things. It is a context of significance, where that significance is relative to the organic interests and ends of the organism.

The continued survival of the organism depends upon its integration with its world and its successful utilization of the resources supplied by that world. This success amounts to the organism's exercise of the ability to respond appropriately, given its interests, to the presence and absence of the instrumentally important features of its environment. That is, to be alive is for the organism to *know how* to make a living and to successfully act on that knowhow, to know how to do what it needs to survive, and to know when to exercise that knowhow. But on the pragmatic understanding of the *as* structure, this very same knowhow also amounts to a revelation of certain aspects of the way in which the things in the world actually are. At the organic level, knowing how to cope with its environment is inextricably involved with the organism's knowledge that the entities in the world have certain features at certain times. But the features of things that the organism must successfully respond to are, as we have seen, holistically fixed through their relations with the other requirements of the organism. And, since for the organism to know how to cope with some feature of its world, and thus to know that the entity with which it is dealing has that feature, it is necessary that it also know how to cope with other features of its world and to know that other entities have other instrumentally important properties. Thus, for the pragmatist, knowledge of the way in which the world is is essentially holistic, because knowledge of the way the world is only exists in the context of knowing how to cope with the world, and knowing how to cope with the world is holistic.

Now none of this directly implies that semantic meanings need to be understood holistically. Nor does it imply that the meanings of sentences are fixed by their pragmatic verification conditions. After all, it is one thing for the ways that things are instrumentally significant for organisms to be holistically related to one another, and quite a different thing for the semantic significance of the words that human organisms use to represent things to be holistically fixed by pragmatically salient conditions of appropriate use. We humans not only treat things *as* this or that by coping with them, we also engage with them *as* this or that by forming justified, conceptual, discursive, judgements. Nevertheless, since pragmatists understand the *as* structure as such as derivative from the conditions on action, in understanding language pragmatists tend to start from the action of actually using language to accomplish various tasks. That is, pragmatists tend to make the strategic bet that the semantic features of language are derivative from the pragmatics of language use. And since action as such has a holistic structure, and in at least non-linguistic action the meanings of things and acts are fixed only by their roles within a context of pragmatic significance, pragmatists are prone to think of the linguistic meanings of linguistic types as also holistically fixed by their roles in language use; that is, pragmatists tend to think that semantic meanings are fixed by inferential roles.

III   HEIDEGGER'S BRAND OF PRAGMATISM

The early Heidegger's phenomenological methodology predisposed him towards a certain scepticism regarding the ontological significance of the fact that we humans are biological creatures. If the primary access to what it is to be an entity to which things are given *as* something is through a self-examination and self-interpretation, then it is at best unclear whether or to what degree 'mere' animals, who perhaps lack the possibility of such self-access, and certainly lack the possibility of sharing the fruits of this self-access with us, share with us this basic *as* structure. Perhaps more importantly, lacking *phenomenological* access to the 'world' of the mere animal, it seems to Heidegger that the only way in which we can approach an understanding of that world is by examining the way in which animals show up for us. And, for Heidegger, animals thus reveal themselves as in some respects *deficient* co-inhabitants with us of that world.

So the early Heidegger firmly rejected the tradition, (which he most closely identified with Aristotle), that understood the *as* structure characteristic of our being as a fundamentally biological phenomenon. And, in this rejection he also rejected the type of naturalistic pragmatism prevalent among American pragmatists. Instead of understanding the human way of engaging with the world as a development and modification of a basic organic inheritance, Heidegger held that to the extent that animals exhibit an *as* structure in their dealings with their environment this biological engagement must be seen as a deficient mode. 'Life must be understood as a kind of Being to which there belongs Being-in-the-world. Only if this kind of Being is oriented in a privative way to Dasein can we fix its character ontologically.'[20]

Nevertheless, Heidegger's understanding of the basic structure of human engagement with the world is, in the crucial sense, thoroughly pragmatic. As Heidegger sees it, the fact that humans engage with entities *as* this or that depends upon the fact that humans *understand* the world and the things in it, and this basic understanding in turn is an aspect of the fundamental constitution of entities like us; we are 'being-in-the-world'. Although the terms translated here as 'world' and 'understanding' are common ones, they serve as part of Heidegger's technical vocabulary. The claim that beings with our kind of being (or 'Dasein') are in-the-world has two sides, but Heidegger insists that the two sides are inextricably connected and only formally abstractable from each other. What we are is 'being-in', and what we are 'in' is the world. In Heidegger's usage, to 'be-in' is to 'inhabit' or to be familiar with. '"I am" thus amounts to saying, I dwell, I abide in the world as with something familiar. Being as in-being and "I am" means dwelling with ... and "in" primarily does not signify anything spatial at all but means primarily *being familiar with*.'[21] The character of this 'dwelling' or 'familiarity' is indicated by the paradigm ways in which it occurs:

> Such possible modes of in-being belonging to everydayness include: working on something with something, producing something, cultivating and caring for something, putting something to use, employing something for something, holding something in trust, giving up, letting something get lost, interrogating, discussing, accomplishing, exploring, considering, determining something.[22]

Heidegger identifies the common factor among these various ways of being-in as concern – we are familiar with something when we are concerned with or have an interest in that something. But in this context another commonality among the items on this list is salient. All of these ways of being-in are ways of *acting*, and most of these ways of acting are necessarily ways of acting overtly with and on things. To be us is to be familiar with an environment and to be familiar with an environment is to know how to cope with it by acting on and with things in light of our concern, or in light of what matters to us.

According to Heidegger, being-in is always primarily being-in the world; being familiar with the world is the precondition for familiarity with things. The 'world' in turn is a context of a certain kind of teleological significance.

> Circumspective concern includes the understanding of a totality of involvements, and this understanding is based on a prior understanding of the relationships of the 'in-order-to', the 'towards-which', the 'towards-this', and the 'for-the-sake-of'. The interconnection of these relationships has been exhibited earlier as 'significance'. Their unity make up what we call 'world'.[23]

Heidegger's technical terminology is never denser than when he is discussing his notion of the world, but the underlying concepts are straightforward enough. The overall context for interpreting the phenomenon of 'world' is that Heidegger is talking about the ways in which we can be familiar with the kinds of things that he calls 'ready-to-hand', tools or pieces of equipment that are to be used for bringing about possibilities that matter to us. 'Involvement' is a catch all term for the various ways in which what a tool is can depend upon how it is to be used along with other things to get things done. When one tool type is defined in terms of what is to be accomplished with it along with other tools with which it is involved it is said to be 'in-order-to' bring about the output of that teleological function. Hammers are 'in-order-to' hammer nails. When the various 'in-order-tos' of a tool chest are interrelated in light of some possible way in which potential users of the tool complex might be, they are said to be 'for-the-sake-of' that possible way of being Dasein. Putting this together, hammers, for example, are involved with nails in so far as hammers are to be used in order to pound nails, so that boards can hang together … for the sake of providing shelter for Dasein. According to Heidegger, when an agent engages with her environment by being familiar with the teleological roles of different kinds of equipment the agent is familiar with the significance of those tools, and, since such significance is holistic in that each tool type is defined only in relation with the others, and the entire complex taken as a whole only makes sense in relation to the human possibility for the sake of which it is, the agent can only be familiar with the particular significance of different kinds of entities by having a prior understanding of the whole structure of significance in which it is embedded. This holistic structure of significance is the 'world'. So Heidegger's overall claim is that what we as Dasein are is a kind of familiarity with how things are to be used as equipment for the sake of bringing about possible ways in which we might be that matter to us.

Heidegger's views regarding the *as* structure of intensionality and intentionality are derived from this basic orientation. 'Understanding' is a fundamental and essential aspect of our being-in, or familiarity with the world, and it is primarily practical. No agent can engage with things or the world without understanding the world and things. An agent is said to understand when it is competent at living (or 'being') in the possible ways of being for the sake of which the world is structured, and the agent's understanding of particular things is part and parcel of this holistic practical competence.

'When we are talking ontically we sometimes use the expression 'understanding something' with the signification of 'being able to manage something', 'being a match for it', 'being competent to do something'. In understanding, as an *existentiale*, that which we have such competence over is not a 'what', but Being as existing.'[24]

One understands just in so far as one can cope with the world and treat the things in it as equipment to be used for the sake of bringing about possibilities of our own being that concern us. It is crucial to Heidegger's view that understanding is not primarily a theoretical understanding that such and such piece of equipment can possibly be used in such and such way, or even an understanding that it is to be used in that way. Rather, the fundamental form of understanding without which there is no other kind of understanding, is understanding how tools are to be used, and such understanding discloses things as capable of being used and to be used in certain ways by actually using them in that way. 'Equipment can genuinely show itself only in dealings cut to its own measure (hammering with a hammer, for example); but in such dealings an entity of this kind is not grasped thematically as an occurring thing'.[25]

The actual use of equipment as equipment requires a perceptual sensitivity to the ways in which tools are usable and to be used, and Heidegger calls this ability to perceptually respond to these aspects of things 'circumspection', which has a definite kind of priority over mere sensation or the perceptual recognition of non-teleological properties of objects; no agent could be perceptually sensitive to non-teleological properties who was not circumspectively engaged with things. And, for Heidegger, the primary way in which we display the *as* structure of our engagement with things is through coping with the world by actually displaying the perceptual-motor abilities involved in our circumspective understanding of those things, by using those things as they are to be used. And for this, judgment that appeals to concepts as concepts is not required.

In dealing with what is environmentally ready-to-hand by interpreting it circumspectively, we 'see' it *as* a table, a door, a carriage, a bridge; but what we have interpreted need not necessarily be taken apart by making an assertion which definitely characterizes it.[26]

It should be obvious even from this brief summary that Heidegger shares with his naturalistically motivated cousins a core commitment to the fundamental anti-representational pragmatic thesis, that the *as* structure of intentional engagement is primarily practical. For Heidegger, as for naturalistic pragmatists, the capacity to judge is not necessary for engaging with things as this or that, and the ability to engage with things as this or that by coping with them for the sake of realizing ends is a necessary condition on the capacity to judge. For Heidegger, the types *as* which the agent engages with things are *primarily practical*. Such types are *practical* both in the sense that they reveal entities as they are relevant to the interests of the agent, that is, relevant to the achievement of the agent's ends, and in the sense that agents engage with things as this or that by actually overtly acting on and with those things. Such types are seen to be *primarily* practical in the sense that it is held that no agent could engage with entities *as* anything at all unless they also engaged with them *as* practically relevant. That is, it is held that engaging with things *as* they are revealed to be in and by the practical interests of the agent is a necessary condition for an agent engaging with things in any way *as* anything at all. The ability to practically cope with things in the world is a necessary condition on being able to form discursive judgements, both 'mentally' and in the overt act of making linguistic assertions. But being capable of making such judgements is not a necessary condition on being able to intend things *as* this or that in and through coping with the world.

The key similarity between naturalistically informed pragmatism and Heidegger's brand of pragmatism is thus the insistence that the *as* structure of engagement is primarily a feature of a practical coping with things in a holistically, teleologically, structured world. For both, treating things *as* something is a byproduct of dealing with an environment in order to achieve ends that the agent cares about or in which she has an interest. But there are striking differences between Heidegger's articulation of the structure of the world of Dasein and the structure of biological environments, and these structural differences are tied to differences regarding both the minimal requirements for an agent engaging with entities *as* something and differences concerning the nature of that intensional engagement.

For Heidegger, there is a teleological structure implicit in the world of Dasein, but that structure does not embody simple means/end relations, nor is that structure anchored in the biological character of the agent. The 'ends' implicit in the world are not states of things that could be realized at a time, such as 'the agent ingests the liquid'. Rather, the for-the-sake-of-which that orients the tool complex of equipment that gives that equipment its significance and gives the world its structure is always a possible way of Dasein's being, and Dasein's way of being is quite different from the way in which tools are.[27] The possible ways of Dasein's being that are the for-the-sake-ofs of the world are always modes of activity that can only occur over time, with the aid of the equipment that is for the sake of that activity. For example, in a classroom the chalk is there in order to write on a blackboard, and the board is there in order to be written on so that students can see what the teacher writes, and the chairs are where they are so that the students can see what's on the board, etc. But the entire complex is for-the-sake-of teaching and learning, which are ongoing activities that are possible ways for Dasein to be. Notice, the actual use of the classroom equipment isn't merely instrumental to the bringing about of some state of affairs. The use doesn't *precede* the teaching in order to bring it about as an accomplishment. Rather, the teaching and the use of the equipment is simultaneous even though the use is for the sake of the teaching, because the use happens in the course of the teaching; that use is part of the activity of teaching itself.

In this respect there is substantial similarity between Heidegger's description of the teleological structure of Dasein's world and certain aspects of Aristotle's characterization of the processes of living things.[28] But Dasein's world is crucially distinct from that of merely biological entities, however that is described, in several other critical respects. The first of these differences can be brought out by first noting a superficial similarity between the for-the-sake-of of a Dasein and the Aristotelian biological essence of an organism. For Aristotle, the answer to the question 'What is it?' when asked of an organism is supplied by appealing to the organism's essence, and that essence coincides with the type of organism the individual is. This type prescribes a certain pattern of organic activity and a certain way of making a living. What Sammie, my pet Sheltie, *is*, is a dog, and being a dog involves him in surviving as a dog by living in a doggie way, structurally, metabolically and behaviourally. No doggieness, no Sammie. Similarly, for Heidegger, the answer to the question 'Who is she?' asked of a Dasein, can be given by alluding to those for-sake-of-whiches that specify a certain pattern of human activity; she is a teacher, or a mother or an American. But (and this is the crucial difference) none of these ways of being are *necessary* to the being of the individual Dasein. Sammie can only be by being a dog. But even if my partner Charlotte is a firmly committed philosopher, it just is not the case that for her to be, she must live the life of a philosopher. Even if Dasein is actually in the process of being a philosopher, being a philosopher is never a necessary way of being that Dasein; it is always a *possible* way of being. And, at some level, every Dasein knows this about herself, if only in and through the temptation to adopt an alternative possible for-the-sake-of-which on which to orient the structure of significance. Who she is is thus an *issue* for every Dasein, as Heidegger puts the point. As opposed to living beings treated as living, the ends that ground the norms that must be satisfied to be in the world in the particular way that the agent is are, for Dasein, always options that are opposed to other possibilities.

This first difference of Dasein's world from the 'world' of biological agents is tied to a second one. As Heidegger sees it, the norms that constrain Dasein as Dasein display a different, essentially non-biological type of normativity and binding power. Both the norms that govern the evaluation of biological action and what things in the environment can be taken to be in and through that action are grounded in the essential biological nature of the organism. As we saw when we were discussing Noe's example of the bacterium, the interest of a biological organism in its own survival, and the fact that the organism can only survive in and through utilizing its environment as a resource in very specific ways in the course of undergoing its continuing life processes, establish a norm against which the actions of the organism, as such, are to be measured. Lions act only as lions, and lions need to eat on a regular basis in order to continue being lions. In light of this fact, various aspects of the lion's behaviour emerge as having a proximate goal, that is, the lion acts in various ways. Acts are acts only if they have a goal, and those goals are always relative to the description of the organism as a type of organism. In light of the fact that it is a lion, some of what the lion does reveals itself as an act with the goal of capturing, killing and ingesting a springbok. That is, the lion hunts, and hunting as hunting prescribes a norm against which the success and failure of the hunting act is to be measured. Because hunting has the goal that it does, when a lion hunts, the lion succeeds if and only if it captures, kills and ingests the springbok; otherwise its hunt fails. The norms that govern the evaluation of the actions of organisms are thus grounded in the biological nature of the organisms that act.

Similarly, when an organism takes something in its environment *as* something in particular, what it takes that thing to be is fixed by its role in the life process of the organism. By hunting, the lion takes the springbok to be food; by hiding its half-eaten prey for another day by placing it under brush, the tiger takes the brush to be camouflage. Since the organism as living can only take the items in its environment as something by acting on and with them, and they can act only in relation to their organically determined essential natures, organisms can only treat things as instrumental or detrimental to their biologically fixed interests.

As we have seen, on Heidegger's description the world of Dasein differs from the environment revealed by the biological activity of organisms in at least one critical respect. In order for an individual Dasein to exist at all, it is never necessary for that Dasein to be in any particular world, oriented by any particular for-the-sake-of-which. An organism is embedded in its environmental niche in such a way that it cannot be at all unless it is as it is, as the kind of organism that it is. One might say, what the animal actually is determines and fixes its possibilities. But for Heidegger this is never true of Dasein. As Heidegger puts it (in an obvious reference to and reversal of Aristotle in *Metaphysics* Theta) for Dasein 'Higher than actuality stands *possibility*'.[29] No matter how embedded an American philosopher is in the world of American philosophy, with its concerns and instrumentalities, it is always possible for that philosopher to cease to be a philosopher and yet still remain Dasein. Every Dasein must be in a world; no Dasein must be in any particular definite world.

For Heidegger this modal fact about Dasein correlates with a distinctive aspect of the way in which Dasein engages with its world. For organisms, what things in the world *can be*, what those things can be treated *as*, is prescribed by their biological natures. An individual organism can make a mistake regarding whether or not some thing is *food* for it, but that it treats some things as food, and what it is to be food, are fixed by what sort of organism it is. For the organic agent as organic, all categories as which things can be engaged are defined by the capacity of an entity to satisfy some instrumental role prescribed by the form of life of the organism. This is not true for the categories revealed in and through Dasein's being-in-the-world. The criteria for being a token of an equipmental type, such as 'hammer', are not defined in terms of an entity's capacity to be useful for a human being in fulfilling some instrumental (biological or non-biological) function, and the form of the organic life of the human organism does not prescribe the equipmental function itself. The function that is involved in the definition of 'hammer' is surely something like 'instrument used to pound nails into wood'. But (1) no individual Dasein must hammer nails into boards on pain of termination, (2) not every entity that can satisfy that function is a hammer (rocks aren't, for example), and (3) not every hammer is capable of satisfying the function (broken hammers might not be, for example). Rather, it is important for understanding what it is to be a hammer to see that hammers are things that are *to be used* to perform the function in question, not things that *can* be used to perform the function. And that something is to be used in this way is not determined by any biological fact about the user.

So what, exactly, does ground the distinctive kind of normativity involved in equipmental types? What can it mean to say that hammers, as hammers, are *to be used* as hammers and thus that to treat some thing as a hammer is to treat it as to be used in acts of hammering? Heidegger's answers to these questions turn on his recognition that Dasein are always historical entities that find themselves always already existing in ongoing culturally constituted and maintained worlds. The structure of the various possible ways of being Dasein that are available for any individual are already determined for that individual by her cultural milieu. What is involved in being a teacher in early twenty-first-century America is already largely prescribed when the individual moves into that social role and practice. How one should act, with what one should act, how one should act with those things, are already built into that form of life in a normative fashion. To be Dasein is to live in a world that is organized in such a way that what is to be done is what any member of the community in which that Dasein exists, what any Dasein with that for-the-sake-of, ought to do; it is to do what *one* does. Heidegger uses the phrase, *das Man* (the One), to express the phenomenal sense of the source of this kind of normativity.

Dasein is for the sake of the 'one' in an everyday manner, and the 'one' itself Articulates the referential context of significance. When entities are encountered, Dasein's world frees them for a totality of involvements with which the 'one' is familiar, and within the limits which have been established with the 'one's' averageness.[30]

Given this understanding of the normative dimension of Dasein's world, to say that some entity is a hammer is to say that it is to be used as one uses 'hammers' to perform the standardized function that is prescribed for 'hammers' within some historically constituted social practice. An act of hammering is successful if it is performed as one hammers within that practice. That these norms arise and are maintained does not depend on the biological character of Dasein. Rather, this kind of normativity depends upon the self-policing ability of the members of a community of Dasein to organize and regularize standardized ways of coping with each other and the non-Dasein environment. For Heidegger, no mere non-Daseinish animal can establish its own niche, and because of this fact, that *as* which the things in the animal world are encountered are limited to those features of things that are directly or indirectly instrumental to the continuing life of the organism. But, for Heidegger, Dasein is not limited in this way. Although no individual Dasein can make up her own form of life from scratch, communal Dasein, through the social capacity to establish norms for what one does, and how one does it, is capable of introducing novel for-the-sake-ofs, novel constellations of practices, equipment and ways of being.

Now it is fairly obvious that most such standardized ways of coping, those that engage with things within the world, could not maintain themselves unless they integrated reasonably well with the non-Dasein environment. These practices are techniques for doing things, not games; one doesn't find grossly ineffective traditions of carpentry. But given those limits, once the social style of normativity is established, there is quite a degree of latitude for how in particular the norms of the 'one' can be determined. And, given that fact, that *as* which Dasein can engage with the entities within the world, the categories in terms of which Dasein can engage with things, are wildly various when compared with the categories as which animals can engage with things. And from Heidegger's perspective, this increased variation extends not only to the number of categories, but also to the kinds of categories. An animal can use a rock to achieve one of its biologically prescribed ends, cracking a nut, for example, and thus treat it as instrumental to achieving that end, but no mere animal can be a carpenter who treats something as a hammer, as something that is to be used in a given way.

Dasein's ability to engage with things as they are to be engaged with is correlated with several other basic aspects of the structure of Dasein's world that, for Heidegger, distinguish it fundamentally from the 'world' of mere animals. Because Dasein can engage with things as they are to be used, Dasein is also capable of a type of second order engagement with the roles that those things occupy. It does so when it no longer uses the things in its world as they are to be used but instead *repairs* or *improves* those things so that they can better perform those functions. Heidegger calls such engagement 'interpretation'. The hammer itself is improved in order to better fulfil its role, and through this interpretative involvement the role of the hammer itself becomes an explicit link in Dasein's world.

> To say that 'circumspection discovers' means that the 'world' which has already been understood comes to be interpreted. The ready-to-hand comes *explicitly* into the sight which understands. All preparing, putting to rights, repairing, improving, rounding-out, are accomplished in the following way: we take apart in its 'in-order-to' that which is circumspectively ready-to-hand, and we concern ourselves with it in accordance with what becomes visible through this process. That which has been circumspectively taken apart with regard to its 'in-order-to', and taken apart as such – that which is *'explicitly'* understood – has the structure *something as something*.[31]

According to Heidegger, Dasein's capacity to make the significance of the things in its world explicit through interpretation also opens up a new possibility for Dasein's engagement with things. Dasein can interpretively engage with a thing by making its significant role explicit in the course of making an assertion regarding that thing: 'This is a hammer'. For Heidegger, assertion is a 'derivative mode of interpretation'.[32] Finally, for Heidegger, this ability to make assertions opens the door for the possibility of engaging with things in ways that are essentially *not* practical, *as* mere objects of possible perception or cognition, *as* merely 'present-at-hand': 'This leveling of the primordial "as" of circumspective interpretation to the "as" with which presence-at-hand is given a definite character is the specialty of assertion.[33]

So, for Heidegger, Dasein's world has a complex of interrelated essential features, features that correlate with distinctive ways in which Dasein can engage with the things in its world, and with distinctive modes as which things in its world can be revealed. Dasein is constrained by social as well as biological normativity; the specific character of Dasein's world is not determined by the fact that the Dasein we are familiar with are biologically human, so no particular world in which Dasein finds itself is ever necessary for that Dasein; Dasein can engage with things as they are to be engaged with within particular cultural social contexts; Dasein can engage with things as belonging to non-biologically instrumental kinds; Dasein can interpretively make explicit the significance of things, that is, make explicit the roles that things are to occupy, that as which things are to be interpreted; Dasein can engage with things as having significance by and through making linguistic assertions regarding them; Dasein can engage with things as belonging to non-instrumental, non-teleological kinds. Heidegger's pragmatism is thus rooted in the social, rather than biological, normative evaluation of action.

IV CONCLUSION: ENGAGING WITH BEINGS AS BEINGS

Heidegger's brand of pragmatism insists that only agents that engage with the world and with the things within it in the full-blown way in which Dasein does, engage with the things in the world *as* anything at all. It is for this reason that Heidegger holds that animal 'worlds' can only be understood as deficient modes of Dasein.

Heidegger is not the only recent philosopher with pragmatic tendencies to hold that only entities that are capable of language use are capable of genuine intentionality, of course. Davidson, Sellars and Brandom all come immediately to mind. But Heidegger's reasons for holding this position are unique. Davidson, Sellars and Brandom all offer versions of an argument that they inherit from Kant. They all hold, first, that it is impossible for an agent to engage with anything as something unless that agent can recognize her own mistakes as mistakes, second, that no agent can engage with mistakes as mistakes unless she is capable of second order intentionality and intend her own intentions as her own intentions, and, third, that no agent who is non-linguistic can be capable of second order intentions. Heidegger, on the other hand, is deeply sceptical of the ontological importance of the capacity for second-order intentions, even denying that such reflective self-awareness is the primary way in which Dasein intends itself *as* itself. Rather, he holds that Dasein engages with itself *as* itself primarily in its engagement with the things within its world that matter to it, through the for-the-sake-of that orients that world. 'The self is there for the Dasein itself without reflection and without inner perception, *before* all reflection ... In everyday terms, we understand ourselves and our existence by way of the activities we pursue and the things we take care of.'[34]

So, whatever reasons Heidegger has for his insistence that only Dasein genuinely engages with things *as* something, they don't turn on the special role of self-directed intentionality. Instead, Heidegger's argument depends, first, upon the claim that only

Dasein's form of being-in-the-world allows an agent to engage with things *as* things that *are*, or as *beings*, and, second, on the assertion that only agents who can engage with things as things that *are* are able to genuinely engage with things as anything at all. In conclusion, I will briefly discuss this line of argument.

Early and late, Heidegger always claimed that the most distinctive feature of Dasein is that only Dasein is capable of an understanding of *being*, and as such, only Dasein can engage with anything *as a being*. '*Understanding of Being is itself a definite characteristic of Dasein's Being. Dasein is ontologically distinctive in that it is ontological.*'[35] At first sight there might seem something odd about the notion that an agent could engage with something as a being. After all, doesn't any engagement by an agent with a thing involve engaging with something that is, on pain of there not being anything for the agent to engage with? Isn't it the case that one can't treat a springbok as food, unless there is a springbok? From Heidegger's standpoint (and plausibly, in fact) this sceptical intuition is doubly misguided. First, it is essential to engagement as such that it doesn't follow from the fact that an entity is of some kind that when an agent engages with that thing it is engaged with *as* that kind of thing. An agent who is ignorant of the game of lacrosse can engage with a ball as a ball, or a spherical thing, without intending it as a lacrosse ball, even if the ball *is* a lacrosse ball. So there is no obvious a priori reason why an agent couldn't engage with a thing that is, but not engage with it as a thing that is. But, second, it is of course also possible for an agent to intend something that is not, in the sense of something that is not actual, and in that sense 'engage with' that which is not. I can contemplate Hamlet, my granddaughter can want to see the tooth fairy, and I can believe that my redeemer liveth, even if there is no Hamlet, tooth fairy or redeemer. Indeed, as we are currently demonstrating, it is even possible to intend the tooth fairy, or Hamlet, or my redeemer, even though one knows full well that they do not exist, and so in that sense intend them not *as* actual beings at all, but rather as merely possible. But if it is possible to engage with something as not (actually) being, then perhaps it is not so strange to think that it is possible to engage with a thing *as* something that is. In that case, to engage with something as something that *is* involves engaging with it against the background of the possibility that it not be. And this is Heidegger's thought.

Only Dasein is capable of engagement with the merely possible as not being, and engagement with the merely possible is a necessary condition on engaging with beings *as* beings, so only Dasein is capable of engaging with beings as being. And this possibility for Heidegger is in turn wrapped up with Dasein's most distinctive engagement; Dasein is the being that understands Being, or what it is to be.

It is at least plausible to maintain, as Heidegger does, that only entities with Dasein's kind of world can engage with possibilities as possibilities.[36] Our only example of Dasein is the human organism, our best example of engaging with possibilities as possibilities involves language use, and we only have experience of humans using language. But Heidegger doesn't follow this argumentative strategy to get to the conclusion that only Dasein can engage with possibilities as possibilities, and thus engage with beings as beings. Perhaps surprisingly, he holds that Dasein's being-in-the-world is a necessary condition on language and assertion, and that Dasein can only engage with things linguistically because it has already engaged with beings as beings non-linguistically.

> Assertion does not as such primarily unveil; instead, it is always, in its sense, already related to something antecedently given as unveiled ... Only because the Dasein exists in the manner of being-in-the-world is some being unveiled along with the Dasein's existence in such a way that what is thus unveiled can become the possible object of an assertion.[37]

Instead, Heidegger's strategy here goes in a quite different direction. For Heidegger, the capacity to use language to represent beings as beings is itself made possible by a deeper ability of Dasein, the ability to engage with *oneself* as something that is. And this ability in turn depends for Heidegger on Dasein's capacity to engage with its own death. So as Heidegger understands it, it is this last ability, the ability of Dasein to engage with its own death by engaging with itself as possibly not being, that grounds the possibility of engaging with any being as something that is. And since only Dasein can engage with itself as possibly not being, only Dasein can engage with beings as beings. In slightly more detail, here is how the argument is supposed to go.

Famously, for Heidegger, Dasein is the being that relates itself to its own being. And, when it does so it engages with itself as a possibility. 'That entity [Dasein] which in its Being has this very being as an issue, comports itself towards its Being as its ownmost possibility.'[38] As this citation makes clear, on Heidegger's reading, Dasein's being is *problematic* for Dasein (Dasein's being is an issue for Dasein), and Dasein engages with its being *as a possibility*. The manner in which Dasein is supposed to engage with its own being as a problematic possibility is made evident in another famous aspect of Heidegger's early thought. For Heidegger, only Dasein can engage with itself as *dying*. 'Dying' is here used as a technical term in Heidegger's vocabulary, although its use is clearly related to the common use of the word. When it engages with itself as dying, Dasein engages with itself in terms of its 'ownmost possibility', the possibility of its not being, and when it engages with itself as possibly not being it engages with its own being as an issue, as problematic. So for Heidegger, the initial engagement with the possibility of non-being, and thus the possibility of engagement with things as beings, is the engagement of Dasein with the possibility of its own death. 'Let "*dying*" stand for the *way of Being* in which Dasein is *towards* its own death.'[39]

With death, Dasein stands before itself in its ownmost potentiality-for-Being. This is a possibility in which the issue is nothing less than Dasein's Being-in-the-world. Its death is the possibility of no-longer being-able-to-be-there. If Dasein stands before itself *as* this possibility, it has been fully assigned to its ownmost potentiality-for-Being.[40]

As Heidegger sees it, Dasein's ability to engage with itself as a being that is, that is, as a being that is not not there, in turn depends upon the unique structure of Dasein's world. Dasein is that for-the-sake-of-which things in the world have the significance that they have, and are as they are. That is, Dasein is in every case a way of being that implicates things and other Dasein in patterns of activity. Because Dasein's world is structured in terms of social rather than biological normativity, however, no for-the-sake-of, no way of Dasein's being is anything other than contingent, and that contingency is evident in the various social roles and various social worlds that Dasein encounters in the course of being itself. Dasein thus always engages with itself as possibly not being as it is. By its very character as Dasein, Dasein's being is an issue for it, or problematic for it, because Dasein always engages with itself as possibly not being there. And, because the for-the-sake-of that Dasein is is also that in terms of which things have their significance, the problematic character of Dasein's being extends to the problematic character of the being of other entities. Things have their significance only in light of a for-the-sake-of, but any for-the-sake-of is engaged by Dasein as possibly not being, so the significance of every thing is engaged by Dasein as possibly not being. And these possibilities in turn allow for the possibility of engaging with the things that in fact *are*, as things that are, as *entities*, as *beings*.[41]

This conclusion leaves the issue between Heidegger and naturalistic pragmatism unresolved, however. For the naturalistic pragmatist, all meaning, all content, all engagement with things as this or that is impossible except for the ability of organisms to utilize their environment, in accordance with their interests, as a resource in order to realize their ends. For this kind of pragmatism, organic activity is both the foundation for and the necessary condition on all kinds of action, and as such, the foundation for and necessary condition on all types of intentionality and intensionality. Heidegger, on the other hand, holds that Dasein is no mere rational animal. As such, he holds that the *as* structure of meaning first enters the world with the social normativity characteristic of Dasein's way of being, which, for Heidegger, is no mere form of life. To get to Heidegger's conclusion, that without Dasein's way of being-in-the-world no mere organic activity can count as an engagement with anything *as* something, one would need an additional argument. The premise for this argument would need to be the preliminary conclusion we have now reached, that only Dasein is capable of engaging with beings *as* beings.

It is anything but obvious, however, how this premise leads to Heidegger's claim that engagement with the entities within the world as this or that is the exclusive preserve of Dasein. And, to be honest, it is unclear to me that Heidegger ever provides the necessary argument. Since the capacity to engage with beings as entities, as things that *are*, correlates with the ability to engage with non-beings *as* mere possibilities, and this ability in turn correlates with the capacity to judge, there is no question that the ability to engage with beings as beings is qualitatively different from any kind of merely organic engagement. And this qualitative difference arguably might be thought to license the decision to terminologically restrict the use of intensional and intentional discourse to the description of Dasein and their activities. But, as Heidegger recognizes, such a terminological decision doesn't relieve one of the burden of coming up with some way of appreciating and accounting for the evident similarities between Daseins' engagement with the things in their world and organisms' engagement with the things in their environment. And, far more importantly, no mere terminological fiat can decide the real issue between naturalistic and Heideggerean forms of pragmatism. Is the Daseinish form of engagement with the world a *sui generis* way of being that uniquely unveils things as this or that by unveiling them as things that are, or is it merely a very distinctive *form of life*?

NOTES

1 'How to Make our Ideas Clear', Peirce, EP1: 132.
2 Peirce, EP1: 131.
3 Heidegger, 1962, p. 189; H. 149.
4 Heidegger, 1962, p. 192; H. 151.
5 Heidegger, 1982, pp. 190–1.
6 Okrent, 1988.
7 I place scare quotes around 'relations' here for the obvious reason that all real relations involve relations between individuals no matter how described, while these intentional 'relations' lack this feature. For that reason it is anything but clear that for an agent to take some entity *as* this or that involves any real relation between the agent and the entity.
8 I will use the blanket phrase 'engagement with' to designate the variety of ways in which we can be 'related' to things when we 'relate' to them as this or that, as when we want to use the hammer, but not the paperweight, although the hammer is the paperweight, or merely treat it as a hammer, by hammering with it, for example. Relations that are not engagements, such as being heavier than, lack this *as* structure.
9 For example, see Donald Davidson's 'Mental Events', in Davidson, 1980, pp. 207–25, especially pp. 210–11, where the linkages are especially clear.
10 This is a bit odd, as he offers us a number of elaborate explicit divisions of the types of representation, most notably in the section on Transcendental Ideas in *The Critique of Pure Reason* (Kant, 1998). For the record, for Kant, concepts are, along with intuitions, one of the two kinds of 'objective perception', where an objective perception is a conscious

representation of an object as an object. The distinguishing differentia of concepts is that they represent the object indirectly.
11 Kant, 1998, p. 232; A. 106.
12 Kant, 1998, p. 399; A. 320; B. 377.
13 It is important to note that the concept of a concept is itself ambiguous. While the majority of philosophers who invoke the concept of a concept treat it roughly in accordance with the Kantian heritage I have described, there is a distinct minority (including myself on most occasions), who accept a more liberal usage. According to this looser sense of 'concept', vervet monkeys who strictly distinguish in their behaviour between their matrilineal kin and all other vervets have something like the concept of 'being matrilineally related', although they are entirely ignorant of the inferential role of the analogous human concept in respect of the biology of reproduction, and my shape-sorting granddaughter has something like our concept of 'triangular' although she doesn't in any sense know the conditions of application of that word. A great deal of confusion and pointless wrangling could be avoided by keeping these senses straight.
14 It should be noted that there are those, and they are many, who hold that the capacity to judge is a necessary condition on intensional engagement with the world, but who also hold that the ability to self-consciously manipulate the inferential linkages among concepts is not necessary for the capacity to judge. There are many varieties of such views, and they differ markedly and pointedly between themselves. Taxonomy of these views is not necessary for my purposes here, however, as they all presuppose a basically representational understanding of what it is to be a concept and a representational understanding of the *as* structure.
15 There is of course a sense in which instruments such as record changers also do things to achieve ends. Nevertheless, there are crucial differences between instruments of that sort and genuinely teleological agents who have ends of their own, and engage with things as this or that. For those interested in the details, see Okrent, 2007.
16 Nor is the crucial difference here between those who hold that what the agent is responding to when she responds to an entity *as* something is not in principle expressible discursively, and those who hold that it is, even if it is not expressible by the agent herself. This is the interpretation of what is basic and important in the early Heidegger that is associated with Hubert Dreyfus and his school. On the view of Heidegger's pragmatism I am presenting here, a decision on this issue is a mere technical detail.
17 Akins, 1996, pp. 337–72.

Heidegger's pragmatism redux   157

18 Cf. Okrent, 2007, esp. ch. 4.
19 Noe, 2009, pp. 39–40.
20 Heidegger, 1962, p. 290; H. 246. There are other thinkers who count as pragmatists under the criterion suggested above who, for reasons different from Heidegger's, also reject a biologically based understanding of intentionality. Wilfred Sellars and Robert Brandom come immediately to mind.
21 Heidegger, 1992, p. 158.
22 Heidegger, 1992, p. 159.
23 Heidegger, 1962, p. 415; H. 364.
24 Heidegger, 1962, p. 183; H. 143.
25 Heidegger, 1962, p. 98; H. 68.
26 Heidegger, 1962, p. 189; H. 149.
27 Tool types are defined by a function that specifies what state of affairs is to be brought about by the use of the tool. This function is the defining 'in-order-to' of the tool type. Hammers are in-order-to hammer nails in the process of making boards fast to one another. Since this defining function is specified in terms of relations with other tool types, Heidegger says that they have an 'involvement' with one another. The *telos* ('*towards-which*') of the entire complex of such involvements, the 'for-the-sake-of-which' of that complex, is a possibility for Dasein's being that has *no* further involvement. That is, the specific for-the-sake-of is not defined by a function that specifies some state of affairs to be brought about as an output. This is Heidegger's way of putting the traditional point derived from Aristotle by way of Kant that beings like us (whether we are conceived as living beings, or rational beings, or Dasein), are ends in ourselves rather than mere means.
28 For example, see Aristotle, *Metaphysics*, book IX, chs. 6–9.
29 Heidegger, 1962, p. 3; H. 38.
30 Heidegger, 1962, p. 167; H. 129. Translation modified.
31 Heidegger, 1962, p. 189; H. 148–9.
32 Heidegger, 1962, p. 195; H. 153. I have argued elsewhere that the ability to use equipment as equipment and the ability to make equipmental roles explicit in interpretation are necessary conditions on the capacity for linguistic assertion, because language use is best seen as a kind of tool use. See Okrent, 2007, ch. 6.
33 Heidegger, 1962, p. 201; H. 158. I outline the steps in Heidegger's argument in somewhat more detail in ch. 3 of Okrent, 1988.
34 Heidegger, 1982, p. 159.
35 Heidegger, 1962, p. 32; H. 12.
36 Despite Heidegger's and others' scepticism concerning the ability of animals to engage with possibilities as possibilities, and beings as

beings, there is now much better evidence than there was in Heidegger's day that some animals do indeed have these capacities. If this is indeed true, then Heidegger would need to count such animals as Dasein.

37 Heidegger, 1982, p. 208.
38 Heidegger, 1962, p. 68; H. 43.
39 Heidegger, 1962, p. 291; H. 247.
40 Heidegger, 1962, p. 294; H. 250.
41 As should be obvious, as presented here there is a certain slippage in Heidegger's argument between two senses of 'to be', and between two senses of 'not being'. That slippage is roughly between what is usually characterized as 'essence' and what is usually characterized as 'existence'. It would seem to be one thing to engage with oneself, or any other thing, as not being as one in fact is, and another thing to engage with oneself or any other thing as not being at all. Early Heidegger has fascinating things to say about this issue, and how it relates to the possibility of Dasein intending beings as beings, but a consideration of that discussion here would take us too far afield.

7 *Practising* pragmatist-Wittgensteinianism

PHIL HUTCHINSON AND RUPERT READ

INTRODUCTION

Much has been written on the continuities between Wittgenstein's later work and pragmatism. Many have argued for there being strong continuity. Of those who see such strong continuity there are those who hold Wittgenstein to be the preeminent – even superior – philosopher of the Wittgenstein–pragmatism nexus (e.g. Hilary Putnam), and others who see Wittgenstein as simply echoing some of what was said with more originality by C. S. Peirce, with the consequent diminution in clarity that echoes bring (e.g. W.V.O. Quine). What Quine and Putnam have in common, however, is the identification of continuity, and in this they are far from alone (see Edwards, *Ethics Without Philosophy* (1985), Richard Rorty, *Philosophy and the Mirror of Nature* (1980), etc.).

We don't necessarily wish to dispute these. However, in a similar manner perhaps to with Wittgenstein's relationship to Freud, there are certain often downplayed aspects of the Wittgenstein–pragmatism nexus that considerably complicate the picture of continuity. Indeed, one question to ask is whether the hold on us of this picture will remain once we've been furnished with certain reminders; that is to say, once we've been taught certain differences between Wittgenstein's philosophy and pragmatism.

Back for a moment to Freud. Many commentators now accept that Wittgenstein's philosophy is best understood as *therapeutic* and in being so is indebted to Freud and the therapeutic method he devised. Wittgenstein's philosophy is characterized as therapeutic in that he seeks to engage his 'interlocutors' (the scare-quotes are necessary, for the voices we hear in Wittgenstein's 'dialogues'/internal monologues might be representative of tendencies of his own, rather than of interlocutors) in dialogue such that he might facilitate their realization that their disquiet stems from unconscious attachment to a picture of how things *must* be. For therapy to be successful, the interlocutor must freely come to acknowledge the picture as that which constrained their thinking and led to their disquiet. Once the picture has been brought to consciousness, it loses its power to effect psychological disturbance.

It's also widely known that Wittgenstein had deep distaste for other aspects of Freudian psychoanalysis: its theory of mind, and the scientific pretensions Freud had for that. So there is a widely acknowledged tension in Wittgenstein's relationship to Freud and Freudianism: Wittgenstein believes the therapeutic method a mark of Freud's genius and constructs his approach to philosophy around that method; (while) he believes Freud's scientistic tendencies to be disastrous and emblematic of the technocratic and scientistic culture of his time (and ours).[1]

Therefore, the Wittgenstein–Freud nexus is only superficially problematic. On inspection it bears up to scrutiny. For one can see the value of the therapeutic method *without* having to accept Freud's metaphysics of mind and his scientistic presentation of that metaphysics. One should be clear about the pretty vast differences between the two, if one is to gain clarity about the genuine continuity.

The question we shall address in the next couple of sections of this chapter is whether (or not) much the same is true of Wittgenstein in relation to pragmatism.

WITTGENSTEIN VS. JAMES

Returning our attention to Wittgenstein's relationship to pragmatism, then, there *is*, it seems, a somewhat similar tension in evidence. For while James and Peirce seem to anticipate some of what one finds in the later Wittgenstein, one also finds Wittgenstein in his writings on the philosophy of psychology discussing William James highly critically. Indeed, James is one of very few philosophers mentioned by name with any frequency in Wittgenstein's later work, such that his words might form one strand – one pole, even – in Wittgenstein's therapeutic dialectic.[2] Wittgenstein, therefore, had read James but chose to bring to the fore the latter's psychological writings as in need of therapy rather than to align himself with James's pragmatism. Put another way: Wittgenstein saw James's writings on psychology as giving voice to a tendency which was to be resisted, combated.

There are two (closely related) questions that might spring forth here:

1. Might one take Wittgenstein's remarks on James and treat them in isolation from any discussion as to the continuity so frequently identified between Wittgenstein and pragmatism? This would be tantamount to saying that there is a pragmatist William James who wrote on philosophy and a scientistic William James who wrote on psychology. Or one might rather hold that Wittgenstein radically misread those psychological writings of James's, which Wittgenstein weaves into his therapeutic dialogue on the philosophy of psychology. We find this latter option implausible. We believe Wittgenstein's criticisms of James to be dead right, in their fundamentals and most of their details.[3] So: one is left it seems having to try to pry apart James's empiricism from his pragmatism (we have our doubts as to whether this can be done).
2. What is distinctly pragmatic about James's philosophy and in what sense might we see Wittgenstein as inheriting it?[4]

James's writings on psychology are distinguished by their empiricism rather than anything distinctively pragmatic. Is pragmatism at core empiricist in its leanings? There is much evidence to suggest so. Of course this need not come as a great surprise. James and Dewey called themselves radical empiricists. What's in a name ... ?

Let us quote a passage from James, from the opening lecture of his famous series on pragmatism, wherein he seeks to explain the distinctiveness of the philosophical movement:

You want a system that will combine both ... the scientific loyalty to facts and willingness to take account of them ... but also the old confidence in human values and the resultant spontaneity, whether of the religious or of the romantic type. And this is then your dilemma: you find the two parts of your quaesitum hopelessly separated. You find empiricism with inhumanism and irreligion; or else you find a rationalistic philosophy that indeed may call itself religious, but that keeps out of all definite touch with concrete facts and joys and sorrows.

(James, 1991, p. 10)

James wants to effect a rapprochement between the language of empiricism and religious and ethical language; that is, between what he sees as the respect for facts, found in the person of empiricist leanings, and the respect for the passions, for the integrity of the immaterial, found in the religious person. These can strike one as laudable aims. They're aims that have appealed to many who have become disillusioned with hard-headed (and often hard-hearted) materialist attitudes and their penetration into every corner of modern life, including philosophy. The penetration can manifest a threat to the integrity of ethics, to the integrity of religious views, to the integrity of philosophy as a discrete discipline and ultimately to the integrity of that which is distinctively human.

Bells will be ringing for the Wittgensteinian. Should the Wittgensteinian allow herself to be summoned by those bells to the (scientifically acceptable) church of pragmatism? Many have suggested so. Rorty is most prominent in having suggested it, Putnam is a little more complicated, but no less prominent;[5] he too does in the end believe that the Wittgensteinian will find a deeply like-minded ally in the pragmatists. We remain cautious.

To be clear, the point is not that James wants to protect Christianity from scientific critique; nor is he advocating that Richard Dawkins become a regular recipient of the sacrament. Rather he is wanting to say that philosophy should acknowledge the integrity of the different domains and find them to be complementary, not fix its gaze on one at the expense of the other. What would such a one-sided diet amount to? Well, we need not speculate; we have positivism, which came after James, to remind us what the consequences of philosophy fixing its gaze on science can do to the status of ethical language. In contemporary guise we have the work of those such as Paul E. Griffiths[6] who wish to eliminate non-scientific language (read: language unsuitable for 'experimental' purposes) from the psychological lexicon. But should Wittgensteinians be Jamesians (pragmatists)? We would argue not ... so fast. For what is needed is an understanding as to *why* the worldviews/mindsets of empiricism and the religious/ethical seem to be in conflict; why it is that ethics feels (or is) threatened by science, why it is that those of an empiricist bent feel the need to attack ethical language or religious language. Such an understanding can only be effected by inviting the empiricist (including the empiricist in each and every one of us) to the therapy session, not by taking empiricism as it has been presented and trying to effect rapprochement between it (as presented by its adherents) and ethical or religious language (as presented by *its* adherents).

This is one important reason why we are very suspicious of the claim that James should be seen as an ally or progenitor of Wittgenstein.

For James does not question the underlying drive to 'imperialism' which is one of the hallmarks of empiricism: its yearning for a universe where all language is amenable to playing an epistemological role, in the narrow empiricist sense of 'epistemological'. To be sure James wants to delimit its imperialist tendencies, and thus protect the integrity of ethical and religious discourse; but he does not get to the nub of the issue. He does not incline to tackling the tendency to imperialism at source. In James's own thinking and writing, the unacknowledged picture at the heart of empiricism remains unacknowledged. Empiricism's underlying appeal remains subterranean, undimmed. This was one key reason why Wittgenstein wrote so critically about James.

It is also why when James writes on matters psychological he writes as an empiricist. Here emotions are the experience of sensations or bodily changes, rather than ways of taking the world in all its conceptual richness.[7] It is these writings of James's to which Wittgenstein addresses himself explicitly in his late manuscripts. James presents us as observers of our own inner states, and those states – sensations – as being the evidence for our having such-and-such an emotion.

There is then in James – *and* we find this in Peirce and Dewey (and in turn in Sellars, Quine, Davidson and Rorty also) – at best a too deferent approach to empiricism and at worst an embracing of empiricism aligned with a myopia regarding problems implicitly inherent in it. Pragmatism supposedly overcomes the subject–object dichotomy; but, in this connection at least, it does so (if at all) only at the unacceptably drastic cost of objectifying – thingifying – the 'inner', the subject, including the lived-body.[8] In James's writing on psychology there is a remarkably full-blooded embracing of empiricism, and to say that the eggshells of this way of thinking are still stuck to his attempts to produce a distinct philosophy in pragmatism would be (too charitable) a way of capturing our misgivings in a way that paraphrases Wittgenstein's own concerns about some of his own earlier work. In short, while we find pragmatism's maxim unobjectionable and consonant with Wittgenstein's approach to philosophy, we find the practice of the seminal figures in the history of pragmatism to represent a failure to have fully broken free of the empiricist tendencies. Again quoting James, the maxim, or principle, is as follows:

> A glance at the history of the idea will show you ... what pragmatism means. The term is derived from the same Greek word, meaning action, from which our words 'practice' and 'practical' come. It was first introduced into philosophy by Mr. Charles Peirce in 1878. In an article entitled 'How to Make Our Ideas Clear'... Peirce, after pointing out that our beliefs are really rules for action, said that to develop a thought's meaning, we need only determine what conduct it is fitted to produce: that conduct is for us its sole significance. And the tangible fact at the root of all our thought-distinctions, however subtle, is that there is no one of them so fine as to consist in anything but a possible difference of practice. To attain perfect clearness in our thoughts of an object, then, we need only consider what conceivable effects of a practical kind the object may involve – what sensations we are to expect from it, and what reactions we must prepare. Our conception of these effects, whether immediate or remote, is then for us the whole of our conception of the object, so far as that conception has positive significance at all.

This clearly has resonance for Wittgenstein(ians) and the prophylactic he offered by recommending responding to questions as to the meaning of a term by looking at the term's use. But such similarities are superficial when one acknowledges the empiricism at the heart of pragmatism (and they are what led some pragmatists, unlike Wittgenstein, toward behaviourism. Quine in this regard was only following a path already dangerously indicated by the classic pragmatists, beginning with Bain and Peirce).

WITTGENSTEIN VS. PEIRCE

Hitherto we have focused our attentions on William James. What of the other two founding figures of pragmatism, Peirce and Dewey? Let us deal with Peirce, so prominently mentioned in the quotation above. Parallels have been drawn between some of Peirce's remarks on meaning and use and some of Wittgenstein's; here again it is important to be clear about the status of some of the parallels being drawn. H. O. Mounce writes:

> It is worth noting that there are striking resemblances between Peirce's theory of the sign and some of the <u>views</u> in Wittgenstein's later work. This is especially evident in the case of Wittgenstein's celebrated <u>argument</u> against the idea of a private language. A private language is precisely one in which there is a first sign. Thus Wittgenstein imagines that someone gives meaning to a sign 'S' simply by associating it with one of his sensations. Thereafter he knows the correct way to take S, by recalling the original act of meaning. Here S is a first sign, since it derives its meaning simply from the relation between the individual's mind and its object ... Now Wittgenstein's criticism of this idea may be expressed in Peirce's terms by saying that meaning is not a dyadic but a triadic relation. On the idea of a private language, meaning is two-term. Thus the correct way of taking S is determined by a two-term relation in which the sign is related directly to an object. For Peirce and Wittgenstein meaning is <u>essentially</u> three-term. A term is related to an object only if there is *already* a correct way to take it. And only if there were already a correct way to take S could it be related to its object.
>
> (Mounce, 1997, pp. 27–8; underlined text is our emphasis)

It might strike some that Mounce has drawn some important parallels here; but he does so at great cost to any understanding of Wittgenstein as the radical philosopher he is. He attributes to Wittgenstein *views* and *arguments* and talks of Wittgenstein, along with Peirce, identifying the *essence* of meaning.

Let's look at what Wittgenstein actually has to say about meaning, in his later work. In the much cited passage 43 from *Philosophical Investigations*, Wittgenstein writes:

> For a <u>large class of cases – though not for all</u> – in which we employ the word 'meaning' it **can** be defined thus: the meaning of a word is its use in the language.
> And the *meaning* of a name is sometimes explained by pointing to its bearer.
>
> (Wittgenstein, 1953; underlined text is ours)

We have argued elsewhere[9] that – rather than selectively interpreting this passage, by ignoring the modals such as 'can' and ignoring the last one-sentence paragraph – one should take Wittgenstein at his word. While many have been tempted to see the phrasing of this remark as a combination of Wittgenstein's dispensable stylistic 'tics' and a definition of meaning, which therefore demands that the reader identify and remove the superfluous clauses and hedging strategies in order to extract the thesis ('Meaning is use'), we have argued something like the opposite. Wittgenstein is deliberately cautious in his wording precisely to guard against reading him as advancing the claim/thesis that meaning is use.

Now, historically, there have been two paths proposed by those who have rightly resisted what we might call the 'theoretical-selective reading' of this passage. The first of these alternatives has it that Wittgenstein identifies or essentially connects the meaning of a word with its use. He does so so as to draw attention to the 'grammatical nexus' between the use of a word and the meaning of a word, such that if one asks for the meaning of a word one is generally satisfied with an account of the word's use. This approach, therefore, reads the phrase 'the meaning of a word is its use in language' as a 'grammatical remark', rather than a hypothetical remark or expression of a philosophical theory. This one might call for shorthand the Oxford reading, as it emerges in the work of Kenny and Hacker, and is defended today by their students.

Both the theoretical reading and the 'Oxford' (or 'grammatical') reading might be treated as supporting Mounce, in claiming that Wittgenstein's account of meaning is the same as Peirce's; for both 'accounts' are, in Mounce's words, 'essentially three-term'.

Talking of the essence of Wittgenstein's account of meaning is rendered redundant when one observes that nowhere does Wittgenstein offer an account of meaning. Much less does he 'argue' (Mounce again) for something being considered the 'essence' of meaning.

How then might one (more successfully) read *Philosophical Investigations* 43? Well, we recommend one reads it as something akin to a prophylactic: it is offered by Wittgenstein as something that might help you when faced with an otherwise vexing philosophical question. Consider the following:

I have suggested substituting for 'meaning of a word', 'use of a word', because *use of a word* comprises a large part of what is meant by 'the meaning of a word'…

> I also <u>suggest</u> examining the correlate expression 'explanation of meaning' ... It is less difficult to describe what <u>we call</u> 'explanation of meaning' than to explain 'meaning'. The meaning of a word is **explained by** describing its use.
>
> (Baker, 2003, p. 121; underlining is ours)

In a similar vein, note also:

> <u>An</u> answer to the question: 'What is the meaning of a word?' would be: 'The meaning is simply what is explained in the explanation of the meaning'. This answer makes good sense. For we are <u>less</u> tempted to consider the words 'explanation of the meaning' with a bias than the word 'meaning' by itself. Common sense does not run away from us as easily when looking at the words 'explanation of the meaning' as at the sight of the word 'meaning'. We remember more easily how we actually use it.
>
> (Baker, 2003, underlining is ours)

We suggest that it is an error to read Wittgenstein as offering an 'argument' for (any kind of theory whatsoever of) meaning, or to be saying anything regarding the putative essence of meaning. In these passages we find Wittgenstein writing that he *suggests* substituting for 'meaning of a word' 'use of a word'. He repeatedly writes 'we' and 'for us': 'we ask ... ', 'what we call ... ', thus he indexes this work to 'us' and 'we', i.e. those who adhere to his conception of philosophy, 'our method' (cf. 'Dictation for Schlick', in Baker, 2003, p. 69). He writes of the meaning of a phrase being *'characterised by us'* as the use made of the phrase. These locutions fall well short of those which one might honestly characterize as indicating identity-claims regarding meaning and use.

The emboldened text in the three quotes (immediately above) should indicate that throughout his discussions of meaning Wittgenstein is very specifically talking about/suggesting a way of going on which will help one avoid confusion. There is something distinctly pragmatic about this – but it is not so in the way Mounce wishes to argue regarding Peirce's theory of the sign. To bring this out fully, we need to first consider another quote from Wittgenstein:

> The meaning of a phrase <u>for us</u> is <u>characterised</u> by the use we make of it. The meaning is not a mental accompaniment to the expression. Therefore, the phrase ... 'I'm sure I mean something by it', which we so often hear in philosophical discussions to justify the use of an expression is **for us** no justification at all. <u>We</u> ask: *'What* do **you** mean?', i.e., 'How <u>do you</u> use this

expression?' If someone taught me the word 'bench' and said that he sometimes or always put a stroke over it ... and that this meant something to him, I should say: 'I don't know what sort of idea you associate with this stroke, but it doesn't interest me unless you show me that there is a use for the stroke in the kind of calculus in which you wish to use the word "bench"'. – I want to play chess, and a man gives the white king a paper crown, leaving the use of the piece unaltered, but telling me that the crown has a meaning to him in the game, which he can't express by rules. <u>I say</u>: <u>'as long as it doesn't alter the use of the piece, it hasn't what</u> I call <u>meaning'</u>. (Wittgenstein, 1969a, p. 65; underlining is ours)

We can now see why, despite the parallels, one will be puzzled if one expects there to be strong continuity throughout the writings of the key pragmatists and Wittgenstein. The puzzlement can stem from two sources we have outlined thus far:

1. To recap: James departs from his own pragmatist principles in his philosophical psychology and in his neutral monist version of empiricism: radical empiricism. Therefore, parallels between Wittgenstein and James need to accommodate this facet of James's work by seeing that when James appears in Wittgenstein's writings he does so as a voice in a therapeutic dialogue, a voice in need of change or reflection. Wittgenstein sees James as highly subject to metaphysical yearnings and in need of therapy. What we have suggested here, however, is that it is not that James's radical empiricism and his empiricist philosophical psychology are anomalous with respect to his pragmatist principles but that the seeds of these views can be found in the way he lays out his pragmatist principles. He is, crucially, too 'respectful' – too inheritative – of empiricism. In this sense one might say either that Wittgenstein completes the pragmatist project or that pragmatism was a stage in a dialectic which Wittgenstein brings to synthesis, or even overcomes.
2. Furthermore (and this is what emerges most clearly in the quotes we have marshalled to problematize the alleged Peirce–Wittgenstein nexus): there is a widespread failure to grasp in full the nature of Wittgenstein's radical approach to philosophy – his 'metaphilosophy'. Failure to see the therapeutic nature of Wittgenstein's philosophizing leads

one mistakenly to draw parallels at the level of substantive 'accounts' or 'arguments'. This is mistaken because in a significant sense there *are* no accounts or arguments in Wittgenstein's work. He does not offer an account of meaning; rather, he *suggests* to us a *way of seeing* meaning which might help us when faced with philosophical problems which are generated from certain pictures of the meaning of meaning. Thus, even where pragmatism and Wittgenstein seem most similar, there remains a crucial difference in conception. Again, we think pragmatism can learn from Wittgenstein here.

HOW TO WRITE MOST AUTHENTICALLY ABOUT PRAGMATISM AND WITTGENSTEIN?

So far, we have chiefly accentuated the negative. The glass is half empty. By our lights, there are significant – founding – strands in pragmatism that are signally inferior to what we find in and is Wittgenstein's philosophy. But, as we mentioned at the outset of this chapter, the glass has often been described also as being half full; *and we don't necessarily want to deny this*. There are significant strands in pragmatism that make it possible and fruitful to be a 'pragmatist-Wittgensteinian'.

How can one write most *authentically* on the Wittgenstein–pragmatism nexus? To set out the things that they agree on would presuppose that they *have* opinions, views, positions, in the ordinary sense presumed and purveyed by most philosophers. Taking seriously that Wittgenstein was a 'therapeutic' thinker,[10] who held philosophy to be an activity rather than a body of views or accounts no matter of what kind,[11] and who had no opinions *qua* philosopher;[12] *and* taking seriously that pragmatism – at least at its best – is a philosophy of and in practice, holding that beliefs *are* nothing other than the practices that they are embodied in,[13] and that the speculative and spectatorial quest for certainty[14] that previous philosophy has mostly been is forever beside the point ... taking these things seriously is incompatible with such a presupposition.

We want now to try to take pragmatism at its best, rather than accentuating the negative. We want in what follows to try to bring pragmatism's metaphilosophy/methodology closer to Wittgenstein's.

Our submission in fact is that one cannot, in the final analysis, write truly authentically on the Wittgenstein–pragmatism nexus except by writing authentically *as* a pragmatist-Wittgensteinian, or at least by seeking to do so and to understand what it really means to do so.[15] Writing, that is, in such a way as to take seriously the conception of philosophy that is actually present – manifest – in Wittgenstein's philosophical activity, and in that of the best of pragmatism, in pragmatism once its (above-adumbrated) scientific weaknesses have been acknowledged and overcome.

The philosopher who has done the most to combine pragmatism and Wittgenstein is, as we mentioned at the outset, Hilary Putnam.[16] Putnam is the best source for any conventional attempt to write (accentuating the positive) on the Wittgenstein–pragmatism nexus. But that isn't the most important thing that Putnam does, to bring Wittgenstein and Pragmatism together. The most important thing Putnam does, in this regard, is to *do* philosophy *as a pragmatist-Wittgensteinian* – it was he who coined this term. In other words, to seek to practise the bringing together of pragmatism and Wittgenstein, not merely to preach it. To produce a *pragma* here, and a use – not merely a meta-discourse.

As Wittgenstein remarked, words are deeds. We do not wish to produce a position statement, a set of theses about 'pragmatist-Wittgensteinian philosophy'. We want to *do some work*.

In the remainder of this chapter, then, we aim to follow Putnam's lead beyond where he has gone. We suggest that ultimately the only serious and worthwhile way in which to write on Wittgenstein-and-pragmatism now is to move beyond the (ultimately unsatisfying) half-empty/half-full debate, and instead to (try to) do some philosophy genuinely in their spirit.

The paper that we take as our jumping-off point we choose, in part, precisely to show how very wide is the applicability of 'pragmatist-Wittgensteinian' thinking. The paper in question is by Jerry Williams and Shaun Parkman; its title is 'On Humans and Environment: The Role of Consciousness in Environmental Problems'.[17] The paper uses 'a framework derived from Schutzian phenomenology' (p. 449) to explore some deep reasons why human beings create 'environmental problems' – and to explore how these problems might be effectively addressed in a way that works with rather than against the grain of human consciousness and living.

Our primary intention, in the remainder of the present chapter, is to explore what is right/helpful in the approach adopted by Williams and Parkman, and some of what is wrong with it, *as* would-be pragmatist-Wittgensteinians. We aim to set out and to correct Williams and Parkman by extending their thinking in directions suggested, we believe, both by Wittgenstein and by pragmatism at its best. We aim, in the process, to set out and *exemplify* how a pragmatist-Wittgensteinian approach to philosophy can help one to think therapeutically about our society and our 'environment' and to clear the ground for pragmatic interventions therein that could actually work to heal it (us). If we are right, then this such would certainly deserve the Rortian honorific term, 'edifying philosophy'.

WITTGENSTEIN-AND-PRAGMATISM IN PRACTICE: 'EVERYDAY ENVIRONMENTALISTS'

Williams and Parkman argue that

> human consciousness is characterized by a dialectic of environmental destruction. On the one hand, enabled by consciousness and scientific rationality, humans produce and externalize their being into the world thus creating environmental damage, yet on the other hand consciousness provides a risk of anomie so great that humans must internalise the social order and thereby make it taken-for-granted and a matter of common sense. Environmental destruction, then, finds its foundation in our very being.
> (Williams and Parkman, 2003, p. 449)

This we think is a helpful if desperately concise summary. The point about internalizing the social order is particularly important: it suggests a basis for a necessarily *political* aspect in how one sees society, whether phenomenologically or through another philosophical lens. There will be an unavoidable need successfully to 'bracket' the taken-for-granted societal ideology, if one wants to achieve liberation from the built-in tendency to ecological damage indexed in this quotation. Liberal individualism, capitalist growthism – we need to find a way to make figural such implicit nativized ideologies, and not allow them simply to be the assumed ground of our existence, if we want that existence to continue, to be able to be sustained. (For these failing ideologies and their associated naturalized newspeaks are the tacit metaphysics of our age.)

How is this to be done? Williams and Parkman claim:

'To solve large-scale environmental problems we must transcend everyday thinking and the discourse of ideas. Effective solutions to environmental problems cannot be based in idealism; rather, they must be framed in very pragmatic ways – in terms of consequences and actions.'[18]

Is this right? It is surely right that, to solve the kind of ecological problems that are assailing the world today, business-as-usual thinking cannot be merely tweaked. The *current* everyday ideologies (the very widespread assumption that growth is good, the ideology of 'development', etc.) need to be transcended. A transformed thinking needs to become common sensical. But the Wittgensteinian in us protests that this change is *not* well characterized simply as the transcending of 'everyday thinking'. What is required rather is to find a way of *turning everyday thinking into naturally ecological thinking* (and to preserve some capacity for thinking outside either of these 'boxes', the mainstream one or the ecological one, for such thinking will surely be needed again). The agenda then, surely, has to be one of creating a society of *everyday environmentalists* or, perhaps better still: everyday ecologists).[19] This process, so far as it concerns language, will begin with 'watering the seeds' of such thinking in our language as we already find it: to give a very simple example, in the case of a catch phrase such as 'waste not, want not'; and in the very idea of 'waste' as something ... wasteful, to be minimized (and, ultimately, one might even say, absurd; nothing can be wasted, in a society that wishes to survive indefinitely in a finite world).[20] Of course, the process will have to concern myriad practical actions in the world too, with which our words inter leave, such as the practice of getting to know our waste better, and finding endlessly better ways of (re-)using it or of reducing it.

We need to bring a whole set of words back from their tacitly metaphysical use (in which growth can be infinite, 'development' means industrialization, 'rubbish' is thrown 'away' and not seen rather as resources, etc. etc.) to their (old-and-new) everyday use.[21] How exactly is this to be done?

The attack on 'idealism'[22] in Williams and Parkman is surely on roughly the right track, in terms of explaining how it *won't* successfully be done. It is quite hopeless – hopelessly 'idealist(-ic)', hopelessly rationalistic – to simply tell people the facts about looming environmental catastrophe and expect them to respond rationally and problem-solve the coming catastrophe away. It is hopeless to adopt *any* strategem which relies centrally only upon changing individual 'hearts and minds', not collective practices and 'language-games'.²³ Furthermore, as Williams and Parkman rightly put it, 'Effective solutions to environmental problems ... must be framed in very pragmatic ways – in terms of consequences and actions.' Yes; without pragmatism, here, we are lost; *provided* that the *deep* 'framing' of such problems is alive to life. That is to say: environmental pragmatism is entirely appropriate, *on the back of* a profound commitment both linguistic, practical, etc. to seeing ourselves as part of our ecosystem, etc.²⁴ We need to forge a new everyday thinking. An environmentalist (better still: an eco-logical) everyday thinking.

Read (2004) argues that the deep affinity between Dewey and Wittgenstein in respect of their being 'deflationary naturalists'²⁵ and 'cultural naturalists'²⁶ is best taken now and extended in the direction of 'environmentalism'.²⁷ We best understand ourselves as through-and-through naturally cultural animals, if we understand our *coping* with the world, our being 'internally-related'²⁸ to it rather than spectators of it, our being always-already doers, through the lens of environmentalism (or, better still, ecologism). We are part of our ecosystem,²⁹ and this is of great philosophical and ethical and political meaning.

(But doesn't Dewey rely on a Baconian (instrumentalist, dangerously hyper-'disenchanted') starting point in much of his philosophizing³⁰? To some extent, yes; Dewey too could be critiqued, as we critiqued James, and Peirce, earlier. We think that the Owl of Minerva has long flown *for certain of Dewey's more Baconian (nature-cutting) formulations*. But we think that the confluence of a Wittgensteinianism and a reconstructed pragmatism *can* nevertheless be fertile.)

Williams and Parkman remark that '[t]he idealism of modern environmental discourse holds little promise for the remediation of large-scale environmental problems' (p. 456). This is true, inasmuch as such discourse often simply abstracts from or ignores or speaks down to the everyday lived experience of many people, at least in the West/North of the world, which is mostly felt in everyday life as relatively unaffected by ecological impoverishment, let alone catastrophe (Crisis? What crisis?).[31] Furthermore, the danger of such discourse is that it frequently abstracts *from* our lived embeddedness in the world, and so can too easily sucker us into a search for techno-fixes and other sticking-plaster solutions to what are deep problems of consciousness and way of life. For we are (or: need to be) looking for a practicable way of living that is co-tenable with such living continuing, and with a sufficient valuing of life (not just one's own) that will enable this.[32] If we fail to act on the (pragmatist-Wittgensteinian) truth of our co-constitution with the world, if we fantasize ourselves as outsiders to that world, if we fantasize ourselves as quintessentially thinking or gazing individuals (as so much philosophy has done), then we will aim, hopelessly and disastrously, to intervene in the world as if *from the outside*, crudely and without awareness of the full complexity and subtlety of the system 'into' which we are intervening.

And Williams and Parkman rightly point up (pp.455 and 457) the dangerous tendency for intellectuals to overly assume that explicit thinking, theoretical insight, etc. is a potent influence upon society, when typically it is quite marginal (much as one might regret that fact). It is the philosopher's *deformation professionelle* to believe that s/he is a figure who ought to be and surely will be listened to, in the society in question. The role of explicit theory/metaphysics is played up, in the course of such belief; our practical engagement in the world and the assumed linguistic and psychological tools that constrain and enable that engagement are played down. *Pragmatist-Wittgensteinian thinkers stand this appealing misconception on its head*. We place the deed first; we return over and over to actual practice. Thus Wittgenstein famously agreed with Goethe's remark that "In the beginning was the deed", and, once more, 'pragmatism' as a term comes of course from the Greek word, *'pragma'*, meaning: deed. (And thus our title: for how could one really think Wittgenstein-and-pragmatism at all, *except* in practice?)

But then doesn't that, even if it is more realistic than one or another 'idealist' fantasy, leave us simply having to accept our impotence? Take one of Williams and Parkman's central two recommendations, on how we ought to intervene so as to create an effective environmentalism:

[L]arge-scale environmental problems like global warming can be translated into immediate consequences ... by addressing them at their foundation, the consumptive behaviour of individuals. ... [F]or example ... the cost of fossil fuel paid by Americans only represent[s] a small share of their actual cost when scarcity and environmental damage are considered ... If those who use fossil fuels were to pay the true cost (enabled by green taxes), consumptive behaviour would change as a matter of economic necessity. Suggestions that urban commuters should pay a 'commuting tax' to account for their consumptive behaviour is [sic] also an example of a pragmatic, consequence driven mechanism of environmental change ... In these cases change occurs when consequences accrue, and consequences accrue when they are linked to our consumptive behaviour, behaviours such as buying gasoline and commuting by automobile.

(Williams and Parkman, 2003, p. 458)

All true enough; but now who is being idealist? Williams and Parkman are; for they have merely pushed the problem back one stage, but have not acknowledged this. For how do we generate the political willpower to put policy instruments such as these into place? How is a democracy (a society in which the people genuinely rule) – or even a command society (for commands are useless unless they are obeyed) – to summon the will to put in place measures in response to what Williams and Parkman have themselves pointed up as the still rather abstract nature of the threat, and given that a society built around the needs of the motor-car now seems normal and 'just how it is' (Williams and Parkman, 2003, p. 454)?

To a pragmatist-Wittgensteinian, it is obvious (as it should be to all – but philosophers often have to relearn what is obvious)[33] that we have to have in mind (and be able to communicate) a workable way to get from *here to there*. Thus there is a pressing need for a movement (more likely: a movement of movements) that will take actions that will help to make the new world seem possible, *and* will help to make the new world be actual. For example: using and strengthening and lobbying for alternatives to the motorcar, and starting to make these the norm, the taken-for-granted, the everyday. This will require vast alterations in everything from our planning system to our cultural icons. The needful change in consciousness to motivate and then to constitute this must itself be fostered, and pursued at first on fertile ground. Just as Marx looked for the class that would be best placed to see reality and to fight for a future in which that reality would be different, so must we.

One such 'class' is perhaps parents and children – for it is children upon which the burdens of an ecologically wrecked future will fall hardest.

This movement (of movements) is to some extent in existence, already.[34] What the pragmatist-Wittgensteinian can do, functioning more or less as what Foucault called a 'specific intellectual', is to work with it, and help it flourish and avoid the many pitfalls inevitably close to any transformative project. This is neither 'idealism' nor philistinism; it is a bold, but realistic and pragmatic approach. It is, we believe, true philo-sophy, today.

Language and practice can be transformed from within. To create the new out of the old, we will need to work relentlessly to expand the 'vanguard' of those whose consciousness is already raised, to use both linguistic reframing[35] and 'non-linguistic'[36] strategems to change the everyday into an eco-logical everyday; in sum, to start to make commonsense compatible with continued existence.

This will be a vastly difficult enterprise, in part for the reasons explored by Williams and Parkman. But we have the right to believe that it can be done; this is what is implicit in James's great paper 'The Will to Believe'.[37] The need of others (and of ourselves) for us to do this, to believe (and then to act), is internally related to our human – individual and social – power to make things possible (by virtue of believing that they are/can become possible) that would otherwise *not* be possible.[38] James, like Wittgenstein, is philosophically revolutionary in considering philosophical issues throughout *from the point of view of the agent(s)*.[39] Such agent-centred thinking is why the philosophies it co-constitutes are not in the end statable as doctrines or theses – it is itself a central reason why we are taking the approach that we are in this essay. Of not trying (pointlessly, even counterproductively) to say what Wittgenstein and Pragmatism *say*, but rather, *doing*. And our point now is: what needs to be done, in order to engender the transformations of discourse and action that becoming a society of everyday ecologists will entail, crucially requires just this same sense of (collective) agent-centredness. A greater sense of possibility than is delivered in the pessimism of Williams and Parkman, as of so much of the present scientistic, techno-fixing, consumeristic worldview, which encourages people to innoculate themselves against the hope that real change could come.

The antidote to (self-fulfilling) pessimism concerning the likelihood that we can collectively make the changes that truly becoming an everyday-ecologist culture will entail can in part be found precisely in being inspired by the agent-centred philosophical thinking of the likes of James and Wittgenstein. We can individually and collectively become autonomous with regard to norms of waste, mutual indifference, short-sightedness of our temporal horizons, etc., through following the example of liberation offered in Wittgenstein's thought and of hope offered in James's, against the background of the understanding of ourselves as thoroughly interdependent and environed that is so prominent throughout Wittgenstein and Dewey. If we intelligently look for allies and 'classes' for which such thinking should make sense, if we work to expand the 'vanguard' of those who see the coming cataclysm with open eyes and open hearts, then the job can be done.

You need to *recognize* yourself in all this; to assess as you go along your resistances to it and its 'cathexes' for and with you. This isn't in the end about us addressing you, the reader; it is about you actually experiencing what we are 'talking about' in the paper. Philosophy is an activity – philosophy that is written down *is* only philosophy waiting to be read and resisted and welcomed and reworked. Reconstructed, renewed. Similarly, the deepest meaning of the agent-centredness and action-centredness (rather than being spectatorial or theoryist) of pragmatist philosophising is that the deed that is done here depends in part on – is to some degree perhaps even *constituted* by – the deeds that are done in response to it. Beginning with the reader's commitment to the 'proposals' presented here; proposals, initially drawn from our reading of Williams and Parkman, concerning the need to remould our everyday worlds of expectation, action, norm and emotionality. We submit that the way that we (humans) *take* the world needs to change – now it is over to you (to us collectively), to think-and-feel this through, and then perhaps to undertake a segment of that re-taking.

By our lights, a work of philosophy, like a work of art, aims to be a therapeutic work, and this means that it speaks *with* rather than at the reader. If it speaks *to* the reader, then that is because the reader finds herself in it. All true philosophy is a deed, a *pragma*; but the deed is not the author's (or the authors') alone.

ANTHROPOGENIC GLOBAL WARMING AS A DIFFUSE OBJECT

So how might this deed look? One of the problems with motivating ourselves (as a society, as a species) to make the changes required to mitigate or prevent climate catastrophe, changes such as the radical shift in our cultures required to move to a decarbonized economy, is that the problem of anthropogenic climate change is so diffuse. There is no clear object for us to fear, and fear needs an object. Therefore, even for those who understand the threat posed by anthropogenic climate change the understanding stays at what one might call an unfelt level. Put another way, fear of a threat to one's existence is a characteristically emotional response: we round the corner while walking in the Pyrenees and are confronted by a bear, and our instinctual fear brings about or is an emotional response. How one characterizes this emotional response, explains it, has been the subject of much discussion. A discussion in which James played a hugely influential role. Contemporary philosophy of emotions can usefully be seen as divided into two camps.[40] In one camp are the Jamesians (or neo-Jamesians) and in the other the cognitivists (or judgementalists).[41] The term 'cognitivism' brings together writers on emotions, some of whom might be termed *pure* cognitivists: e.g. Sartre as discussed by Solomon (1976 and 2003a), Taylor (1985) and Nussbaum (2003); and some of whom might be termed *hybrid* cognitivists: e.g. Goldie (2000), Greenspan (1995), Nash (1989) and Stocker (1987). (Roughly: 'pure' cognitivists believe that emotions are beliefs; while 'hybrid' cognitivists believe that they are belief/bodily-feeling admixtures, and that beliefs etc. alone are not enough to explain them. 'Hybrid' cognitivists thus can easily appear the sensible 'middle-ground' between the 'excesses' of a James and a Sartre. But our thought is that Jamesianism (and cognitivism) need to be brought into the therapy session; not just 'happily' melded together.)

What of those who build upon James's groundbreaking work? The neo-Jamesian camp comprises philosophers and psychologists who advance a contemporary variant of James's account of emotion and in doing so often align themselves with the research program initiated by Darwin (1872) and later Ekman (1972); those Darwinian claims are often supported by theoretical claims drawn from neuroscience and cognate theories of mind: e.g. Damasio (1995), Prinz (2004) and Robinson (1995).

In short, cognitivists take emotions to be centrally, and explain them in terms of, appraisals, judgements or evaluative beliefs; neo-Jamesians explain emotions in terms of awareness of bodily changes, usually patterned changes in the autonomic nervous system (ANS). How the debate is polarized can be captured by returning to a passage from William James's paper in *Mind*, published in 1884, a passage frequently quoted and/or referred to by those on either side of the debate:[42]

Our natural way of thinking about ... emotions is that the mental perception of some fact excites the mental affection called the emotion, and that this latter state of mind gives rise to the bodily expression. My thesis on the contrary is that *the bodily changes follow directly the* PERCEPTION *of the exciting fact, and that our feeling of the same changes as they occur* IS *the emotion.*[43]

(James, 1884, pp. 190–1; emphasis in original)

This is of course James in empiricist 'rather than' pragmatist mode. However, we will not dwell further on that kind of point, here. Rather we wish to show how a pragmatist-Wittgensteinian (or better, Wittgensteinian-pragmatist?) approach to this debate might help and in turn throw light on bringing about genuine change.

On a (neo-)Jamesian account one might characterize the fundamental problem facing humanity today thus: the threat posed by anthropogenic global warming (AGW) and explained to us by climate science just does not provide the environmental triggers for our physiological response (sensations, changes in the ANS) to be triggered. Now, if one takes a purely Jamesian approach hereabouts, then there is nothing we can do about this but wait until there is an event of such magnitude and which is unequivocally climate-change related which will serve as an environmental (in both senses of that word) trigger. (Or we can try to mimic such an event by means of scaring people witless via artistic renditions of possible futures, etc.) The problem with such a sit-and-wait approach is that waiting for such an event will probably be to wait until it is too late (to prevent fatal runaway overheating).

On the cognitivist account it seems difficult to make sense of our inaction. The science is unequivocal, the precautionary principle invokes rational grounds for acting now, yet we are simply failing to act in any meaningful way. Surely an understanding of the science would lead to a forming of the evaluative beliefs such that one would fear the consequences of failing to act to mitigate climate change and thus take action to absent that fear?[44] Yet fear it seems is lacking. Now fear, like many emotions, can often lead to a form of paralysis and this *could* be what is happening, but our suggestion to follow will meet this point also. For (extending the logic of Williams and Parkman) what we wish to highlight is that the threat posed by AGW is one we need to feel in an emotionally engaged way if we are to be motivated to act rationally to mitigate it before it is too late.

So, our problem is this:

1 If we're Jamesians, then we sit and wait, because until there are the environmental triggers to initiate our physiological response to AGW we will not be in a position to acknowledge the threat in an emotionally engaged way (one might say in the Cavellian sense of the term, 'acknowledgement', as we must acknowledge one another, and not merely 'know' (about) one another) and thus will not be motivated to act until it is likely too late to avert catastrophe.
2 If we are cognitivists, then we seem to have no way of accounting for the current inaction: the ingredients are there for us to form the requisite evaluative beliefs but they either remain unformed or they are formed in a peculiarly detached and unemotional way.

The problem we suggest is the problem of diffuse objects. Our emotional/psychological make-up as human beings seems prejudiced in favour of simple objects with which we are directly acquainted. The threat posed by AGW, though no less real, is something akin to a threat that we might characterize as having a complex diffuse object. Does this mean, as many have argued, that cognitivism is wrong, and that we must give ourselves up to the truth in Jamesian approaches to these matters? As we noted, doing so would be to simply sit and wait for an ecological trigger. Thus, probably, to merely *wait* for our predictable doom.

CONCLUSION: 'WORLD-TAKING COGNITIVISM'

There is a true middle way here (not the bet-hedging middle-ground – which does not therapeutically reconceive the terrain – of 'hybrid' cognitivism). One might invoke a more nuanced, methodologically radical version of cognitivism: what one of us has dubbed 'world-taking cognitivism' (see Hutchinson, 2008b for a full treatment).

World-taking cognitivism is offered both as a possible framework for understanding and as itself a therapeutic device. It *is* a pragmatic strategy for aiding us to overcome tensions in our thinking about certain matters. The idea is that emotions are 'world-taking' to the extent that they are answerable to the way the *meaningful* world *is*. In this sense this framework enables one to see that, *contra* James, emotions are cognitive to the extent that they are not truly characterized as passive: something that afflicts the being. For our emotions are neither truly passive (affective: James) nor plainly chosen by us (judgements: Solomon, Sartre), nor even some blended combination of the two. Emotions are ways of reading and of taking (grasping) the world; more precisely they are ways in which we acknowledge loci of significance in the world. Our taking of the world is enabled through our conceptual capacities: our second nature. Thus given our nature, our *Bildung*, the loci of significance that we co-create bear down on us. We are both answerable for our emotions and subject to them.

Important proviso: the term cognitivism/cognitivist is employed here in the way in which it is in meta-ethics and thus does not imply any appeal to 'the cognitive sciences'. The term is not used, therefore, to denote the existence of cognitive processes. This is how we as Wittgensteinians are comfortable to speak of an -ism, and a cognitivism at that, that we endorse; whereas obviously much of what 'cognitive science' calls 'cognitivism', we would reject or recontextualize.[45]

Thus none of this amounts to the advancement of a philosophical theory of emotion. 'World-taking cognitivism' is merely a suggestion as to a pragmatic way of seeing our relationship to our world and to others through a reflection upon our conceptual capacities and the internal relations holding between concepts, on occasions of use.

Let us elaborate this final remark. Identifying the relations holding between concepts, such as those between fear and threat, is not to propound a theory. It is to describe how the grasping of one concept might need to carry with it, in a particular context, another. Grasping fear entails, on some occasions, in some contexts, also having grasped the concept of threat, maybe the concepts of vulnerability, fragility, etc. Invoking concepts as internally related is simply a perspicuous way of noting, describing, the nature of our conceptual capacities.[46] Again, we here merely invoke the truism that goes somewhat grandiosely by the name of the identity theory of truth. Not knowing (e.g.) that fire is hot, that fire burns, is to fall short of fulfilling one side of the equation; thus one has failed to grasp the concept.

Now, one can employ the word 'fear' in some contexts and on some occasions whereby the internal relation between it and, say, 'threat' does not hold, to the extent that the relation is not active on that occasion of use. The internal relations that might hold on an occasion between 'fear' and other concepts such as 'threat', 'anxiety', 'human needs', 'hope', 'pain', 'love', do so only given a degree of cultural specificity: a specificity regarding the enculturation of the expresser of fear: the afraid person. The cultural specificity demanded by fear is much less than that demanded by an emotion such as shame, but it is still something that can operate at the cultural level, or in response to a meaningful world, and not merely at the brute causal level (see Hutchinson, 2008b, chs. 3 and 4).

To return us to our problem. What is required to motivate action is an *engaged acknowledgement* of the problem we face. The problem, of how to stop the planet burning – in being complex and diffuse – seems to fall short of bringing about such a response, and neither (standard) cognitivist accounts of emotion nor Jamesian empiricist accounts help us to understand and effect the required change. 'World-taking cognitivism' helps in the sense in which it rejects the Jamesian implication that emotions are passive (essentially affective) while also providing a way of understanding how they might be responses to a meaningful world without inferring from that that they are chosen.

What might this do for us in practical terms? Well, it might tell us how best to frame the way in which we communicate the threat, so that it brings about the integrated engaged response we require (and here one might return to the discussion begun in the 'Everyday environmentalists' section, above). It might show us the kind of *cultural prerequisites* for individuals being in a position whereby and wherein they acknowledge the threat. Let us draw an analogy with the notion of prejudice. We noted above that there seems to be a human prejudice whereby complex diffuse objects (e.g. threats that are not before us and which are a concatenation of different smaller non-fear-invoking-threats spread over time but ultimately comprising a threat of huge magnitude) do not seem to bring about our acknowledgement of them as threats in the engaged and emotionally integrated manner that would bring about fear and motivate action. What is required therefore is not mere stating of the current scientific facts about AGW, but rather a shift in the culture and in our practices, for currently our culture has led to a deep-seated prejudice (a judgement formed in advance of the facts, and remaining largely untouched once the facts are in) in favour of certain already mentioned dogmas of cultural 'commonsense', which militate against acknowledgement of the threat and against mitigating the threat. The important point we wish to convey here, as Wittgensteinian-pragmatists, is that what is required are strategies whereby *we might collectively be brought to a position whereby we acknowledge those deep-seated ways of taking the world as contingent 'pictures' of the world*. And thus can we start to midwife a new world, one in which our world-takings are healthier, and thus in which we (as a species, one among many) can be sustained, through-and-through environed more self-consciously and securely.

The emotional transition might be one of (first) shame at our realization that we have suppressed our acknowledgement, based on unconscious commitment to these dogmas (the world as disposable resource for human use, the world as object (and us as subjects), economic growthism, consumerism, materialism, short-termism, liberal individualism and so on) and (second) fear as we come to perceive and acknowledge the magnitude of the threat.

Assenting that shame and fear will be a giant leap away from the abyss, and toward true human flourishing.

NOTES

1 See Bouveresse, 1996 for extended discussion of this seeming tension in Wittgenstein's relationship to Freud.
2 See Michael Stern, 2004 and Hutchinson and Read, 2005 for more on Wittgenstein's employment of dialogue and dialectic in his therapeutic practice.

3   It is worthy of note that James is the doyen of empiricists in the philosophy of emotions, who often term themselves Jamesians (or neo-Jamesians). See Hutchinson, 2008b and the closing sections of the present chapter.
4   Hilary Putnam's work on dissolving the fact–value dichotomy and the reason–emotion dichotomy (see especially his 2002) can be helpful here, in making possible pragmatist-Wittgensteinianism, rather than just an opposition between classical pragmatism on the one hand and Wittgenstein on the other.
5   Others too are legion; see the bibliography of Malachowski's *The New Pragmatism* (2010).
6   See his *What Emotions Really Are: The Problem of Psychological Categories* (Griffiths, 1997).
7   See the early chapters of Hutchinson, 2008b, for detail.
8   We are thinking here for instance of *Philosophical Investigations* 293 and 339. There is absolutely no anticipation in James of Wittgenstein's 'grammatical' reminders concerning the profound difference between the 'inner' and the 'outer'. To the contrary.
9   See especially our 'Towards a perspicuous presentation of "perspicuous presentation"', in Hutchinson and Read, 2008.
10 See e.g. Hutchinson and Read, 2010.
11 See e.g. *Tractatus* 4.112, and Hutchinson and Read (forthcoming).
12 See e.g. p. 103 of Wittgenstein, 1975.
13 We are here drawing upon and extending the following famous statement of Peirce's, concerning 'Bain's definition of belief, as "that upon which a man is prepared to act." From this definition, pragmatism is scarce more than a corollary; so that I am disposed to think of him [Bain] as the grandfather of pragmatism.' For the full source and a detailed treatment, see Wernham, 1986, pp. 262–6.
14 See e.g. Dewey, 1933. Peirce and Dewey argued powerfully that certainty is simply not required for – and is in a certain important sense irrelevant to – knowledge. Wittgenstein's *On Certainty* (1969b) can be seen as close indeed to this vein of pragmatist thought.
15 Or at least, by trying and failing, or alternatively: by setting out why such failure is (some might hold) inevitable.
16 For all his own innovativeness and brilliance, Rorty himself was the first to acknowledge, modestly, that Putnam, rather than he (Rorty) himself, deserved this laurel. (Lectures heard by and personal communications with Rupert Read.)
17 By Jerry Williams and Shaun Parkman (2003). We will not dwell here on some more obvious shortcomings of their paper, such as its (at times) cod sociobiologism. We are trying here to draw from it what is

worthwhile, and thus taking its glass to be half-full, so as to develop out of the useful points and issues that it starts to raise a more fully adequate pragmatist-Wittgensteinian rendition of the same terrain.

18 It is perhaps important to point out in passing that the term 'idealism' here is to be heard as close to the use of that term in Marx. That is, the criticism is not of the idea that it is a good thing to be idealistic (*provided* that one is also profoundly realistic, and not in denial about *material* considerations); without at least some idealism in *that* sense, there is no basis for or enthusiasm for change. Nor is the criticism directly of 'Idealism' in the sense of the metaphysical system (of Fichte, Bradley, etc.) commonly opposed to 'Realism' – though again there is a connection (for after all, Hegel too was an Idealist in this sense; and Idealists are very prone to overemphasizing the importance of mind, as opposed to that of world/body). Rather, the worry about 'idealism' being raised here is that it gives false hope, and can distract attention from the material (and pragmatic) considerations that are likely to govern success or failure.

19 See for instance Trainer, 1995.

20 Consider this moving story of how this is possible, how the spirit of 'Everyone is downstream' can come to be lived: 'Soon after I had arrived in Ladakh, I was washing some clothes in a stream. Just as I was plunging a dirty dress into the water, a little girl, no more than seven years old, came by from a village upstream. "You can't put your clothes in that water", she said shyly. "People down there have to drink it". She pointed to a village at least a mile further downstream. "You can use that one over there, that's just for irrigation."' This is from Helena Norberg-Hodge's remarkable and perhaps prophetic book, *Ancient Futures: Learning from Ladakh* (2000), p. 24; and see the revisioning of the term 'frugality' on the subsequent pages.

21 Cf. *Philosophical Investigations*, section 116. Cf. also the approach taken by Read (2007b) in ch. 6; and his *Handbook* on 'green' reframing (in preparation).

22 Cf. once more n. 20, above.

23 It might be objected at this point that philosophy 'leaves everything as it is' (*Philosophical Investigations* 124) – isn't Wittgenstein a 'quietist'? Isn't it quite hopeless to use him for radical political ends? But this is based on a misunderstanding of *Philosophical Investigations* 124 in particular, and of Wittgenstein's philosophy in general. See Read's (2002) account of how Wittgenstein is quite compatible with and in fact a natural companion to radical political change.

24 For some examples of this, see for instance Tom Crompton's work, such as www.wwf.org.uk/research_centre/research_centre_results.cfm/

uNewsID=2224. See also http://greenwordsworkshop.org/, and especially Read's contribution at http://greenwordsworkshop.org/node/7. See also Light and Katz, 1996. For a primer on 'ecologism' as the 'ideology' which such thinking adds up to, see Dobson, 2000.
25 This term is owed to Jerry Katz (1990) – see the introduction. 'Deflationary naturalism' is not really an 'ism' at all, in the sense that it is simply *non*-supernaturalism.
26 For Dewey's use of this term to describe himself, see p. 20 of his *Experience and Nature* (1929a). For this term as describing Wittgenstein, see p. 240 of Baker and Hacker (1985). Cf. also the entire argument of Read, 2004.
27 Read's (2004) argument does not go as far as we now would. We (now) believe that weak anthropocentrism must dissolve entirely into 'deep ecology'. The latter sometimes fails to succeed in not taking up an adversarial stance toward the planet through a fantasised alienation from it (and, in such cases, recoils into a biocentrism that tacitly *excludes* humans). But, even if one's 'main concern' is human beings, then one will not be pursuing a genuinely sustainable approach unless one truly places the ecosystem first. That is to say: to care for future generations, etc., it is not enough to place society as conceptually prior to the individual, and to think like a society. It is not enough, even to place society firmly in its environmental context. One has (We have) to *think like an ecosystem*. The only way in which we can have a society that can be sustained is to pursue the flourishing of the ecosystem in which the society is nested (and which it co-constitutes). A viable anthropocentrism of necessity coincides with a strong ecologism, which intrinsically values nature (including but not restricted to ourselves).
28 The scare quotes are advised. See Read, 2007a.
29 See ch. 1 of Read, 2007b.
30 See e.g. the early chapters of Dewey, 1957.
31 Cf. here Williams's and Parkman's valid criticisms of Ulrich Beck (Williams and Parkman, 2003), at p. 457.
32 See the account of William James in Stephens, 2009, which is directly salient to this point: 'William James's radical empiricism and pragmatism constitutes a philosophy that can reconcile the split between intrinsic value theorists ... and pragmatists who have favored a more direct emphasis on environmental policy and application' (p. 228). Stephens's paper helps to dissolve the apparent clash between the need for radical change and the danger of drift toward compromise inevitably present in the concept of 'environmental pragmatism' due to Light and Katz, 1996. It is crucial, of course, in all of this, not to fall into the crude

misreading of pragmatism (as a philosophical stance) as necessarily involving (excessive) compromise or an abandonment of principle.

Furthermore, Stephens touches on an aspect of James's radical empiricism which for us yields a very promising, 'glass half-full' moment in James's pragmatist thinking. The emphasis (in 'radical empiricism') on explaining our experiences not just in terms of sense data, etc. but in terms of their felt-meaningfulness. In *this* regard, 'radical empiricism' is close to a broadly Wittgensteinian 'world-taking cognitivism', as we present that, below. (As noted earlier, the trouble is that James typically doesn't *follow through* on this moment, this emphasis; which is a key reason why Wittgenstein subjects him to critical scrutiny.)

33 Cf. Wittgenstein's 'A philosopher is a man who has to cure many intellectual diseases in himself before he can arrive at the notions of common sense' (Wittgenstein, 1980, p. 44), and cf. also *Philosophical Investigations* 129: 'The aspects of things that are most important for us are hidden because of their simplicity and familiarity. (One is unable to notice something – because it is always before one's eyes.)' Somewhat similarly, James, the philosopher who Wittgenstein cites in his *nachlass* more than any other, discussed with great subtlety and poignancy the sentimentalist fallacy of professing deep concern for abstract justice while being blind to concrete injustice in front of one's eyes in his *Pragmatism* lectures, and also in the *Principles of Psychology* (James, 1950).

34 See for instance issue 5 of *Turbulence*: http://turbulence.org.uk/
35 See e.g. George Lakoff's writings.
36 See for instance the Transition Movement: www.transitionnetwork.org.
37 And here is a great confluence with Wittgenstein, whose remark that philosophical problems are really problems of the will, not of the intellect, is nothing if not Jamesian. What is needed is a Jamesian (one might also call it a Pascalian, or Kierkegaardian) step of faith in our ability to act together successfully to change our common future into a liveable one. Without such faith, such willed-belief, our mutual (self-)destruction is assured.
38 As explicated in our Wittgenstein-inspired book, *There is No Such Thing as a Social Science* (Hutchinson *et al.*, 2008), this touches on the fundamental misconception of human activity in 'social science' as predictable and delimitable. For knowledge of what is 'humanly impossible' can act as a stimulus to *make* it possible, or as a self-fulfilling prophecy (i.e. such 'knowledge' can depress us into its being true). It is 'objectively impossible' to know where human society is going, because we mutually make it, and any such knowledge therefore would be self-refuting.
39 For a lovely account of James as the apogee of this philosophical revolution, see Sydney Morgenbesser's remarks, at p. 88 of Bryan Magee's

The Great Philosophers (2000). For Wittgenstein's shift to seeing the agent, the person, as the fundamental unit, rather than theory or anything like it, see our accounts of philosophical therapy as person-relative, in Hutchinson and Read, 2010 and forthcoming.

40 See Hutchinson 2008a 'Emotions-Philosophy-Science'.
41 There is much debate over the most appropriate term for this group of theorists: for an overview see Hutchinson 2008b.
42 See, for example, Prinz, 2003b, p. 5 and Solomon, 2003b, p. 12.
43 It is telling to note, given the widely held assumption that Wittgenstein was an anti-Jamesian proto-cognitivist (see, for example, Griffiths's (1997) account of the emergence of cognitivism in Kenny's *Action, Emotion and Will* (2003)) that Wittgenstein would find neither of the options presented by James to be satisfactory. Both options, as presented in the quote from James, suggest or imply a mind–body dualism.
44 Of course, one typical fear response, is flight (fleeing the threat). This is simply not an option in this context. It seems the option left to us is to fight, which would in this context entail forgoing certain luxuries to which we have become accustomed so as to bring about the change required to mitigate the threat. That is correct: but it doesn't usually feel like fighting ('the climate war'). This is where (for instance) reframing and the normalisation of new practices come in.
45 For such rejection, see for instance the March 2008 (25(2)) special issue of *Theory, Culture and Society* on (criticisms of) cognitivism in this sense.
46 Cf. *On Certainty* Wittgenstein, 1969b, sections 472–4.

DAVID MACARTHUR

8 Putnam, pragmatism and the fate of metaphysics

Hilary Putnam refuses the title of 'pragmatist' on the grounds that he is critical of the central tenets of classical pragmatism. He finds the early pragmatist accounts of truth confused and Peirce's pragmatic maxim of meaningfulness hopelessly verificationist. None the less, we can rightly call Putnam a neo-pragmatist on the basis of three themes that have loomed large in his recent writings: the anti-sceptical notion that epistemology is to be understood in terms of a fallibilist theory of inquiry; the entanglement of fact and value which involves a denial of any metaphysically substantial fact–value dualism; and the general methodological principle that philosophy should do justice to our practices and the agent's point of view. Admittedly, these are all features of classical pragmatism but they come to the fore in neo-pragmatist thought when not encumbered with the false views of truth and meaning that went hand in hand with the rise of the pragmatist movement.

Indeed, the more one looks the more one can find parallels between Putnam and classic pragmatism. For example, and significantly, Putnam joins the pragmatist tradition in aspiring to a philosophy that does equal justice to our scientific knowledge, our religious experiences and the irreducible variety and complexity of our ethical lives. In this chapter I want to examine another, although widely overlooked, respect in which Putnam's thinking is indebted to the pragmatist tradition: a deep ambivalence towards metaphysics. In order to make room for this reading, let me dispel a tempting misreading of Putnam that sees him as simply preaching the end of metaphysics.

In *Renewing Philosophy* (1992), having surveyed a number of metaphysical programmes in contemporary analytic philosophy, including Bernard Williams's appeal to an absolute conception of the world (Williams, 1985), Ruth Millikan's attempt to reduce intentionality to biological function (Millikan, 1984), and Nelson Goodman's irrealism (Goodman, 1978), Putnam concludes as follows:

> I have argued that the decision of a large part of contemporary analytic philosophy to become a form of metaphysics is a mistake. Indeed, contemporary analytic metaphysics is in many ways a parody of the great metaphysics of the past. As Dewey pointed out, the metaphysics of previous epochs had a vital connection to the culture of those epochs, which is why it was able to change the lives of men and women, and not always for the worse. Contemporary analytic metaphysics has no connection with anything but the "intuitions" of a handful of philosophers. It lacks what Wittgenstein called "weight".
>
> (Putnam 1992, p. 197)

Not implausibly, the renewal of philosophy that Putnam calls for can be read as a vision of a non-metaphysical form of philosophizing – what we might call philosophizing without philosophical 'musts'. That would certainly fit with Putnam's invocation of John Dewey, whose therapeutic and socially reconstructive aims seem to stand in stark contrast to the programme of constructive metaphysics.[1] And it is undeniable that at least part of Putnam's vision of what philosophy ought to be involves resisting the revisionist tendencies of substantial metaphysical programmes, especially those of the analytic tradition, in order to do justice to our everyday life-world. Philosophy, unlike contemporary analytic metaphysicians, ought never to lose contact with the question of how we ought to live or with forms of thought that have 'weight' in our lives.

One might even read Putnam as adopting something like the spirit of logical positivism for which metaphysical expressions are meaningless pseudo-statements lacking any cognitive meaning or truth-value.[2] Such a conception is consistent with Putnam's long-running battle with metaphysical realism, which he describes on more than one occasion as 'a metaphysical fantasy' (Putnam, 1999, p. 6). And it also seems to fit Putnam's status as a leading neo-pragmatist, the kind of philosopher who, in the words of Richard Rorty, 'does not think of himself as *any* kind of metaphysician' (Rorty, 1982a, p. xxviii). Furthermore, Putnam's work for more than two decades has shown a strong sympathy with the writings of Ludwig Wittgenstein, who describes his own philosophical project as 'bring[ing] words back from their metaphysical to their everyday use' (Wittgenstein, 1953, §116).

On this way of looking at things, Putnam's claim that traditional metaphysics had a 'vital connection' to the cultures in which it flourished can be glossed as a statement about a time when philosophical reflection had yet to reach a stage of maturity from which it could see its way past the construction of metaphysical systems. The recent recrudescence of metaphysics in analytic philosophy, then, involves a failure to see that there is no longer any question of returning to the grand old days of traditional metaphysical inquiry. Metaphysics, on this reading, is nothing but *luftgebäude*, as Wittgenstein puts it, castles of air (Wittgenstein, 1953, §118).[3]

Although there is more than a grain of truth in this reading, I take it that it misses the depth and complexity of Putnam's attitude to metaphysics. We might say that although Putnam preaches the end of contemporary analytic metaphysics he is far more circumspect in his attitude to metaphysics as a whole. The guiding idea of this chapter is that clarity can be shed on this difficult region of Putnam's thought only if it is understood as a version of a pragmatist approach to metaphysical systems exemplified in different ways by the work of William James and John Dewey.

The pragmatist approach to metaphysics has been unjustly neglected in contemporary philosophy for two main reasons, both having to do with the rise of logical positivism. In the first place the prestige of pragmatism has suffered on account of a widespread misreading which regards it as little more than an implausible analysis of truth in terms of verifications and practical benefits.[4] Secondly, the pragmatist approach was eclipsed in the twentieth century by the powerful and sweeping logical positivist conception of metaphysics as meaningless pseudo-statements.

The chapter concerns itself, then, with the question of what is the fate of metaphysics according to Putnam? It is divided into three parts. The first considers James's appeal to practical factors to help determine whether a metaphysical claim is true. The second turns to Dewey's more sceptical diagnostic approach which focuses attention on the meaningfulness of metaphysical pronouncements. And the last part argues that Putnam can be located on the unstable ground that lies between these two positions where the undermining of metaphysics is curiously associated with its rehabilitation.

Before turning to consider James, however, it is worth providing a brief sketch, however incomplete and preliminary, of the traditional conception of metaphysics since it is this conception, first and foremost, that the pragmatists are suspicious of.

I TRADITIONAL METAPHYSICS: A SKETCH

The term 'metaphysics' was first used to refer to certain works of Aristotle. Traditional metaphysical inquiry as practised in Europe from the middle ages through to the nineteenth century retains a connection to Aristotle's idea of a science of *being qua being*, the most general study of existence or reality distinct from, and supposedly more fundamental than, any special science. In this traditional conception it is an a priori inquiry concerned to provide a complete and comprehensive explanation of the way the world *appears* to be in terms of some particular conception of an underlying *reality*. The metaphysical distinction between appearance and reality departs significantly from the everyday understandings of these terms as concretely applied to, say, the motives of politicians, the shapes of distant objects or the looks of colours. The 'reality' the metaphysician is concerned with is something hidden and only revealed through some combination of intuition (or revelation) and a priori argument. A crucial assumption of the metaphysician is that if we could comprehend or know this underlying reality then we could provide *an absolute or final explanation* of the 'appearances' of things, one that is basic and supposed to hold once and for all.[5] Plato's Forms, Leibniz's monads, Kant's things-in-themselves, and Descartes's mental substances are familiar examples of metaphysical entities employed to play a role in this kind of explanation.

A representative contemporary metaphysician, Frank Jackson, writes:

Metaphysics ... is about what there is and what it is like ... Metaphysicians seek a comprehensive account of some subject matter – the mind, the semantic, or most ambitiously, everything – in terms of a limited number of more or less basic notions ... ['Serious metaphysics'] attempt[s] to explain it all ... in terms of some limited set of fundamental ingredients.

(Jackson, 1994, p. 25)

Note the typical features of traditional metaphysics: the unfamiliar use of the appearance/reality distinction; the claim that some (few) things are fundamental; and the claim that everything can be explained in terms of such things.[6] In this explanation 'appearances' are either to be eliminated or reduced to (or 'located' in) the 'reality' that the metaphysician recognizes as fundamental.

II JAMES AND THE TRUTH OF METAPHYSICS

In his famous volumes *Pragmatism* and *The Meaning of Truth* (1998) James presents pragmatism, in the first instance, as opposing what he calls intellectualist metaphysics:

> [A pragmatist] turns away from abstraction and insufficiency, from verbal solutions, from bad a priori reasons, from fixed principles, closed systems, and pretended absolutes and origins.
>
> (James, 1998, p. 31)

This dimension of his thought appears to be a rehearsal of the Kantian strategy of eliminating a dogmatic kind of metaphysics in favour of another more rationally acceptable kind. The application of the pragmatic principle – to clarify our ideas or concepts of an object by 'consider[ing] what conceivable effects of a practical kind the object may involve' (James, 1998 p. 29) – is advertised as undermining rationalist metaphysics but leaving empiricist metaphysics relatively unscathed. Thus James speaks of pragmatism as representative of 'the empiricist attitude' (1998 pp. 4, 31), an attitude which has 'anti-intellectualist tendencies' (1998 p. 5). Although he presents pragmatism as 'a method only' (1998 p. 31), not a metaphysical position, James regards his own metaphysics of experience – the doctrine of *radical empiricism* – as fitting particularly well with it. Consequently, although inimical to intellectualist metaphysics, pragmatism is presented as at least compatible with, perhaps even sympathetic to, empiricist metaphysics.

But there is another side to James's pragmatism that is in tension with this. In applying the pragmatic maxim to metaphysical claims, if there are no specific experiences to be expected, one must consider the conduct to be recommended and any emotional or other reactions that the object under consideration, supposing it exists, would elicit. James's liberal understanding of what constitutes practical effects puts pressure on him to acknowledge that a pragmatic defence of the intellectualist metaphysics he officially opposes is available.

On James's view it is a significant advantage of pragmatism that traditional metaphysical disputes, which would otherwise be interminably irresolvable[7] on grounds of a priori reason or empirical evidence, are able to be settled by appeal to pragmatic considerations.[8] Thus James writes, 'in every genuine metaphysical debate some practical issue, however conjectural and remote, is involved' (1998, p. 5).

Furthermore, James suggests that it is not retrospectively but *prospectively* that the practical value of metaphysical systems reveals itself. For example, on this basis he argues that the dispute between materialism and theism, which cannot be decided by appeal to epistemic considerations of evidence or explanatory power, can decisively be settled in favour of theism. His ultimate claim is that belief in God can satisfy a widespread desire for a philosophy of promise or hope when we consider the *future* course of the world since 'the notion of God ... guarantees an ideal [moral] order' (p. 6).

Similarly, when James examines the traditional metaphysical topics of substance, the Absolute (of German idealism), design in nature and free will, the *only* thing that he decisively rejects on pragmatic grounds is substance, the mere bearer of properties that Locke suspiciously called a we-know-not-what.[9] All the rest provide *some* basis for an attitude of hope, either by implying that there is an eternal rational order in the universe that does not depend on us or, in the case of free will, by implying that there will be novelties in the future. As these examples demonstrate, a metaphysical topic that might have seemed pointless from either a rational or empirical point of view is revealed as having, at least for a certain class of minds, beneficial pragmatic effects such as feelings of confidence or comfort, particularly when the *future* course of the world is taken into account.

Like the positivists, James holds that metaphysical disputes are not settled by appeal to empirical evidence or a priori reason. His invocation of pragmatic value makes available non-epistemic reasons to help decide in favour of the truth of one side or the other of a metaphysical dispute that would otherwise be undecidable. That is, James treats the benefits of believing in some metaphysical posit as being part of the rationale for so believing. Consequently, the unreality and unwieldy abstraction of the Absolute, say, which counts against it as far as truth is concerned, is balanced by the fact that since it 'yield[s] a religious comfort to a class of minds ... [it is] true "in so far forth"' (James, 1998, p. 12).[10]

James's pragmatism, then, ultimately has very little antimetaphysical bite. While he *claims* to stand opposed to empty intellectualism, whether in the form of merely verbal disputes or metaphysical posits that lack practical value, he is forced to admit that most intellectualist metaphysics is, upon reflection, free of these deficiencies. Pragmatism, for James, makes available new opportunities for discovering which metaphysics is true all things considered.

III DEWEY AND THE CONTENT OF METAPHYSICS

Dewey is a more robustly anti-metaphysical thinker than James although, as we will see, there is an important qualification to be made. By conceiving philosophy as a broadly empirical method of inquiry, Dewey renders traditional metaphysics (or 'absolutistic philosophies') obsolete.[11] Dewey's experimentalism leaves no room for any purely a priori inquiry into the (putatively) hidden and fixed nature or essence of the world. Of the problems of traditional metaphysics Dewey writes, 'We do not solve them; we get over them' (1965, p. 7). In contrast to James, he does not think that a consideration of the practical significance of metaphysical systems provides any vindication of them. Two main points of difference are worth noting: (1) for James, practical significance is a criterion of the *truth* of a metaphysical system, whereas for Dewey it primarily bears on the question of its *content*;[12] and (2) Dewey's conception of the practical significance of a metaphysical system is rooted in the social and historic conditions under which that system was invented and flourished. James's account, alternatively, focuses on the relation of metaphysics to allegedly trans-historic human needs such as 'the need of an eternal moral order' (1998, p. 6). Dewey remarks,

Metaphysics is a substitute for custom as the source and guarantor of higher moral and social values – that is the leading theme of the classic philosophy of Europe, as evolved by Plato and Aristotle ... [and] renewed and restated by the Christian philosophy of Medieval Europe.   (EW12: 89)

Metaphysics is here seen as the illusion of a timeless foundation for what are in fact local and changeable moral and social values. At the same time it is, together with traditional epistemology, a consolation of the purely speculative mind for its demoralizing inability to change the world:

> In truth, historic intellectualism, the spectator view of knowledge, is a purely compensatory doctrine which men of an intellectual turn have built up to console themselves for the actual social impotency of the calling of thought to which they are devoted.
>
> (Dewey, 1957, p. 117)

Of course this conception of metaphysics is not one that the metaphysician himself could reflectively endorse without undergoing something akin to an apostasy. Dewey's diagnostic approach implies that metaphysics characteristically involves self-deception. It is not really a study of the timeless, universal or necessary features of reality, as it takes itself to be, for there is no such thing on Dewey's view. Metaphysics plays an imaginary role of apparently securing a transcendent account of the source and authority of what is, in reality, attributable to custom and human history. It thus consoles us for its inability to play any *genuine* or *authentic* moral or social function.

This account, far from vindicating metaphysics, is no less destructive of it than logical positivism is. Metaphysical questions lack genuine empirical or practical value, and the apparent authority they provide for a community's moral and social values is a grand illusion. Perhaps one should add that Dewey is sensitive to the way in which such illusions can, none the less, be forces in world history. But he is the last person to want to perpetuate these myths. So, if the moral function of metaphysics cannot be appealed to as a defence of it and one has followed Dewey in abandoning a priori inquiry, what hope is there for the future of metaphysics? In this vein he writes,

> Is there not reason for believing that the release of philosophy of its burden of sterile metaphysics and sterile epistemology instead of depriving philosophy of problems and subject-matter would open a way to questions of the most perplexing and the most significant sort?
>
> (Dewey 1957, p. 126)

None the less, in spite of the strongly anti-metaphysical tendencies of his thinking, Dewey surprisingly follows James in attempting to articulate what he calls a 'metaphysics' of experience. The tension in Dewey's position is mitigated to some extent by an explicit attempt to employ the old metaphysical vocabulary in a new, more pragmatic spirit. Thus, what he calls 'metaphysics' is not concerned with fixed essences, ultimate origins or ends but with what he calls 'the more ultimate traits of the world' which he goes on to identify with 'certain irreducible traits found in any and every subject of scientific inquiry' (1967–90, vol. 8, 4). Examples of the objects of metaphysical inquiry in this sense include diversity, interaction and change. Whereas traditional metaphysics typically concerns itself with the fixed and final, Dewey's metaphysics concerns itself with the fluid and incomplete. The impression that Dewey has cut off the branch he is attempting to sit on is confirmed when we ask what this new metaphysics consists in. What are its discoveries or insights? Dewey provides nothing but vague and disappointing generalities which do not have any of the power of his diagnostic claims or, for that matter, of the great metaphysical systems of the past.[13] In a particularly revealing passage he writes:

> This is the extent and method of my "metaphysics": – the large and constant features of human sufferings, enjoyments, trials, failures and successes together with the institutions of art, science, technology, politics, and religion which mark them, communicate genuine features of the world within which man lives. The method differs not a whit from that of any investigator who, by making certain observations and experiments, and by utilizing the existing body of ideas available for calculation and interpretation, concludes that he really succeeds in finding out something about some limited aspect of nature.
>
> (Dewey, 1927, p. 59)

What are the 'large and constant features' of the human condition or, more broadly still, of what he elsewhere calls 'the generic traits manifested by existences of all kinds' (Dewey, 1929a, p. 412)? And even if we can give content to such vague and general pronouncements about the human condition or all existences, why call it metaphysics rather than anthropology or history, especially if the method is the same as that of the social scientist?[14]

Dewey eventually gave up his attempt to reinterpret metaphysics to fit his own pragmatist standpoint. The tension in Dewey's conception finally led to his complete renunciation of metaphysics. In replying to a critic in 1949, Dewey writes,

I now realize that it was exceedingly naïve of me to suppose that it was possible to rescue the word ['metaphysics'] from its deeply ingrained traditional use. I derive what consolation may be possible from promising myself never to use the word again in connection with any aspect of any part of my own position.

(Dewey, 1949, pp. 712–13)

To take this remark seriously is to see Dewey as having a fundamentally therapeutic attitude to metaphysics all along. His mistake was to suppose there was any point in trying to rescue the term 'metaphysics' in the radically new setting of pragmatism.

IV PUTNAM AND THE INSIGHTS OF METAPHYSICS

Let us sum up the pragmatist stance to metaphysics as exemplified in James and Dewey. The pragmatist is presented as a critic of the traditional intellectualist metaphysician and of the merely verbal disputes often associated with such metaphysics. He is more congenial to a metaphysics of experience. More importantly, pragmatism is perhaps the first philosophical movement to seriously consider the *practical* function of a metaphysics: as a source of spiritual comfort; or an apparent guarantor of the moral and social order; or a consolation for political and social impotence. For James these functions provide some reason to think a metaphysics is true; for Dewey, on the contrary, they shows that metaphysics is inescapably bound up with self-deception or what existentialists call bad faith. For Dewey the illusion that there is a fixed, underlying realm of Being is a consequence of the human capacity to transcendentalize or eternalize the time-bound values of a particular society. Thus James's appeal to the pragmatic significance of metaphysics tends to be vindicatory, whereas Dewey's tends to be undermining.

Now let us ask: where does Putnam stand on these issues? Is he a Jamesian apologist for metaphysics or a Deweyan critic of the enterprise? As I hope will become clear I read Putnam as sharing aspects of *both* the positions of James and Dewey, an uneasy position that is not without internal tension. I shall end this chapter by raising some questions about how this tension might be overcome.

In the first place, Putnam is certainly a strong critic of the foundationalist and essentialist pretensions of traditional metaphysics. A representative passage reads:

the long history of failures to explain in metaphysical terms how mathematics is possible, how nondemonstrative knowledge is possible ... and so on, suggests nothing much follows from the failure of philosophy to come up with an explanation of anything in 'absolute terms' – except, perhaps, the senselessness of a certain sort of metaphysics.

(Putnam, 2002, p. 45)

Putnam reserves his strongest criticisms for the many and various attempts to explain away or denigrate our everyday ethical thought and talk in metaphysical terms whether by way of the contrasts between cognitivism and non-cognitivism (e.g. Simon Blackburn), facts and values (e.g. A. J. Ayer), or absolute and perspectival knowledge (e.g. Bernard Williams).

Perhaps Putnam's best-known anti-metaphysical programme has been his attempt to salvage a small 'r' realism – qualified at one time as 'internal' and, more recently, as 'pragmatic' or 'natural' – from big 'R' Metaphysical Realism. His criticisms are too familiar and too various to rehearse again in this context. What I want to call attention to is that Putnam explicitly avoids the Kantian strategy: he is careful to distinguish natural realism from *any* kind of metaphysical theory that might be imagined to superannuate Metaphysical Realism.[15] Natural realism is, rather, an attempt to salvage a commonsense attitude towards the world that metaphysics (and scepticism) is thought to ultimately deny or denigrate. We might think of this as representing the Deweyan dimension of his approach.

Like both James and Dewey, and in contrast to the logical positivists, Putnam does not regard traditional metaphysics as totally lacking in cognitive content. He explains:

To call upon us to renounce ... the dreams of metaphysics ... is not at all to join the logical positivists of yesteryear in calling ... metaphysics ... 'nonsense'. There is much of permanent value in the writings of ... traditional metaphysicians. It would be false to Dewey's own spirit to deny that there is.

(Putnam, 2004b, p. 105)

But what does Putnam mean by 'permanent value' in this context? Putnam takes himself to be following Dewey here but his thought is, in fact, much closer to James. Putnam is inclined, for all of his criticisms of traditional metaphysics, to think that this region of philosophy contains valuable insights. Dewey, as we have seen, takes a more Wittgensteinian or diagnostic approach which attempts to explain metaphysics as an understandable intellectual distortion or 'divination' of aspects of our familiar world for understandable reasons such as our fear of change or the theorist's need for consolation for being unable to change the world for the better. Dewey, in short, does not look to metaphysics as a rich seam of insights; he looks to it, rather, as an all-too-human indulgence in mythology and consoling self-deception.

To illustrate this difference it is worth comparing the different ways in which Dewey and Putnam think about the role of the imagination in metaphysics. Dewey holds that a human being is 'primarily a creature of the imagination' (Dewey, 1957, p. 118) and that this has an important bearing on the way in which we understand what motivates metaphysical speculation. On his view, an important difference between metaphysics and scientific inquiry lies in two different employments of the same idealizing function of the imagination.[16] In metaphysical thinking there is a tendency to treat ideals and idealizations as realities by forgetting that they are products of human intellectual activity, often arising out of everyday experiences but, as Dewey puts it, 'with their blemishes removed, their imperfections eliminated, their lacks rounded out, their suggestions and hints fulfilled' (pp. 105–6). Plato's Forms are a classic example. The metaphysician Plato not only treats these ideals as perfect, singular and unchangeable entities but as more real than the mundane realities of the world in which we live our lives. For a scientist, or a scientifically minded pragmatist, however, ideals and idealizations are seen as imaginative tools that help to explain or understand highly complex real-world objects or events. An ideal or idealization, like an architectural model, is not to be assessed as simply true or false. Its role is, rather, to illuminate by way of analogy some, but by no means all, of the important features of the target phenomena.[17]

The moral is that although metaphysics arises from a natural, indeed laudable, capacity for idealization – a capacity that includes the construction of models and imagined possibilities – Dewey sees metaphysical system-building as an undisciplined employment of this capacity, one that depends on forgetting the schematic character of ideals, and their context-sensitive utility in highlighting some features of a particular thing to the exclusion of others. Dewey's diagnostic approach is not a matter of seeing metaphysics as containing various truths, however indirect. It would be better to say that metaphysics has its source in a useful capacity which, when properly employed (e.g. in scientific theorizing), can lead to fruitful discoveries.

Putnam follows Dewey (and Wittgenstein) in thinking that the imagination plays a central role in motivating metaphysical thinking but he conceives this role in a more Jamesian spirit. To explain the role of the imagination in this context Putnam adopts Wittgenstein's notion of a *picture* which can be variously understood as what we would ordinarily call a picture e.g. a drawing or diagram; a mental image; a rough and ready conception; an engineer's or architect's model e.g. of a bridge or house; and so on. A picture, we might say, is a rough or schematic way of seeing things, especially highly complex things, that is to be contrasted with a fully elaborated theory.

What, then, is the relation between pictures and metaphysics? Consider the following passage in which Putnam is comparing what he calls the picture of Metaphysical Realism with the idealist picture of truth as consisting in idealized warranted assertibility:

> I think the idealist 'picture' calls our attention to vitally important features of our practice – and what is the point of having 'pictures' if we are not interested in seeing how well they represent what we actually think and do.
> (Putnam, 1990, p. 42)

This passage strongly suggests a representationalist conception of pictures according to which they represent the world well or badly. I take it that the pictures themselves are not simply true or false but that they can, through a certain use or employment, bring 'vitally important features of our practices' to our attention, and, in that sense, represent the world. The Jamesian suggestion seems to be that traditional metaphysics, in so far as it is a matter of using pictures, can indirectly represent features of the world that we would otherwise miss. This constitutes part of its 'permanent value'.

V THE END OR THE RENEWAL OF METAPHYSICS?

Where do these reflections leave the fate of metaphysics? We have seen how Dewey, despite some equivocation, is charitably interpreted as having an end of metaphysics stance. His equivocation is not a matter of thinking that traditional metaphysics has any life left in it; it is, rather, a matter of thinking that metaphysics can be reconceived and to some extent rehabilitated on a pragmatist basis. As we have seen, Dewey has a more nuanced approach to traditional metaphysics than the positivists. He provides a rich account of its motivations in various entrenched human capacities, needs and desires but, for all that, his account is not a vindication of metaphysics, as James's account tends to be. A central part of his view is that metaphysicians do not realize the nature or sources of their own thinking. If they did, they would be out of business.

Putnam's attitude to the fate of metaphysics seems to be located somewhere between Dewey and James. He writes:

> I take it as a fact of life that there is a sense in which the task of philosophy is to overcome metaphysics and a sense in which its task is to continue metaphysical discussion.
>
> (Putnam, 1988, p. 457)

The difficulty in interpreting this comment is to understand in what sense it is the task of philosophy to *continue* metaphysical discussion. Putnam has made it quite clear that he thinks almost all current analytic metaphysics, and large tracts of traditional metaphysics, are a matter of 'dreams', 'fantasies', 'confusions' and 'ridiculous' ideas. This fits well with the Deweyan (and Wittgensteinian) idea that an important task for philosophy is to overcome metaphysics. But, like James in particular, he has also claimed that there are salvageable insights in at least some of the great systems of traditional metaphysics. These insights, however, were certainly not the insights the metaphysicians themselves believed they had discovered. For Putnam, there is no fixed realm of essences or necessary truths of the sort the metaphysicians of old dreamed that they had discovered. One example is worth considering further.

In lectures delivered at Harvard, Putnam held that the insight in Metaphysical Realism (an insight owed to James, in fact) is that words do indeed correspond to realities but that there are *many different kinds* of correspondence relation in question not a single relation, as the Realist had supposed. But note that this insight salvaged from the metaphysical picture of a single word–world relation is not a distinctively *metaphysical* insight and it is certainly not the insight the Metaphysical Realists themselves supposed they had found.

Putnam follows Dewey and Wittgenstein in holding that the metaphysician is subject to the illusion of taking products of his own imagination for realities. If that is so, then how could a contemporary metaphysician engage in metaphysical discussion *without* illusion, or self-deception, or forgetting that his pictures are pictures? In approaching this question it is worth reflecting that throughout the discussion we have been assuming that metaphysics is a fairly well-circumscribed concept for an a priori inquiry into eternal essences or fixed and necessary structures of the world. But what of a philosopher who holds that what reality is *really* like does not include essences? Surely this is still a metaphysical stance even if it is anti-essentialist? Or one could hold that there are essences or fixed necessities but they are in the mind or language rather than the external world. Surely that counts as metaphysics too? Or what of a philosopher like Quine who claims to forgo a priori theorizing but retains a kind of empiricism and physics worship that seem like elements of a first philosophy (in so far as they are not subject to revision)? One is tempted to call these elements metaphysical too. The point is that since there are many forms that the metaphysical aspiration to explain *appearances* in terms of some underlying *reality* can take, the concept of the metaphysical is itself not fixed but evolves. It is what Wittgenstein calls a family resemblance concept. The traditional search for essence prompted by the Socratic question 'What is X?' is simply the most important historical paradigm of metaphysics. But metaphysics also includes Kant's transcendental question 'How is X possible?' as well as the modern search for the necessary and sufficient conditions for the application of a concept; and other things besides.[18]

Consequently, it can be hard to say what counts as a metaphysics in any given case, especially if Wittgenstein is right in thinking that metaphysics often dresses itself up as science.[19] So one reason for thinking that we will continue metaphysical discussion is that it is often unclear whether certain expressions are being employed for metaphysical purposes or not. The question of discerning what is metaphysical and what not thus becomes an important matter for philosophical investigation. But even if that is so it is not obvious that this exhausts what Putnam means by speaking of the continuation of metaphysical discussion – although it does seem clear that his renewed vision of philosophy is incompatible with the metaphysical system-building of, say, a David Lewis or a David Armstrong.

Putnam's remarks suggest that philosophy will always engage in metaphysical discussion in at least the relatively weak sense that we are creatures who, given the facts of our human nature – our wants, wishes, imaginings, etc. – will inevitably drift into asking metaphysical questions and urging metaphysical answers. This view is compatible with a primarily therapeutic conception of philosophy that sees its aim as one of exposing and interrogating metaphysical pronouncements with a view to overcoming them, endlessly, one by one. This would be to embrace an end to metaphysical system-building while acknowledging that there will be no end to the *urge* to metaphysics.

Alternatively, Putnam may think, as Dewey sometimes did, that there is a viable reconception of metaphysics that is distinct from traditional metaphysics. In the same vein, Strawson (1959) supposed that an investigation of the general features of our conceptual network is a kind of metaphysics, which he called 'descriptive metaphysics'. We might think of it as contributing to a conception of philosophy as the attempt 'to understand how things, in the broadest possible sense of the term hang together in the broadest possible sense of the term' (Sellars, 1963, p. 1). But this attempt to redefine the term 'metaphysics' is prone to lead to confusion, as Dewey finally saw. The aim of 'descriptive metaphysics' is to describe something that lies open to view – uses of language, concepts as employed in judgements on specific occasions – not to explain the 'appearances' in terms of something hidden, i.e. some underlying metaphysical reality. And it has no trouble accepting that our concepts are contingent, changeable and responsive to human needs. If one *is* tempted to make this move it is important not to lose sight of the great difference between, on the one hand, engaging in traditional metaphysics and, on the other, responding to traditional metaphysical questions by, in effect, changing the subject to engage in piecemeal descriptions of our concepts and their uses.

NOTES

1   For example, Dewey writes: 'Philosophy forswears inquiry after absolute origins and absolute finalities in order to explore specific values and specific conditions that generate them' (Dewey, 1965, p. 13).
2   At best they have some non-cognitive (or emotive) meaning but Carnap explains that this meaning would be better expressed in the arts rather

than masquerading as a product of a genuine theoretical enterprise. Carnap writes: 'Our conjecture [is] that metaphysics is a substitute, albeit an inadequate one, for art' (Ayer 1959, p. 80).

3 Here the important differences between the attitudes of Wittgenstein and the logical positivists towards metaphysics are being set aside.
4 In fact, James and Dewey (and, arguably, the later Peirce) really defend not a logical analysis but what James called a 'genetic theory of what is meant by truth' (James, 1998, p. 37), a theory that is only *one* application of the general pragmatic method for clarifying concepts in science and philosophy.
5 Mary Warnock speaks of 'the claims of metaphysical systems ... to provide a total explanation of everything' and goes on to say 'that some such claim is essential to a metaphysical system' (Warnock, 1962, p. 143).
6 There have been many candidates for what constitute the fundamental aspects of metaphysical reality including first causes, universals and the essences or natures of things.
7 James (1998, p. 28): 'The pragmatic method is primarily a method of settling metaphysical disputes that might otherwise be interminable'.
8 This is best seen as a widening of the scope of reason.
9 James believes that even substance has pragmatic value in the Eucharist since, for believers at least, the wafer exchanges its bread-substance for divine-substance.
10 Of course, to be counted as true *simpliciter* the Absolute must, in addition, 'run the gauntlet of all our other truths' (James, 1998, p. 7) which James does not think it does.
11 Dewey calls traditional metaphysical problems 'hopeless puzzles' (EW3: *Reality as Experience*).
12 When considering metaphysical posits James does not appeal to pragmatic significance to reconceive their content or meaning, as the pragmatic maxim might lead one to suppose, but to help to determine their truth. They are, as he puts it, true *in so far* as they have such and such pragmatic value.
13 This is essentially Rorty's argument in his (1977).
14 Rorty (1977, p. 72): '[Dewey] occasionally came down with the disease he was trying to cure'.
15 Putnam (1999, p. 41): '"The natural realist account" urged on us by Austin and Wittgenstein, is, in the end, not an "alternative metaphysical account"... Winning through to natural realism is seeing the needlessness and the unintelligibility of a picture that imposes an interface between ourselves and the world. It is a way of completing the task of philosophy, the task that John Wisdom once called a "journey from the familiar to the familiar".'

16 See Godfrey-Smith (2006).
17 Dewey's idea here fits well with recent work on model-based theorizing in the philosophy of science including Cartwright's (1999) view that laws of physics are models rather than representations of fact and Godfrey-Smith's (2006) work on the role of models in biological theorizing.
18 On Wittgenstein's view criteria for metaphysical uses of words include: the attempt to formulate a special non-logical non-empirical kind of necessity; the use of words without significant antitheses; non-scientific statements being used as if they were scientific; the assumption that the use of words is grounded in the supposed fixed natures of things; and so on.
19 Wittgenstein (1967, 458).

ALAN MALACHOWSKI

9 Imagination over truth: Rorty's contribution to pragmatism

Richard Rorty claims that 'philosophy makes progress not by becoming more rigorous but by becoming more imaginative'.[1] While making such claims, he has, over the past forty years or so, done more than anyone else to both revive pragmatism and stimulate greater optimism regarding its prospects going forward.[2] But in doing this, he has also provoked a great deal of controversy. On matters of historical interpretation, for example, his writings are heavily criticized for distorting, misconstruing or simply ignoring, some of the key ideas of pragmatism's founding figures. Similar condemnation is frequently made of his treatment of those previous and later thinkers he is keen to include within the pragmatist fold – the most noteworthy being, in the former case, Hegel, Nietzsche and Heidegger, and in the latter, Davidson, Sellars and Wittgenstein.[3]

In addition, and presumably many of his detractors would argue that this is more important, Rorty is commonly vilified over matters of philosophical substance. The brand of pragmatism he creates out of his disputed construals and controversial appropriations is claimed to suffer from a woefully inadequate conception of truth, one form or another of self-refuting relativism, and various related forms of scholarly licentiousness.[4] Should philosophy take the pragmatist low road he has carved out, it will end up destroying its own intellectual credentials. Such, at any rate, is the view of many of Rorty's fiercest critics.

Rorty's notoriety has been one of the precipitating causes of pragmatism's greater visibility of late.[5] And much of that notoriety stems from his very attempts to blur distinctions such as the one just alluded to between historical interpretation and philosophical substance. However, for the purpose of elucidating his approach to pragmatism and the philosophical motivation behind that approach, we will initially assume that the distinction holds some water. Later, as these considerations become clearer, we can dispense with it.

RORTY WITHIN THE PRAGMATIST TRADITION

'The pragmatist thinks that the tradition needs to be utilized, as one utilizes a bag of tools' is one of Rorty's maxims.[6] But many dedicated and knowledgable scholars of the pragmatist tradition complain that Rorty abuses it in pursuit of his own, largely adventitious, ends.[7] Some claim, for example, that by overlooking Peirce's importance, Rorty untethers pragmatism from one of its key anchor points in rational deliberation and disciplined inquiry, thereby setting it adrift on the rough seas of unscientific musings.[8] Others are more worried that, whether by accident or design, Rorty deforms the main aims of both James and Dewey, bending the content of their thoughts and texts into shapes that they would themselves have found abhorrent – shapes that have little or no proper historical context. In James's case, one of the main bones of contention is Rorty's attempt to lift his pragmatism out of the empiricist tradition and turn it into a strong form of anti-epistemology.[9] As for Dewey, a principal concern is that in freeing his work from its deep and serious attachments to notions of experience, method, metaphysics and science, Rorty leaves us with an hollowed out shell of pragmatism, one within which Dewey's own views become no more than a distant echo of protest.

There are cases where it seems quite obvious that Rorty is unfair to Peirce,[10] and others where he appears to play unmercifully loose with the actual words of both James and Dewey. This is partly a consequence of his magpie-like handling of quotations. Rorty is quick to seize upon and then repeatedly advertise any word, phrase or passage that catches his eye because it appears to support a cause he wishes to advance or undermines one he wants us to reject.[11] And at times, this becomes something of a rhetorical bad habit, leading him to ignore ancillary details that are patently inhospitable to his underlying motivational strategy. However, broader objections to Rorty's use of the pragmatist tradition frequently fail to grasp, or even acknowledge, the nature of his relationship to it. When that relationship is unravelled and clarified, it becomes more difficult, and often less appropriate, to pin labels of intellectual irresponsibility on his efforts.

Rorty's relationship to the pragmatist tradition is a self-consciously pragmatic one, as depicted in the characteristically pithy maxim that kicks off the present section. For Rorty, this style of relationship is all to the good. It exemplifies the philosophical importance he attaches to practical relevance and utility, and it also rounds off his approach in the sense that he does not need to refer to extra-pragmatic motivation in invoking his forebears. However, for those who are hostile to pragmatism, or at least Rorty's version of it, this characterization is exasperating. Indeed, at first blush it cements much that they already find objectionable. If textual, doctrinal and contextual innacuracies are to be pragmatically licensed, then something must surely be gravely wrong. It is time to do some explaining.

The pragmatic value that defines Rorty's main links with classic pragmatism has two aspects: instrumental and inspirational. Some of the views of James and Dewey have instrumental value for Rorty because they enable him to develop and sustain an antirepresentationalist critique of epistemology and, by extension, the whole of philosophy as it has been practised by those following in the footsteps of Plato, Descartes, Locke, Hume and Kant. But again, it is necessary to divide things up. Two things are going on. Some such views have *straightforward* instrumental value for Rorty; that is, without him having to put too much contemporary spin on them. Dewey's concerted attempts to undermine what he calls the 'spectator theory of knowledge' and push the 'epistemology industry' out of business provide prime examples of this. In other cases, where the value is less obvious, Rorty can only cash it out by extracting the views in question from their original setting at the risk of overriding the philosophical intentions behind them. Rorty generally treats James's approach to truth in this way. He extrapolates from James's views on the multifarious connectons between truth and utility as well as other considerations such as fidelity to 'funded experience' and established traditions, in order to shore up his own view that truth is neither a legitimate goal of inquiry[12] nor something that we should try to create an all-embracing theory of. From James's lengthy, complex and sometimes nuanced discussions of truth, Rorty draws the rather quick lesson that truth is actually something we should not feel obliged to say much about. It is, he surmises, precisely the kind of topic philosophers now need to get away from. And, he regards this lesson as being reinforced by a salutary realization to be gained from Donald Davidson's work: 'nobody should even try to specify the nature of truth'.[13]

Although his own account of pragmatism is more conventional than Rorty's, H. S. Thayer's account of its achievements indicates why someone like Rorty might wish to emphasize, above all else, its inspirational value: its capacity to stir the imagination. For Thayer maintains that pragmatism 'has helped shape the modern conception of philosophy as a way of investigating problems and clarifying communication *rather than as a fixed system of ultimate answers and great truths*'.[14] And, he further claims that having 'achieved permanence', it 'has a future though as *a suggestive body of ideas*'.[15] In *Philosophy and the Mirror of Nature*, Rorty launches a sustained attack on the very notion of philosophy being a source of ultimate answers and great truths.Taking analytic philosophy to be the apotheosis of the tradition that started with Plato, Rorty tries to show how it has, no doubt mostly unwittingly, undermined itself from within.[16] Between them, two of its stalwart practitioners, Wilfrid Sellars and W. V. O. Quine, have left analytic philosophy bereft of substantial or methodological foundations.[17] For in his systematic demolition of the idea of 'the given', Sellars[18] removes the possibility of attaching any interesting or important epistemological value to unadorned experience. This punctures the foundational and reductive pretensions of empiricism. Then, by emasculating the analytic/synthetic tradition, Quine[19] displaces reason-based alternatives. Neither pure experience nor pure thought can provide grounds for establishing ultimate answers and great truths.

This conception of philosophy's limitations comports with a general difficulty that Rorty perceives at the very outset of his serious philosophical thinking when he begins to worry whether 'one could possibly get a non-circular justification of any debatable stand on any important issue' because 'there seem[s] to be nothing like a neutral standpoint from which alternative first principles could be evaluated'.[20] It also fits in with an approach to pragmatism that views it as above all 'a suggestive body of ideas'. It fits for Rorty because he believes philosophy, honestly conceived, can be *no more than that*. And, it fits *well* because the writings of James and Dewey provide him with plenty of ideas as to the direction philosophy can take if it is to live in self-conscious honesty within its own limitations. These early pragmatists strike Rorty as primarily inspirational figures – thinkers who are liable to spark off new and exciting ideas, rather than purveyors of fixed doctrines or methods. It is their capacity to vividly imagine, and help others so imagine, a different kind of future, one unencumbered by certain highly problematic philosophical presuppositions, that chiefly interests him rather than the details or even the truth of their doctrines. For this reason, then, it can be a mistake to chastise Rorty because of his apparent textual infidelities. His relationship to the tradition of classic pragmatism is, at one and the same time, both loose enough to allow for creative reinterpretations of the classic pragmatists' writings and strong enough to embody their spirit of inquiry. It can be likened to that of, say, an artist's relationship to the impressionist tradition.

Consider a painter with little previous training who starts her career off by tackling landscapes, but soon encounters some tricky technical problems that cause her to vacillate between realism and abstraction, while finding neither satisfactory. Suppose she then discovers Cézanne, and finds him a source of inspiration for tackling landscapes without either sticking rigidly to realistic detail or veering off into complete abstraction? Further suppose it turns out that Cézanne inspires this artist to eventually produce paintings that appear to go against the grain of Cézanne's own approach to art. Whether she should then be criticized for betraying the impressionist tradition will depend on the usefulness of the story that can be told about the supposed deviations. She or others may, for example, weave a narrative around her work that supports the view that she is carrying Cézanne's impressionism to another level or updating it in some way (perhaps by incorporating innovative materials and techniques that were not available to Cezanne himself). Rorty's appropriation of James and Dewey likewise needs to judged on the story that can be told about the utility of its inspirational upshot rather than on some fixed model of conceptual or textual fidelity.

GETTING PRAGMATISM BACK INTO SHAPE

The slack in his inspiration-based relationship to pragmatism leaves Rorty room for textual manoeuvre in his dealings with James and Dewey. But, there are other reasons why he does not want to swallow whole what they have to say. In the first place, he feels that both philosophers tend to take the early objections to their work too seriously, in the sense, that is, of invariably meeting with their critics on their own ground where concerns and interests that are alien to pragmatism dominate the landscape. Rorty has little time for this, and wants to push pragmatism forward into new territory where the assumptions that enticed James and Dewey out of their comfort zone and on to foreign battlefields no longer hold.[21] At the same time, in pushing it forward, he wants to unburden pragmatism of other attachments to the philosophical past. In particular, he wants to set aside what he regards as its long-standing obsessions with both experience and scientific method. He sees these as keeping pragmatism trapped within the empiricist problematic so that it is unable to take advantage of the progress that has been made in bringing language into play as a key subject for investigation and reflection:

There are two great differences between the classical pragmatists and neo-pragmatists. The first ... is the difference between talking about 'experience' as James and Dewey did, and talking about 'language'. The second is the difference between assuming that there is something called 'the scientific method', whose employment increases the likelihood of one's beliefs being true, and tacitly abandoning this assumption.[22]

Experience is always liable to become philosophically troublesome. Construed as a psychological intermediary of epistemological significance, it paradoxically opens a chasm between the subject and his or her environment into which wholesale scepticism is all too easily sucked. And, considered as something of an entity in its own right, it becomes an enigma: unknowable from without and thereby also effectively cut off from the world at large. Both scepticism and idealism can feed heartily on this isolation.

James and Dewey make concerted efforts to formulate conceptions of experience that ward off the possibility of estrangement and overcome problem-mongering dualisms. And they do this by stressing both its natural and social embeddedness. Dewey, for instance, insists that experience 'is no infinitesimally thin layer or foreground of nature, but ... penetrates into it, reaching down into its depths'.[23] Rorty, however, doubts whether such characterizations are worth the effort. He points out that they tend to beg the very questions of interest to those wanting to develop theories of epistemology to help defeat or prevent radical scepticism about knowledge. Moreover, although Rorty does not state the motivation for this very crisply, he leans towards the view that if experience *can* be described in suitably non-dualistic terms, terms that do not generate any of the usual epistemological concerns, it will lose its uniqueness and render itself, philosophically disposable.[24] On Rorty's understanding, then, experience is either a source of problems that have now become stale or it is surplus to philosophical requirements. This is one of the main reasons that he finds Davidson's approach to philosophy so attractive. For Rorty believes that it shows us how to proceed with no intermediate terrain of philosophical inquiry, not even language itself:

Davidson's account of linguistic communication dispenses with the picture of language as a third thing intervening between self and reality.[25]

In ruling out such bugbears as 'ideas', 'meanings' and 'experience', Davidson's approach thus encourages us to 'forget empiricism rather than radicalize it'.[26] And, erasing 'the boundary between knowing a language and knowing our way around the world generally',[27] leaves no gap for traditional scepticism to occupy with squatters' rights.[28]

In response, some scholars have lept instantly to the defence of Dewey's treatment of experience. Shustermann, for instance, argues that Rorty's critique ignores the importance Dewey attaches to 'immmediate non-discursive experience'[29] and its intimate relationship to the quality of life in all its manifestations. Relatedly, Bernstein claims that Rorty is badly mistaken in thinking that Dewey allocates a narrowly foundational role to experience.[30] Such defences may well succeed in showing that Dewey's approach to experience is more complex and multi-purposed than Rorty allows. But in the context within which Rorty raises his objections, they are beside the point. For he wants to guide us towards a mode of philosophizing within which experience has no deeply significant *epistemological* part to play. That it can be invoked on other grounds is largely irrelevant.[31]

When experience is set aside, over-inflated conceptions of science follow in its wake. The arguments of Sellars and Quine just alluded to leave it with no unimpeachable experiential foundations, no links to reality that cannot be reasonably overidden, and no theoretical claims that cannot be rejected or revised if circumstances so dictate. However, it is important not to exaggerate the upshot for the status of science. These are *anti-scientistic* considerations. They are not meant to cast shadows on the common practices of science itself. Under their influence, these remain as important and useful as ever. What changes is the perception of science as the fountainhead of a unique method that provides a model for all other modes of inquiry. This perceptual shift reveals that science should enjoy no uniquely privileged position within discourse, pragmatist or otherwise. It needs to compete for attention with other means of inquiry. To those who complain that even so, Rorty's approach to science betrays a lack of sympathy with, or even understanding of, its central role in Dewey's work, he voices a reply that is both interesting and challenging:

> Granted that Dewey never stopped talking about "scientific method," I submit that he never had anything very useful to say about it. Those who think I am overstating my case here should, I think, tell us what this thing called "method" – which is neither a set of rules nor a character trait nor a collection of techniques – is supposed to be. Unless some reasonably definite element can be specified, and chapter and verse cited from Dewey showing that this is what he had in mind, I shall stick to my claim that Dewey could have said everything he needed to say if he dropped the term "scientific method".[32]

To my knowledge, no one has met this challenge. And, from my own reading of Dewey, I can see little prospect of much success being achieved on that score.

In an interview in 1982, Rorty said 'I think Dewey and James are the best guides to understanding the modern world that we've got, and that it's a question of putting pragmatism into better shape after thirty years of super-professionalism'.[33] We are now in a somewhat better position to see what putting pragmatism into better shape means for him. It means recognizing that pragmatism is best regarded as a relatively autonomous, practical approach to philosophy, one that now needs to forget the details of its early quarrels with the founders of the analytic movement and divest itself of any incipient attachments to empiricism. It should do this by dispatching philosophically laden notions of experience while also ceasing to regard science as a methodological touchstone. The interesting thing here is that Rorty's reformist tendencies are themselves partly inspired by the pragmatism that he claims needs reforming. Failure to appreciate this can compound the mistakes that too many of his critics are inclined to make when they object to his version of pragmatism on narrow textual and/or conceptual grounds, assuming that what Rorty wishes to dispose of is somehow part of the defining essence of pragmatism.

When Rorty expounds what he calls epistemological behaviourism, for instance, in what he rightly considers to be the pivotal chapter of *Philosophy and the Mirror of Nature* (1980), he is already starting to give us an indication of how pragmatism should begin to look when it has been updated and reformed along the lines he will later come to make more explicit. But, in concentrating on how this kind of behaviourism fails to square with a straightforward interpretation of the writings of James and Dewey, critics have missed Rorty's pragmatist point.

Epistemological behaviourism attempts to explain 'rationality and epistemic authority by reference to what society lets us say, rather than the latter by the former' (Rorty, 1980, p. 174) and Rorty claims that in doing so it manifests an 'attitude common to Dewey and Wittgenstein' (p. 174). In an insightful general assessment of his approach to pragmatism, Gary Brodsky says that for Rorty, this attitude licenses a form of behaviourism which can be usefully broken down into four claims:

1 Knowledge must be understood holistically and not atomistically.
2 Rational criticism of knowledge claims can only proceeed on an historicistic basis, i.e., in the light of the problems and existing norms human beings possess during particular epochs.
3 Philosophy cannot tell us any more about knowledge and truth than common sense supplemented by biology, history, etc.
4 There is no neutral ahistorical framework containing wholesale constraints on inquiry which philosophy can articulate and establish.[34]

Brodsky then asserts that pragmatism, as it should be understood, neither 'contains nor implies' epistemological behaviourism thus construed. In particular, he claims, the pragmatist orthodoxy does not explicitly endorse historicism and it would have been very odd for Dewey to have written so much about knowledge if he believed anything like (3). Earlier in his discussion, Brodsky mentions the difficulty in distinguishing between Rorty's interpretations of historical figures and his philosophical position. Difficulties there may be, but it is important not to compound them by forcing an overly conventional framework of interpretation on the conception of pragmatism Rorty prefers. He does not claim that the work of the classic pragmatists contains or implies epistemological behaviourism. His view is rather that pragmatism *ought now* to embrace this position. It is, if you like, a *normative* view, one that prescribes how those who are faithful to the spirit of classic pragmatism should be inclined to think of pragmatism if they want it to thrive in present intellectual circumstances. When we examine the aspirations of James and Dewey in the light of the philosophical developments that have occurred since they were writing, then *on this understanding* we should realize that pragmatism will be better off if it moves in the direction Rorty suggests.

Furthermore, we should then see that it makes good sense for Rorty to claim that James and Dewey actually inspire agreement on this. Here, the imperative of making practical progress in philosophy, thus linking it more closely to the kind of human problems that are generated by life itself rather than an independent tradition of thinking, is the driving force. Witness Dewey's famous test of the value of a philosophy:

> Does it end in conclusions which, when they are referred back to ordinary life-experiences and predicaments, render them more significant, more luminous to us, and make our dealings with them more fruitful?[35]

Take out the reference to experience here, making life itself the focal point, and we have Rorty's own reformist criterion of worthwhile philosophy.

IMAGINATION OVER TRUTH

For Rorty, pragmatism functions best as an 'instrument of cultural change',[36] and thus cultural change is where the philosophical action ought to be. But, pragmatism so functions only when it recognizes that the imagination provides a better map of the future than truth. This all sounds highly implausible to Rorty's critics, and many of them have not hesitated to say so before examining the details and implications of what he proposes.

Interpreting pragmatism as an instrument of cultural change is one of Rorty's ways of finessing pragmatism's traditional concern with practicalities. Some critics are convinced that the very first move Rorty makes here can only lead to pragmatism's ruin. And those who are hostile to pragmatism in any case precisely because of its very emphasis on practicalities see the introduction of an imagination-based model of cultural change as yet a further step in the wrong direction. Others regard it as inimical to the nature of pragmatism. But Rorty is concerned to introduce a notion of practicality that is both more philosophically innocent and more pragmatically useful than that targetted by the first type of critic or adequately recognized by the second.

Since he does not, and nor does he want to, deny the significance of what we might call everyday practicalities, Rorty is happy to elevate one philosophical claim over another if there is an obvious practical advantage to doing so in that plainly understood sense. Indeed, the search for such advantages is his usual starting point or default position: 'Pragmatists think that if something makes no difference to practice, it should make no difference to philosophy.'[37] But Rorty does not hold that when it arms itself with such advantages, pragmatism can achieve much more than put an end to, or draw attention away from, rather esoteric, and in the end pointless, philosophical disputes. James and Dewey wanted to do that. But they wanted to do more than that. They wanted to create a broader-based, social difference that was all to the greater good. And one interesting and useful way of viewing Rorty's approach to pragmatism is to see it as an attempt to resurrect the agenda for such large-scale social change.

To make that kind of larger ambition realistic, pragmatists need to gain a better understanding of cultural change and its relationship to practicalities ordinarily conceived. However, this requires another shift in philosophical perspective, one that gravely disturbs critics precisely because it involves a substantial appeal to the wild powers of the imagination rather than relying on what they regard to be the sterner and far more reliable forces of rational argumentation.

Rorty's position invokes a particular picture of both our ongoing relationship to the world and our notions of how culture moves forward on the basis of that relationship. Immediate practical gains of the everyday variety can be philosophically advantageous, but they will only take pragmatists so far. If such gains are given absolute priority in the task of driving widespread social change, then pragmatism is liable to fall into philosophical disrepute and impotence – disrepute, because it leaves itself hostage to local prejudices and impotence because it will inevitably be tightly constrained by the conservatism inherent in those very prejudices. Moreover, as practicalities lose their immediacy and are more broadly construed, deeply investigated or generalized, they shade over from the natural to the noumenal world, the world of mind-independent reality, the world that causes so much philosophical fuss because, naive realists aside, nobody dares claim direct epistemic access to it. Conceptions of that reality, though they may follow the contours of transcendental deductions or scientific theory, are nevertheless saturated with value judgements born of social practices and historical traditions. Moreover, since pragmatists cannot simply reach out beyond its everyday features to these wider practical aspects of the world in order to read off, or fashion for themselves, appropriate recommendations for social change,[38] they need to do something very different. They need to find ways of redescribing things in general that both make them amenable and yield greater, long-term social benefits. Such redescription requires appropriately vivid acts of imagination and the creation of correlatively fresh ways of talking. James famously says that philosophers being pathfinders are like poets. Rorty is only too happy to take him both literally and prescriptively.

Notice that Rorty's picture sticks closely to practicalities ordinarily conceived, but does so only up to the point where radical change occurs or is possible or necessary and would be beneficial. On the picture he opposes, philosophers help build railtracks to the future by constucting arguments as to where these should go. Those arguments are causally answerable to the nature of the terrain – or reality itself (which some claim already contains reasons that need to be catered for). But radical change opens up new territory, the features of which cannot be anticipated, and it does so partly by *creating* that territory. In this sense, our earlier talk of a superior map of the future was misleading. The split between map and territory is akin, philosophically speaking, to unhealthy dichotomies like the appearance/reality division and the scheme/content distinction. As such, the pragmatist will wish to avoid doing any heavy lifting with this split. Recognition of this latter point keeps Rorty close to the classic pragmatist idea, made much of by James in particular, that truth is something we help shape for ourselves, as is the incomplete, because still unfinished, world we inhabit. But his handling of this idea distances him from the kind of criticisms it originally received and, unfortunately, continues to provoke. These object that it automatically licenses idealism because the very idea of creating truths and worlds overlooks both the recalcitrance factor (reality has its own agenda and is not subservient to our will) and the independence condition (reality has its own nature quite separate from our conceptions of it). However, this familiar line of complaint presupposes the fundamental subject/object dualism that Rorty, in keeping with both James and Dewey, abjures. More to the point, he shows that by setting empiricist concerns aside and drawing on other resources that were simply not available to their classic forebears prior to the famous linguistic turn, pragmatists can operate effectively without such dependencies.

Fusing a Wittgensteinian approach to words, one that considers them to be tools rather than representational items, with what he takes to be a thoroughly Davidsonian conception of language,[39] Rorty dispenses with concerns that he is still peddling some form of idealism, albeit of a linguistic variety. He does this by invoking arguments derived from Davidson's own contentions that we have already touched on:

1. Language is not any sort of intermediary, and certainly not one that insulates us from reality.
2. To know our way about a language is tantamount to knowing our way about the world.

In using language to deal with the world, we are in the practical position of someone using, say, a screwdriver to fix a broken piece of electrical equipment: language works for us if we achieve our aims in using it, and similarly the screwdriver. Nothing is added in either case, indeed confusion will then reign, if we posit the existence of a representational relation to explain what is going on. Such a relation runs straight into a general verification problem that Rorty has long drawn attention to: we cannot step outside the representational realm to assess how it stands in connection with the world. This also has implications for the role of the imagination.

The general verification problem cuts little or no ice with many of Rorty's critics. Indeed, one of the main reasons why some of them are highly suspicious of the priority he affords the imagination is that it is not subject to the kind of representational constraints required for sensitivity to how things actually are. They tend to argue for this as follows. If the imagination is in control, objectivity vanishes – and truth along with it. For there is no proper sense of getting things right rather than wrong, there is no answerability to how things really are. But this argument puts the imagination out on a limb, as if it operates in its very own fantasy world, needing to pay no heed to the real one. This is a mistake born of an inadequate conception of how language works. On Rorty's understanding, the imagination, in operating, as it must, over the domain of language, never operates in complete isolation and hence can never operate without constraints. However, the constraints it meets are contextual, causal and holistic rather than representational. This gets to the heart of Rorty's contribution to pragmatism. But it needs unpacking. To do that we need to go back over some previous ground and take another look at why it is that Rorty's anti-representational approach to language does not saddle his pragmatism with anything that amounts to a form of idealism.

The picture the critics we have alluded to are all too inclined to construct from what Rorty says about language is one that depicts human beings as creatures who encase themselves, and cannot do otherwise, in free-floating, word-spun webs thereby losing all contact with the things, *everything* in fact, outside those webs. The absurdity of this linguistic idealism that allows no contact with a world beyond words is captured by David Foster Wallace in his first novel *The Broom of the System*:

Apparently she was some sort of phenomenon in college and won a place in graduate study at Cambridge, no small feat for a woman, in the twenties; but in any event, there she studied classics and philosophy and who knows what else under a mad crackpot genuis named Wittgenstein who believed that everything was words. Really. If your car would not start, it was apparently to be understood as a language problem. If you were unable to love, you were lost in language. Being constipated equaled being clogged with linguistic sediment.[40]

But, to pin this kind of absurdity on Rorty, as if he is also some mad crackpot, is a mistake. And it is one that any careful reader of his work should be able to easily avoid.

In the first place, there is nothing in Rorty's writings that suggests language is a free-floating phenomenon. On the contrary, it is, to use William James's famous phrase, 'pent in', and on all sides.[41] This is why the web metaphor for language works, and why it should never be closely associated with idealism. Webs gain their strength and utility from their links. But these need to be both internal and external. A strongly interconnected web that is tethered to nothing outside iself is useless for ordinary practical purposes. Likewise, a frail, diaphonously interwoven contraption that happens to be hunkered down at some point. Language gets its grip on meaning courtesy the inferential links between sentences. These are an important part of the contextual constraints we alluded to earlier. Individual language users are constrained by such links. Speakers cannot launch themselves into linguistic free space and expect to carry meaning along with them. However, meaning is not just a horizontal affair, so to speak. It is not just a matter of dealing linguistic tokens sideways among those who are willing attach similar semantic values to them. Language use has to be 'hunkered down' by causal sensitivity to the world at large. A key indicator of such sensitivity, made much of by Rorty, is practical efficacy: the linguistic key turns the lock of worldly success. In dispensing with representational connections to the world, Rorty's pragmatism does not present us with an insular, disconnected version of language. Words, people and the world are hooked up together.

This emphasis on language and its causal relationship to the world has an important additional aspect that marks out Rorty's contribution to pragmatism: it embeds a *special* role for the imagination. And this is best understood in the context of Rorty's preference for a Romantic conception of philosophy.

On this conception, metaphor is the engine of cultural history. It was the Romantics who paved the way for proper recognition of this. The priority they afforded to the imagination was not the product of wishful or fanciful thinking, but rather a consequence of realizing at first hand the causal power of language, a power that Rorty believes outruns any account of its representational potential. Taking heed of this power, 'we should try to think of imagination not as a faculty that generates mental images but as an ability to change social practices by proposing advantageous new uses of marks and noises'.[42] Metaphors epitomize such uses and thrive on the social advantages they confer.

Of course, the pervasive fear of those who worry about being trapped in the dungeon of language, stimulated by the fantasies it invokes but starved of contact with the real world, is unlikely to be assuaged by such blithe talk of metaphors. But closer inspection of Rorty's pragmatist account of their function might help. He holds that metaphors embed no special meaning that explains their uniqueness. Indeed, they evade conventional patterns of meaning, and they do this not by introducing something semantically new, but rather because they have no meaning at all, or no literal content, as we might best put it. What makes them special is that they can prod us into seeing and doing things differently: their causal power. This ability yields results that transcend what can be achieved by merely juggling combinations of inferential and perceptual content. Hence it provides an additional source of beliefs. The worry for Rorty's critics, of course, is that since metaphors are the work of the imagination, the additional source is irrational.[43] But this begs the question against the kind of practical, results orientated account of rationality Rorty wants to introduce. As with meaning conventionally conceived, so with rationality: metaphors start on the periphery, risking isolation, but their causal efficacy eventually brings them into the fold of normality where they assume a common significance and begin to play a part in ordinary speech and standard methods of reasoning.

Thinking of metaphors in this way makes it easier to think of language as a whole in non-representational terms. For though they are, of necessity, semantically estranged at first, metaphors do not *ever* operate in a linguistic vacuum. They latch on to the causal capacity of ordinary words and bend that capacity to create a fresh way of achieving behavioural purchase on the world. To get a feel for how this works, take Rorty's Wittgensteinian metaphor of words as tools literally, and then consider the effect of reshaping and amalgamating some of those tools: in certain cases the result will be a new tool for achieving unheard of practical aims. But there is no hope of specifying rules for identifying the cases in question in advance or a general theory that will yield rules for making such tools. This holds for metaphors too: they are the upshot of free imaginative play with language. We cannot set out to create a good metaphor by simply wanting to achieve a particular practical result by non-standard linguistic means and then trying to find combinations of words and parts thereof that will generate that result. If we succeed at all on those terms, we will have to fall back on standard meanings (because they are linked to known and predictable behavioural outcomes) and then the effective element of what we produce will consist in large part of normal rather than metaphorical meanings. An imaginative leap in the dark is always necessary at some stage. How does all this point us in the direction of a non-representational approach to language as a whole?

Those who are familiar with Rorty's work will recognize that this account of metaphors is intended to be Davidsonian: they have no meaning as such, though they get traction through their use in the context of ordinary meanings.[44] It is a small step from seeing that metaphors have no meaningful content to seeing that the way they function does not depend on representational content. And once we get the hang of the idea that the efficacy of metaphors is not dependent on such factors, it is not such a large step to then entertain the notion that all language functions non-representationally, that words, phrases and sentences are best thought of as tools rather than pictorial artefacts. Recall that Rorty wants pragmatists to take all this on board so that they can benefit from the linguistic turn, dispense with empiricist baggage, and hence elude a host of traditional philosophical problems. If they do so, then in his view they will be able to develop fresh modes of philosophical discourse, ones that address the common problems of life, in line with Dewey's deepest wishes, and come closer to the limits of the imagination where our only source of redemption now lies.[45] Working in the new territory opened up by such discourse, philosophers will find it easier to cross the boundaries of various other disciplines and override the kind of splits that have threatened to turn philosophy itself into a series of separate subjects – the most notable being the divide between analytic and continental approaches. In this latter case, one of Rorty's important achievements has been to encourage cross-fertilization between pragmatism and thinkers such as Hegel, Nietzsche, Heidegger and Derrida even in the face of objections to his own interpretations of their work.

Failure to recognize when Rorty is operating in or showing us the way towards new territory explains why so many critics so often miss the particular point he is trying to make. Thus, for example, even his friend and sympathetic commentator Richard Bernstein disputes the value of some of the distinctions Rorty has introduced, 'systematic versus edifying; public versus private; argument versus redescription; finding versus making', and so on,[46] without appearing to recognize that it is too soon to pass such judgement on them because they are designed to operate in a different philosophical environment, one within which the familiar standards of argumentative rigour, intellectual illumination, relevancy and so forth that Bernstein nostalgically gestures towards will themselves need to shift ground to cater for new circumstances

Rorty's contributions to pragmatism have been manifold. He has helped classic pragmatism resurface as a live philosophical option even though this has not been one of his avowed aims. By highlighting the inspirational power of the classic pragmatists' ideas, Rorty has enabled philosophers to see how those ideas can be adapted to current historical circumstances in order to create a new form of pragmatism.[47] But perceived problems with his own adaptations have also made it clear to others that those ideas, having an interest and force in their own right that has been overshadowed by Rorty's interventions, need to be released from the grip of his new brand of pragmatism. In this sense, he has strengthened the case of those who believe that the true value of classic pragmatism has yet to be appreciated.

In expounding a non-representational account of both knowledge and language, Rorty has created an intellectual space within which pragmatism can perhaps develop a new philosophical agenda once it reforms itself along the lines he suggests. At the same time, he has stimulated some thinkers to fashion fresh pragmatist aspirations of their own that involve conserving some of the very constraints on the conversations of philosophy that he wants abandoned. While not wishing to return to the empiricist framework of classic pragmatism or any associated metaphysics of realism, they are nevertheless keen to construct, within the space Rorty has created, a more substantial conception of objectivity, one that is, as Jeffrey Stout puts it, 'hospitable to the cognitive aspiration to get one's subject matter right'.[48]

Revivals of classic pragmatism and hence the ideas of Peirce, James and Dewey, new forms of pragmatism that break out on their own into uncharted territory, and revisionist attempts to mediate between such approaches, perhaps to the extent of reconciling pragmatism and analytic philosophy[49] – these are just some of the intriguing prospects that Rorty has made possible by his own endlessly fruitful, insightful and provocative encounters with pragmatism.

NOTES

1 Richard Rorty, 1998a, p. 8.
2 'In the 1970s Richard Rorty single-handedly brought into being a renaissance for pragmatism': Misak, 2010c, p. 27. Interestingly, the very first sentence of one of Rorty's first published academic papers, now half a century old, tells us 'Pragmatism is getting respectable again' (Rorty, 1961).
3 To be more accurate here, Rorty tends to rely on Sellars for wholesale ammunition against some of the presuppositions of the analytic tradition and does not try to induct him into the pragmatist hall of fame, whereas he does try to make Davidson and Wittgenstein into honorary pragmatists.
4 The bulk of the vast and ever-growing critical responses to Rorty's work since the publication of *Philosophy and the Mirror of Nature* (1979) have been negative, and rather dismissively so. However, it is worth mentioning that there has been something of a turning point in the quality and seriousness of Rorty criticism, with a number of prominent scholars, including Brandom (2000a), Ramberg (2000) and Price (2010), showing why Rorty's views merit serious consideration on a variety of fronts. The more substantial commentaries by Gascoigne (2008) and Tartaglia (2007) are also symptomatic of this encouraging development.
5 And, to state this a bit more carefully, as Rorty began to draw more attention to pragmatism, he kick-started a process of scholarly debate and investigation that must have gratified even some of those who dispute his whole conception of it. For there were at least two consequences that promised gratification. First, if only in the service of attempts to refute Rorty, the primary texts of pragmatism were explored in greater detail – witness the concerted efforts to show that Rorty misinterpreted Dewey in his controversial chapter 'Dewey's Metaphysics' (1982b, pp. 72–89): e.g. 'What Is the Legacy of Instrumentalism? Rorty's Interpretation of Dewey' (Gouinlock, 1995, pp. 72–90). And second, many philosophers who had no interest in, or were hostile to pragmatism, began to see various kinds of merit in it whether independently of Rorty's version or because of it.
6 Rorty, 2010a, p. 211.

7   Given that, as Richard Bernstein rightly says, 'the history of pragmatism has always been a conflict of narratives' (Bernstein, 1995a), it is worth pointing out that the 'pragmatist tradition' is itself still something of a contentious phrase. For further discussion of what is contentious here, see the introduction to the present volume.
8   One of Rorty's final comments on Peirce is indicative of why, despite having spent considerable time on his writings early on in his career, he later became rather scornful of them: 'Sellars and Peirce are alike in the diversity and richness of their talents, as well as in the cryptic style in which they wrote. But Sellars, unlike Peirce, preached a coherent set of doctrines' (Rorty, 2010a, p. 8).
9   For a well argued objection on these grounds see Nevo (1995a).
10 Most famously, and most provocatively: '[Peirce's] contribution to pragmatism was merely to have given it a name, and to have stimulated James', Rorty (1982a), p. 161.
11 Hence it is not surprising to see Richard Shusterman recently reporting that Rorty's well-known discussion in *Contingency, Irony, and Solidarity* (1989a) of a passage from a Philip Larkin poem was written on the basis of having lifted the lines in question from a magazine article and with no knowledge of the poem itself (Shusterman, 2011, p. 11).
12 Rorty, 1998c.
13 Rorty, 1998a, p. 3.
14 Thayer (1967, p. 435).
15 Thayer (1981, p. xviii).
16 The criticisms involved target distinctions, methodologies, positions and so forth within the analytic tradition without drawing conclusions that questioned the tradition as a whole.
17 A full account would also include Wittgenstein who Rorty reads as an arch debunker of both the foundations and general aspirations of analytic philosophy as formulated by Frege, Russell and his own earlier self.
18 Sellars, 1997.
19 Quine, 2004c.
20 Rorty, 1999a, p. 10.
21 Rorty, 1982a, p. 494. See Malachowski (2002b).
22 Rorty, 1999a, p. 35.
23 Dewey, 1958a, p. 3a.
24 This is not to deny that experience can be a very useful, and at times indispensable, reference point.
25 Rorty, 1989a, p. 14.
26 Rorty, 1998b, p. 292.
27 Davidson, 2006b, p. 265.

28 This moves rather quickly past the objection that closing the gap in this way amounts to linguistic idealism. A further worry is that Davidson is trying to do for the language/world gap what James and Dewey try to do for the experience/world gap.
29 Shusterman, 1999, p. 194.
30 Bernstein, 2010b.
31 Rorty's objections to the philosophical use of notions of experience focus on their connections with what he regards as defunct models of mind and of the mind's relationship to the world. These models embed the visual metaphors and the metaphysical apparatus of realism that he believes pragmatists can and should dispense with.
32 Rorty, 1995, p. 94.
33 Rorty, 2010b, p. 494.
34 Brodsky, 2004, p. 187.
35 Dewey, 1981, vol. 1, p. 18.
36 Rorty, 1989a, p. 7. Although Rorty has always adopted the melioristic stance of pragmatism and tied the idea of pragmatic success to social benefits, it is only in his later work that he explicitly identifies cultural change as the primary task of philosophy and cultural politics as the appropriate means. Rorty uses the term "cultural politics" as early as 1995 (see Saatkamp, 1995) but his considered views on what this term involves are only expressed later (see Rorty, 2007a).
37 Rorty, 1998b, p. 19.
38 Rorty's further point here is that in its pure practicality, as it were, the world cannot simply tell us or in any sense automatically determine for us what social policies we should adopt.
39 For an account of Davidson's philosophy of language that seems to have greatly influenced Rorty, see Ramberg (1989). It is important to note that while Rorty claims pragmatists can benefit from the linguistic turn, he does not want them to regard that turn as a turn in the direction of *having to* regard philosophical problems as just linguistic problems. See 'Wittgenstein and the Linguistic Turn', in Rorty, 2007d.
40 Wallace, 2011, p. 73. It should be pointed out that this is satire. Wallace probably did not think, and certainly did not want the reader to think, that Wittgenstein himself was overly eccentric in this way in his view of language.
41 James uses the phrase in describing how the pragmatist is more constrained 'than anyone else sees himself to be' (see p. 44 of the present volume).
42 Rorty, 1989a, p. 107.
43 For an interesting and well-developed argument to the effect that Rorty is wrong to regard metaphors as an additional source of motivation for belief revision over and above inference and perception, see Nevo, 1995b.

44 Davidson, 2006c.
45 Rorty, 2007c.
46 Bernstein, 2010a, pp. 214–15.
47 Malachowski, 2010.
48 Stout, 2009 p. 7.
49 Revisionist suggestions are made in Misak, 2009 and the possibility of rapprochement with analytic philosophy is explored in Brandom, 2010.

PART III

Pragmatism at work

MARJORIE C. MILLER

10 Pragmatism and feminism

There are standard ways to discuss feminism and pragmatism: who are the women whose voices need to be recovered to adequately understand classic pragmatism? How did these women, not merely as females, but as feminists, influence the development of classic pragmatism? What are the ways in which classical pragmatists repeated, and sometimes reinforced, the patriarchal biases of their day? What does classical pragmatism have to offer feminist philosophers today? And what are current feminist pragmatists contributing to both feminism and pragmatism? These are important questions, but good work is already addressing them. I would encourage all interested readers to begin with Judy Whipps's fine article 'Pragmatist Feminism' in the *On-Line Stanford Encyclopedia of Philosophy*, followed by reading Charlene Haddock Seigfried's fundamentally important work: *Pragmatism and Feminism: Reweaving the Social Fabric*.[1] I would hope the reader might follow up with the rich bibliographies each of these works offer. What I want to do is to take this opportunity as a committed pragmatist feminist to speak about some philosophical issues that matter to me just *as* a pragmatist feminist. In the course of my discussion I hope to make clear just how pragmatism and feminism can intersect effectively in addressing issues of concern to each.

The first topic of discussion has got to be to address just what can count as philosophy. In recent years some have questioned the philosophical bona fides of feminism. Pragmatism has often, especially during the mid-twentieth century, been looked upon askance – its right to be understood as serious philosophy doubted. Those of us who are writing in the twenty-first century are perhaps less preoccupied with these matters than earlier folk, but it still does seem important to be clear about what we are trying to do. Yes, both pragmatism and feminism have agendas. We pragmatists and we feminists engage in reflection in order to reconstruct the situations in which we find ourselves. We are not merely political – it is not enough to produce change. We are philosophical in that we want to analyse and understand and theorize in ways which will help us to produce intelligent change, and to learn from and redirect the changes which result from our actions. Both pragmatism and feminism reject the traditionally radical separations between thought and action, between theory and practice, between projects and objectivity. Feminists and pragmatists do not think that holding values antecedent to the theorizing which explores them is a problem for genuine philosophizing. Struggling for greater and freer growth for women, or struggling for flourishing human communities, does not seem at all inimical to careful and logical analyses of the sorts of general concerns and relations which are bound up in the problems we are trying to sort through. Philosophizing, for feminists and pragmatists, is a highly general sort of undertaking – but is not necessarily a second-order or third-order activity. It always, as James was wont to say, reaches down into experience, and returns to experience for its validation (that, of course, is a large part of why Jane Addams and Ella Flagg Young and Lucy Sprague Mitchell and Jessie Taft were busy being activists for and with women while learning from and developing the movement known as pragmatism).

Having addressed the question of how these two movements can be philosophy, I now need to address the strange question of how feminism can tackle a problem which appears to offer 'women' as a category. All of us who have engaged in feminism in the last thirty-or-so years know that the category is itself contested. The flourishing of human communities perhaps entails less of a conceptual problem than trying to further the flourishing of women. Who are women? Are we a biological grouping? A cultural construction? A sex? A gender? Does 'woman' mean the same thing, identify the same sort of person, in Seoul, in Soweto, in Lhasa, in New York, in Birmingham? In a village in Burundi? Is the need for women's growth even similar when discussing the glass ceiling for large industrial corporations or the burdens of child-rearing for a Bolivian villager? Surely, the differences matter. So feminist analysis is complicated, and insists always on being local and connected to the situations in which feminist issues emerge. It insists on intersections between economics, politics, race and gender. It is always historically and culturally engaged when analysis is undertaken. But the same is true for pragmatist theorizing. Pragmatism has always refused to deliver metaphysical, epistemological or ethical principles true for all times and places.² All the categories to be discussed are expected to be local and situated. So I needn't worry too much about conflict between my feminist and pragmatist methodologies.

The problem I want to address is the problem of democratic community. This is one of the central problems of pragmatism and I shall argue that it is also a central problem for feminism. Understood adequately, democratic community is the problem of our age. The lack of such community diminishes the opportunities for peaceful flourishing for all people, and it especially impinges on women's well-being. I hope to show that this is a crucial area, and one which is perhaps most effectively addressed in the intersection of feminism and pragmatism.

I shall begin by saying what I mean by democratic community, and then hope that I can develop its significance from the description. For Jane Addams, democracy is the way of life which entails genuine communication between all the parties concerned in an action or an outcome. Dewey credits Addams with teaching him that democracy is a way of life, rather than a particular political system of elections. What is this democracy as a way of life? It means that those engaged in a common project find their meaning and selfhood through the inter-determination of roles involved in pursuing the project. As Jane Addams said, in the two-part statement below:

[W]e have learned to say that the good must be extended to all of society before it can be held secure by any one person or any one class; but we have not learned to add to that statement, that unless all men and all classes contribute to a good, we cannot even be sure that it is worth having.

And she notes that it is because of a lack of democracy that 'In spite of many attempts we do not really act upon either [part of this] statement.'³

This description seems vague; but contrast it, if you will with projects undertaken by a leader who herself or himself decides what would be best for those whom the project is meant to serve. Such a project may be entirely benevolent in intent, but it is paternalistic and not democratic in nature. It is quite different from a project in which the needs and desires of all involved are mutually discussed and communicated, and in which the design of the project reflects those conjoint needs and desires. The latter model of action is, for Addams, Royce, G. H. Mead and John Dewey, the meaning of democracy, but it is also the meaning of community. John Dewey argues that 'Regarded as an idea, democracy is not an alternative to other principles of associated life. It is the idea of community life itself.'[4]

So a democratic community, according to the classic pragmatists, is a communicating community: one in which individuals become individuals by virtue of the ways in which they interact with and mutually determine the others with whom they are in communication.[5] Communities are more than associations. They entail shared meanings and shared purposes, with respect to which the members of a community find their own meanings and purposes in furthering the action of the community. This all sounds rather nice, but seems hardly an urgent matter. Why is it urgent? I take the Deweyan stance that without community we human beings lack secure individuality. We cannot become full selves unless we function in recognized and recognizable ways with others in functioning communities.[6] We find ourselves without identities. Notice that both communities and identities are given in the plural form. To be a fully developed individual, I must have a range of secure identities in relation to a plurality of functioning communities, which are able to communicate with one another – if I am not to be an individual alienated, closed, to my multiple locations; or a being lacking individuality altogether; or a being with a restricted individuality, limited to the one community in which I genuinely have a role.

Feminists certainly contest the desirability of community, but nevertheless its importance is generally recognized. As Audre Lord has said: 'Without community there is no liberation, only the most vulnerable and temporary armistice between an individual and her oppression.'[7] One of the problems in claiming that democratic community is a crucial issue is that the definition of community is so elusive. Clearly various communities can be profoundly oppressive. But I think *democratic* community, in so far as it is indeed democratic community, is *not* oppressive. Its precise shape, its relation to the various cultural, historical, geographic and purposive settings cannot be defined in advance. One of the features of pragmatism which makes it so useful for feminist analysis is, as we have noted, the intimate relation between theory and practice. Hence, we cannot theorize community in advance of the practical engagement with many communities, out of which theory grows. And it is only with the growth of theoretical understanding that the practices can be changed and organized to better promote the liberatory projects of feminism and pragmatism.

The simplest (and most controversial) of communities is the family – that association in which each member has a clearly defined role and an assured identity within that role. In a well-functioning family, each member shares in the development of the well-being of the whole community, each has a role to play, each has a contribution to make, each cares about the well-being of the community, each helps to determine the success of the community. Of course, not all families are well functioning. In fact the family has been perhaps the greatest source of patriarchal oppression in history. But, just assuming that there could be a well-functioning and non-patriarchal family, we still have a problem. For many cultures and in many times women have been limited to the family as the *only* community in which they have individuality. Clearly this is a diminishment of the development of women's flourishing. In most cultures, in most places, men have been part of school communities, work communities, political communities and economic communities. So there is a long and varied history of the ways in which the lack of multiple community involvements for women does indeed become a feminist issue. But further, in the much more open societies of the present developed and developing worlds, there is still a serious problem of community – for women and men. I want to focus first on the problems that impinge on all of us, and then to talk more specifically about the problems that weigh disproportionately or uniquely on contemporary women.

John Dewey began his work *The Public and its Problems* with a chapter called 'The Divided Mind'. He argued that the values we are taught, the values we as individuals hold or would like to hold, are in direct conflict with the values which animate and promote the socio/cultural/economic lives in which we participate. The dominant direction of the development of social institutions has only been fiercely reinforced since Dewey's day. We participate in a world driven by corporate and media values of material, pecuniary, quantitative, competitive attempts to achieve the life presented for us as both necessary and ideal. But, as Dewey pointed out, our individual satisfaction, the accomplishments which can bring us individual realization, can be made real only within the context of the societies within which we function. Social habits and social institutions must be capable of promoting the realization we crave as individuals. And currently (in both the 1920s when Dewey was writing, and today, in the twenty-first century) they do not. Dewey describes what he calls 'pathological social phenomena' writing in 1930. We would have no trouble describing such phenomena by summarizing the articles in our current newspapers, by watching the behaviour of our students, or by examining our own discontents. But Dewey says that: these are

> evidence, psychologically, of abnormality, and it is idle to seek for their explanation within the deliberate intent of individuals as it is futile to think that they can be got rid of by hortatory moral appeal. Only an acute maladjustment between individuals and the social conditions under which they live can account for such widespread pathological phenomena.[8]

Restructuring is required. And, Dewey argued, genuine restructuring requires not revolution but community and community action.

Why community? Each of us who has participated in community knows all too well the number of failures our attempts at real change have produced. Why stress community, then? In large part because whatever successes have been achieved in reconstructing the social order (limited and imperfect though these changes may be) have only come about through community involvement: labour communities, civil rights communities and feminist communities have made a difference in the structures and institutions which now are interacting to realize individuals who are positioned to continue to change. Will they be fully effective? I am not optimistic. But it does seem to me that it is only in and through democratic communities that evolving change can be intelligently directed and can ameliorate the oppressions and diremptions which alienate us from ourselves and from each other.

Democratic community is difficult to achieve. In some sense, it is epitomized by the face-to-face local community which allows for relatively supportive deliberative determination of the direction and actions of the whole community (not a majority rule, but a strong communicative community which allows all voices to be heard and responded to). But this notion of face-to-face community has been critiqued by some as absurdly unrealistic, and by feminists as insisting on precisely the locality, the localization, which has always given some power to women, but has made us impotent with respect to the larger national and multinational institutions which are the traditional province of men, and which do, in fact, make the determinations which most affect our lives.[9] While I appreciate the critique, I want to argue that it is in face-to-face communities that we are able to develop the habits of democratic communication which then allow us to join other communities – less localized, less limited in time and space, in culture, or in history. But this process of communicating with ever-wider communities is not continuous. It is our base in a given community that allows us to join other communities. Communities, to be effective and meaningful, demand that we have some loyalty to both the shared values the particular community embodies and to the members of the community as far as they share in these values. As we join multiple communities, we must be able to help those communities to communicate with one another, in order to avoid completely chaotic loyalties. As Dewey puts it in developing what he calls the 'democratic idea in its generic social sense':

> From the standpoint of the individual, it consists in having a responsible share according to capacity in forming and directing the activities of the groups to which one belongs and in participating according to need in the values which the groups sustain. From the standpoint of the groups, it demands liberation of the potentialities of members of a group in harmony with the interests and goods which are common. Since every individual is a member of many groups, this specification cannot be fulfilled except when different groups interact flexibly and fully in connection with other groups ... There is a free give-and-take: fullness of integrated personality is therefore possible of achievement, since the pulls and responses of different groups reinforce one another and their values accord. Regarded as an idea, democracy is not an alternative to other principles of associated life. It is the idea of community itself.[10]

This notion of community is of course an ideal. But Dewey indeed recognizes it as an ideal. 'Democracy in this sense is not a fact and never will be. But neither in this sense is there or has there ever been anything which is a community in its full measure.'[11] Still, the ideal has a great deal of value in encouraging us to see what community does mean and could, if projected into full and unimpeded development, become. The value of community is not dependent on the realization of the ideal. The ideal is, in this sense, a prescription for the ultimate meaning of community, rather than a specific description of current behaviour. It is developing the direction of those actions through which we work at creating *greater* community out of the associations in which we participate. It encourages us to go on meliorating – rather than holding a utopian vision irrelevant to our present situations.

I would like to examine three more of Dewey's claims before going on to the more directly feminist discussions of community. First, Dewey claims that an adequate understanding of freedom, of liberty, must not be taken as 'freedom from'. He argues that:

> Liberty is that secure release and fulfillment of personal potentialities which take place only in rich and manifold association with others: the power to be an individualized self making a distinctive contribution and enjoying in its own way the fruits of association.[12]

In short, it is in and through community that freedom is meaningfully realized. As noted below, this may be problematic if we are discussing oppression – feminists want very much to insist that 'freedom from' matters here! But ending oppression is hardly possible, I think, without a vision of what liberatory existence would be – and Dewey is here arguing that liberatory existence is meaningful only in the sorts of democratic communities he is envisioning. Free existence is played out in such communities, though freedom from oppression may require us to reconstruct the institutional structures which oppress us. It is by working toward ideal communities that the ideal of liberty becomes realized in effective action.

The second point I want to make is that Dewey takes community life as moral – he argues that association is physical and organic and always present, but 'community life is moral, that is emotionally, intellectually, consciously sustained'.[13] If we take seriously the notion that community life is moral, we take seriously, I think, the importance of finding ways not merely to accommodate ourselves or others to the community's methods and goals, but to further precisely those goods which community life makes possible: 'the fulfillment of personal potentialities ... the power to be an individualized self making a distinctive contribution and enjoying in its own way the fruits of association'. The moral demand is that we develop ourselves in this way, and develop all the others with whom we are in community. Further, the demands of morality, as Dewey notes them, are that we develop social intelligence supported by commitment consciously furthered, to enhance the goals and values of the community. We are to be enabled not only to work toward the accomplishment of future projects but to experience in the present recognition of immediate enjoyments: to have aesthetic and consummatory experiences. Such experience, for Dewey, requires conscious awareness of the relations between the actions we participate in, the feelings we encounter, and the achievements of the deliberative harmony which is possible.

Finally, before leaving Dewey I want to discuss his conception of equality as it applies to communities. Dewey argues:

> Equality denotes the unhampered share which each individual member of the community has in the consequences of associated action. It is equitable because it is measured only by need and capacity to utilize, not by extraneous factors which deprive one in order that another may take and have ... Equality does not signify that kind of mathematical or physical equivalence in virtue of which any one element may be substituted for another. It denotes effective regard for whatever is distinctive and unique in each, irrespective of physical and psychological inequalities. It is not a natural possession but is a fruit of the community when its action is directed by its character as a community.[14]

This is a rich and wonderful and open description. It echoes much that I would argue for as a feminist. But it is clearly dangerous for feminists. Such views have too often, in too many situations, depended on the way the community defined 'need' and 'capacity to utilize' – and the definitions arrived at were all 'normally' those severely detrimental to women. It sounds so inspiring. But all we need think about is the way in which such an early figure as Aristotle might have subscribed to such a view: for Aristotle, clearly women's capacities, their limited ability to utilize reason, made their needs such as to require direction from those competent to direct. Namely, of course, free men. I am confident that Dewey would not have worked it out this way. Nevertheless, while I am reasonably sure that his prejudices were not consciously held, some of the patriarchal prejudices Dewey possessed allowed him to benefit inequably from communities which women developed and fostered. Jane Addams in Hull House, Lucy Sprague Mitchell in Bank Street, to name only two examples, contributed quite significantly to the growing pragmatist tradition, and particularly to Dewey's ideas about community and education. But their contributions were only nominally acknowledged in his work. The benefits of communal association between these women and Dewey resulted in less than full equality. Dewey seems to have defined their capacities and needs in ways that did not allow them full and public acknowledgement for their influence on his ideas.[15] What this demonstrates is not only the patriarchal side of ostensibly feminist John Dewey, but the fact that communities, as Dewey himself noted, are always less than ideal. Problematically, their failings tend precisely towards the disempowering of those belonging to the marginalized: women and men from minority groups, economically disadvantaged groups, and women as a class. Indeed an appropriate concern for the anti-community feminists!

Then why, as a pragmatist-feminist, am I arguing for democratic community? Because I think the rich roles for community as developed by pragmatists – by the Dewey whose theories I have been quoting, but also by Jane Addams and Ella Flagg Young and Lucy Sprague Mitchell – serve as an irreplaceable visioning of liberatory models. Imperfect, to be sure. But crucial for the reconstruction of oppressive and restrictive institutions. Yes, such communities imperfectly realized may indeed themselves prove oppressive and restrictive. But they are the loci from which intelligent and committed reconstruction can continue to take place.

What matters, I think, is that undercutting of binaries, of either/or's, which is common to both many feminists and to all the pragmatists. The most basic binary, here, is the separation of a 'bad' past from a 'good' future. This move is made as if there is a sharp dividing line between past and future, as well as a sharp division between 'good' and 'bad'. I think it better to talk of continua: the future moves into the present, and itself becomes the past. There is no sharp dividing line. The crucial thing is not to establish the future as absolutely Other than the present or past. Evolution, that powerful notion which was so central a stimulus to the development of pragmatism, makes clear that changes accumulate. Changes of all sorts produce the introduction of new species, the development of some species, and the destruction of others. There is no end to changing. There is no final stage which we can pronounce good or bad, as James would have it, until the last person has had her experiences and said her say.[16] So the task is, as pragmatists insist, to make better, to meliorate. We can make our situations better, we can address the problems which discourage and frustrate us. We can resolve some problems, though, of course, new ones will emerge. Making things better does not require that we achieve the ideal. It requires that we address particular problems and situations now. We will have successes and failures. They will matter only in so far as we are able to utilize the experiences as the basis for more effective theorizing of the nature of the institutions that oppress us, the nature of the oppression, and the actions to be undertaken in response. We can then test those theories in further action, and so refine the theories. But, as the pragmatists make clear, we cannot test the theories as isolated individuals. It is only in the context of the experiences of the communities and environments in which we act that our theories are validated or disconfirmed. This is a view shared by all of the pragmatists. This view is central to pragmatic metaphysics, epistemology and ethics.

This view of community depends on something too often ignored in the contemporary communitarianism which so often elicits feminist ire.[17] That is, this view depends on diversity, on pluralism, on difference. It sees community not as a locally rooted stronghold of traditional shared values, but rather as an interdependent set of relationships between individuals in which participants act to create the values they share; to join their wisdom and their voices in challenging the problems they discover themselves to be facing together; to participate in the sort of debate which clarifies their own positions and allows them to learn from one another. Community as the source and the arena for testing theories and beliefs is crucial to the creation of more enduring truths. Not final truths. Fallible truths. But more reliable truths! Truths need to be enacted and reacted to. They need to play out among diverse experiences and diverse subjects in order to be intersubjectively supported. Further, it is only in diverse communities that novelty can be both born and sustained. Pluralism, difference, are the bases of interdependence and social intelligence. Homogeneity does not preclude new ideas, but it discourages them. It has less space for imagination than heterogeneity provides. Values that are taken for granted in homogenous communities are effectively critiqued when confronted by different values, developed in experiences which reveal different possibilities and conditions. Dewey and other pragmatists, even including William James, indeed do discuss the benefits of diversity. But it is Jane Addams and others of the feminist pragmatists who tie the notion of diversity most closely to their understandings of community.

Jane Addams is a prime example of an early feminist pragmatist whose view of community remains of value for continued feminist work. She began with a location: Hull House, set intentionally in the middle of the Chicago slums. She was determined to mix classes and cultures and ethnicities, in an interdependent community wherein the classes and groups could learn from one another. She and the women who settled with her in the house – educated, accomplished, by-and-large bourgeois women – depended on their poor, mostly immigrant neighbours, to teach them about cultures and views and needs and habits which were not their own. They depended on the slum-dwellers to help them to live more meaningful lives than the bourgeois marriages that their families foresaw would have allowed them to live. The neighbours depended on the women of Hull House to help them to become open to the world of possibilities that Hull House represented: they communicated their needs and the women of Hull House got them clubhouse and gym facilities for their kids, open kitchens where cooking and food preparation could be more effectively learned and shared, nurseries to care for their children, help with difficult births, the opportunity to make art, and the negotiating skills to obtain better social services (among an enormous number of other interactions between the women of Hull House, the people of the neighbourhood, and the many visitors who came to give lectures or readings or to chat and participate). The community around and in Hull House is example enough of a democratic community which did not reinforce traditional values, but worked to create new values out of the interdependence of the diverse community. But much more happened. Addams's involvement in the local neighbourhood of Hull House became entwined with her involvements in other communities – in Chicago, in the nation, in the world. She became an activist for workers' rights, working with trade unionists in community. She joined women across the nation and internationally to fight for suffrage rights. She involved herself in educational communities beyond the Hull House community. Eventually she became co-founder of the Women's International League for Peace and Freedom, and worked with other communities committed to peace work in Europe and America during the First World War (for which she received the Nobel Peace Prize in 1931). The communities Addams built or was engaged in were always diverse, and they were always critical and creative. They were not warm, fuzzy, nests of tradition. They were bold and experimental and aimed at melioration of mutually recognized problems and the creation of shared possibilities. They were not all local, and they were not all face to face. But it was her engagement in the Hull House community that gave Addams the base from which to develop the social intelligence which allowed her to recognize continually new problems – not just to generate new solutions.

Her experimental work produced new theoretical understandings – of the intersections of class and gender, for example, and of the relation between war and women's roles. And the new theoretical understandings produced new communal activities and new communities. And these, in turn, continued to contribute to renew theorizing. The communities in which Addams was engaged were not maws in which her autonomy was devoured. They were settings which genuinely liberated her, and her fellows, to develop themselves as productive and significant individuals.

Feminists and pragmatists, pragmatist feminists, have limited energy, however. While the sorts of activities in which we are engaged cannot be sharply divided between theory and action, the majority of our time may be spent in communities of social reformers or in academic communities. As philosophers, we pragmatist/feminists take perhaps a broader view, engage in more abstract discussion, commit to a more critical approach, than that taken by our sisters whose primary engagement is with social workers, or lawyers, or protest groups or neighbourhood associations or international reform movements. But this is again a matter of continua: our focus on philosophy is invalidated if it does not take account of the diverse experiences provided by those primarily focused on 'field' work, and it is equally invalidated if it does not provide greater understanding of the connections and bearings and meanings that feed back into that 'field' work. Our philosophy is incomplete if it does not bring us into contact with that experience which feeds it and which it is reordering. Pragmatist feminists discover both a philosophic and a moral duty to involve our flesh and our spirit as well as our brains, to engage in the organizing work which makes community possible and enriching. Pragmatist feminists discover the moral duty of solidarity in community with diverse others – without diversity our communities become settings for indoctrination rather than sources of social intelligence.

Interestingly, many of us engaged in contemporary academic communities do have access to diversity within our communities if we consciously undertake to create communities in our classrooms, among our majors, across the faculty, with the senior citizens who may take our classes and interact with us and our students, to say nothing of the larger academic communities created by our philosophical interests – across national and international lines. We have diversity of age, diversity of experience, diversity of culture, race, class and gender. This is especially true for those of us who teach in state universities or near big cities. These communities can be nourishing and liberating if they are seen and experienced *as* communities by all involved. But this does require conscious, active, emotional, and intellectual commitment.[18]

Before leaving the discussion of pragmatist-feminist community there are two points that we need to go back to: the discussion of equality and my claim that community in this democratic sense is both a good thing and an urgent thing. First, the question of equality. Above, I provided a quotation from Dewey which read, in part:

Equality does not signify that kind of mathematical or physical equivalence in virtue of which any one element may be substituted for another. It denotes effective regard for whatever is distinctive and unique in each, irrespective of physical and psychological inequalities. It is not a natural possession but is a fruit of the community when its action is directed by its character as a community.[19]

There was an additional piece of the quotation which claimed that 'it is equitable because it is measured only by need and capacity to utilize'. It is this part of the quotation that gave rise to the problems that I think feminists might find in the attempt to define 'equitable'. Saying that 'the community' decides 'need' and 'capacity to utilize' invites the sorts of power distortions from which disadvantaged groups continually suffer. Because of these distortions, many feminists have insisted on 'absolute' equality in any feminist community. The avoidance of any hint of hierarchical power distribution has come to be a hallmark of the intentional communities which feminists support. But is this either necessary, or always appropriate or productive of the sorts of communities which will function to liberate individuals and reconstruct social institutions? My feminist training says always pay attention to where the power is and how it is being exercised; my pragmatist training says that there are productive re-visionings to be made here.

Let's go back to the classroom community, and the academic community, alluded to before. A study group differs from a classroom community. The classroom does include a member with more extensive experience, more thorough reflection on a particular subject, and more training in a discipline than most others in the classroom. That person, the professor, is neither infallible nor omniscient, of course, but nevertheless the professor is, and should be, in a position of leadership in the community. Leadership means that the professor takes responsibility for providing reading lists, selecting appropriate texts, and providing an interpretative framework. But in so far as the classroom is a community, the students' needs and interests have some role in the ongoing debate about the meanings of what is read, the procedures to be followed, and the engagement with the values the material opens up. When the community is diverse, the perspectives brought to bear may open new channels of interpretation; the students may have suggestions for procedures which help the community as a whole to deal with the material in ways which enrich the dialogue. The dialogue is valued by the whole community as deepening the grasp of the issues that the professor has pointed to as requiring interpretation and debate, and which the students have come to recognize as goods to be grasped. The community shares the values of inquiry and values the understanding to be gained. But its members are not, as Dewey noted, mathematically equivalent or substitutable. In addition to the expertise of the teacher there will be differences in the contributions students can make: some are too shy to want to talk freely, others are perhaps overly eager to monopolize the discussions. Some are widely read, others much less so. Some have had a great deal of experience, being older, and some have had less. The exchanges will depend, indeed, on capacity to participate and the need to become informed. It cannot be 'mathematically equal'. Such equality would undermine community, not support it. The kind of equitable engagement which allows for shifting hierarchies depending on the situations of the persons involved is not at all anti-feminist, it is crucial to genuine community.

So, how do we address distortions of power in communities? Dewey once said that the cure for democracy is more democracy. In some sense this is rather glib. But there is some legitimacy to it. If, as is indeed often the case, there are oppressions in the communities in which we participate, sometimes the answer is to form new communities. This is, I think, what happened in Addams's own engagement with new communities, with the civil rights movement and the feminist movement and in third wave feminism. Sometimes, in order to gain the power of sisterhood, sisters must form distinctly feminist communities. Sometimes, in order to gain the power of black sisterhood, or lesbian sisterhood, black women or lesbian women must form separate communities. But, as Dewey noted before the notion of identity communities was so prevalent, we belong to many communities. Some lesbians are black women. Some black women are lesbians. I am now both an ageing woman and a partially disabled woman. I find that I am in solidarity with some groups of ageing persons, and some groups of disabled persons, as well as with many feminist groups. Our communities are communities within which we genuinely communicate – they are democratic communities. However, as we noted early on, our communities must be capable of communicating with each other, or our necessarily multiple identities become fragmented and begin to fall apart. It is in the communication of communities with each other that we have the opportunity to speak truth to power. It is in the power which solidarity gives us that we are empowered to challenge the power distortions in other communities in which we find ourselves oppressed.

But why see community as an urgent need right now? I am currently sitting in South Korea as North Korea threatens to 'see Seoul in flames'. I am an American who cringes with shame and horror as drones, decorated with American flags, wreak havoc in Pakistan and Afghanistan. I am saddened as I read of the plight of the people and animals of the Gulf of Mexico as oil continues to spurt inexorably into the waters. I am depressed by the inaction of the world in the face of the global warming which will cause certain pain to the dwellers on the sea islands and which is already causing dangerous changes to weather patterns and loss of species and diversity on our planet. And I am deeply pained as I see the widening gulf between rich and poor, between those who live in luxury and those who suffer starvation and deprivation and misery. I am shocked at the increases in senseless, horrific violence in almost every country of the world. And I am alarmed at the high suicide rates in developed and developing countries. Finally, I am concerned for my sisters who still suffer the physical, emotional and financial consequences of misogyny – the costs are overwhelming, and continue to be felt by women around the globe. So what can community have to do with these very powerful challenges to human well-being? Why worry about community when the world appears to be falling apart?

We need to worry about community because it is all we have. It is only, I have argued, through community that we become individuals capable of changing the situations in which we find ourselves, capable of creating social change as communities create us. We create our communities as they create us – and it is through our communities that we have the possibility of effecting social reconstruction. Pragmatism insists on this. As a pragmatist feminist I find the philosophical commitments which help me address the feminist projects I am engaged in through the resources and models pragmatism and pragmatists have provided.

NOTES

1 Whipps, 2008; Haddock Seigfried, 1996.
2 A carefully nuanced discussion would show that there are problems with my claim, here, if applied as a blanket claim to all that Peirce, James, and Dewey have written (to identify the major classic pragmatists). But I believe my claim can be defended against the problematic instances if the defence is sufficiently developed. But that is the subject for another chapter!
3 Addams, 2002, p. 97.

4 Dewey, 'Search for the Great Community', in *The Public and Its Problems*, LW2: 328.
5 'To learn to be human is to develop through the give-and-take of communication an effective sense of being an individually distinctive member of a community': LW2: 330.
6 See Dewey, LW2:330.
7 Lorde, 1984, p. 112.
8 Dewey, 'The Lost Individual', *Individualism Old and New*, LW5: 67.
9 See, for example the discussion of Barbara Ehrenreich's critique offered by Penny Weiss in the introduction to Weiss and Friedman, 1995.
10 Dewey, LW2: 328.
11 Dewey, LW2: 328.
12 Dewey, LW2: 328–9.
13 Dewey, LW2: 329.
14 Dewey, LW2: 329.
15 I should not like to be inaccurate here. Indeed Dewey did give effusive acknowledgement to the communities (and their female members) to whom he is indebted for his own ideas. But the acknowledgement tended to be in letters, or at best in prefaces – not in the body of the works for which he became so well known as a philosopher. See, for further discussion of this point, especially the work of Charlene Haddock Seigfried, noted earlier.
16 From William James, 1979, p. 141, shamelessly modified to eliminate the sexist language of the original.
17 Note particularly the views of Amitai Etzioni as particularly connected to the term communitarianism, especially his early work: *The Spirit Of Community Rights, Responsibilities and the Communitarian Agenda* (1993). His views are particularly conservative and problematic for feminists – who often take his work as the work defining the advocacy of community.
18 Recall the earlier quote from Dewey, 'community life is moral, that is emotionally, intellectually, consciously sustained'.
19 See above, p. 239.

CAROL NICHOLSON

11 Education and the pragmatic temperament

The 'pragmatic temperament' is a flexible habit of mind that is not committed to any ideology or philosophical system and is compatible with a variety of philosophical approaches. Many interpreters have attempted to capture the spirit of pragmatism in a definition, which has resulted in some interesting paradoxes. 'Pragmatism cannot be defined', wrote the Italian pragmatist Giovanni Papini in 1906. 'Whoever gives a definition of pragmatism in a few words would be doing the most antipragmatic thing imaginable.' According to Papini, the dominant feature of pragmatism is 'the plasticity or flexibility of theories and beliefs, that is, the recognition of their purely instrumental value ... their value being only relative to an end or group of ends which are susceptible to being changed, varied, and transformed when needed'.[1] In 1908, when Arthur O. Lovejoy (1965) distinguished 'thirteen pragmatisms', some of which contradicted each other, the British pragmatist F. C. S. Schiller welcomed the idea that 'there are as many pragmatisms as there are pragmatists'.[2] A century later, after the ideas of C. S. Peirce, William James and John Dewey had been further developed by later twentieth-century philosophers and recently revived by Richard Rorty, there are many more pragmatists and many more varieties of pragmatism and neo-pragmatism. A reviewer of the *Blackwell Companion to Pragmatism* recently pointed out that there is so much disagreement among scholars about the nature of pragmatism that readers of the literature on the wide-ranging debate may 'be left with the impression that pragmatism is something so broad that it is hard to fathom'.[3]

I am grateful to Catharine Forbes, Lucien Frary, Robert Good, and Guy Stroh for their comments and helpful suggestions.

There is no consensus about what sets pragmatism apart from other philosophical movements or about its most significant contribution to the history of philosophy. According to Robert Westbrook, 'American pragmatism has always been less a coherent philosophical school or movement than a philosophical family – often a contentious family – of thinkers holding distinct if related positions on the "workmanlike" nature of knowledge, meaning, and truth.'[4] Philosophers debate about such issues as whether Peirce's or James's version of pragmatism is the best one to follow and whether or not Rorty's version of neo-pragmatism betrays the legacy of Dewey. In their views on education the differences between pragmatists are so stark as to be apparently in complete contradiction. Dewey argues that 'philosophy is the theory of education as a deliberately conducted practice', and thus all philosophy is philosophy of education.[5] Rorty, on the other hand, is 'dubious about the relevance of philosophy to education', suggesting that there is no such thing as philosophy of education.[6] John Patrick Diggins describes pragmatism as having a 'split personality' because of the many internal disputes between contemporary philosophers who call themselves pragmatists.[7]

The standard interpretation of pragmatism is that it is an American philosophical movement that emerged in the early 1870's in regular meetings near Harvard University of the 'Metaphysical Club,' an informal group of young intellectuals including C. S. Peirce and William James. This account is somewhat misleadingly narrow and simplistic, because pragmatism is not exclusively American, its main themes are much older than the nineteenth century, and it is not even primarily 'philosophical', at least in the academic sense of the term. I interpret pragmatism as an international, multicultural and interdisciplinary movement of thought and social practices which has had a profound cultural impact; but in spite of a brief period in the early twentieth century during which Dewey's ideas were popular (and in many circles notorious), its success in making lasting changes in education has been minimal. My hypothesis is that the prevailing interpretation of pragmatism as a movement within philosophy departments of American universities has limited its potential to influence education in the ways that the early pragmatists anticipated. I propose a broader view of pragmatism as a habit of mind that is open to uncertainty, change and different points of view, which I call the 'pragmatic temperament'. Many philosophical theories (e.g. naturalism, historicism, the pragmatic theory of truth, pluralism,

Education and the pragmatic temperament 251

anti-foundationalism, etc.) have been adopted by those who call themselves pragmatists. The intention here is to identify the least common denominator of the many varieties of pragmatism as a way of thinking that is best described in terms of adverbs rather than nouns ending in 'ism'. I shall explore some of the implications of this 'adverbial' interpretation of pragmatism for education in the hope that a broader view of pragmatism will contribute to a better appreciation of the potential of the movement for educational change.

Many intellectual historians assume that pragmatism is a distinctively American movement and explain its origins as a response to the new challenges of the frontier[8] or a reaction against the ideological certainties of the Civil War.[9] These approaches are useful for understanding the intellectual climate in which pragmatism arose in the United States, but they do not take account of British pragmatism, represented by F. C. S. Schiller, and the many pragmatists in France and Italy in the late nineteenth and early twentieth centuries. Schiller acknowledged the influence of James, but he claimed to have arrived at his pragmatic position independently in reaction to the absolute idealism of the British Hegelians. The Italian pragmatists, particularly Giovanni Papini and Giuseppe Prezzolini, borrowed from Schiller and James, but their versions of pragmatism arose in the context of their criticism of politics in Italy, which at that time was dominated by oratory instead of action. A number of French philosophers, including Henri Bergson, Maurice Blondel, Emile Boutroux, Pierre Duhen, Edouard Le Roy, Henri Poincaré and Georges Sorel, were receptive to James's views, but most of them had already developed similar lines of thought.[10]

The early pragmatists did not believe that their ideas were new or revolutionary. Schiller looked back to Protagoras in the fifth century BCE as the first pragmatist. Peirce called Jesus a pragmatist and thought that the saying 'By their fruits ye shall know them' was an early version of his pragmatic maxim that the meaning of ideas is to be found in their practical consequences. The subtitle of James's *Pragmatism* was 'A New Name for Some Old Ways of Thinking', and he dedicated the book 'To the memory of John Stuart Mill from whom I first learned the pragmatic openness of mind and whom my fancy likes to picture as our leader were he alive to-day'. James suggests that Peirce's pragmatic rule only made explicit the empirical attitude of the British philosophers, but Peirce claims that his term 'pragmatism' was derived from Kant's distinction between *praktisch* and *pragmatisch*. Although they disagree on the details, Peirce and James agree in thinking that pragmatism is a further development of ideas already present in British and European philosophy.

Recent interpretations of pragmatism place the movement in a broader context by challenging the idea that it is a product of exclusively European influences and exploring its wider social origins outside academic philosophy. Cornel West argues that Ralph Waldo Emerson was an 'organic intellectual' who anticipated the main themes of American pragmatism and encouraged it to 'swerve from mainstream European philosophy'.[11] I have argued elsewhere that Emerson was an important influence on landscape architect Frederick Law Olmsted, whose vision of the connection between public parks and the ideal of democracy inspired Walt Whitman's poetry and anticipated pragmatic themes later developed by John Dewey.[12] According to West, the most important twentieth-century successors in Emerson's pragmatic project of social transformation towards a 'culture of creative democracy' were 'no longer white Yankees but rather two second-generation Jewish Americans, Sidney Hook and Lionel Trilling, a second-generation American of German extraction, Reinhold Niebuhr; an Irish Southwesterner, C. Wright Mills; and a fifth-generation American of African descent, W. E. B. Du Bois'. West argues that 'Du Bois provides American pragmatism with what it sorely lacks: an international perspective ... that highlights the plight of the wretched of the earth'.[13] Charlene Haddock Siegfried highlights the influence of women's experiences and the early feminist movement on pragmatism, especially Jane Addams's writings and work at the Hull House settlement in Chicago, which deeply influenced James's and Dewey's ideas on education and social reform.[14] Scott L. Pratt points out that ways of thinking indigenous to North America, in addition to European ideas, were an important influence on the climate of thought in which American pragmatism emerged. He argues that such figures as Roger Williams and Benjamin Franklin, who had close contact with Native American communities, were instrumental in communicating to early European settlers the indigenous peoples' attitude of openness to different points of view and their concept of a pluralist community. Pratt suggests that pragmatism in America originated 'along the border between Native and European America as an attitude of resistance against the dominant attitudes of European colonialism'.[15]

Philosophers may object that if pragmatism is so broad as to include poets, community organizers, gardeners and American Indians, the concept is in danger of becoming meaningless. It might seem reasonable to assume, as most interpreters do, that because Peirce, James and Dewey (as well as Rorty and other neo-pragmatists) are all part of the same tradition, there must be a common core of doctrines that they agree upon, or at least some beliefs that pragmatists share in the way of 'family resemblances'. This assumption can be challenged, however, on the grounds that pragmatism was not originally intended to be a 'philosophy' in the usual sense of the word. All of the early pragmatists emphasized that pragmatism is not a system of thought or a specific solution to philosophical problems, but it is an attitude or a way of thinking. According to Papini, 'Pragmatism is really less a philosophy than a method of doing without philosophy.'[16] Peirce's 'The Fixation of Belief' gives the clearest (and wittiest) introduction to pragmatism by contrasting the pragmatic habit of mind with the other available means of forming opinions – the 'method of tenacity', the 'method of authority', and the 'a priori method'.[17] He defends the 'scientific method' of treating ideas as hypotheses to be tested by their publicly observable consequences as the only way of fixing belief that is self-correcting and does not stand in the way of the progress of knowledge. The contemporary reader might be misled by the term 'method' into thinking that pragmatism is a formal set of rules of philosophical procedure, but clearly Peirce had in mind the commonsense meaning of the term 'method' as simply a way of doing things. Pragmatism is a 'method', as Peirce describes it with tongue firmly in cheek, in the same sense that stubbornness, bowing to political and religious authorities, or going along with what seems reasonable are 'methods' of arriving at beliefs. He proposes pragmatism as an alternative to traditional ways of thinking in terms of the following rule: 'Do not block the way of inquiry', which he thinks 'deserves to be inscribed upon every wall in the city of philosophy' and is perhaps the only 'categorical imperative' with which every pragmatist and neo-pragmatist would agree.[18]

According to James, pragmatism 'stands for no particular results. It has no dogmas, and no doctrines save its method.' It is 'only an attitude of orientation ... the attitude of looking away from first things, principles, categories, supposed necessities; and of looking towards last things, consequences, facts'. James argues that although pragmatism is 'only' a method, 'the general triumph of that method would mean an enormous change in ... the "temperament" of philosophy'.[19] Dewey describes pragmatism as a

> disposition ... as obnoxious to ultimate philosophic truth as it is repellant to certain temperaments ... It discourages dogmatism and its child, intolerance. It arouses and heartens an experimental spirit which wants to know how systems and theories work before giving complete adhesion.[20]

He argues that one of the main goals of pragmatic education is to encourage 'intellectual hospitality', defined as 'an attitude of mind which actively welcomes suggestions and relevant information from all sides' and 'points of view hitherto alien', a disposition necessary to intellectual growth. Good educational methods, according to Dewey, develop 'flexible intellectual interest' and an 'open-minded will to learn', but

> open-mindedness is not the same as empty-mindedness. To hang out a sign saying, "Come right in; there is no one at home" is not the equivalent of hospitality. But there is a kind of passivity, willingness to let experiences accumulate and sink in and ripen, which is an essential of development.[21]

Peirce, James and Dewey disagree in many of their philosophical views, but they all agree that the pragmatic approach can best be described as a habit of mind, an attitude, or a disposition of being open to new ideas and experiences, rather than as a definitive solution to philosophical problems.

Richard Bernstein argues that pragmatism should not be interpreted as 'a set of doctrines or even a method'. He writes, 'We can best appreciate the vitality and diversity of this tradition when we approach it as an ongoing engaged conversation consisting of distinctive – sometimes competing – voices.'[22] In my own view, the most successful attempts to identify the unifying themes of pragmatism follow Bernstein's advice that the movement should not be treated as a school of thought, as well as Papini's earlier warning about the difficulty of defining it. By this criterion, Louis Menand gives one of the best brief summaries of the common core of the pragmatists' attitude: 'The belief that ideas should never become ideologies – either justifying the status quo, or dictating some transcendent imperative for renouncing it – was the essence of what they taught.'[23] But the temptation to view pragmatism itself as an ideology has been difficult to avoid, even for some of its most distinguished interpreters. Bernstein seems to forget his own admonition against thinking of pragmatism as a set of doctrines when he lists a series of 'isms', including anti-foundationalism, fallibilism and pluralism, in identifying the themes that characterize the pragmatic style of thinking.[24] Similarly, Rorty somewhat inconsistently relies on "isms" to characterize his version of neo-pragmatism. In the preface to his last book of collected essays, he endorses Dewey's view that 'Philosophy is not in any sense whatever a form of knowledge.' It is instead, 'a social hope reduced to a working program of action, a prophecy of the future'. And yet, on the same page, Rorty describes his revival of pragmatism as an attempt to weave together 'Hegelian historicism' with a Wittgensteinian 'non-representationalist account of language'.[25] The prevalence of the language of 'isms' in discussions of pragmatism may seem to be a relatively minor lapse in form of expression, rather than a misunderstanding of the spirit of pragmatism, but it has contributed to the tendency to view pragmatism as a philosophical school, rather than as a way of thinking that is compatible with any number of different philosophical approaches. The attempts of Bernstein, Rorty and others to capture the essential insights of pragmatism are useful, but only if we keep in mind that the central themes common to the work of Peirce, James, Dewey and their followers are aspects of an intellectual style or habit of mind, rather than a philosophical theory that is in competition with traditional philosophies and contemporary analytic methods.

The widespread tendency to think of pragmatism as a 'school of thought' that can be compared and contrasted with other philosophies such as idealism, materialism, utilitarianism and analytic philosophy is an example of a bad philosophical habit that has a long history. Ever since Aristotle criticized Plato for separating the Forms, it has been noted that philosophers have a tendency towards reification, which is a type of category-mistake involving treating abstractions as if they were substantial entities. Alfred North Whitehead called this the 'fallacy of misplaced concreteness', and Jacques Barzun referred to the same error as 'misplaced abstraction'.[26] One version of this fallacy treats qualities of things and ways of doing things as if they were actual things; to put the point in linguistic terms, the fallacy is in the confusion of an adjective or adverb with a noun. According to Aristotle, Plato made this type of mistake in thinking that something called 'Justice' existed apart from the way in which just individuals and fair systems of government operate. This intellectual move is analogous to inferring from the fact that a dancer moves gracefully that there is a transcendent Form called 'Grace' that she miraculously received from the goddess of beauty or that she is graceful by virtue of her knowledge of aesthetic principles. The common tendency to interpret pragmatism as a philosophical school commits a category-mistake analogous to Plato's in confusing a concrete way of thinking with a collection of abstractions.

The classic American pragmatists were in large part responsible for leaving themselves open to this kind of misinterpretation by appearing to derive various philosophical theories – e.g. Peirce's speculations on Evolutionary Love, James's pragmatic theory of truth, and Dewey's philosophy of education – from the pragmatic habit of mind. As Peirce pointed out, the idea that 'truth is what works' does not logically follow from adopting the pragmatic way of thinking. Peirce failed to recognize, however, that his own theory of truth – the point of view that the community of inquirers are fated to agree upon in the infinitely long run – does not follow from adopting the pragmatic habit of mind either. No rhetorical sleight of hand can conjure up the logical derivation of even a single proposition, let alone an entire philosophical theory, from a way of thinking, any more than a system of aesthetic principles can be deduced from the quality of gracefulness. We can avoid the fallacy of reifying pragmatism by thinking of the distinctive stance of the pragmatists as a style of thinking rather than as a set of doctrines or conclusions. To put the point linguistically, if pragmatism is a habit of mind or a disposition, it is misleading to try to define it in nominative terms, as if it were a fixed entity or ideological 'ism'. We can better express the significance of pragmatism by using adjectives that modify a habit of mind or, better yet, adverbs that qualify an active way of approaching the process of thinking.

William James remarked that 'The history of philosophy is to a great extent that of a certain clash of human temperaments',[27] and he argued that pragmatism could be the 'happy harmonizer' between two types of temperament, which he described as follows:

The Tender-Minded	The Tough-Minded
Rationalistic (going by 'principles')	Empiricist (going by 'facts')
Intellectualistic	Sensationalistic
Idealistic	Materialistic
Optimistic	Pessimistic
Religious	Irreligious
Free-willist	Fatalistic
Monistic	Pluralistic
Dogmatical	Sceptical

If we assume for the sake of argument that James is right in thinking that different philosophical approaches are associated with different types of temperament, we should be able to identify the 'pragmatic temperament' in contrast with its opposite. I interpret pragmatism 'adverbially' as a style of thinking that is flexible and open to new ideas, as opposed to an ideological way of thinking that is firmly committed to a set of philosophical doctrines. Using James's model, we can articulate the main characteristics of these two types of temperament in the following way:

The flexible-minded (pragmatic)	The firm-minded (ideological)
holds beliefs lightly	holds beliefs tightly
treats beliefs as hypotheses	treats beliefs as fixed principles
looks to consequences	looks to origins and foundations
accepts uncertainty	seeks certainty
recognizes ambiguity	makes sharp either/or distinctions
welcomes new ideas	stays loyal to tradition
adapts to change	remains steadfast
respects different points of view	requires unity and uniformity

These personality types are easily recognized and much studied by psychologists, but, of course, nobody is a pure example of either one. We are all a mixture of both types and switch from one to the other depending on the circumstances. In our spouses, for example, we usually expect steadfast adherence to the vow of fidelity, but we prefer a more flexible attitude when planning holidays with the in-laws. We want our doctors to change their beliefs and practices in the light of new advances in medical knowledge, but we hope that they will remain firmly committed to the Hippocratic Oath. We elect politicians who we think are open to the different points of view of their constituencies, but we wish that they would stand by their campaign promises. Nobody can survive for even an hour without both kinds of temperament, and so, as James points out, 'it is a difference rather of emphasis, yet it breeds antipathies of the most pungent character between those who lay the emphasis differently'.[28] From the flexible-minded point of view, the firm-minded are thought to be rigid blockheads, antiquated stick-in-the-muds, or authoritarian intellectual fascists; from the firm-minded point of view, the flexible-minded seem to be rudderless boats, spineless relativists or dangerous nihilists whose attitude is, as James puts it, 'a mere mess of anarchy and confusion ... so much sheer trash, philosophically'.[29] On my reading, the pragmatists had no intention of denying that both the flexible and the firm habits of mind are necessary to life, but they were making the radical suggestion that we should try treating our philosophical theories in a way that is more like the scientist's entertaining of a hypotheses to be tested or the way we plan holidays in a large family than it is like the attitude we take towards our marriage vows or the doctor's commitment to doing no harm.

The 'pragmatic temperament' is primarily an attitude of plasticity and flexibility of mind, rather than firm adherence to an ideology or philosophical system, which is why Papini correctly points out that the spirit of pragmatism cannot be captured in a definition. Although Papini is right in thinking that we cannot define any particular doctrines, methods or results that all those who adopt the pragmatic temperament will agree upon, we can specify three main characteristics of this habit of mind: willingness to accept doubt and uncertainty, openness to change, and recognition of a wide plurality of perspectives. In contrast, the firm habit of mind seeks certainty, fixity of principles, and a single, all-encompassing point of view. The difference between the flexible and firm types of temperament cuts across James's distinction between the tough- and tender-minded personalities. Tender-minded people can be firm (e.g. religious fundamentalists and the Pope) or flexible (e.g. Emerson and the 'prophetic pragmatist' Cornel West). Tough-minded people can be firm (e.g. dogmatic atheists like Richard Dawkins and Christopher Hitchens) or flexible (e.g. scientists who adopt Karl Popper's criterion of falsifiability).

The most obvious contemporary examples of the flexible and firm habits of mind are President Barack Obama and his predecessor

George W. Bush, both of whom would be classified as 'tender-minded' in James's scheme, because they are religious believers; but they have distinctively different ways of thinking. Bush is a good example of the fixed type of temperament, because he holds tenaciously to his ideas about good and evil in spite of all obstacles. He believes in 'a divine plan that supersedes all human plans' and thinks that 'Moral truth is the same in every culture, in every time, and in every place.' He describes his religious faith as 'a foundation that will not shift', an attitude that helped him as president to 'pick a course and not look back'. According to his former speechwriter David Frum, in the Bush White House 'attendance at Bible study was, if not compulsory, not exactly noncompulsory'. Bush opened Cabinet meetings with a prayer, and in ordering the invasion of Iraq, he asked God to bless him and the troops. Greg Thielmann, of the State Department's Bureau of Intelligence and Research, says that his administration had a 'faith-based intelligence attitude': 'We know the answers, give us the intelligence to support those answers', adding that 'When you sense this kind of attitude, you quash the spirit of intellectual inquiry and integrity.'[30]

Obama, on the other hand, has often been described as a pragmatist, and there is much debate about whether that means a "postpartisan" politics that moves to the centre or involves a Deweyan progressive approach.[31] It is clear, however, that Obama illustrates the flexible habit of mind that I call the pragmatic temperament. He believes that implicit in the framework of the American Constitution was

a rejection of absolute truth, the infallibility of any idea or ideology or theology or "ism," any tyrannical consistency that might lock future generations into a single, unalterable course, or drive both majorities and minorities into the cruelties of the Inquisition, the pogrom, the gulag, or the jihad.

He thinks that the Constitution is 'designed to force us into a conversation, a "deliberative democracy" in which all citizens are required to engage in a process of testing their ideas against an external reality, persuading others of their point of view, and building shifting alliances of consent'. He says that

the process of making laws in America compels us to entertain the possibility that we are not always right and to sometimes change our minds; it challenges us to examine our motives and our interests constantly, and suggests that both our individual and collective judgments are at once legitimate and highly fallible.

Obama admires the American Founders because they 'were suspicious of abstraction and liked asking questions ... it was their realism, their practicality and flexibility and curiosity that ensured the Union's survival'.[32]

Obama does not think that his reading of the American constitution as a framework for democratic deliberation requires 'abandonment of our highest ideals, or of a commitment to the common good'. He argues that

> The rejection of absolutism implicit in our constitutional structure may sometimes make our politics seem unprincipled. But for most of our history it has encouraged the very process of information gathering, analysis, and argument that allows us to make better, if not perfect, choices, not only about the means to our ends but also about the ends themselves. Whether we are for or against affirmative action, for or against prayer in schools, we must test out our ideals, vision, and values against the realities of a common life, so that over time they may be refined, discarded, or replaced by new ideals, sharper visions, deeper values.

Obama's flexibility of mind is further illustrated in the subtlety and nuance of his analysis, which recognizes the limitations of pragmatism. He writes that 'it has not always been the pragmatist, the voice of reason, or the force of compromise that has created the conditions for liberty'. It has sometimes been 'the cranks, the zealots, the prophets, the agitators, and the unreasonable – in other words, the absolutists' – like William Lloyd Garrison, Frederick Douglass and Harriet Tubman, who 'first sounded the clarion call for justice' and 'fought for a new order'. He succinctly captures the inevitable irony of the pragmatic attitude by saying, 'I am robbed even of the certainty of uncertainty – for sometimes absolute truths may well be absolute.'[33]

In 'The Will to Believe' James describes the most important choices that we make in life as 'genuine options' that are live, forced and momentous, and he argues that we cannot avoid making a choice in these circumstances, even if we do not have sufficient scientific evidence upon which to base our decision.[34] The decision whether to think pragmatically or ideologically is a 'genuine option' in James's sense. A 'live option' is a choice between two hypotheses, each of which an individual takes seriously as a possible basis for belief and action. 'Believe in Zeus or believe in Jupiter' is like a dead rather than a live wire that makes no 'electric connection' with people's belief systems today, but 'Imitate Bush or Obama' represents a choice between real possibilities. A 'forced option' is one that cannot be avoided by choosing a third alternative. We could decide not to imitate either Bush or Obama, but refraining from thinking either flexibly or firmly would mean refusing to think at all. A 'momentous option' presents a unique and irreversible opportunity with important consequences. Choosing whether to think pragmatically or ideologically is not a once-in-a lifetime decision, but the results of making this choice are far from trivial.

Bush's tenacious adherence to his view of traditional religious principles is admirable to those who expect their ideas of right and wrong to be absolutely clear and unchanging, and it is comforting to those who want their philosophies to give them security amid the vicissitudes of life. Obama's flexible, pragmatic way of thinking is liberating to those who want their philosophies to give them the freedom from obsolete ideologies to develop new solutions to problems. If the crucial issue in debating about pragmatism is deciding between different types of temperament, rather than between systems of knowledge, then the question 'Is pragmatism true?' becomes as meaningless and inappropriate as asking 'Is gracefulness true?' The philosophically interesting question has nothing to do with how people feel about pragmatism. Whether we like or dislike this habit of mind is irrelevant to the issue. The important philosophical question is, 'Should we try to think flexibly or should we remain firm in our convictions?' Once we open this question up for discussion, the even more important question that arises is, 'Should we try to teach the pragmatic temperament?'

Peirce's views on this question were quite different from those of James and Dewey. Peirce was a self-described 'ultra-conservative' who thought that the pragmatic temperament should be the privilege of an elite class of scientists and philosophers. In a letter of 1908 he wrote, 'The people ought to be enslaved; only the slaveholders ought to practice the virtues that alone can maintain their rule.' He characterized himself as an 'opponent of female suffrage and of universal male suffrage ... [and] a disbeliever in democracy'.[35] In

'The Fixation of Belief' he wrote, 'for the mass of mankind' the method of authority is perhaps the best way of forming beliefs. 'If it is their highest impulse to be intellectual slaves, then slaves they ought to remain.'[36] Even for the elite scientific class, Peirce thought that sentiment and instinct were better guides than reason for practical decision-making and action. What is usually called belief, he thought, 'has no place in science at all', and 'pure science has nothing at all to do with action'. The metaphysician, like the scientist, has a duty to be a 'genuine, honest, earnest, resolute, energetic, industrious, and accomplished doubter' on theoretical issues, but practical 'matters of vital importance' require 'full belief' and 'must be left to sentiment, that is, to instinct'.[37] James and Dewey had far more faith than Peirce did in the ordinary person's ability to adopt the pragmatic way of thinking, and they were also more sanguine about the value of the pragmatic temperament for addressing the urgent practical problems of life. James thought that everyone could benefit from the way in which pragmatism 'widens the field of search for God', and he concluded 'What Pragmatism Means' by saying: 'But you see already how democratic she is. Her manners are as various and flexible, her resources as rich and endless, and her conclusions as friendly as mother Nature.'[38] Dewey hoped that pragmatism would lead to a more democratic society by transforming our system of education so that it would aim primarily to teach open-mindedness, creativity and democratic citizenship.

There are many arguments to be made on both sides. On Peirce's side, it could be maintained that powerful psychological and social forces make James's and Dewey's democratic vision dangerous to attempt and impossible to achieve. Even if one disagrees with Aristotle and Peirce that some people are naturally born to be slaves, it might be argued that there are good reasons why people do not want to change their traditional beliefs and why parents are opposed to any educational programme that would encourage their children to challenge them. Teaching the pragmatic temperament, according to this argument, would destroy social order, because pragmatism entails relativism about religious beliefs and ethical values. Much ink has been spilled on this pseudo-problem, which does not arise if we interpret pragmatism as a habit of mind, rather than a set of doctrines. I have argued that no propositions logically follow from adopting the pragmatic temperament, and therefore pragmatism, so interpreted, cannot entail the view that any opinion is as good as any other, that 'anything goes', or any other kind of relativistic philosophy. On the adverbial interpretation, pragmatism does not entail relativism any more than the scientific method does, and it is no more disruptive to society. Adopting the pragmatic temperament, as Obama points out, does not mean giving up our ideals or the ability to make strong commitments to them, but it enables us to refine and deepen our ideals in the practice of 'deliberative democracy'. Bernstein challenges 'the unjustified and outrageous claim that without an appeal to absolutes and fixed moral certainties we lack the grounds to act decisively in fighting our real enemies. There is no incompatibility between fallibilism and a passionate commitment to oppose injustice and immorality.'[39] A flexible mind can choose between firm commitment and openness to new ideas, but a fixed mentality has only one habitual way of thinking and thus fewer options for adaptation to change.

The widespread tendency to identify pragmatism with relativism has resulted, at least in part, from confusing pragmatism as a philosophical movement with the variety of different ordinary language uses of the words 'pragmatic' and 'pragmatism'. Because of the ambiguity of the word, many have argued that 'pragmatism' was perhaps an unfortunate choice for the philosophical movement, and even James wrote in the preface to *Pragmatism* in 1907, 'I do not like the name, but apparently it is too late to change it.'[40] In Roman law 'pragmatic' denoted a ruler's fundamental decree, e.g. the 1438 Pragmatic Sanction of Bourges.[41] In the seventeenth and eighteenth centuries the term was used to mean overly busy and interfering, e.g. 'Common estimation puts an ill character upon pragmatic medling people' (1674). Oddly enough, a pragmatic person also meant one who is opinionated, dictatorial and dogmatic, e.g. 'She is as pragmatic and proud as the Pope' (1771), which is the exact opposite of one of the word's primary meanings today.[42] All of these older meanings are obsolete, but the terms 'pragmatism' and 'pragmatic' are still extremely ambiguous. In current discourse 'pragmatic' is sometimes used very broadly as a synonym for 'practical', e.g. 'The politician made a pragmatic decision.' In this trivial sense, as Martin Gardner points out, everybody is a pragmatist, at least some of the time, and the term becomes useless.[43] More interestingly specific uses of the term 'pragmatic' contrast it either with 'principled' or with 'dogmatic'.[44] As the opposite of 'principled', the term often carries the negative connotation of 'opportunism' to mean abandoning ethical standards to further immediate interests that are convenient, profitable or popular, e.g. 'We need to be pragmatic about the arms trade to protect jobs.'

In 1983 Jacques Barzun claimed to have found well over two hundred uses of the word 'pragmatism' in books, the press and casual conversation, nearly all of which contained or implied disparagement, and he suggested that the 'wretched word' be dropped from the common vocabulary.[45] If Barzun were to conduct his informal survey again twenty-five years later, he would find that the term 'pragmatism' often carries an honorific rather than a pejorative connotation when used as the opposite of 'dogmatism'.

A pragmatist, as contrasted with an ideologue, can mean a person who is not wedded to a particular school of thought and takes an open-minded approach to solving problems by using ideas from a variety of sources, and it is in this third sense that Obama is pragmatic. In her confirmation hearing as Obama's secretary of state, Hillary Clinton promised to 'return to a foreign policy based on "principles and pragmatism", not rigid ideology'. The *New York Times* praised her choice of words, after the last eight years under the Bush administration, as 'cool water in the desert'.[46] Clearly, Clinton was using 'pragmatism' to mean open-mindedness (the opposite of dogmatism), rather than opportunism (the antithesis of principle), or else her statement would be an oxymoron. To summarize, in current discourse the word 'pragmatic' is used in a number of different ways, including the very general sense of 'practical' and the more specific senses of 'opportunistic' and 'not dogmatic or ideological'.

Enormous misunderstandings have resulted from confusing the use of the word 'pragmatism' in ordinary language with the name of the philosophical movement. The confusion of the philosophy with mere practicality has led some critics to view pragmatism as a long-winded statement of the obvious. Gardner seemed to make this error when he wrote, 'Pragmatists were momentarily at the center of a storm in the United States and England until finally it dawned on philosophers that the pragmatists were not saying anything revolutionary at all. They were only saying the same old things in a bizarre way.'[47] Bertrand Russell confused it with the second sense of 'opportunism' when he described it as the philosophical expression of American commercialism. Dewey's reply, a classic in the genre of hilarious refutation, was that Russell's suggestion was

> of that order of interpretation which would say that English neo-realism is a reflection of the aristocratic snobbery of the English; the tendency of French thought to dualism an expression of the alleged Gallic disposition to keep a mistress in addition to a wife; and the idealism of Germany a manifestation of an ability to elevate beer and sausage into a higher synthesis with the spiritual values of Beethoven and Wagner.[48]

Eliminating misinterpretations based on confusion with the first two ordinary-language senses of the word makes it clear that philosophical pragmatism is closest in meaning to the third sense in which a pragmatist is the antithesis of a dogmatist or an ideologue. Far from entailing relativism, pragmatism is as opposed to this naive ideology as it is to every other ideology.

While all good teachers encourage bold inquiry, systematic teaching of the pragmatic temperament has never been tried except on a very small scale. Noam Chomsky writes that he was 'very lucky to have gone to a school based on democratic ideals, where the influence of John Dewey was very much felt and where children were encouraged to study and investigate as a process of discovering the truth for themselves'.[49] Few schools have the opportunity to implement Dewey's programme of educating for democracy, largely because of the trend towards standardized testing, which has increased dramatically in the United States, following the enactment of former President Bush's 'No Child Left Behind' policy. Dewey was not much interested in education beyond the first few years of elementary school, believing that by the time students entered college 'their mental habits were pretty well fixed'.[50] Rorty, on the other hand, argues that 'education up to the age of 18 or 19 is mostly a matter of socialization – of getting the students to take over the moral and political common sense of the society as it is'. He thinks that it is not until college that students should be taught the pragmatic attitude by 'inciting doubt and stimulating imagination, thereby challenging the prevailing consensus'.[51] Here both Dewey and Rorty seem to violate Peirce's first rule of logic – 'Do not block the way of inquiry' – in assuming that pragmatism cannot or should not be taught at some levels of education. A more pragmatic approach would try teaching it at every level to see if it works.

Empirical research has shown the advantages of teaching openness to uncertainty, change and different points of view in the training of doctors and pilots. A large NASA study in the 1970s concluded that

> many cockpit mistakes were attributable, at least in part, to the 'God-like certainty' of the pilot in command. If other crew-members had been consulted, or if the pilot had considered other alternatives, then some of the bad decisions might have been avoided. As a result, the goal of CRM [Cockpit Resource Management] was to create an environment in which a diversity of viewpoints was freely shared.[52]

As Jonah Lehrer points out in *How We Decide*, many hospitals now realize that the same decision-making strategies that can prevent pilot error can also prevent medical error and have adopted CRM techniques in their training programmes.

> The reason CRM is so effective is that it encourages flight crews and surgical teams to think together. It deters certainty and stimulates debate. In this sense, CRM creates the ideal atmosphere for good decision-making, in which a diversity of opinions is openly shared. The evidence is looked at from multiple angles, and new alternatives are considered. Such a process not only prevents mistakes but also leads to startling new insights.[53]

In *How Doctors Think* Jerome Groopman argues that most medical schools do not adequately prepare doctors to accept the uncertainty that is inevitable in the diagnosis and treatment of patients. Instead of using exposure to controversy as an exercise in teaching uncertainty, there is a 'culture of conformity and orthodoxy' in medical training that does not encourage open-mindedness but educates for 'dogmatic certainty, for adopting one school of thought or the other, and for laying the game according to the venerable, but contradictory, rules' that each institution seeks to impose on staff, students, and patients. Groopman concludes that:

> Paradoxically, taking uncertainty into account can enhance a physician's therapeutic effectiveness, because it demonstrates his honesty, his willingness to be more engaged with his patients, his commitment to the reality of the situation rather than resorting to evasion, half-truth, and even lies. And it makes it easier for the doctor to change course if the first strategy fails, to keep trying. Uncertainty sometimes is essential for success.[54]

Given that teaching the pragmatic temperament has been so successful in postgraduate education, we should be willing to entertain the hypothesis that it might be a good idea to try teaching it in schools, colleges, and universities. How can this best be done? I do not claim to have the answer to this large question, and it is in any case beyond the scope of this chapter, but I think that we can find some clues in the works of Plato, who is universally acknowledged to be the greatest philosopher of education who ever lived. Plato's Socratic dialogues give a model of teaching by means of asking questions in an open-minded conversation. My experience in over thirty years of teaching philosophy has convinced me that teaching the pragmatic temperament is most likely to be successful in so far as we aspire to the Socratic ideal in our classrooms; it will probably fail in large lecture classes where students sit in rows facing the teacher, rather than each other, and in which they are evaluated primarily upon their ability to pass standardized tests. In a Socratic classroom there are strict rules governing the conversation: all students must be made to feel welcome to contribute; they must listen respectfully to the points of view of others, never interrupting or dominating the conversation; asking questions is encouraged and valued more than insisting on being right; making mistakes is not something to be afraid of, nor is changing one's mind, because correcting errors is the key to learning. The teacher must follow the same rules as the students, not talking all of the time, listening and asking questions often. In grading policies and giving feedback in class, the teacher should encourage and reward demonstrations of the flexible habit of mind and correct breaches of conversational etiquette. Students who catch the teacher in making an error should not be penalized, but should be publicly praised and given extra credit! It could be argued that the Socratic model of education is not as appropriate for every subject as it is for teaching such disciplines as philosophy, civics, literature and creative writing; furthermore, it is expensive, because it depends upon relatively small classes and a larger investment of teachers' time than does the method of evaluation by standardized testing. On the other hand, if teaching the pragmatic temperament is thought to be an important educational goal, then perhaps this model should be adopted as an experiment for all students in at least some classes.

I have argued that the least common denominator of the many varieties of pragmatism is a way of thinking that is flexible and open to uncertainty, change and different points of view and that we should make this an explicit goal in our teaching. The 'adverbial' interpretation resolves some of the paradoxes of pragmatism. It reconciles the seemingly contradictory statements of Dewey and Rorty on the relationship between pragmatic philosophy and education with which this chapter began.

Rorty is right in saying that pragmatism does not logically entail any specific implications for the curriculum, teaching methods or government policies on education, but Dewey is also right in saying that pragmatism is intimately connected with education, because teaching the pragmatic temperament would radically transform how we think about what we are doing in our schools and universities and how we attempt to do it. Adopting the pragmatic temperament as an educational ideal could help to overcome the division in philosophy of education between analytic and historical methods of treating philosophical texts. In an excellent recent article, 'Pragmatist Philosophy of Education', Randall Curren argues that many contemporary neo-pragmatist philosophers of education fail to grasp the main significance of pragmatism for education because of their 'problematic embrace of systematic philosophy' and 'misbegotten attempts to glean educational lessons from metaphysics and epistemology'. He writes that

'to the extent contemporary analytic philosophers of education ... integrate 'the empirical, the normative, and the contextual' (especially the sociocultural) ... it is within analytic philosophy that the basic pragmatist message about how to do philosophy of education lives on ... If philosophy is a tool, then let it be sharp and efficient in cutting to the chase.'[55]

I have tried to show, on the contrary, that there is no one way of philosophizing that exclusively captures the main significance of pragmatism, but that both analytic and traditional methods of philosophizing are compatible with the pragmatic temperament. As Papini puts it, one of the main features of pragmatism is its 'armed neutrality'.

This means that it does not decide upon questions, but it only says: given certain goals, I suggest you to use certain means rather than others. It is, thus, a corridor theory – a corridor of a large hotel where a hundred doors open into a hundred rooms. In one of those rooms there is a kneeler and a man who wants to reconquer the faith; in another there is a desk and a man who wants to kill all metaphysics; in a third there is a laboratory and a man who seeks new 'handles' to grasp the future ... But the corridor belongs to all and everybody walks through it: if from time to time conversations start among the guests, no waiter will be so impolite as to break them up.[56]

An even better analogy than the corridor is Dewey's image of a 'hospitality room' where all lovers of wisdom are greeted and welcomed.

On my reading, Rorty and Bernstein 'cut to the chase' in recognizing that pragmatism is a radical shift in our way thinking, rather than in the content of our thought. Bernstein argues that the real clash in the post 9/11 world, contrary to Samuel Huntington's theory of the clash of civilizations, is a clash between competing 'mentalities'. He writes,

The time is ripe – indeed it is urgent – for a revitalized, passionate commitment to furthering a genuine democratic faith that eschews the appeal to dogmatic absolutes and simplistic dichotomies; a democratic faith that fosters tangible public freedom where debate, persuasion, and reciprocal argumentation flourish; a democratic faith that has the courage to live with uncertainty, contingency, and ambiguity; a democratic faith that is thoroughly imbued with a fallibilistic spirit.[57]

James describes his hopes for the impact of pragmatism as follows:

See, I say, how pragmatism shifts the emphasis and looks forward into facts themselves. The really vital question for us all is, What is this world going to be? What is life eventually to make of itself? The centre of gravity of philosophy must therefore alter its place ... It will be an alteration in 'the seat of authority' that reminds one almost of the Protestant Reformation.[58]

To many readers James's comparison of pragmatism to the Protestant Reformation has seemed preposterous. Rorty writes, 'In an exuberant moment, James compared pragmatism's potential for producing radical cultural change to that of the Protestant Reformation. I would like to persuade my readers that the analogy is not as absurd as it might seem.'[59]

The apparent paradox that a philosophical approach with no direct and immediate results could have the potential to bring about an intellectual revolution does not appear so absurd if we interpret pragmatism adverbially as a habit of mind rather than a philosophical theory. There is a chance that teaching the pragmatic temperament might result in a paradigm shift with important implications both within and outside the academy. James, Dewey and their followers, like Nietzsche, envision a future in which there would be greater individual freedom of thought; unlike Nietzsche, they are democratic in emphasizing the inseparable relationship between strong individuals and a strong sense of solidarity with human communities of inquiry. Those of us who advocate self-consciously adopting and teaching the pragmatic temperament do not claim to know that it would be better for humanity in the long run to try out this intellectual and social experiment. We imagine that this way of thinking could lead to a future society in which people are freer and happier, because they will be better able to adapt to uncertainty, change and a plurality of points of view. I have argued that the most valuable legacy of pragmatism is its clear presentation of the choice between the flexible and the firm habits of thinking as 'live, forced, and momentous'. If my argument has been successful, teaching the pragmatic temperament will begin to receive serious consideration at every level of education.

NOTES

1 Wiener, 1973, pp. 552, 563.
2 Wiener, 1973, p. 553.
3 Pappas, 2007, p. 123.
4 Westbrook, 2005, p. 1.
5 Dewey, MW9, p. 342.
6 Rorty, 1990, p. 41.
7 Diggins, 1994, p. 455; Westbrook, 2005, p. 175.
8 De Waal, 2005, pp. 2–3, 176.
9 Menand, 2001, p. x.
10 De Waal, 2005, pp. 52, 67–8.
11 West, 1989, p. 9.
12 Nicholson, 2004; see also Rybczynski, 1999, p. 7.
13 West, 1989, pp. 112, 147.
14 Haddock Seigfried, 1996.
15 Pratt, 2002, pp. xi–xviii.
16 Papini, 1907, p. 354.
17 Peirce, 1877, pp. 1–15; Peirce, 1878, pp. 286–302.
18 Peirce, EP9, p. 48.

19 James, 1955, p. 45-7.
20 Dewey, MW13: 308.
21 Dewey, MW9: 182–3, 187.
22 Bernstein 1988; Bernstein 1992, p. 324.
23 Menand, 2001, p. xii.
24 Bernstein, 1992, pp. 326–9.
25 Rorty, 2007a, p. ix.
26 Barzun, 1983, p. 62.
27 James, 1955, p. 19.
28 James, 1955, p. 21.
29 James, 1955, p. 86.
30 Bush, 1999, pp. 6, 136–9; Singer, 2004, pp. 91, 96–100, 208–12.
31 Packer, 2008, p. 86; Hayes, 2008, p. 13.
32 Obama, 2006, pp. 110–12.
33 Obama, 2006, pp. 112–16.
34 James, 1948, pp. 88–109.
35 Westbrook, 2005, p. 25.
36 Peirce, EP1: 118.
37 Peirce, EP1: 31–3.
38 James, 1955, pp. 61–2.
39 Bernstein, 2005, p. viii.
40 James, 1955, p. 13.
41 Barzun, 1983, p. 90.
42 *The Shorter Oxford English Dictionary*, 3rd edn, 1973. Oxford: Clarendon Press, 1973, II, p. 1646.
43 Gardner, 1983, p. 47.
44 Williams, 1983, pp. 240–1.
45 Barzun, 1983, p. 89.
46 *The New York Times*, 14 January 2009.
47 Gardner, 1983, p. 44.
48 Dewey, MW13: 307.
49 Chomsky, 2000, p. 27.
50 Ryan, 1998, p. 405,
51 Rorty, 1999a, pp. 116–18.
52 Lehrer, 2009, pp. 253–5.
53 Lehrer, 2009, pp. 255–6.
54 Groopman, 2007, pp. 153–5.
55 Curren, 2009, pp. 481–99.
56 De Waal, 2005, p. 86.
57 Bernstein, 2005, p. 124.
58 James, 1955, p. 86.
59 Rorty, 2007a, p. x.

12 Dewey's pragmatic aesthetics: the contours of experience

It is with no less than an 'ironic perversity' (Dewey, 1958b p. 3) that John Dewey initiates the greatest philosophical examination of the arts in the pragmatic tradition, his now classic *Art as Experience*.[1] Because works of art are products that possess an external, physical existence, the whole work of art is, in 'common conception' (although he means common misconception), identified with the 'building, book, painting, or statue in its existence apart from human experience' (p. 3). The true work of art, the full elucidation of which is for Dewey the central aim of aesthetic theory, is in fact – and for Dewey this very often means in *practice* – 'what the product does with and in experience' (p. 3). That ironic condition – in which the very physical existence of works of art blocks our arrival at an accurate aesthetic theory to explain those objects – is only exacerbated by the attainment to a classic status by some of those objects, since such a status further isolates the work from the human conditions and contexts from which it emerged as well as from the human consequences it engenders in actual life-experience' (p. 3). Art, thus 'remitted to a separate realm' (p. 3), is placed beyond the reach of the relational sinews that would reveal its true connections to a vast range of human aims, efforts and achievements, and that would disclose an experiential continuity between works of fine art as we shall see, of refined and intensified forms of *experience*, not of objects) and the substance of the ordinary;[2] the 'everyday events, doings, and sufferings that are universally recognized to constitute experience' (p. 3). Aesthetic theory has thus, for Dewey, traditionally cloaked the very subject it tries to illuminate; hence Dewey's central philosophical motivation in his expansive and multifaceted study is to reveal the truths of practice behind the cloak of theory. Indeed,

Dewey, in one respect as a latter-day Plato, is determined to lead us from opinion to knowledge, and (also like Plato, if in very modernized form) to show us that what we find behind the veil is not an elevated, separate or autonomous fine object, but rather a kind of mirror held up to the reality of our human, lived experience.[3]

I THE 'LIVE CREATURE' AND THE PREFIGUREMENT OF ART IN HUMAN EXPERIENCE

Dewey instructs us that, if we are to appreciate a work such as the Parthenon, we must first appreciate what the people within whose lives that building figured have in common with us 'in our own homes and on our own streets' (Dewey, 1958b, p. 4). This experiential commonality is something we comprehend, at least initially, not through a focus on great aesthetic achievements, but through a return to the aesthetic impulse in its most raw state. A vast multiplicity captures our attentive eyes and ears: Dewey offers the example of a fire engine rushing by, construction machines excavating enormous holes in the earth, a human fly climbing the steeple, construction workers perched high on thin girders throwing and catching red-hot bolts, the 'tense grace' (p. 5) of a ball player, the tending of plants, and watching the flames and poking the coals of a fire. In such experiences, he reminds us – in a way not unlike Wittgenstein's[4] methods of assembling reminders of what we already know in order to reveal the breadth of our knowledge against the false strictures and limitations imposed by a philosophical theory, and to disclose the actual diversity of practices under a given heading against the illusory uniformity artificially imposed by theory – that we find ourselves imaginatively engaged over and above the practical reasons we may give for our actions if asked about them, e.g. our poking the embers is 'to make the fire burn better' (p. 5). The engagement, and the fascination, that we display in such cases constitute our everyday entries into the unrefined, or indeed raw, forms of aesthetic experience. And these are not external objects, seen from a distance, viewed atop a pedestal: we are not 'cold spectators' (p. 5), but rather imaginative participants.

While such a list reminds us of the roots of aesthetic practice, it by no means undercuts the distinction for Dewey between fine and vulgar aesthetic engagements; indeed he offers an explanation of society's appetites for the aesthetically cheap in terms of the illusory severance of art from lived experience. Because of the irrepressible human impulse for aesthetic 'experiences enjoyable in themselves' (Dewey, 1958b, p. 6), if we mistakenly believe the achievements of the fine arts to be cold, remote[5] and, in their isolation from the rhythms of our own inner experience, anaemic, we naturally turn to more crude (but apparently more humanly connected) forms of engagement (e.g. 'the comic strip', 'newspaper accounts of love-nests, murders, and exploits of bandits' (p. 6), and if Dewey were writing today, surely much of what television[6] offers, and probably sports). Thus a removal of the misconception of the estrangement of fine art from lived experience would not only offer the illuminating philosophy of art we need, it would also restore society to a state in which the higher forms of aesthetic edification are instinctively sought out, while simultaneously restoring art to a state in which an experiential or pragmatic mimesis is commonplace.[7]

If we need to newly understand the nature of the work of art, however, and if that nature is experiential, then we may well need to better, if not newly, understand ourselves. Such an understanding Dewey pursues under the heading of 'the live creature'. 'The first great consideration', he writes, 'is that life goes on in an environment', and lest we interpret this remark in terms of a Cartesian duality[8] wherein an isolated and autonomous self only contingently interacts with the externalities of its environment, Dewey quickly adds 'not merely *in* it but because of it, through interaction with it' (Dewey, 1958b, p. 13). At every moment the live creature is exposed to danger, draws upon its environment's resources to fulfil needs, and indeed develops its 'destiny' through intimate interactions with its immediate and extended environs. Death is the result of a gap between organism and environment that has grown too wide; subsistence is the result of a minimally successful interactive mediation between organism and environment; life well lived is the result of a wholly successful mediation. 'These biological commonplaces', Dewey claims, 'reach to the roots of the esthetic in experience' (Dewey, 1958b, p. 14).

It is an organism, a live creature, that not only successfully manipulates the objects of its environment, but that is in part constituted by its multiple relations to those objects, that secures the 'stability essential to living' (Dewey, 1958b, p. 15). And this dynamic self-constitutive interaction is indeed mirrored in the experience of the work of art:

The rhythm of loss of integration with environment and recovery of union not only persists in man but becomes conscious with him; its conditions are material out of which he forms purposes. Emotion is the conscious sign of a break, actual or impending. The discord is the occasion that induces reflection. Desire for restoration of the union converts mere emotion into interest in objects as conditions of realization of harmony. With the realization, material of reflection is incorporated into objects as their meaning. Since the artist cares in a peculiar way for the phase of experience in which union is achieved, he does not shun moments of resistance and tension. He rather cultivates them, not for their own sake but because of their potentialities, bringing to living consciousness an experience that is unified and total.

(Dewey, 1958b, p. 15)

Through this dynamic interaction with the materials and relations of the contexts of our practices we experience fractures, fissures and ruptures, and by the awareness of those and the drive for the restoration of equilibrium we develop conscious purposes that are motivated or charged by emotion, all of which in turn invest the objects of our environment with meaning. The patterns of tension and resolution are reflected in – or, better, embedded in – works of art, and the rhythms of the systolic and diastolic changes move toward a state of 'inner harmony' (p. 17). But the emotional charges of the objects in our environment, and the accompanying teleology towards harmonic resolution, are not, as Dewey is careful to say, *projected* on to those objects. On the contrary, 'Nature is kind and hateful, bland and morose, irritating and comforting, long before she is ... a congeries of "secondary" qualities like colors and their shapes' (p. 16).[9] Emotive charges, positive or negative (in any of a multitude of ways located along a vast continuum stretching between these poles), are given in experience; Dewey underscores that by pointing out that even seemingly inert terms such as 'long' and 'short', 'solid' and 'hollow', carry emotional connotations, and that early uses of terms such as 'sweet' and 'bitter' were employed more to distinguish the favourable from the hostile than to denote sensory qualities.[10]

Further under the heading of better understanding ourselves, i.e. our lived experience, as a way of newly understanding art, Dewey claims that, just as we do 'not have to project emotions into the objects experienced' (p. 16), so we do not have to carry the weight of the past as a burden. The past, for many mortals, can haunt the present (and thus obtrude onto our futures) as a repository of regret, opportunities not taken and undesirable consequences we impossibly 'wish undone' (Dewey, 1958b, p. 18). Dewey's live creature, by contrast, adapts to its own past as a storehouse of resources, and to be fully alive is to be fully present (Dewey makes the analogy to an alert animal), standing on the foundation of an acknowledged and integrated past that emanates significance as present experience calls it up explicitly through similarity or implicitly through the 'hushed reverberations' from the past of which Santayana wrote.[11] The past, for the live creature at its best, is 'absorbed into the present' (p. 19) just as, for that creature, the complex elements that make up the environment are absorbed, through ever-unfolding interaction and the overcoming of any solipsistic impulse towards disassociation, into the self. And *experience itself*, properly understood as the 'fulfillment of an organism in its struggles and achievement in a world of things' and integrative of all of the foregoing raw or indeed animal[12] elements of Dewey's reorientation of aesthetic theory, is 'art in germ' (p. 19).

Dewey's fundamental project of reconnecting the aesthetic with lived experience, he is the first to acknowledge, is in imminent danger of meeting with contempt by those who regard the supreme achievements of fine art as well above the life of the 'live creature'. But this objection would be registered only by those, as he is also quick to point out, who regard the lived, embodied, contextualized life we live as 'an affair of low appetite' and of 'gross sensation' (Dewey, 1958b, p. 20). A full explanation of this unjustifiable contempt for the embodied, implicit in their anticipated criticism, would require a full examination of the history of morals that have caused a fear of the senses,[13] tracing the genesis of that position back to the dichotomized opposition[14] of flesh to spirit. On one level, a response can be given in terms of the false analogy between morality and art that arises here. On the ethical side, even if we do harbour a contempt, or at the very least a dismissive attitude, toward the sensory, that in itself is no reason to cross over to the aesthetic side of the analogy and hold the physical objects that are works of art in contempt, precisely because they may constitute the very things that stimulate the higher forms of cognition and affective experience that the moralist is eager to defend. Indeed, a cultivated aesthetic sensibility may require for its continued cultivation and maturation an acquaintance with the many sensory particulars that happen to be works of high art. But on another level, and in a way more in accord with Dewey's larger aesthetic vision, works of art are simply not, as we have seen him assert, *physical* objects; they are complex *experiences* that arise through mutually interactive engagement with the work by a contextually situated live (aesthetic) creature. Thus on that level, the work of art is not in danger of being mistakenly identified with a purely sensory object[15] and accordingly held in contempt. And on still another level, most in accord with Dewey's vision of aesthetic life, it is those very conditions under which 'sense and flesh get a bad name' (p. 21) that need to be reconsidered.

We presently live, he believed, in an age in which the theological distinction between spirit and flesh, in all its various ethical and aesthetic manifestations, is widely acknowledged, and this acknowledgement, particularly under contemporary economic and industrialized conditions, assumes the character of a self-fulfilling prophecy.[16] The sensory dimension of lived experience is greatly diminished, reduced down to 'sensations as mechanical stimuli or as irritated stimulations', and this wholesale reduction of our sensory engagements precludes our gaining 'a sense of the reality that is in them and behind them' (Dewey, 1958b, p.21). We 'use the senses to arouse passion but not to fulfill the interest of insight', and this, Dewey assures us, is 'not because that interest is not potentially present in the exercise of sense but because we yield to conditions of living that force sense to remain an excitation on the surface' (p. 21). And this forced exclusion, not of untutored and unmediated sensation but of contextualized sensory experience, blinds us to the epistemic, ethical and of course aesthetic value of such experience; this inward banishment, having become an immobile obstacle to the processes of self-integration Dewey believes aesthetic experience can and should engender,[17] is externally reinforced by hierarchies of power and prestige in social structures. Dewey encapsulates the point nicely: 'Prestige goes to those who use their minds without participation of the body and who act vicariously through control of the bodies and labor of others' (p. 21). Again, it is the entire dichotomy between flesh and spirit that, according to Dewey, requires re-examination, and it becomes clear that one way of undertaking this is through a re-examination of the fundamentally *experiential* nature of the aesthetic.

We have seen Dewey speak of the enduring presence of the past within the present, and the need for temporal integration on the part of the adaptive organism. Does aesthetic experience take place in the present? The answer, as we may now anticipate, is as complex as his larger conception of human experience in general. The question invites both affirmative and negative answers. Aesthetic experience can be in one sense blindingly immediate, and thus powerfully situated in an immediate present. But this can be like 'a flash of lightning illuminat[ing] a dark landscape' (Dewey, 1958b, p. 23), where – although there is indisputably a momentary recognition of known or familiar objects – there is also the lingering presence of a lengthy process of visual and recognitional maturation, which in turn have the attendant emotional charges, themselves the results of prior experience. So the apparent suddenness of visual experience, or of any particular aesthetic experience, may be, as Dewey suggests, like Hamlet's 'the rest is silence': meaningless in isolation, but heavily laden with meaning as the conclusion to a drama enacted through time and thus, in a sense, present in those heavily laden words. Form in the arts, Dewey suggests, is present to our aesthetic sensibilities in just that way, containing its own past evolution of organization in its present. And it is a kind of form that is prefigured in the very structure of lived experience. 'Art,' he says, 'is thus prefigured in the very processes of living' (p. 24).

Yet prefiguration is not invariably the correct concept to employ, because some of those processes of living are themselves aesthetic experiences, of a kind that spontaneously arise without any expectation or without any deliberate pursuit of the aesthetic. One such experience is recorded by Emerson, who wrote 'Crossing a bare common, in snow puddles, at twilight, under a clouded sky, without having in my thought any occurrence of special good fortune, I have enjoyed a perfect exhilaration. I am glad to the brink of fear' (Dewey, 1958b, pp. 28–9). Dewey believes that the great multitude of experiences of that kind empirically confirm the power that immediate sensuous experience has to 'absorb' (p. 29) meanings and values – thus again subverting the distinction between the sensory level and the intellective, spiritual or ideal level of experience. The continuity between those is also readily visible in, he says, rites, ceremonies and myths.[18] Dewey sees the same convergence of levels in a remark of Walter Pater, who wrote 'The Christianity of the middle ages made its way partly by its esthetic beauty, a thing so profoundly felt by the Latin hymn writers, *who for one moral or spiritual sentiment had a hundred sensuous images*' (p. 31). And, as Dewey has intimated, such experiences are anything but epistemologically inert. First, he observes that human reasoning itself is not a detached and ideal category of intellective experience, but rather, as he finds well expressed in Keats,[19] that '"reasonings" have an origin like that of the movements of a wild creature toward its goal' (p. 33), and that even '"the greatest philosopher" exercises an animal-like preference to guide his thinking to its conclusions' (p. 33). Thus for Dewey the very idea of pure ratiocination is suspect, in that such rarefied cognition would reinforce the false belief in the detachment of the rational from the sensory and the logical from the instinctive. Second, and here too employing Keats, Dewey claims that in equating truth with beauty, Keats's *Ode* refers not to truth in a modern, scientific, or positivistic sense of verification, but rather in the sense of the wisdom by which people live, indeed 'the lore of good and evil' (p. 34). Keats's words show a good deal, Dewey believes, about both the nature of experiential (and for Dewey that means genuine) knowledge and its relation to beauty. It was, Dewey claims, in his moments of 'most intense esthetic perception' that Keats found simultaneously his 'utmost solace and his deepest convictions' (p. 34). Far from being epistemologically neutral, aesthetic experience – and thus art – is a central source of knowledge[20] in human life.

II EXPERIENTIAL DEPTH AND ITS REFLECTION IN THE MIRROR OF ART

Any critic, even a sympathetic one, could ask of Dewey at this point if indeed his conception of experience was so broad and encompassing, or to a sterner critic so vague and undefined, as to render unilluminatingly general the theory of art that so clearly depends on that conception of experience. Dewey's next philosophical aim is to provide the requisite specificity.

Experience, of course, occurs continuously, because the live creature is in constant interaction, and in a constant process of self-creation or self-renewal, with the conditions of the environment. But often, Dewey now adds, the 'experience had is inchoate' (Dewey, 1958b, p. 35). He suggests that encounters with the inchoate are failures of *composition*, i.e. they are not 'composed into *an* experience' (p. 35). But when the content of experience runs its course, when it achieves fulfilment, when it is internally integrated, and when it is marked off as distinct from the rest of the stream of experience,[21] it constitutes *an* experience. A piece of work is satisfactorily completed, a distinct problem is solved, a game is played to its conclusion, a meal is finished, a conversation is kept on track to its conclusion, a political campaign is completed: in all of those and countless other cases, *closure* is reached with a sense of having followed a given course, with the sense of having moved through an organizing sequence to a consummation. That sense of an ending[22] stands in contrast to the mere fact of cessation, which follows a disorganized series (not a *sequence*) or episodes that happen to follow on each other, without any teleological thread.[23] Experiences of the kind that prefigure and constitute art (depending on whether the content of the experience is analogous to or within the realm of the aesthetic) display two generally defining characteristics: they possess an individuating quality,[24] and they exhibit self-sufficiency. In the best of such experiences, every successive part 'flows freely, without seam and without unfilled blanks, into what ensues'[25] (p. 36). The *integrated* quality of the experience is also essential:

As one part leads into another and as one part carries on what went before, each gains distinctness in itself. The enduring whole is diversified by successive phases that are emphases of its varied colors.

Because of continuous merging, there are no holes, mechanical junctions, and dead centers when we have *an* experience. There are pauses, places of rest, but they punctuate and define the quality of movement. They sum up what has been undergone and prevent its dissipation and idle evaporation ... In a work of art, different acts, episodes, occurrences melt and fuse into unity, and yet do not disappear and lose their own character as they do so ...

The existence of this unity is constituted by a single *quality* that pervades the entire experience in spite of the variation of its constituent parts.

(Dewey, 1958b, pp. 36–7)

It is clear that in this part of his aesthetic theory, Dewey is not far from espousing the traditional aesthetic values of uniformity amidst variety and organic unity, nor is he far from the thesis that a work achieves its completion when anything added or deleted either detracts rather than adds to the work or diminishes its coherence.[26] And he is verging on, or over, the edges of Gestalt psychology[27] in emphasizing perceptual integration and the fusing into unity. It is no more surprising to see those elements of past aesthetic theory integrated into Dewey's philosophy than it is to see the various ways in which Dewey anticipated a number of developments in the field; pragmatism has been since its inception a philosophy simultaneously accepting of external influences, of internal developmental processes and progress, and of constant renewal, change and self-recreation through appropriation and reformulation. But it has also been a philosophical movement that has – here too like a live creature interacting with its environment – defined itself oppositionally,[28] and Dewey does so in his examination of experience by setting himself directly against the empiricism of Locke and Hume.

The classical empiricists' philosophy ultimately reduced all experience to the twin categories of sensation and reflection (or impressions and ideas); experience was there described as separate, distinct inscriptions on the senses (impressions), or as imaginative recollections of those sensory impacts (ideas), the two being differentiated (in Hume) by the force and vivacity of the experience. Dewey is opposed to that conception both in its explicit content and in what it philosophically engenders: regarding content, he has consistently argued that experience as given is not fragmented, not a mosaic (if it is assembled at all) of isolated sense data; regarding what it engenders, in that the Humean conception of experience renders us blind to the 'developing underlying quality' (p. 37) of given experiences and to the containment of the past in the present. Indeed, on empirical grounds, the *coherence* of the better kind of experience is missed; *all* experience would be demoted to the variety of inchoate sensation that it is the purpose of the live creature to overcome. Aesthetic experience of the kind Dewey is articulating would be impossible on classically empirical grounds.

But Dewey, in oppositionally defining his position, must place his view against not only historical empiricism; he must also place it between, and thus also against each of, what he identifies as the twin poles of the nonaesthetic. 'At one pole', he writes, 'is the loose succession that does not begin at any particular place and that ends – in the sense of ceasing – at no particular place. At the other pole is arrest, constriction, proceeding from parts having only a mechanical connection with one another' (Dewey, 1958b, p. 40). And what he is most strongly encouraging us to resist is the inundation by the non-aesthetic of the prosaic contexts of ordinary life; there are so many assaults on the sensibility by the two polar varieties that we can come unconsciously to accept them as the 'norms of all experience' (p. 40), thus again reinforcing the illegitimate separation of the aesthetic from the ordinary. And the primary enemies of the aesthetic, he claims, are not the mistaken enemies of traditional theory, i.e. the practical on the one hand and the purely intellectual on the other, both of which we have seen Dewey to have found problematic.[29] The enemies are the 'humdrum; slackness of loose ends; submission to convention in practice and intellectual procedure'. We find 'abstinence, coerced submission, tightness on one side and dissipation, incoherence, and aimless indulgence on the other' (p. 40). Here Dewey appropriates a part of Aristotle's philosophy, suggesting that in this sense the proper location of the aesthetic, like that of virtue in the *Nicomachean Ethics*,[30] is the mean between the two polar vices placed at each end of a continuum, but he also emends the appropriated element, suggesting that what constitutes the mean cannot be decided without recourse to the developmental movement towards consummation as sensed within a particular aesthetic experience.

In giving further specificity to his concept of experience, both in the positive respects of what it is and the negative respects of what it is not, Dewey delivers an indictment of modern life as it is too frequently lived: in a hurried and impatient social environment our experience becomes 'thin' because it fails to integrate what he calls the 'underdoings' of our experience, i.e. the resonances with the past, the anticipation of the future, the integral teleology of the structure of the experience, the emotive charges of the event and so forth. No one experience reaches maturation, nor does understanding suffuse it, because we suffer not only from an internal 'excess of receptivity' (p. 45) but also from an external bombardment by a miscellany of episodic distractions that yield at once a surfeit of thin, and a paucity of real, experience. Art is thus, for Dewey and for us if we suffer from the maladies he has diagnosed, one of the primary tools available in life to restore experiential depth.

III EXPRESSION, CREATION AND THE CREATIVE ROLE OF THE SPECTATOR

Experience, of the requisite sort, prefigures art, and art provides a mimetic embodiment of that prefigurative experience as it offers a new, distinctively aesthetic experience, through its invitation to engage in a dynamic interaction between self and artwork. What then of the *making* of art? Is artistic creativity patterned after Dewey's conception of genuine experience? The answer is precisely what we would expect: 'the esthetic experience ... is thus seen to be inherently connected with the experience of making' (Dewey, 1958b, p. 49). And the connection, for Dewey, is complex, and again one way of understanding it is gained through an understanding of what it is not. If the artist's hand and eye are engaged in making, so that the response of the eye to what the hand has just done guides the hand to its next move (as in painting or etching, for example), there is a part – but only one part – of the whole of aesthetic creativity it is Dewey's desire to illuminate. This partial scenario produces only a *'mechanical* sequence of sense and movement' (p. 50, emphasis mine), and reduces the creative act to an analogue of walking that is 'automatic', i.e. that is directed but in a sense unconscious. However, when this partial scenario is filled in with the rest of the picture, we arrive, Dewey suggests, at a much fuller account of creativity than is otherwise available. While it is true that the eye very closely attends to what the hand has done (and thus partially assumes the role of the spectator), subsequent movement is first, not a matter of whim or caprice, but guided by the 'logic' of the work; second, not a matter of routine or any approximation of creative automatism; third, mutually interpenetrating, so that the movement of the hand controls the perception of the eye, and – approximating but not arriving at a kind of creative paradox – simultaneously vice versa, so that the perception of the eye controls the movement of the hand; and fourth, guided by 'the whole being' (p. 50), where 'hand and eye ... are but instruments through which the entire live creature, moved and active throughout, operates' (p. 50); fifth, the artist 'perfect[s] a *new* vision' (emphasis mine) rather than repeating an old model warehoused in the creative imagination; and sixth, the artist simultaneously builds up an experience that is, in the previously discussed senses of experiential quality, internally coherent while still maintaining a sense of constant forward motion and change in its development teleologically guided towards the kind of experiential consummation indicated above.

That would perhaps seem rather a lot in terms of elucidating the creative act, but if we recall the great value we place on artistic achievements, and if we recall the full critical and attentive absorption such works can repeatedly – in the same observer – occasion, then indeed we should expect rather a lot: it would be far more puzzling a state of affairs if we did not expect as much, and yet still value creative work as we do. And although Dewey is not generally given to adducing linguistic evidence or appealing to linguistic practice, he observes in passing that there is a piece of verbal support for his position: it is, he says, no linguistic accident that the artistic terms 'building', 'construction', and, most generically, 'work' refer both to a process and to its completed product (Dewey, 1958b, p. 51). If, to grammatically encapsulate Dewey's point, we did not have the content of the verb, the noun would be empty.

Is the work entirely the artist's? Given what we already know about Dewey's overarching aim of placing aesthetics back into the realm of lived experience, and his accompanying desire to place aesthetics within the sphere of pragmatic action rather than to leave it in the over-rarefied realm of (imagined) pure contemplation or intellection, the answer is clearly negative. Dewey shows little patience for those who, bypassing an experiential apprenticeship prerequisite to genuine aesthetic perception, would try to *see* art by passively *looking*, perhaps learning to attach correct names and dates to images. Only if we perform the *work* required for seeing, work involving what he calls the 'continuous interaction between the total organism and the objects' (Dewey, 1958b, p. 54), can we say there has been a genuine case of aesthetic perception. And that work is *itself* creative, and the sustained act of creative interpretation must, he claims, 'include relations comparable to those which the original producer underwent' (p. 54). The perceiver, for Dewey, is not given licence to construct the work for himself or herself in just any way; the creativity assigned the viewer on Dewey's theory is not by any means unconstrained in the style posited by recent poststructural theorists and reception theorists. Yet the exact recovery of the intentional state of the artist Dewey would find too strict and insufficiently creative.[31] Thus again the pragmatist charts a middle course between polar extremes. The perceiver, he suggests, must order the various elements of the work that is in general form – but not in exact details – the same as that consciously experienced by the artist in the creative process outlined above.[32] On a moment's reflection it becomes clear that only the general organizational scheme or form could be similar; the details of the emotional charges of the elements, and the resonances and whisperings from past experience elicited by the work, would be idiosyncratic to each individual.[33] Thus this is creative work that, in different senses, is dependent and independent, and it is essential to aesthetic experience: 'Without an act of recreation the object is not perceived as a work of art' (p. 54). Creativity in art is not the sole province of the artist, yet the creative acts are related, if not identical. Does a similar relation hold for the expressive content of art?

Like other twentieth-century theorists of expression,[34] Dewey is quick to draw the distinction between discharging and expressing an emotion. Discharging is simply an unmediated venting of some perturbation; expressing, by contrast, is to carry forward through a developmental process, and to work out to a completion that possesses the sense of closure described above, an emotional state or condition. The former is of no aesthetic interest (although it may be of moral interest through the ability of such emotional discharges to reveal character). The latter, for the artist, is the emotive element of the creative process; for the viewer, reader, or auditor, it is the emotional process that loosely constrains the interpretation of emotional content in the work, and more importantly it is the element of the work that offers the appreciator his or her individualized experience of emotional 'working through', the aesthetic experience of emotional imagination (in that we can imaginatively enter into emotional states foreign to our own experience)[35] and the aesthetic experience of emotional maturation (in that we can come to terms, through dynamic relational interaction, with the emotional states and conditions that we harbour).

It is again important to recognize that Dewey's position in the philosophy of mind behind his aesthetic position is *not* one of Cartesian dualism. He is most assuredly not claiming that emotional states are private, inward experiences whose content and quality we know immediately through privileged first-person introspective access.[36] On the contrary, and in a way consistent with the mental philosophies of a number of his fellow pragmatists, notably G. H. Mead and C. S. Peirce, he believes that the expressive act need not follow, logically as well as temporally, the inner emotional meaning.[37] Often the meaning, or, more broadly, the human significance, of the expressive act is learned inwardly *after* the expressive gesture in action is interpreted to have meaning to an outside observer. That is not, however, behaviourism, i.e. not a theory of expression that *removes* the inner life from consideration. It is a position, here too, that charts a middle course between the polemical extremes of Cartesian dualism and behaviourism. The self gains self-knowledge with regard to the significance of expressive action through, again, dynamic mutually constitutive interaction with the environment. One particular passage of Dewey articulates this position clearly:

> The transition from an act that is expressive from the standpoint of an outside observer to one intrinsically expressive is readily illustrated by a simple case. At first a baby weeps, just as it turns its head to follow light; there is an inner urge but nothing to express. As the infant matures, he learns that particular acts effect different consequences, that, for example, he gets attention if he cries, and that smiling induces another definite response from those about him. He thus begins to be aware of the *meaning* of what he does. As he grasps the meaning of an act at first performed from sheer internal pressure, he becomes capable of acts of true expression. The transformation of sounds, babblings, lalling, and so forth, into language is a perfect illustration of the way in which acts of expression are brought into existence and also of the difference between them and mere acts of discharge.
>
> (Dewey, 1958b, p. 62)

That is a model, taken from the learning of expressive language,[38] that applies directly to the learning and developing of an expressive artistic language by an artist; what we need to remember is that the artist can assume the role of the spectator, the analogue to the 'outside observer' in the passage above, in the development and maturation of the expressive style. And the passage, perhaps less obviously, calls attention to the role of the *medium* in artistic expression; a mere act of emotional discharge 'lacks a medium' (Dewey, 1958b, p. 63), whereas the infant comes to shape and use language ('the transformation of sounds') in a purposeful and controlled way, in the interest of intentional emotional signification. The artist, Dewey suggests, uses the medium in the analogous way (which also explains why we would not find artistically compelling the employment of a medium in an instantaneously discharging, indeed unmediated, manner). What is more striking, beyond what Dewey explicitly suggests, is that it makes a way for the appreciation of the work to enter *into* the expressive 'language' of the work and not merely passively 'listen to' or 'hear' it, precisely because, as we have seen, the appreciator's re-creative role requires that the work of perceptual assemblage, in part, be accomplished by him or her. The artistic analogue to the language of the infant – the artistic medium – is used, and is hence meaningful, by both artist and viewer.

There are, to be sure, a number of questions calling for answers. What, to take one fairly rudimentary question, shall we say concerning the specificity of the emotional content of the work of art? Dewey is fully aware of the philosophical subtleties surrounding the question of the specificity of emotional experience itself, and he suggests that there *is* no such thing as '*the* emotion of fear, hate, love' (Dewey, 1958b, p. 67).[39] There are only unique and, as he says, unduplicated emotional states: there are only countless and different instances of fear of this particular oncoming automobile at this particular time and place in precisely this frame of mind with precisely this background of memory, precisely these resonances from past episodes of fear, and so forth through countless nuances. 'A lifetime', he suggests for good reason, 'would be too short to reproduce in words a single emotion' (p. 67). Is then the emotive content of the work unique and particularized? The answer is necessarily affirmative, because as it is an emotion, it *must* be uniquely particularized. But this is where, as Dewey suggested earlier, the form of the interpretation on the part of the viewer needs to follow the artist, but the particularized content need not. The viewer will still see what we call e.g. fear in the work, and so in general form it corresponds to the expressive content invested in the work by the artist. (To see joy would be formally discordant with the work, and thus constitute an interpretive error.) But the fear will be particularized, and made unique, by the experiential stock[40] of the viewer; the expressive content is, in large and general terms, that of the artist, and in fully particularized and humanly contextualized terms, his or her own.

Another question worth asking is what precisely is the role played by the emotional content of the work in terms of the work's structure and design. It is apparent that Dewey has strong feelings concerning the matter. He suggests that one quite common way of failing artistically is to attempt to regulate, in a most deliberate way, the emotive impact of the work, and thus to order and arrange the elements of the larger Gestalt in a formulaic way. We feel, in the presence of such works, emotionally manipulated, and we accordingly take offence. In such works no inner 'logical necessity' (Dewey, 1958b, p. 68) of the work's structural coherence is sensed; if one thinks of the successes, e.g. the feeling of inexorability often conveyed in Greek drama,[41] or the sense of necessity exhibited in the unfolding of the most successful development sections of the sonata form,[42] it becomes clear what Dewey means by the failures. 'We are irritated', he says, at the feeling generated by our recognition within aesthetic experience that the artist is 'manipulating materials to secure an effect decided upon in advance' (p. 68). An *external* force holds the various structural elements of the work together; it is only the sense of necessity, the inspired *internal* force, which will yield successful work. In making that claim Dewey is implicitly protecting the concept of artistic inspiration,[43] giving it a secure place within his theory. In uninspired work, we have 'foisted upon us ... something that we feel comes from outside the movement of the subject matter' (p. 68). Indeed, it is for Dewey the subject matter, and *not* the author, that should serve as the arbiter of the work. And as to the explicit shaping power of the emotion on the structure and design, he says the 'determination of the *mot juste*, of the right incident in the right place, of exquisiteness of proportion, of the precise tone, hue and shade that helps unify the whole while it defines a part, is accomplished by emotion' (p. 70). And that will be not merely any emotion: it will be, in the cases of high artistic achievement, an emotion that has undergone the full process of developmental maturation.

Still another question arises: is this particular process of emotional development and maturation one that occurs before entry into the creative process, or does it occur during and within that process? We know that in one sense the maturation must occur prior to the work, because the emotive content exhibited in the work will to some extent incorporate the past; the resonances of related past experience will inevitably be felt, particularly if the emotive content of the work is sufficient to serve as arbiter, sufficient to structurally organize it, sufficient to have the work, as we say, 'take on a life of its own'. And Dewey believes that one vital part of this maturation occurs in our 'underdoings': 'Subconscious maturation precedes creative production in every line of human endeavor' (Dewey, 1958b, p. 73). Direct effort, not stabilized by such experiential ballast, 'never gave birth to anything that is not mechanical' (p. 73). So it appears that the maturation, an essential condition of artistic success, precedes the work.

Yet it is only, as one may also now expect, part of the larger creative truth Dewey is attempting to elucidate. Once again, a middle way is found. It is also compatibly true that the *work* of artistic creativity involves emotive maturation in a way internal to the work in progress; if we were able to proceed back to the earliest manifestations of the work of art, to proto-artistic stirrings, we would discover 'an emotion *comparatively* gross and undefined' (Dewey, 1958b, p. 75, emphasis mine), and the 'assumed definite shape' only as it worked through a developmental process of expressing itself, or being captured, in various changes to real and imagined material in the given artistic medium. What is required is an ability Dewey believes common to all accomplished artists, the ability not merely to experience the inceptive emotion, nor merely the technical ability to manipulate and order the materials of a medium, but the 'capacity to work a vague idea and emotion over into terms of some definite medium' (p. 75). So art, or the artistic process, certainly has – in that particular sense also – great epistemological value (and one might add a therapeutic value) for the artist. Artistic expression is 'the clarification of turbid emotion' (p. 77), and the process it requires, a process sufficient to transcend the formulaic and the shallowly manipulative, is productive of self-knowledge and self-integration.

Is it, in those precise respects, valuable for the appreciator also? Going back to the question of the temporal priority versus the simultaneity of emotional maturation with the creation of the work, it is in the appreciator's case plainly evident that the *artist's* maturational processes precede the appreciator's engagement with the work. But that by no means diminishes the epistemological or therapeutic dimensions of the aesthetic experience for the appreciator. We come to know our appetites, Dewey says, 'when they are reflected in the mirror of art' (Dewey, 1958b, p. 77), and for the viewer too, as we gain self-knowledge of those appetites through mimetic enjoyment, 'they are transfigured'. The experience of emotional transfiguration is not 'a form of sentiment that exists independently from the outset', it is rather a distinctively aesthetic emotion induced in the viewer by expressive artistic material. Hence there is, in cases of genuine aesthetic experience, epistemic and therapeutic gain in terms particularly of emotional maturation. But in all of this it is again important, in understanding Dewey, to avoid the trap of interpreting him in terms of Cartesian dualism. Those processes, the emotive content of the epistemic gain that art affords, do not occur in the twin (and separate) categories of inner emotion and outward artistic material. They occur in an indissolubly interactive fashion; the live creature does not possess a fully formed identity separate from and prior to its environment. In regard to the developmental changes that occur in physical materials and in expressive emotion (the materials of the aesthetic environment), Dewey writes 'Nor are there in fact two operations, one performed upon the outer material and the other upon the inner and mental stuff' (p. 75). Dualism, as Dewey has shown us in a number of respects, can only obfuscate the very creative processes (on the parts of both the artist and the viewer) it is his goal to illuminate.

Two further questions arise from the expressionistic dimension of Dewey's aesthetic theory. The first concerns spontaneity in art, particularly if the insistence on expressing – with all that we have seen this concept to entail – over and above the discharging of emotion, precludes spontaneity. Works of art, Dewey readily acknowledges, do in empirical fact exhibit 'an air of spontaneity' (Dewey, 1958b, p. 70), yet we know that our most spontaneous emotional outbursts are decidedly not aesthetic, or not expressive in the aesthetic sense. And if any seeming outburst *is* expressive, then it is not an unmediated function of 'momentary internal pressures' (p. 70). Spontaneity in art, even if seemingly self-contradictory given what he has heretofore said, is possible, Dewey posits, through a complete absorption in subject matter that is fresh. It is true, he claims, that reflection on the material, and its processes of maturation, may have been long and arduous, but nevertheless an artistic expression will 'manifest spontaneity if that matter has been vitally taken up into a present experience' (p. 70), i.e. if the particular expressive content takes a place within the larger Gestalt of the developing work and satisfies all the demands of genuine experience as delineated above. Any amount of labour, he says, is compatible with spontaneity in art, but only in so far as the resultant artistic work maintains the 'freshness' of the emotion – which must mean an emotion that is still in the active processes of negotiation with the structure of the work and continual maturation and clarification. 'Staleness of matter', he writes, along with the 'obtrusion of calculation' (p. 70), are the enemies of spontaneity in art; his theory, properly understood and integrated (bringing the expressionistic and the experiential dimensions of the theory into alignment), is not.

The final brief question concerns a relation already intimated, specifically that between linguistic meaning and emotive content, or – broadly stated – between verbal and artistic meaning. We already know that Dewey believes that it would require, as experiential prerequisite, a lifetime to get into a position from which we might capture an emotion fully in words. Dewey displays strong feelings on this topic as well, and treats it forcefully and succinctly. After clarifying the assertion that thought, in the materials of colours, tones and images, is distinct from linguistic thought,[44] he adds that only superstition would hold that because the thought contained in paintings or symphonies cannot be given translations into linguistic form, or that of poetry into prose, that the only real thought is linguistic or verbal thought, that the intellectual content we find on canvas and in sound cannot thus genuinely constitute thought. There are, Dewey insists, values and meanings that can *only* be experienced by 'visible and audible qualities' and 'to ask what they mean in the sense of something else that can be put into words is to deny their distinctive existence' (Dewey, 1958b, p. 74). And, like numerous others in the history of aesthetic theory, he preserves an expressive *necessity* in the genesis of the arts in civilization: if the values and meanings recorded in our greatest artistic achievements could have been expressed in linguistic form, the arts, he suggests, would never have come into existence.

Dewey began his philosophy of art by observing the 'ironic perversity' that would keep our understanding of art remote from the lived human contexts that constitute the locus of genuine aesthetic engagement.[45] After an examination of Dewey's conception of the live creature, his philosophy of experience, and his analysis of artistic expression, it does indeed become easier to see precisely why he found so perversely ironic the particular circumstance aesthetic theory found itself in, before he brought the resources of pragmatism to the philosophy of art. The elevation of a masterpiece, figuratively and literally, to a high and remote pedestal only severs the multiform linkages to human experience, thus removing the very possibility of self-constitutive and mutually transformative experience of the kind Dewey finds not only of the greatest human value but also necessary to the very condition of arthood. Aesthetic emotion, properly understood, is undeniably distinctive, yet it is 'not cut off by a chasm from other and natural emotional experiences' (p. 78); that would constitute one kind of latter-day Platonic banishment of the arts from society. One can see in Dewey's thought a pragmatic realism competing with a kind of idealism: he writes

> "In an imperfect society – and no society will ever be perfect – fine art will be to some extent an escape from, or an adventitious decoration of, the main activities of living. But in a better-ordered society than that in which we live, an infinitely greater happiness than is now the case would attend all modes of production"
>
> (Dewey, 1958b, pp. 80–1)

That greater happiness would come, he suggests, with the advent of a social organization that is not externally imposed, but rather of a kind that grows from within the structures of human experience, a kind that 'involves ... the whole of the live creature, toward a fulfilling conclusion' (p. 81). And it is only works of art – apart from and supplementary to the great values of the arts that we have had pointed out to us by Dewey – that have the capacity at once to reflect the best of social experience and to contribute substantially to the creation of that collective experience. 'The remaking of the material of experience in the act of expression is not an isolated event confined to the artist and to a person here and there who happens to enjoy the work' (p. 81). On the contrary, it can be the 'remaking of the experience of the community' (p. 81).

There is a great deal more in Dewey's philosophy of art than it is possible to examine here, but again (1) the recontextualization of human life as lived within his discussion of the live creature, (2) his full account of the structures and forms of valuable lived experience, and (3) his analysis of the tightly intertwined processes of aesthetic expression, artistic creation and the creative role of the spectator, are

Dewey's pragmatic aesthetics 293

the three pillars upon which his full theory stands.[46] It would indeed constitute yet another particularly unfortunate irony if, from the vantage point of contemporary aesthetics, we rendered ourselves unable to hear his constructive and – in terms of the great and distinct power of the arts to remake social experience in the interest of the collective good – prescient voice because we have elevated his writings to the pedestal of lofty and remote historical significance, above and beyond the active field of aesthetic discourse today.

NOTES

1 Dewey, 1958b. This book had its origins in the William James Lectures that Dewey delivered at Harvard University in 1931.
2 In a number of differing ways this fundamentally pragmatic imperative to recover the ordinary has been furthered both in philosophy in general and in aesthetics in particular in the time since Dewey wrote. Although perhaps not all these authors would explicitly acknowledge a conceptual linkage to Dewey (i.e. there is a similar strain running back to Wittgenstein and J. L. Austin), the manifestations of this imperative in twentieth-century philosophy would make a lengthy and fascinating study in their own right. See Cavell, 1988a, particularly ch. 6, 'The Uncanniness of the Ordinary', pp. 153–78; Cavell, 1990, particularly ch. 2, 'The Argument of the Ordinary', pp. 64–100; Cavell, 1988b, particularly 'The Ordinary as the Uneventful (A Note on the *Annales* Historians)', pp. 184–94. Much of Cavell's work relevant to this theme is helpfully anthologized in Mulhall, 1996; see also Mulhall, 1994. See also many of the writings of Arthur Danto relating to this theme, including Danto, 1981, particularly 'Works of Art and Mere Real Things', pp. 1–32; Danto, 1997, *passim*; see also the essays, many of which touch on the theme of the relations between the art object and the ordinary object, in Danto, 1986. While it is true that Danto is principally concerned with the *difference* between the art object and the ordinary (non-art) object (e.g. Duchampian snow shovels and bottle racks versus their non-Duchampian counterparts), the larger point is that the difference is retinally indiscernible: thus to that extent the ordinary *has* been, in a way and for reasons Danto finely articulates, ontologically elevated.
This tradition of recovering and unveiling the significance of the ordinary runs back at least to Wordsworth, as has been discussed in Leonard, 1994; for a brief discussion see Hagberg, 1996a, pp. 295–7, and for a brief discussion of Danto's method see Hagberg, 1991, pp. 221–30. For an

explicit development of this fundamental pragmatic imperative see Shusterman, 1992, *passim*, and for a framing of the issue in terms of aesthetic egalitarianism, see Krieger, 1981, *passim*.

3   It would not be difficult to press the analogy to Plato too far. This is in truth at once Platonic and anti-Platonic; the ascension from illusion to truth constitutes the former, as does the idea of art as a mirror held up to reality. But while Plato's theory would emphasize the immutable, the autonomous, the trans-historical, Dewey's theory of course emphasizes the opposite. Emphasizing the similarities, Dewey writes 'it is not surprising that the Athenian Greeks, when they came to reflect upon art, formed the idea that it is an art of reproduction, an imitation', and noting that, although there is much to criticize in that conception of the arts, still 'the theory is testimony to the close connection of the fine arts with daily life; the idea would not have occurred to any one had art been remote from the interests of life' (Dewey, 1958b, p. 7).

4   In addition to Ludwig Wittgenstein's *magnum opus*, *Philosophical Investigations* (1953), in which – as a vast album of such assembled reminders – it is claimed of philosophical problems that they 'are solved, not by giving new information, but by arranging what we have already known' (section 109); see particularly in connection with art Barrett, 1972. For a profound use of the method in epistemology, see *On Certainty* Wittgenstein, 1969b; for an acute elucidation see Stroll, 1994.

5   See, on this problem, Sparshott, 1982, pp. 127–36.

6   For a recent insightful discussion see Cavell, 1998c.

7   Dewey suggests that that was a commonplace in Plato's time, during which 'art for art's sake' would not have been comprehensible. Indeed 'no contemporary would have doubted that music was an integral part of the ethos and the institutions of the community' (1958b, p. 8). Dewey observes that the conditions of mass production in industrialized society have proven inimical to the proper placement of art in society: the artist, pushed to one side, develops in self-defence an aesthetic of individualism and a corresponding theory of self-expression that only widens the gulf between ordinary and aesthetic experience, which stands as an analogue to, or as Dewey sometimes suggests, a manifestation of, 'the gulf which exists generally between producer and consumer in modern society' (p. 10).

8   For a strongly anti-Cartesian position at the heart of pragmatism, see Peirce, 1987, pp. 32–3. For an anti-Cartesian conception of the self, see the writings of G. H. Mead in Stuhr, 1987, pp. 430–76. For a recent discussion of pragmatism as it incorporates and builds on this non-dualistic stance (in language, epistemology, and other areas of philosophy, and particularly in relation to recent debate), see Putnam, 1995.

9 It is important to note that Dewey's pragmatic empiricism stands in contrast to Lockean and Humean empiricism; in this respect Dewey's position is of a piece with William James's conception of *radical* empiricism as it supplants classic empiricism. For full articulation of that position see James, 1976, pp. 21–44, reprinted in Stuhr, 1987, pp. 125–35. In brief, James's position 'differs from the Humean type of empiricism in one particular which makes one add the epithet radical. To be radical, an empiricism must neither admit into its constructions any element that is not directly experienced, nor exclude from them any element that is directly experienced' (Stuhr, 1987, p. 125). As James continues, it becomes clear that it is the continuous nature of conscious experience that he is underscoring, and that his position, in its inclusion of the various 'conjunctive relations' that integrate lived experience, opposes the experiential atomism implicit in classical empiricism; for James (and Dewey) experience is not analyzable into discrete, isolated units. See also the excerpt from James's *The Principles of Psychology* on the 'sensibly continuous' character of thought (in Stuhr, 1987, p. 113).

10 Dewey's position again relates clearly to that articulated by James; see the full excerpt from *The Principles of Psychology* in Stuhr, 1987, pp. 108–24, particularly on the nuanced alterations in the feeling state, the 'pulse of subjectivity', in the utterance of a seemingly objective, factual, and (allegedly) emotionally inert statement of fact (Stuhr, 1987, pp. 120–2).

11 See also the remarkable passage from George Eliot's *The Mill on the Floss* in Dewey, 1958b, p. 18: 'These familiar flowers, these well-remembered bird-notes, this sky with its fitful brightness, these furrowed and grassy fields, each with a sort of personality given to it by the capricious hedge, such things as these are the mother tongue of our imagination, the language that is laden with all the subtle inextricable associations the fleeting hours of our childhood left behind them. Our delight in the sunshine of the deep-bladed grass today might be no more than the faint perception of wearied souls, if it were not for the sunshine and grass of far-off years, which still live in us and transform our perception into love.'

12 This element of Dewey's thought connects to a view articulated by Santayana, 1955; the excerpts reprinted in Stuhr (1987, pp. 277–303) provide the fundamentals of the fuller position to which Dewey is alluding and upon which he is relying. This incidentally is another point of similarity between the pragmatic and Wittgensteinian traditions; on the role of 'animal knowledge' in epistemology see the works cited in nn. 33 and 34 below.

13 For a discussion of such fear of the senses as it has been manifested in aesthetic thought and then diagnosed in Nietzsche's critique, see Hagberg, 1995a.
14 On the matter of the repudiation of entrenched dichotomies (e.g. mind/matter, appearance/reality, theory/practice, facts/values, individual/community, etc.) as a defining characteristic of pragmatic thought, see Stuhr, 1987, pp. 3–12.
15 Thus the work of art is not defined as a repository of secondary qualities, consistent with classic pragmatism's larger opposition to Lockean and Humean empiricism.
16 Dewey relates the separation of the lived from the fine to the separation of the beautiful from the useful, which he identifies as yet another pernicious distinction in aesthetic theory (as well he should from the vantage point of pragmatism). In this connection see his pointed remark 'The story of the severance and final sharp opposition of the useful and the fine is the history of that industrial development through which so much of production has become a form of postponed living and so much of consumption a superimposed enjoyment of the fruits of the labor of others' (1958bp. 27).
17 This relates closely to the issue of the integration of the self's past discussed above. Specifically, if the past experience in a given case was *sensory* in nature, and the sensory is, under the influence of the position here criticized by Dewey, repudiated on the very grounds that the sensory is intrinsically morally objectionable and epistemologically insignificant, then the kind of past-integration (and thus self-integration) Dewey (and aesthetic experience of the kind he adumbrates) encourages is rendered impossible from the outset. Again the pragmatic and Wittgensteinian tradition intersect: a pernicious philosophical 'picture' can, as Wittgenstein put it, 'hold us captive' (see *Philosophical Investigations*, section 115).
18 See, for example, Dewey, 1958b, p. 30: 'Myths were something other than intellectualistic essays of primitive man in science.' For a fascinating set of compatible observations on the meaning and understanding of myth and ritual (and marking another point of convergence between those traditions), see Wittgenstein, 1979.
19 See the quotations from the letter to Keats's brother, particularly 'The greater part of men make their way with the same instinctiveness, the same unwandering eye from their purposes as the Hawk' (Dewey, 1958b, p. 32), as well as, again, the writings of Santayana on animal faith.
20 Indeed one of the virtues of pragmatic philosophy is that it has significantly broadened the scope of epistemology; virtually all of the classical

and most recent contributors to the field have written on knowledge in the broadening way suggested by Dewey here. For a representative sampling of Dewey on the subject, see 'The Pattern of Inquiry', from *Logic: The Theory of Inquiry*, LW12, cited in Stuhr, 1987, pp. 369–77; see also 'Education as Growth', from *Democracy and Education*, MW9, in Stuhr, 1987, pp. 377–83. See also Smith, 1992, where pragmatic epistemology is illuminatingly contrasted to Marxist positions.

21 The *locus classicus* within pragmatism of this notion is of course William James's writings on the 'stream of thought' in *The Principles of Psychology*; see the excerpt in Stuhr, 1987, pp. 108–24. See also Smith, 1970.

22 I borrow Frank Kermode's title phrase; see *The Sense of an Ending: Studies in the Theory of Fiction* (1968) for an examination of the concept in literary contexts.

23 For a full discussion of the sense of teleology and continuity within the concept of the self, see Wollheim, 1984.

24 See more recent discussions, to which this view of Dewey's directly relates, of qualia (as irreducibly individuating characteristics of phenomenal experience); a number of them are conveniently anthologized in Rosenthal, 1991.

25 Here too Dewey's discussion anticipates more recent work, in this case in psychology; see Csikszentmihalyi, 1991.

26 The aesthetic value of uniformity amid variety was championed principally by Hutcheson, *An Inquiry into the Original of Our Ideas of Beauty and Virtue* (1725), reprinted frequently; see for example Dickie *et al.*, 1989, pp. 223–41. The notion also plays a role later in the eighteenth century (1755) in Moses Mendelssohn's views on aesthetics; see Gilbert and Kuhn, 1956, pp. 296–7, and in Hogarth, *The Analysis of Beauty* (1772). The value of organic unity in the work of art traces back to Aristotle in the *Poetics* (Barnes, 1984), vol. II, pp. 2316–40; the notion of completion as the point of equilibrium where nothing can be added nor taken away without damage to the work also derives from Aristotle, and becomes particularly influential in the seventeenth and eighteenth centuries, with the architectural works of Palladio serving as the model exemplars of this feature; see Paulson, 1975, esp. pp. 33–4.

27 For the full development of Gestalt psychology in aesthetics see the writings of Arnheim, principally his *Art and Visual Perception* (1965).

28 For an excellent specimen of the oppositional self-definition in pragmatism, see Mead, *Mind*, 1934, conveniently excerpted in Stuhr, 1987, pp. 430–54.

29 Dewey identifies enemies of the aesthetic *within* the arts as well: a sculptor who does not care deeply for his subject matter, and thus for his work, and whose 'perception is not ... esthetic in nature' (1958b, p. 48) will have 'only a colorless and cold recognition of what has been done, used as a stimulus to the next step in a process that is essentially mechanical' (p. 48). This 'coldness' of process, identified as an enemy of the aesthetic, is contrasted to the artist who perceives that the work's internal developmental teleology controls the production of the work. This artist 'embodies in himself the attitude of the perceiver while he works' (p. 48). Thus Dewey's position holds great significance for the philosophy of creativity as well. For an independent discussion of the last point, see Wollheim, 1987.

30 In *The Complete Works of Aristotle*, Barnes, 1984, vol. II, esp. pp. 1747ff.

31 For an independent examination of this thesis, see Wollheim, 1980, pp. 185–204.

32 Although not by any means written as a development of Dewey's idea, we could see the development of the combination of interpretive restraint-with-freedom endorsed here in Walton, 1989; the practice is articulated in terms of standard, variable and contra-standard properties, where the aesthetic properties an object possesses depend to an extent on the category within which it is perceived. Mistaken judgements arise from the misperception of the work by seeing it 'through' the wrong category, not unlike the degree of perceptual correctness emphasized by Dewey.

33 This is, however, *not* to say that the emotional content is *private* to each individual. Dewey is careful to make that clear, and is thus not in this respect vulnerable to Wittgensteinian attacks on the (allegedly) meaning-determining private inner object, the inner sensation: '[E]motions ... are not, save in pathological instances, private' (Dewey, 1958b, p. 42). This is still another respect in which the Deweyan and Wittgensteinian positions are deeply compatible.

34 I refer to e.g. C. Ducasse, S. Langer and R. Collingwood, among others; for examination of those positions, see Hagberg, 1995b, pp. 1–74.

35 The development of the moral imagination by means of aesthetic experience is an idea with a rich past; for two recent studies giving a central place to that view in literary and musical experience respectively, see Palmer, 1992, and Ridley, 1995; for a discussion of the latter see my review (Hagberg, 1996b).

36 In this particular respect Dewey is closer to Wittgenstein than to William James – although Dewey's positions can oscillate according to the needs of the context.

37 For the classic sources of this fundamental pragmatic position, see the writings of Peirce and Mead in Stuhr, 1987.
38 The significance of a re-examination of the learning of language for aesthetic understanding has not been lost on a number of other writers in the field; see Wollheim, 1974, pp. 130–51; and – although the Wittgensteinian issue of entering language fans out throughout much of Cavell's work (see Mulhall, 1996, *passim*), see Cavell, 1995, pp. 125–86.
39 Dewey notes, interestingly, that that is why the novelist has an advantage over the psychologist in dealing with emotion: the novelist can construct a concrete, detailed, fully contextualized situation, and let *it* evoke the emotion, rather than attempting to describe it directly.
40 I adapt this phrase ('experiential stock') from Wollheim's 'cognitive stock', which he has helpfully employed to refer to the complex of ideas, attitudes, expectations, background knowledge, etc. in the mind of the beholder; see Wollheim, 1987.
41 Often the sense of inexorable progression and foreboding are generated simultaneously; see e.g. *The Medea*, 1955, pp. 56–108.
42 For clarifying studies of the inner logic or thematic cohesion generated in such musical sections, see Rosen, 1988.
43 Thus there is again one sense in which Dewey's conception is Platonic while in another sense being simultaneously strongly anti-Platonic; for Plato's view of artistic inspiration, with which Dewey's view does in this particular respect resonate, see *Ion*, in Hamilton and Cairns, 1961, pp. 215–28.
44 My own view is that it is a significantly more complex matter than suggested here. See Hagberg, 1994, chs. 1 and 2.
45 See Berleant, 1991, *passim*, for a recent expansive examination of the idea of aesthetic engagement.
46 Consider Dewey's own early summary of his project: 'I have tried to show in these chapters that the esthetic is no intruder in experience from without, whether by way of idle luxury or transcendent ideality, but that it is the clarified and intensified development of traits that belong to every normally complete experience. This fact I take to be the only secure basis upon which esthetic theory can build' (1958b, p. 46).

ANTON A. VAN NIEKERK

13 Pragmatism and religion

INTRODUCTION

The pragmatist appraisal of the intellectual respectability of religion as a human endeavour represents some of pragmatism's most controversial claims and positions. In certain circles, the view persists that pragmatism is in fact indifferent or even inhospitable to religion.[1] Many other commentators (of whom Bertrand Russell[2] was the first, if not still the most prominent), however, argue that the way in which pragmatism clearly can be utilized for a defence of religion is indicative of its very intellectual susceptibility – a susceptibility that is closely identified with the widely feared 'subjectivism' that a pragmatist position allegedly implies. In this sense, religion is the soft underbelly of pragmatism – the arena that demonstrates above all else that pragmatism represents an intellectual stance that has relinquished the canons of strict and consistent rationality and that is engaged in an irresponsible, yet also unavoidable flirtation with relativism. Others, to the contrary, hail the pragmatist evaluation of religion as exactly indicative of the openness and tolerance that a pragmatist life orientation facilitates in both societal and intellectual circles. For example, Giles Gunn in an article dealing with religion and the recent 'revival' of pragmatism, remarks that 'philosophers like John E. Smith, Richard J. Bernstein and John McDermott view pragmatism not only as a philosophical theory in need of defense but also as an intellectual method capable of keeping open the lines of communication between philosophy and some of the other departments of the intellectual life'.[3]

Although Charles Sanders Peirce (1839–1914), the 'founding father' of pragmatism, did not develop his original ideas as a defence of religion, the latter gained an unquestionable prominence in the reflections of William James. (James wrote about many other topics as well.) Although there are many references and discussions of religion in a number of Dewey's writings,[4] he wrote only one complete book on religion,[5] and he deals with the subject in a way that differs quite markedly from that of James (and, for that matter, from the way pragmatists generally deal with religion). The most prominent recent exponent of pragmatism was, of course, Richard Rorty. In stark contradistinction to his earlier work that revealed an outspoken disregard and critique of religion in any form, the way in which he turned to not only a discussion, but to an eventual distinctly pragmatist defence, of religion remains one of the most remarkable aspects of Rorty's philosophical work in the terminal phase of his life.[6]

In this chapter I will firstly deal with the way James understands and defends religion. This is followed by a discussion of Dewey's understanding and evaluation of religion – a position that dwells far less than the Jamesian view on the nature of religious belief, but rather concentrates on the relevance of religion for human action. Thereafter I deal with Rorty's current-day appraisal and critique of the classical pragmatist defences of religion. The chapter will be concluded by a short critical appraisal.

WILLIAM JAMES: RELIGION AS MOMENTOUS OPTION AND CONNECTION WITH HIGHER POWERS

As has been pointed out in earlier chapters in this volume, the fundamental presupposition of pragmatism as a philosophy is that all ideas (including beliefs, propositions, convictions and theories) are instruments that human beings design and use in order to so organize their environment that they can adapt it to their practical and existential needs. Ideas function in human lives for the sake of the removal of difficulties or the solution of problems or disconcerting puzzles. Ideas or beliefs, consequently, are true when they work, i.e. when they meet with success in pursuing the goal for which they were invented. This implies a distinct rejection of the age old correspondence theory of truth, in terms of which a knowledge claim is true when it 'corresponds with how things actually are in the world' (*veritas adaequatio rei et intellectus*; literally: truth is the correspondence between a thing (in the world) and the intellect). Richard Rorty claims that the founding proposition of pragmatism is that there is no difference of any real consequence, no 'difference that makes a difference' between the statements 'it works because it is true, and it is true because it works'.[7]

This idea draws on the radical insights of C. S. Peirce. In a famous essay with the title 'How to Make our Ideas Clear',[8] Peirce develops the idea that the 'sole motive, idea and function' of thought is 'to produce belief'. What, then, is a 'belief'? Peirce ascribes three properties to a belief: 'First, it is something that we are aware of; second, it appeases the irritation of doubt; and, third, it involves the establishment in our nature of a rule of action, or, say for short, a habit'.[9] In short, beliefs are habits of action. His point is that there exists the closest possible relationship between what we think or believe, and some action that is precipitated by that belief. Beliefs always and necessarily arise and function within the ambit of some practical goal that we seek through concerted action. For Peirce, as for all the pragmatists, the idea that belief is divorced from action and arrived at purely for its own sake or for the sake of inherent intellectual insight or gratification is inconceivable.

Gunn rightfully claims that 'religion played a not inconsiderable, if not always obvious, role in the thinking of the founding generation [of pragmatism]'.[10] Of no one is this more true than of William James, who applied Peirce's idea of beliefs as 'habits of action' directly to religious beliefs. James's best-known exposition of his pragmatist view of religion is to be found in his essay 'The Will to Believe'.[11] This very title seems to suggest the implausibility of thinking about beliefs as 'habits of action'. Would the implication of such a view not be that, if there is that close a bond between what we believe and some goal we wish to achieve through action, we could literally believe whatever we please, i.e. we could 'will to believe' anything that facilitates some practical project? This possibility does concern James in this essay. He refers to the famous proof for God's existence known as 'Pascal's wager'. This is the argument that claims that it would be foolish not to believe in God, for if God does not exist, belief in him would have brought us no harm, whereas if he indeed exists and we choose not to believe, we forfeit the significant benefits that belief in Him would have brought us. Pascal's wager is often put forward as a good example of a pragmatist view of religion:[12] we believe in God, according to such an argument, not because God's existence can 'objectively be demonstrated', but purely for the sake of practical expediency.

James rejects Pascal's wager as a persuasive argument; religion cannot be defended with 'the language of the gaming table'.[13] While he defends the claim that (also religious) beliefs are 'habits of action', the relationship between beliefs and action needs to be specified more closely. For this purpose, he introduces a threefold distinction that needs to be applied to beliefs in order for them to attain the status of justifiable religious beliefs. Beliefs can, according to these distinctions, be regarded as hypotheses that we accept or reject according to three sets of options presented to us. These options are living or dead, forced or avoidable, and momentous or trivial.[14] James uses the following examples: the choice between being a theosophist or a Mohammedan is, for Christians, dead, since neither is in any way a realistic possibility. But the choice between being a Christian and being an agnostic does make some appeal to our belief, and is thus live. The choice between leaving the building with or without an umbrella is an avoidable choice; one need not leave the building. If a perfect stranger confronts me with the choice 'love me or hate me', it is similarly not forced, since I can, without any problem, continue to be completely indifferent towards that person.

But if I say, 'Either accept this truth or go without it,' I put on you a forced option, for there is no standing place outside of the alternative. Every dilemma based on a complete logical disjunction, with no possibility of not choosing, is an option of this forced kind.[15]

Lastly, momentous options are those choices that we take seriously because they offer unique or unrivalled opportunities. The offer to partake in space travel is momentous for a NASA pilot; he cannot be indifferent to it, since it comes once in a lifetime and would be the culmination of an ideal that any such pilot works for in his/her career. The option, on the other hand, is trivial when the opportunity it offers is not unique. James's example is: 'A chemist finds an hypothesis live enough to spend a year in its verification: he believes in it to that extent. But if his experiments prove inconclusive either way, he is quit for his loss of time, no vital harm being done.'[16]

These distinctions, which dominate James's arguments in 'The Will to Believe' explain why he does not support Pascal's wager as a defence of religion. It represents an option which, for most people, is dead. But while the idea that we believe purely on the basis of volition, seems, prima facie, to be both 'silly' and 'vile', James nevertheless defends it. 'The Will to Believe' is, to a significant extent, a reponse to W. A. Clifford's insistence that 'it is [morally!] wrong always, everywhere, and for every one, to believe anything upon insufficient evidence'.[17] This James cannot accept. Following Peirce's idea of beliefs as 'habits of action' that are always motivated by some social goal or practical project within which they function, he insists that we disbelieve all facts and theories for which we find no use.[18] Our 'non-intellectual nature' does influence our convictions. 'Pure insight and logic' are not, for James, the only things that produce that which we believe in. James's central thesis in 'The Will to Believe' is stated as follows:

Our passional nature not only lawfully may, but must, decide an option between propositions, whenever it is a genuine option that cannot by its nature be decided on intellectual grounds; for to say, under such circumstances, 'Do not decide, but leave the question open' is itself a passional decision – just like deciding yes or no – and is attended with the same risk of losing the truth.[19]

In order to motivate this claim, James distinguishes between what he calls an 'absolutist' and an 'empiricist' way of believing in truth. The absolutists in this matter 'say that we not only can attain to knowing truth, but we can know when we have attained to knowing it'[20] (his emphasis). This is the position of traditional philosophy, what Rorty would later call the 'Fach'[21] or subject that engages, not only in the attainment of (true) knowledge, but that specifically engages in the activity of 'knowing about knowing', i.e. formulating the alleged indubitable grounds for knowledge.

Over against philosophy, which traditionally tended to be absolutist, stands science, that is empiricist. James sides with empiricism: the position that is willing to settle for no more than what actual experience delivers. He asks: 'Objective evidence and certitude [as sought by absolutism] are doubtless very fine ideals to play with, but where in this moonlit and dream-visited planet are they to be found?' In a Cartesian move (later also to be again taken up by

Husserl), he claims 'There is but one indefectibly certain truth, and that is the truth that phyrrhonistic skepticism itself leaves standing – the truth that the present phenomenon of consciousness exists'.[22] There is no such thing as the absolute certainty that absolutists seek. With reference to Clifford, James notes the two 'laws' that are valid for all 'would-be knowers': (1) Believe truth! and (2) Shun errors! Clifford insists that the second takes precedence over the first; one can only accept a truth when there can be absolutely no doubt that all errors have been eliminated. But this James finds a 'fantastic' requirement. We cannot live that way. Clifford's demand 'is like a general informing his soldiers that it is better to keep out of battle forever than to risk a single wound'.[23]

For James, this demonstrates persuasively that what he calls 'our passional nature', i.e. our emotions and our practical goals, inevitably influence our beliefs. This does not mean that we can simply 'will to believe anything'. But we sometimes are confronted with choices for or against beliefs that are indeed momentous or forced. In science we can mostly avoid this; we need not commit to the 'truth' that all metals everywhere expand when heated; we can settle with what has empirically been established. The same goes for the decisions of a court of law: the certain knowledge that an accused is guilty of a crime, is avoidable; the court only evaluates the available evidence and makes a decision beyond reasonable doubt. Both science and judicial process can function well by sticking to the task of avoiding or eliminating error, and are not normally confronted by momentous options in terms of committing to truth.[24]

James's argument is that, in spite of this, there are sometimes forced options that present themselves in the speculative questions that we ask, i.e. options that cannot simply be dealt with by the continued effort to avoid error, but that bestow on us the responsibility to choose truth, even if that choice lacks absolute certainty. Moral questions pose one example; they are questions 'whose solution cannot wait for sensible proof'. The doctor who is confronted with an HIV positive patient who refuses to inform his sex partners of his condition, and also forbids the doctor to do it on his behalf, is confronted with the moral dilemma posed by the conflict of which principle to apply: doctor–patient confidentiality or beneficence. 'Proof' of the right decision is too much to ask here; a momentous and forced decision is asked for. Writes James: 'Moral skepticism can no more be refuted or proved by logic than intellectual skepticism can. When we stick to it that there is truth (be it of either kind), we do so with our whole nature, and resolve to stand or fall by the results.' There simply are situations in life in which we cannot abide by continued scepticism and mere error elimination. We have to know truth. Think of personal relations: is it tolerable to hinge on contrary possibilities when a man and a woman need to know whether they love each other? And although error elimination is the basic business of science, is continued scepticism sustainable when we, as in the Bellarmine–Galileo controversy, need to decide whether empirical evidence weighs heavier than ecclesiastical authority? James's point is that, in all these examples (though not all of them are his) the 'will to believe', i.e. the intricate pragmatic link between belief and action or social goals, is decisive.

James then applies this idea directly to religion. Religion, he asserts, says essentially two things. (1) 'The best things are the more eternal things ... Perfection is eternal ... (an affirmation which obviously cannot be verified scientifically at all)', and (2) '[we] are better off even now if we believe [the] first affirmation to be true'.[25]

The question is: is the religious hypothesis true? James tests it against his earlier noted distinctions. Whether it is a living option, each individual must decide; James only addresses his argument to the 'saving remnant' for whom it is alive. If so, the hypothesis must also be 'momentous'; 'we are supposed to gain, even now, by our belief, and to lose by our non-belief, a certain vital good'. Religion is also a 'forced option': we cannot indefinitely postpone a decision about it. The Cliffordian strategy is one that is so committed to persistent efforts to eliminate error that it boils down to a position that regards it better to prevent error than to ever admit a truth. 'To preach skepticism to us as a duty until sufficient evidence for religion be found is tantamount therefore to telling us, when in the presence of the religious hypothesis, that to yield to our fear of its being error is wiser and better than to yield to our hope that it may be true.'[26] The essence of James's argument therefore is that he cannot accept an intellectual strategy ('rule of thinking') that, if applied, would simply and in principle prevent one from committing to certain kinds of truth 'if those kinds of truths were really there'. He finds such a prohibition irrational.

In the concluding chapter of his book *Varieties of Religious Experience*,[27] James creates the impression that he departs from the 'purely' pragmatist defence of religion as just described. He now develops a defence of religion that is justified in terms of a more traditional theory of truth than the pragmatist insistence that nothing meaningful could be said about truth if divorced from identifiable practical projects of social goals. Religion now is for James the outcome of an 'uneasiness ... that there is something wrong about us as we naturally stand', and a 'solution' that consists of a sense 'that we are saved from the wrongness by making proper connection with the higher powers'.[28] James's argument in this conclusion is not always that clear, but it amounts to an idea of religion as the experience of being moved by some higher power[29] and being in connection with 'a wider self', a disposition that he also calls an 'over-belief',[30] i.e. a belief that cannot be verified in a scientific manner. He then continues with a strong claim: 'we have in the fact that the conscious person is continuous with a wider self through which saving experiences come, a positive content of religious experience which, it seems to me, is literally and objectively true as far as it goes'.[31] Note that the notion of truth which is implored in this observation is no longer the earlier pragmatist linkage of belief and social project, but the idea of something being 'literally and objectively' true – much more akin to the correspondence theory of truth. This shows a marked inconsistency in James's views.

JOHN DEWEY: RELIGION(S) VERSUS THE RELIGIOUS

Dewey's assessment of the intellectual respectability of the idea and practice of religion is more radical than that of James. Although Dewey (1859–1952) fully shares James's and Peirce's pragmatist strategy of apportioning belief to human needs, he concerns himself much less with epistemology. His discussions and appraisal of religion occur much rather in the context of his sustained concerns about human practice, particularly in the broader contexts of civil life, education, politics and the theory and praxis of democracy. From his reflections on the latter a much more critical stance towards conventional religion emerges in his thought than in that of James.

For Dewey, pragmatism as both a philosophy and a political disposition is born from a fundamental scepticism of authority. As democracy is not born from the question 'who should rule?' (a question that suggests the possibility of a highest authority), but rather from the concern 'how do we best protect ourselves against bad government?',[32] so pragmatism as a philosophy is born from a deep-seated distrust of traditional sources of authority. Dewey appreciates democracy as a theory and practice of 'self-reliance', and therefore has little patience with religion in respect of the latter's tendency to promote dependence on superhuman powers. Central to Dewey's thought is also his emphasis on contingency, humility and his rejection of the possibility of certainty.[33] The pragmatist Dewey's thinking always remains oriented to the domain of practical action; philosophy, for him, only makes sense to the extent that it impinges on human praxis.

As regards religion, the fundamental question for Dewey, as formulated by Rogers in the latter's recent book, is: 'How should we conceive of our religious lives given that our fundamental orientation proceeds from the domain of practical action?'[34] His position could be circumscribed as a 'religious naturalism' that draws much more strongly on Emerson than on Peirce or James. Dewey's philosophy of religion can in essence be understood as a conversation between religious experience and political life – a conversation that is necessary since religion prima facie threatens democratic practice. In his 1908 essay 'Religion and our Schools' Dewey indeed argued for a prohibition on religious instruction in American public schools. His concern in this regard has to do with religion's strong, often dogmatic claim to truth. He writes:

The characteristic of religion from their [religious believers'] point of view, is that it is – intellectually speaking – secret, not public; peculiarly revealed, not generally known; authoritatively declared, not communicated and tested in ordinary ways.[35]

The title of Dewey's best known work on religion, *A Common Faith*, embodies the suggestion that religious faith, if it is to be taken seriously, must be 'common', not in the sense of ordinary or 'not extraordinary', but in the sense of shared and open to intersubjective scrutiny – 'common' in the way that resembles values and beliefs that are put to the test in the sustained critical conversation that a democratic society essentially is.

Dewey's religious naturalism is first of all characterized by a rejection of the supernatural claims of traditional religion. From the first pages of *A Common Faith* he resists the 'extremist' view 'that with the elimination of the supernatural not only must historic religions be dismissed but with them everything of a religious nature'.[36] His task in the book is to 'develop another conception of the nature of the religious phase of experience, one that separates it from the supernatural'. He hopes that the upshot of his analysis will be that 'what is genuinely religious will undergo an emancipation when it is relieved from [the supernatural]; that then, for the first time, the religious aspect of experience will be free to develop freely on its own account'.[37]

Dewey's position on religion hinges on a fundamental distinction that dominates the argument in the book – the distinction between a religion and the religious. He claims that the trouble in which religion generally finds itself in the modern world might well be the effect of the way in which religions (without which he can do) prevents the religious quality of experience (which he regards as invaluable) from coming to consciousness and finding an appropriate moral and intellectual expression. How are the two to be distinguished?

> [A] religion ... always signifies a special body of beliefs and practices having some kind of institutional organization, loose or tight. In contrast, the adjective 'religious' denotes nothing in the way of a specifiable entity, either institutional or as a system of beliefs ... it does not denote anything that can exist by itself or that can be organized into a particular and distinctive form of existence. It denotes attitudes that may be taken toward every object and every proposed end or ideal.[38]

To clarify what he means by 'the religious', Dewey describes existential attitudes closely associated with religion such as 'adaptation', 'orientation' and 'accommodation', and claims that people often think that these attitudes are brought about by embracing particular religions. He, however, prefers to 'turn the statement around'. His counterclaim is that whenever the changes in human attitudes designated by these phenomena occur, there is a religious attitude. 'It is not a religion that brings it about, but when it [i.e. adaptation, orientation and accommodation] occurs, from whatever cause and by whatever means, there is a religious outlook and function.'[39] The religious also has to do with an imaginative process bent on the harmonizing of the self, in a way that is akin to Santayana's observations about poetry. 'The implication is that faith is a kind of anticipatory vision of things that are now invisible because of the limitations of our finite and erring nature.'[40] In this process, morality is also involved: 'The religious is "morality touched by emotion" only when the ends of moral conviction arouse emotions that are not only intense but are actuated and supported by ends so inclusive that they unify the self.'[41]

What therefore is of value in religion for Dewey is not a set of beliefs in some supernatural power, but a discernment springing from a certain type of experience. Religions do not bring about this experience; the experience has a certain nature that might be called 'the religious'. The experience emanates from our efforts to imaginatively harmonize and unify our inner selves, to 'introduce perspective into the piecemeal and shifting episodes of existence'. What must be understood is that 'whatever introduces genuine perspective is religious, not that [a] religion is something that introduces it'.[42]

'The religious' is that which connects us, in wonder and humility, with our environment and with nature. Dewey abhors the fact that religions are so often born out of fear and a sense of hopelessness that can only be alleviated by committing to a supernatural force that can safeguard us against 'the powers of dark'. That notion of a religion tends to isolate people from the world of physical nature and one's fellow beings. Such an isolation is something that Dewey describes as distinctly unreligious. Again, it must be clearly distinguished from what he calls the religious: 'Our successes are dependent upon the co-operation of nature. The sense of dignity of human nature is as religious as is the sense of awe and reverence when it rests upon a sense of human nature as a cooperating part of a larger whole.'[43]

Let us conclude the discussion of Dewey's contribution by referring to the fascinating evaluation he offers of the alleged debate between religion and science. We live in times when religious faith that based itself on factual claims is consistently finding itself losing ground to science. Dewey judges the role that liberal theologians have played in this process harshly. Whenever a key doctrine or factual claim of a religion (e.g. the virgin birth of Christ) comes under fire from science, the liberal strategy almost infallibly is to deny that the doctrine was ever central to the faith. For this reason, Dewey is unimpressed by the intellectual antics of traditional religions. For him, religious qualities and values, if they are of any real consequence, are not dependent on or to be derived from 'any single item of intellectual assent, not even that of the existence of the God of theism'.[44] His claim is that the religious function in experience 'can be emancipated only through surrender of the whole notion of special truths that are religious by their own nature, together with the idea of peculiar avenues of access to such truths'.[45] What happens in religious faith, is not a process of establishing truths that are epistemologically well founded. Religious faith is exactly what the adjective suggests: 'religious'. 'The religious' has nothing to do with the assertion of facts, but much rather with the 'unification of the self through alliance to inclusive ideal ends, which imagination presents to us and to which the human will responds as worthy of controlling our desires and choices'.[46]

Whereas this 'religious' ideal of the unification of the self might seem individualistic, Dewey, in the later parts of *A Common Faith*, makes it clear that the unification, facilitated by imagination, is not conceivable outside the interactions of a dynamic human community. 'The religious' is exactly that quality of experience that acknowledges our personal incompleteness and our dependence upon the solidarity of fellow human beings to realize the values that bind us together. The concluding passage of the books reads:

Ours is the responsibility of conserving, transmitting, rectifying and expanding the heritage of values we have received [so] that those who come after us may receive it more solid and secure, more widely accessible and more generously shared than we have received it. Here are all the elements for a religious faith that shall not be confined to sect, class or race. Such a faith has always been implicitly the common faith of mankind. It remains to make it explicit and militant.[47]

RICHARD RORTY: PRAGMATISM, RELIGION AND ROMANTIC POLYTHEISM

Richard Rorty (1931–2007) was in his lifetime, and through his work remains, the pragmatist with the highest current-day international profile. Since the publication of his now almost classical *Philosophy and the Mirror of Nature* in 1980, he has, in a wide range of books and articles, promoted pragmatism as the most significant critique of foundationalist (Rorty increasingly preferred the epithet 'Platonic') epistemology. For most of the 1980s and well into the 1990s Rorty wrote very little about religion, and when he did, he came across as a relatively sharp critic of any agenda that pertains to defend religion. Nicholas Smith points out that 'in his more unguarded moments, Rorty gives the impression that he thinks we would be better off without religion altogether'.[48] Such an 'unguarded moment' occurs, for example, in an essay with the provocative title 'Religion as Conversation-Stopper' where he refers to himself and like-minded intellectuals as 'we atheists'.[49] But in spite of such moments, one of the most remarkable aspects of Rorty's writings is the way in which, in the last decade of his life, he became an enthusiastic promoter of the reconcilability of pragmatism and religion, and hence of the intellectual respectability of religious convictions and attitudes generally.

Rorty's 'defence' of religion, however, has very little, if anything, to do with any effort to prove the existence of a superior being, let alone the specific doctrines of Christianity or any other religion. In this sense Smith is correct when he claims that Rorty's apology for religion must not be confused with a defense of theism.[50] In his reflections on religion Rorty draws strongly on James,[51] eventually prefers Dewey,[52] and is increasingly influenced by the inferentialism of R. B. Brandom.[53]

Rorty affirms Peirce's and James's claim that beliefs are 'habits of action'. His way to press the point is encapsulated in the following question: 'How do we tell when, if ever, an issue about what exists should be discussed without reference to any socio-political goals?'[54] And Rorty's answer to that question, embracing the spirit of Peirce and James, is a clear-cut: 'we can't'! He fully supports James in the latter's dispute with Clifford, as discussed earlier. Clifford insists on 'enough evidence' whenever anything is to be believed. But the counter question is: Is 'evidence' something which floats free from human projects? Can the requirement of 'evidence' amount to anything more than the responsibility to continue arguing until your interlocutors accept your claim? The claim to evidence is the claim to rationality, and rationality, for Rorty, amounts to no more than to submit one's beliefs to the 'judgement of one's peers'.[55] 'James's criticism of correspondence theories of truth boils down to the argument that a belief's purported fit with the intrinsic nature of reality adds nothing which makes any practical difference to the fact that it is universally agreed to lead to successful action.'[56] What Rorty appreciates in James, is the latter's deliberate effort to 'blur the distinction between belief and desire'. We have beliefs exactly in order to gratify desires.

He also approvingly refers to Hume's claim that reason ought to be the slave of the passions.[57] The upshot of these arguments is that, for Rorty, the quest for truth and the quest for happiness are not that distinct. Rorty makes no secret of the appeal that Mill's utilitarianism has for him. James did indeed advocate a 'utilitarian ethics of belief'.[58] We do whatever we do in society in one or another in order to promote happiness. Writes Rorty:

James and Nietzsche did for the word 'true' what John Stuart Mill did for the word 'right'. Just as Mill says that there is no ethical motive apart from the desire for the happiness of human beings, so James and Nietzsche say that there is no will to truth distinct from the will to happiness. All three philosophers think that the terms 'true' and 'right' gain their meaning from their use in evaluating the relative success of efforts to achieve happiness.[59]

There is no such thing as 'truth in itself' which compels us to look for it irrespective of the effects that that quest will have on our social well-being. Rorty unabashedly defends the idea that successful intellectual endeavours, which includes religion, are always the outcome of 'cultural politics'. Consider controversial scientific projects, such as research on the splitting of the atom, the relationship between skin colour and intelligence or the question whether Holocaust denial ought to be tolerated in a society such as current-day Germany. Rorty's argument is that all decisions about these and other intellectually worthwhile endeavours are the outcome of 'cultural politics'. These investigations occur, if they occur, as a result of a societally mediated conviction about what is, and what is not good for us, and not because they are to continue because they are sure to yield something that is 'inherently true'. Truth and reality exist for the sake of social practices, not the other way round.[60] According to Smith's interpretation of Rorty in this regard: 'Something is "culturally desirable" if it conduce to human happiness. And so the true measure of theism is not whether some preternatural, non-human power exists, but whether or not theism conduces to human happiness.'[61]

In spite of his stringent criticisms of theism, which, in its traditional Western guise operated fully within the Platonic, fundamentalist framework that he finds so deeply problematic, Rorty nevertheless believes that pragmatism and religion do 'mix'. His pragmatist defence of religion occurs within the ambit of the broader development, in his later work, of a philosophy of social hope.[62] The force of pragmatism is its ability to, anew, take seriously the third of the famous threefold questions that Kant formulated for the philosophical enterprise (What can I know? What ought I to do? What may I hope?).[63] In a striking formulation Smith claims that 'Just as Kant sought to establish the limits of knowledge so as to make room for faith, Rorty tries to show how a proper understanding of the scope and significance of belief makes room for hope.'[64] Like utilitarianism, pragmatism looks to and is mainly concerned with the future. It gives precedence to the attainment of human happiness over the attainment of truth on the basis of indisputable foundations; it expresses, in the title of one of Rorty's earlier essays, the 'priority of democracy to philosophy'.[65] The precedence given to hope highlights pragmatism's practical intent and import: what is important, is not primarily what we can 'find out' about the world, but what we can, in intersubjective dialogue and cooperation, make of the world; in another earlier essay, Rorty argued for the replacement of 'metaphors of finding' with 'metaphors of making'.[66]

Rorty's pragmatist defence of religion, is first an argument for the desirability of 'romantic polytheism' over theism.[67] He draws on Matthew Arnold's rejection of the 'Hebraist' tradition of monotheism in favor of the 'Hellenistic' culture of polytheism. For Arnold, polytheism does not reside in the worship of a range of deities, but in the acknowledgement of a range of human ideals that, for him (Arnold) comes best to expression in the work of poets. 'A romantic utilitarian [read: Rortyan pragmatist] probably drops the idea of diverse immortal persons, such as Olympian deities, but she will retain the idea that there are diverse, conflicting, but equally valuable forms of human life.'[68] This, according to Rorty, is also the kind of polytheism promoted by James when the latter writes: 'The divine can mean no single quality, it must mean a group of qualities, by being champions of which in alternation, different men may all find worthy missions.'[69] What James means by 'the divine', clearly simply means 'the ideal'.[70] But the notion of polytheism does not only capture the idea of variety, but also the idea of a lack of hierarchy.

> You are a polytheist if you think that there is no actual or possible object of knowledge that would permit you to commensurate and rank all human needs ... All you need to do is abandon the idea that we should try to find a way of making everything hang together, which will tell all human beings what to do with their lives, and tell all of them the same thing.[71]

Rorty's 'polytheism' is also characterized as 'romantic'. This not only refers to his admiration of poets and poetry. It first of all tries to capture his plead, shared with James, that religion can play an optimal role in people's lives when privatized. Religion, for Rorty, must, as in the case of poetry, be best understood as an instrument of imaginative redemption in the sense of self-improvement. Religion is an instrument of hope – the hope for what we might become. Religious beliefs have value to the extent that they enable us to project onto the future an image of what both we and our world might optimally be or become. Rorty therefore goes beyond Dewey's idea of religion as the harmonization of the self; for him, religion essentially consists in the idealization of the self. This redemptive force in religion requires, on the one hand, its 'privatization' in order to create space for all people to pursue their own ideals.

> For human perfection becomes a private concern, and our responsibility to others becomes a matter of permitting them as much space to pursue these private concerns – to worship their own gods, so to speak – as is compatible with granting an equal amount of space to all. The tradition of religious toleration is extended to moral toleration.[72]

Yet, on the other hand, Rorty's pragmatist idea of religion also recognizes the redemptive role of other humans. When religion entails little more than the acknowledgement of revelation and 'contact with non-human, preternatural forces', there is 'no need to engage with other people, and for this reason both redemptive truth and the primitive religious impulses are "egotist models" of redemption'.[73] The model of religion that Rorty promotes amounts to a 'redemption from egotism'. Smith explains this as follows:

> For whereas the dialogical or social character of knowledge involves the idea that it can withstand public scrutiny and criticism, and that it is the outcome of a common endeavor, redemption from egotism is not a matter of justifying

to others at all ... One is not redeemed from egotism, in Rorty's sense, by being able to defend oneself in relation to another. The redemption rather arises from being able to imagine oneself as enlarged, or made better, or perhaps transfigured and made complete through the mediation of the lives of other people, including the fictional lives of people found in literature, the arts, and other cultural artefacts [including religious images].[74]

The worth of religion, for Rorty, therefore is located in its cultural desirability and potential contribution to human happiness; it embodies and articulates the hope for what we may become if we are able to embody and materialize the best that our imaginations can come up with. In this effort, we need to create optimal space for other people to pursue their ideals. But the very business of imaginative self-creation is as much a dialogical process in which we foster ourselves through the intersubjective self-formation that dialogue and interaction facilitates. To quote Smith again:

The more people are able to pursue projects of self-creation and personal redemption the better. But the very goal of maximizing the scope for individual variation entails a commitment to leaving individuals alone – in the sense of free from interference – to pursue such projects themselves. In acting collectively to improve the quality of their democracy citizens are better off not having to deal with whatever it is that they separately seek redemption from. In this sense, Rorty reconciles religion with pragmatism by turning the former into a source of 'private' hope ... and he presents the 'privatisation of religion' as if it were a corollary of the democratisation of politics ... There is, however, one exception: democracy itself as the highest hope and the object of religious awe and devotion. Rorty envisages a civic religion of democracy that keeps social hope alive sitting alongside many private religions sustaining private hopes about what individuals may become.[75]

I conclude with Rorty's summary, in four points, of his pragmatist philosophy of religion in his essay 'Philosophy as Cultural Politics'.[76] First, the anti-representationalist view of belief that James developed for the first time frees us from the responsibility to unify all our beliefs into a single worldview. That opens the door for Rorty's 'romantic polytheism' in which the religious impulse becomes the vehicle for imaginative self-improvement. Second, pragmatism enables us to replace the age-old distinction of the cognitive and the non-cognitive with the distinction between 'projects of social co-operation and projects of self-development'. And whereas consensus or intersubjective agreement is a requirement for the former, it is not a requirement for the latter; Rorty suggests natural science and law as examples of projects of social cooperation, and romantic art and religion as examples of projects of individual self-development. Third, the claim that religion is 'intellectually irresponsible' or unfounded, is mainly undergirded by the requirement that we should 'love Truth'. But for Rorty, there is no such thing as the 'love of Truth'. What has been proposed in the past as the 'love of truth', in fact amounted to little more than 'the love of gaining mastery over a recalcitrant set of data, the love of winning arguments, and the love of synthesizing little theories into big theories'. Rorty cannot accept that it can ever be a legitimate objection to religious belief that there is no evidence for it. 'The only possible objection to it can be that it intrudes an individual project into a social and cooperative project, and thereby offends against the teachings of On Liberty [by J.S. Mill].'

Finally, Rorty makes a point about the way in which the quest for Truth is nothing but a secularized version of the 'traditional religious hope that allegiance to something big, powerful and non-human will persuade that powerful being to take your side in your struggle with other people'. Whereas this hope, for Nietzsche, was simply a sign of weakness on the side of religionists, pragmatists have another objection to it: that it represents a betrayal of the ideal that democracy inherits from the Judaeo-Christian religious tradition. His formulation of this ideal is that, following Mill and James, 'every human need should be satisfied unless doing so causes too many other human needs to go unsatisfied'. The pragmatist objection against religious fundamentalism is not that the latter is intellectually irresponsible to ignore the findings of natural science, but that it is morally irresponsible 'in attempting to circumvent the process of achieving democratic consensus about how to maximize happiness', i.e. through taking serious the broad consensus that the project of natural science is our best answer to understanding the world in a way that best serves human interests.

CRITICAL REMARKS

Space limitations leave us little room for critical discussion. This author appreciates the pragmatist insistence on the link between belief and action or human social goals, as well as James's good point against Clifford that to insist on definitively sufficient evidence for all beliefs that one holds is unrealistic and will result in the forfeiture of choices that we need to make in order to live fulfilling lives. Yet James, as was pointed out earlier, in the final passages of *Varieties of Religious Experience*, again yields to a foundationalist notion of truth that is inconsistent with the more 'purely' pragmatist position that he developed in "The Will to Believe". Rorty does criticize James for this inconsistency, but also is less impressed by James's idea of 'perfection as eternal', since it smacks of reliance on (a) power outside of ourselves. Rorty himself, drawing more strongly on Dewey's appraisal of the liberation that democracy brings to culture, therefore proposes his idea of 'romantic polytheism' and its concomitant insistence not only on self-reliance and democratic cooperation, but also on the freedom of every individual to pursue unprecedented privatized self-improvement through religious and artistic imagination.[77]

Whether the beliefs of actual religious believers would be able to significantly resonate with any of the ideas proposed by pragmatists as discussed above, is, of course, a serious question. As far as Rorty's 'romantic polytheism' is concerned, one is left with the question as to why Rorty really needs the notion of religion in order to achieve the self-enhancement that he hopes might be facilitated by the religious imagination. Rorty is often quite outspoken about the fact that the vehicle for this kind of self-improvement can, if not most often in fact is, artistic imagination, poetry and the like. The question is what exactly it is about religion that bestows on its utilization a transformative power that is not as easily reachable or achievable by other means.

In addition, it is a question whether Rorty does justice to the phenomenon of the religious in his unmitigated critique of a sense of dependence that religious experience provides, and his concomitant insistence on the virtues of self-reliance and self-responsibility. As Smith records in this regard, Rorty 'makes a vice of the very idea that there is an order in which human beings are set and upon which they depend for spiritual sustenance'. This has to be at odds with *de facto* religious experience and perspectives. The religious impulse is, in essence, an acknowledgement that human beings are not self-sufficient; for Rorty to therefore exclusively appreciate religious believers' (possible) disposition to imagine and realize their ideal selves (even following role models such as Jesus, Mohammed or the Buddha), is nevertheless to deny or disown a fundamental trait of the religious orientation. Smith rightfully remarks:

> The religious sense of dependence is not just directed at a non-human sense of authority, although this is the way Rorty typically characterizes it. When Rorty praises self-reliance, the contrast he has in mind is with obeisance, servility and submission ... But this is not only a very narrow conception of what the religious sense of dependence consists in, it also excludes an idea which seems to be at the heart of distinctively religious modes of human self-interpretation: the non-self-sufficiency of the human with respect to its spiritual needs.[78]

This tendency to appreciate the specificity of the religious orientation is also evident in Rorty's rather naive assertions that both tolerance and a promotion of a democratic social practice has always been part and parcel of the Judaeo-Christian tradition. Whereas the light in terms of these lofty ideals has certainly dawned upon most strata of current-day Christianity, one need only to be reminded of the Crusades, the Inquisition and the history of Northern Ireland to be not only sceptical of Rorty's claim, but under the impression of the disingenuousness of some of his more sweeping arguments.

A more fundamental question about the pragmatist enterprise as such is the issue as to whether the search for truth can that easily be equated with the search for human happiness. Rorty's and James's analyses in this regard are sometimes impressive, and offer much food for thought. Yet, they are not convincing throughout. For example: why are we to prefer Copernican astronomy to a religious fundamentalism in terms of which the earth is the centre of the universe, no more than 6000 years old, and which asserts that the moon is none other than, as Genesis 1:14–16 describes it, a 'light' given to us at night? Rorty's answer would obviously be that Copernican astronomy is a *sine qua non* for a host of human projects with admirable and pursuable social goals; in fact, it enabled us to land on the moon (and see for ourselves!) and to, maybe, in the near future, travel to Mars. Yet, if the fundamentalist worldview offers the kind of emotional security that is associated with belief in a God that 'holds the whole world in His hand', if only we believe His Word literally, why could, in purely pragmatist terms, an argument not be construed in defence of such fundamentalism? Put differently, if adherence to positions/beliefs that make people happy are really the prime motivation for ascribing to positions and beliefs, how can the pragmatist avoid the accusation that he/she promotes an intellectual orientation that could well justify irrationalism? Rorty's answer to this problem would have been that there are no non-circular arguments to defend pragmatism, other than the actual, *de facto* comparisons of the results yielded by the two sets of beliefs and the hope (it can never be more than hope; hence the growing importance of this notion in his later thought) that what 'we' take for granted, will also be shared by those doing the comparison. But there must be more to it than that.

To conclude: I tend to agree that there is no such thing as 'final truth', either in a religious or in a scientific sense. That agreement, however, does not compel us to accept that the definitive requirement of justified beliefs is to conduce to human happiness. There are instances of beliefs, attained in a series of prolonged intellectual, historical settlements, that we can take as given – not because they represent 'Truth' in any final sense, but because worthwhile inquiry, also in religious affairs, cannot meaningfully proceed without them. That does not mean that these 'settlements' are non-revisable; they always are. But their revision requires, as Habermas[79] has persuasively argued, a kind of discourse very different from that of ordinary or scientific inquiry. Until that inquiry is embarked upon, they remain the 'hinges' that, as provocatively stated by Wittgenstein, must stay put if the door of ordinary intellectual inquiry wants to turn.[80]

NOTES

1 Cf. Diggins, 1994, as also discussed by Gunn, 1998, p. 406.
2 Cf. Russell, 1946, pp. 766–782.
3 Gunn, 1998, p. 405.
4 Cf. for example his educational essay 'Creative Democracy: The Task before Us' (Dewey, MW14: 224–30) in which he deals extensively with the relationship between religion and democracy.
5 Dewey 1934.
6 Cf. Rorty 1997b, 1999a and 2007a.
7 Rorty, 1982a, p. xxxvii.
8 Peirce, 1878.
9 Peirce, 1878, CP5: 397.

10 Gunn, 1998, p. 407.
11 James, 2005.
12 Cf. Jordan, 1997, pp. 353–5.
13 James, 2005, p. 97.
14 James, 2005, pp. 95–6.
15 James 2005, p. 96
16 James, 2005, p. 96.
17 Clifford, 2001, p. 18.
18 James, 2005, p. 99. James uses the example of telepathy which is not only not accepted by scientists, but about which many scientists believe that, even if it there really is something like telepathy, it ought to be withheld from becoming general knowledge since it would compromise fundamental assumptions of the scientific enterprise, such as belief in the uniformity and predictability of nature. James, on the other hand, argues that if the use of telepathy could be demonstrated to scientists, it would be accepted by them, even if the 'scientific basis' of the practice remains obscure.
19 James, 2005, p. 100.
20 James, 2005, p. 101.
21 Rorty, 1982a, p. 26.
22 James, 2005, p. 101.
23 James, 2005, p. 103.
24 James, 2005, p. 104.
25 James, 2005, p. 107.
26 James, 2005, p. 107.
27 James, 2002 (this work was originally published in 1902; my references are to the centenary edition).
28 James, 2002, p. 392.
29 James, 2002, p. 395.
30 James, 2002, p. 396.
31 James, 2002, p. 397.
32 In this respect, and in spite of other differences between them, Dewey's political thinking shows marked resemblances to that of Karl Popper. Cf. Popper, 1947 and 1957, as well as Magee's discussion of Popper's social and political philosophy in Magee, 1973, pp. 74–108.
33 Cf. Dewey, 1929b. It is also in his rejection of the possibility of certainty that Dewey's thinking shows remarkable resemblances to that of Popper.
34 Rogers, 2009, p. 107.
35 Dewey, as quoted by Rogers, 2009, p. 112.
36 Dewey, 1934, p. 1.
37 Dewey, 1934, p. 2.

38 Dewey, 1934, pp. 9–10.
39 Dewey, 1934, p. 17.
40 Dewey, 1934, p. 20.
41 Dewey, 1934, p. 22.
42 Dewey, 1934, p. 24.
43 Dewey, 1934, p. 25.
44 Dewey, 1934, p. 32.
45 Dewey, 1934, p. 33.
46 Dewey, 1934, p. 33.
47 Dewey, 1934, p. 87.
48 Smith, 2005, p. 82.
49 Rorty 1999a, p. 169.
50 Smith, 2005, pp. 78–82.
51 As in e.g. Rorty, 1997b.
52 As in Rorty, 2007a, pp. 27–41.
53 Cf. Brandom, 1994
54 Rorty, 2007a, p. 4.
55 Rorty, 1997b, p. 6.
56 Rorty, 1997b, p. 5.
57 Rorty, 1997b, pp. 6–7.
58 Rorty, 2007a, p. 5.
59 Rorty, 2007a, p. 28
60 Rorty, 2007a, p. 7
61 Smith, 2005, p. 80.
62 Cf. his book *Philosophy and Social Hope*, Rorty, 1999a.
63 Cf. Kant, 1929, p. 635 (A805/B833).
64 Smith, 2005, p. 91.
65 Rorty, 1991a, pp. 175–96.
66 Cf. Rorty, 1985, pp. 10–11. It must, however, be noted, that Rorty acknowledged the invalidity of this distinction in his later essay 'Relativism: Finding and Making' (Rorty, 1999c, pp. xvi–xxxii) on the basis of the legitimate counter question: 'How can we establish whether this is a cogent distinction? Is it something that anybody [Rorty himself?] found to be the case'?! This latter essay is also remarkable for another reason, viz. that Rorty here for the first time embraces the notion of 'relativist' as a self-description, something that he resisted fiercely in his earlier work, e.g. Rorty, 1985. For a further discussion of this issue, see Van Niekerk, 2005.
67 For Rorty's argument in this regard, see Rorty, 2007a, pp. 27–41. For an enlightening discussion of the way in which monotheism replaced polytheism in the Roman Empire, and its profound (mostly negative) implications, see Freeman, 2003, pp. 34–205.

68 Rorty, 2007a, p. 29.
69 James, 2002, p. 377.
70 Note James's definition of religion in 'Varieties of Religious Experience': 'Religion ... shall mean for us the feelings, acts and experiences of individual men in their solitude, so far as they apprehend themselves to stand in relation to whatever they may consider the divine' (James, 2002, pp. 29–30).
71 Rorty 2007a, p. 30. Again, in this passage he, by implication, refutes his earlier proclaimed view that, in as far the continued existence of philosophy and philosophers is still justifiable, it derives merely from their efforts to show 'how things hang together'. Cf. Rorty 1982a, p. xl.
72 Rorty, 2007a, p. 30.
73 Smith, 2005, p. 83.
74 Smith, 2005, pp. 83–4.
75 Smith, 2005, p. 84.
76 For these points, one of which I leave out for the sake of space limits, see Rorty, 2007a, pp. 34–5.
77 For Rorty's criticism of James, see Rorty, 1997b, pp. 14–16, and for his arguments in favour of Dewey, see Rorty, 2007a, pp. 36–41.
78 Smith, 2005, p. 89.
79 Cf. Habermas, 1976 and Bernstein, 1983, pp. 185ff.
80 Cf. Wittgenstein, 1969b.

14 Radical pragmatism

'[P]ragmatist theory of law is, like much pragmatist theory, essentially banal.'[1] So wrote Thomas Grey at the dawn of pragmatism's renaissance in legal theory.[2] Even Richard Rorty, the philosopher frequently credited with reviving pragmatism, concurs.[3] Richard Posner could not agree more. For well over a decade, Posner has been the leading proponent of legal pragmatism. He proclaims that 'pragmatism is the best description of the American judicial ethos and also the best guide to the improvement of judicial performance – and thus the best normative as well as positive theory of the judicial role'. For Posner, pragmatic adjudication boils down to 'reasonableness'; it is '[n]ebulous and banal, modest and perhaps even timorous – or maybe oscillating unpredictably between timorous and bold'.[4]

Following the classical pragmatists, many contemporary pragmatists reject philosophy as a method for securing unshakeable foundations for knowledge. Yet these pragmatists part ways with classical pragmatism by rejecting the possibility of developing a thicker theory of the good and viewing pragmatism as a thin non-theoretical method of approaching issues. On this account, pragmatism is a relatively commonplace set of ideas and should hardly be shocking to the contemporary mind. According to Posner, 'pragmatism is more a tradition, attitude, and outlook than a body of doctrine'; it is more of a 'mood' than a substantive philosophy. Posner insists that pragmatism has 'no inherent political valence'.[5] Likewise, Rorty contends

---

The work published in this chapter is derived and modified from portions of a review article previously published in the *Yale Law Journal*. See Michael Sullivan and Daniel J. Solove, 'Can Pragmatism be Radical? Richard Posner and Legal Pragmatism', *YLJ* 113, 687.

that pragmatism 'is neutral between alternative prophecies, and thus neutral between democrats and fascists'.[6] Under this view, pragmatism generally leads to cautious commonsense policies. It is far from radical and unsettling, for it is too grounded in practice and too lacking in substantive value commitments to be otherwise.

In this chapter, we contest this account of pragmatism held by many neo-pragmatists and articulated most directly by Posner. We offer a thicker account. Pragmatism does indeed have a political valence. It has substantive values. And, far from being banal, it is radical at its core.

THEORY AND PRACTICE

According to Posner, pragmatism's 'core is merely a disposition to base action on facts and consequences rather than on conceptualisms, generalities, pieties, and slogans'.[7] Posner observes that pragmatism 'is not hostile to all theory ... [It] is hostile to the idea of using abstract moral and political theory to guide judicial decisionmaking.'[8] In contrast, 'theories that seek to guide empirical inquiry are welcomed in pragmatic adjudication'.[9] Although the pragmatist is open-minded to insights from a variety of disciplines, she should be wary of philosophy, which for Posner is little more than 'intellectual pretension' that isn't helpful in grappling with legal and policy issues.[10] Therefore, the pragmatist should reject philosophical theory as having any role to play in the law.

Posner is not alone in his view that pragmatism urges the abandonment of philosophical theorizing. Indeed, pragmatism is often criticized for being anti-theoretical. For example, Steven Smith argues that '[l]egal pragmatism is best understood as a kind of exhortation about theorizing'.[11]

This thin account of pragmatism runs into serious problems, however, when it comes to guiding the normative ends we should adopt. These problems emerge most explicitly when Posner discusses how the pragmatic judge should adjudicate cases. In articulating his account of pragmatic adjudication, he describes pragmatism as a method that is helpful in analysing whether the means we select can further our ends. But Posner's pragmatism has little to say about the normative ends we choose to adopt. Critics of pragmatism often attack pragmatism on this basis, dismissing it as empty. Pragmatism, on this account, is nothing more than a tool that can be used by anybody to achieve whatever ends they have in mind.

Posner begins his account of pragmatic adjudication by defending it against charges that it counsels judges to ignore precedent and decide cases simply based on personal views about the best outcome. Ronald Dworkin, legal pragmatism's well-known nemesis, argues that pragmatism is disrespectful of the past in general, and precedent in particular. In *Law's Empire*, he writes, 'The pragmatist thinks judges should always do the best they can for the future, in the circumstances, unchecked by any need to respect or secure consistency in principle with what other officials have done or will do.'[12]

Posner correctly rejects this account of pragmatic adjudication. He notes that it is true that the pragmatic judge does not feel any special duty to follow past precedent: 'The pragmatist values continuity with past enactments and decisions, but because such continuity is indeed a social value, not because he feels a sense of duty to the past.'[13] This does not imply that the pragmatist will simply do whatever she pleases, without any respect for precedent. Posner correctly contends that the pragmatist has instrumental reasons for adhering to precedent. Failure to follow precedent will undermine the stability of the legal system, which depends upon predictability and fairness (understood as treating like cases alike).[14] Moreover, past decisions may helpfully inform our present investigations. Thus, Dworkin and other critics of pragmatic adjudication fail to recognize that the pragmatist has good reasons to respect precedent.

Nevertheless, despite Posner's dispute with Dworkin, it turns out that they both share an impoverished notion of pragmatism rooted in a similar mistake. After Posner refutes the argument that judges should respect precedent for its own sake, he then goes too far in the other direction. He argues that '[t]he past is a repository of useful information, but it has no claim on us. The criterion of whether we should adhere to past practices is the consequences of doing so for now and the future.'[15] Posner's insistence that the past has no claim on us is problematic, especially in our constitutional democracy. It conjures up images of the judge arriving on a scene armed with a storehouse of 'facts' from the past, and then rendering her choice in light of whatever ends she has in mind. The origin of these ends apparently doesn't need to be accounted for. Dworkin therefore has a valid criticism when he argues that for adjudication in a constitutional democracy, these ends *do* need to be accounted for. Thus, both Posner and Dworkin view the pragmatist judge as deciding according to unjustified ends.

If pragmatism can't help us assess the goodness and badness of our ends, then it seems fair to say that the pragmatist simply accepts (or inherits) her ends uncritically. This reduces the contribution of pragmatism to merely aiding the selection of means to achieve particular ends. When asked about which ends to choose, Posner has nothing to say.[16] For him, pragmatism is value-neutral and 'has no moral compass'.[17] The notion that pragmatism is neutral hearkens back to William James, who wrote that pragmatism 'stands for no particular results. It has no dogmas, and no doctrines save its method.'[18]

This account of pragmatism is shared by many neo-pragmatists as well as their critics. For example, Brian Tamanaha has stated that 'pragmatism is empty of substance', and he contends that '[p]ragmatism does not say what the good is, how to live, what economic or political system to develop, or anything else of that nature'.[19] Lynn Baker's critique of the pragmatism of Richard Rorty goes even further, suggesting that contemporary pragmatism not only lacks substance, but is also merely an exhortation to privilege action over theory: 'In the end, pragmatism appears to be useful in achieving progressive social change to the extent that one profits from statements such as, "There is no method or procedure to be followed except courageous and imaginative experimentation." Or, as the Nike people say, "Just do it."'[20]

It is this account of pragmatism that Dworkin critiques, and rightly so. Dworkin is correct that we must justify the legitimacy of the ends we select to guide our adjudication. Since citizens do not vote on every issue, and since we are bound by a Constitution that circumscribes our ordinary lawmaking, it is important for judges to demonstrate the legitimacy of the principles, ends and ideals they invoke.

Dworkin's concerns have merit, but his critique is misplaced when he speaks of pragmatism beyond the thin account held by neo-pragmatists and exemplified by Posner. At the heart of Posner's pragmatism is a particular understanding of the relationship between theory and practice. For Posner, theory has little to offer practice. According to Posner, academics are insulated from the 'real' world and tend to become easily infatuated with empty abstractions such as justice, fairness and equality. Legal pragmatists reject 'abstract theorizing of which professors of constitutional law are enamored, in which decisions are evaluated by reference to abstractions common in law talk such as fairness, justice, autonomy, and equality'.[21]

One can understand Posner's concerns. Much theoretical academic work participates in a private conversation far removed from the pressing social problems of the day. Philosophical discourse, whether in academic philosophy or in legal theory, can be overly abstract, filled with jargon and disconnected from current practice.

In making this criticism, Posner echoes Dewey, who also staunchly criticized the academy for theorizing abstractly without attempting to connect theory to current practice.[22] Dewey criticized philosophy that attempted to treat itself as something more lofty than other forms of knowledge, as 'a realm of higher Being' with 'air purer than that in which exist the making and doing that relate to livelihood'.[23] Like Dewey, Posner is right to criticize academic theorists who view their theorizing as a higher and purer activity than disciplines that employ empirical methods of analysis.

Dewey was very critical of academic departments for creating pseudo-problems – taking problems from general experience and converting them into philosophical puzzles with a life of their own, disconnected from their origins in experience. Philosophy should begin in ordinary life with the concerns, pressures and facts of contemporary existence.[24] For Dewey, '[p]hilosophy recovers itself when it ceases to be a device for dealing with the problems of philosophers and becomes a method, cultivated by philosophers, for dealing with the problems of men'.[25] Dewey believed a 'first-rate test' of the value of any philosophy consists in its answer to this question: 'Does it end in conclusions which, when they are referred back to ordinary life-experiences and their predicaments, render them more significant, more luminous to us, and make our dealings with them more fruitful?'[26]

If a philosophy is to meet this challenge, it must take as its starting point the problems generated by our everyday practices. Likewise, a philosophy of law, as Dewey observes, 'cannot be set up as if it were a separate entity, but can be discussed only in terms of the social conditions in which it arises and of what it concretely does there'.[27] Thus, as a pragmatist, Posner is right to suggest that those interested in improving legal methods and procedures should not look to academic philosophy or law departments for ready-made answers. He is also right to insist that constructive solutions usually require in-depth investigations of the facts.

Posner also astutely argues that work should be done in what he calls the 'empirical lowlands'.[28] As Posner observes, '[t]he theoretical uplands, where democratic and judicial ideals are debated, tend to be arid and overgrazed; the empirical lowlands are fertile but rarely cultivated'.[29] The uplands are thus theoretical discourses that ask questions about the nature of justice, equality and the good. The lowlands are efforts to explore empirically the results of our social practices. It is one thing to argue about the justification for policies such as affirmative action by sparring over competing conceptions of fairness, but more important to the pragmatist is understanding the consequences of such rhetoric in practice. Posner, like Dewey, thinks that theoretically minded individuals concerned with questions of justice and the like could accomplish much more by investigating these conceptions in the context of particular practices. Not only would they help to ameliorate present problems, but they would also be submitting their ideals to the test of experience. Indeed, law is an excellent field for the pragmatist since it provides a forum to investigate concretely the meaning of our ideals.

However, Posner then takes a wrong turn. He equates philosophy exclusively with the work of academic departments in universities, and then he rejects philosophy wholesale. The practice of philosophy, however, is much broader than the practice of professors in academic institutions, and even the philosophy of the academy is far from monochromatic. Whether someone is a philosopher is a function of the questions she asks and the writing she does, not whether she is employed by a philosophy department. Philosophy isn't the exclusive domain of academic philosophers; rather, it is the development of intelligent, critical and reconstructive methods for approaching the problems of lived experience. Philosophy is something that everyone does or at least can do, not an insular club that only those in the ivory tower can join. Therefore, although the academic practice of philosophy can be often overly technical and disengaged from the problems of society, this does not imply that philosophy should be abandoned.[30]

Posner's account of pragmatism, as rejecting a role for philosophical theory, stems in part from a misunderstanding of the pragmatic reconstruction of the theory and practice relationship. Under the traditional model of the theory–practice relationship, philosophical theory is seen as offering a foundation for practice. One should learn the theory and then put it into practice. But pragmatists, such as Dewey, never expected theory to guide practice in this way and never pretended that practice was independent of theory. Rather than embrace this dualism, the classic pragmatists sought to make practice more intelligent and more critical, in part by recognizing its theoretical dimension. This does not require theoretical reason capable of determining its goals outside of historical practices; rather it requires a critical and reconstructive approach to social institutions and practices.

In so far as the language of 'justice' has been dominated by Kantian moralists who believe that our regulative ideals are the product of pure reason, then one can understand Posner's reservations. Terms like 'justice' and 'freedom' are not backed up by reference to Platonic forms, but are the products of our human experience and contested history.[31] We don't look to theory to tell us what 'democracy', 'justice', 'equality', and 'freedom' mean. We look to our experience of past practices. Under this view, 'theory' is a statement of the insights, often generalized, formed as a result of the success and failures of these practices.

The risk with Posner's anti-abstraction strategy is that it silences meaningful community discussion. Terms such as 'justice' and 'equality' are not only used in the academy, but also are part of popular social discourse. Whereas Dewey offers us tools to reconstruct the meaning of these terms by giving priority to experience, Posner advises us to avoid the terms. The result may be that they remain to do mischief having been insulated from critical attention.

By eliminating philosophical theorizing, Posner discards pragmatic tools for transforming existing institutions, customs and social norms. Without a role for philosophical theorizing, Posner's pragmatism looks less to opportunities for criticism and reconstruction of unsatisfactory practices, the two hallmarks of Deweyan pragmatic approach, and more to opportunities for affirmation and acquiescence to the status quo. Such an account of pragmatism leads critics such as David Luban to conclude that: 'Pragmatism represents in the arena of conceptual change what Burke represents in that of political change: a cautionary voice protesting those who seek to overthrow the amassed wisdom of generations on no better basis than the trifling speculations of philosophers.'[32]

Because it rejects any way to discuss the selection of ends, Posnerian pragmatism has little choice but to accept uncritically the dominant ends of society. This result is rather ironic considering Posner's claim that pragmatism has no political valence. Since Posner's pragmatism lacks the tools to engage in more radical social reform, it becomes a rather conservative philosophy in the Burkean sense. It ends up inhibiting the kinds of philosophical inquiries necessary to question the status quo. Therefore, the effects of Posnerian pragmatism are anything but neutral.

MEANS AND ENDS

Posner's pragmatism fails to point us toward productive inquiries for resolving legal and policy issues, for these issues involve the choice of ends. In contrast to Posner's account, Deweyan pragmatism provides for a more fruitful inquiry into our selection of ends. Under this account of pragmatism, philosophy plays an essential role. Dewey sees philosophy as critical inquiry, which aims to unsettle status quo assumptions and then provide guidance for projects of social reconstruction. Dewey observed that we often act out of habit, which is 'an ability ... formed through past experience'. While we need habit in order to function, habit can restrict the 'reach' of our intellect, and can 'fix its boundaries'.[33]

Social customs are aggregation of habits. They 'persist because individuals form their personal habits under conditions set by prior customs'. The problem with customs is that they can be 'inert' and can readily lead 'into conformity, constriction, surrender of skepticism and experiment'.[34] Maintaining institutions without change can lead to social stagnation. The goal of philosophical inquiry is thus to make habits 'more intelligent', by which Dewey means 'more sensitively percipient, more informed with foresight, more aware of what they are about, more direct and sincere, more flexibly responsive than those now current'. Rather than be controlled by habit and custom, we must strive toward the intelligent control of habit.[35] This involves criticizing current institutions and finding ways to reconstruct them. Of course, Dewey observed, we cannot abandon our institutions, as this would lead to 'chaos and anarchy'; rather, we must 'make over these institutions so that they serve under changing conditions'.[36]

As a pragmatist, Posner is wrong to shrug off the hard work of justifying the ends our legal system pursues. The pragmatist *does* have something to say about our ends. The pragmatist justifies her value commitments, in part, by analysing their historical genesis. Guiding ideals such as 'fairness', 'justice', and 'freedom' must be critically examined by looking to past experience. Posner complains that such ideals are empty abstractions, useless for assisting us in decisions. Yet they are rendered useless not because they are abstractions, but because insufficient effort is made to critically explore their genesis and the consequences of their deployment in various contexts.

Pragmatists are committed to finding substantive sustenance for their guiding ideals through experiential inquiry. This requires difficult historical investigation and interpretation. There is no guarantee that one account will emerge as superior to all others, although many accounts, upon careful investigation, are shown to be wanting. If a particular view of justice or democracy is to be favoured, it should be favoured because of its past consequences and in light of its anticipated future consequences. Those in disagreement over political ends need not refrain from invoking considerations of justice, freedom, equality and democracy, but they must not let matters rest there. They must explain the experiential basis for their choices.

The pragmatist need not be a shallow empiricist who has something to say about means but nothing much to say about ends. The pragmatist need not eschew philosophical theorizing or discussion of regulative ideals. Far from being a mere method that provides little guidance as to our normative ends, pragmatism facilitates philosophical debates about them in ways that avoid appealing to hollow abstractions.

Posner is mistaken, therefore, when he proposes that there is nothing useful to be done in terms of critically assessing our value commitments. He appears to view ends as little more than mere tastes. As a result, he does not seem to believe that discussion about our ends will be very fruitful. This is why Posner ultimately recommends a diverse judiciary; at least different ends can be represented, even if discussing them won't lead us anywhere.

If Posner simply treats the selection of ends as the product of a judge's individual choice, those ends become insulated from critical scrutiny. Pragmatism, by contrast, demands the critical assessment of our ends. Where did they come from? What conditions were they responding to? What have been the results? Who has benefited from their adoption? Who has suffered? Have they been democratically selected?

As a result, the pragmatist would understand that any view of the best future must be informed by a view of who we are as a people – and this depends upon an interpretation of our history.[37] Pragmatists recognize that ends are not ahistorical. Dewey noted that 'personal desire and belief are functions of habit and custom'.[38] We do not get our ends from some a priori source; they emerge from experience. And our values originate not just from our own experience, but from collective social experience, which has a long history and is embodied in our current habits, customs and traditions. In this way, the past perpetuates itself; it has a hold on us. We can't simply wipe the slate clean. We adopt the ends we do often because they are transmitted to us by our parents, education, and culture. Dewey argued that we must consider the history of any social end in both directions: its past and its future. 'We must consider it with reference to the antecedents which evoked it, and with reference to its later career and fate.'[39] We must look to the genesis of a particular end because:

> [i]t arises in a certain context, and as a reaction to certain circumstances; it has a subsequent history which can be traced. It maintains and reinforces certain conditions, and modifies others. It becomes a stimulus which provokes new modes of action. Now when we see how and why the belief came about, and also know what else came about because of it, we have a hold upon the worth of the belief which is entirely wanting when we set it up as an isolated intuition.[40]

Since ends do not emerge from a transcendent realm, the pragmatist should not simply accept her own ends uncritically. She must subject them to critical inquiry. This involves understanding the origins of our ends, the reasons for their existence, and whether these reasons warrant continued allegiance today. Through pragmatic criticism, we may discover that particular ends have merely survived through inertia or that the reasons for their existence no longer apply to our present situation.

Therefore, to the extent that pragmatism is an 'attitude', it is one that is radical, for it is sceptical and experimental. The pragmatic temperament is one that is constantly prodding and questioning; it focuses on change and transformation. Although the pragmatist need not be committed to radical ends, she is committed to a radical kind of criticism and experimentation. This doesn't mean that pragmatism must reject the status quo; but it does mean that the pragmatist must be wary of accepting inherited ends uncritically. Far from being mundane and banal, pragmatism takes up the hard work of removing the blinders of existing habits, customs, and conventions by testing accepted beliefs and 'truths'. The result of this attitude is a critical edge.

In this manner, pragmatism is not empty and devoid of substance. Pragmatism has substantive commitments that are not separable from method. In other words, no method of inquiry is neutral. All inquiry begins with a particular direction, some preconceived notion of what is being sought. Inquiry is thus not a wide open process that can lead anywhere. To embark on an inquiry (or to adopt a method of inquiry) is already to head in a particular direction. The starting points of pragmatic inquiry are certain critical stances toward the status quo. This does not mean that one must reject the status quo, but it requires an inquiry into certain assumptions and basic social institutions. In the end, one of the consequences of Posner's pragmatism is that it discourages understanding debate over social ends as a worthwhile critical activity, and therefore entrenches past results, insulating dominant social structures from criticism.

DEMOCRACY

After articulating his account of pragmatism, Posner devotes the core of his book to discussing democratic theory. He contrasts two concepts of democracy, which he refers to as 'concept 1' and 'concept 2' democracy. Posner defines concept 1 democracy, which is often called 'deliberative democracy', as 'political democracy conceived of as the pooling of different ideas and approaches and the selection of the best through debate and discussion'. According to Posner, concept 1 democracy views all legally competent adults as having an equal 'moral right' to participate in societal governance. Citizens have the responsibility to be informed about the issues, engage in open-minded dialogue with other citizens, and vote based on 'what is best for society as a whole rather than on narrow self-interest'.⁴¹

In contrast to concept 1, Posner advances an alternative notion of democracy, which he calls 'concept 2' democracy. Concept 2 democracy is based on Joseph Schumpeter's theory of 'elite democracy'. Concept 2 democracy is representative democracy, in which the bulk of the population has little political involvement except for casting a vote every now and then. 'Concept 2 rejects the idea that democracy is self-government. Democracy is government subject to electoral checks.' Interest groups and elites run the show. 'Successful [political] candidates are not random draws from the public at large. They are smarter, better educated, more ambitious, and wealthier than the average person.'⁴²

Despite its reliance on elites, concept 2 democracy is populist, Posner argues, because it takes people as they are. Ordinary people simply don't have the expertise or time to be engaged in a robust political life. Concept 1 democracy is too idealistic and utopian. It wants people to be more educated, more concerned about politics, more civic-minded. In contrast, concept 2 is realistic and takes people as they are. Concept 2 democracy is thus 'the democracy of the pragmatists'.⁴³

Since Posner justifies his choice of concept 2 democracy based on pragmatism, he attempts to explain why Dewey chose concept 1. Posner argues that Dewey's views of democracy are entirely separate from his pragmatic ideas. Thus, Posner contends, Dewey's political views 'have no organic relation to his philosophy' and belong instead 'to his career as a public intellectual'.⁴⁴ This move is essential for Posner, because Posner accepts many of Dewey's pragmatic ideas yet eschews Dewey's liberal political philosophy.

Since Posner and other neo-pragmatists believe pragmatism has no political valence, he argues that there is no necessary connection between the pragmatic ideas of John Dewey and his political philosophy: 'The connection between the liberal-visionary and the pragmatic is purely historical and contingent.'⁴⁵ According to Posner, Dewey's faith in deliberative democracy was misplaced, for Dewey wanted people 'to think about political questions the way scientists think about scientific ones – disinterestedly, intelligently, empirically', but he 'succumbed to the intellectual's typical mistake of exaggerating the importance of intellect and of associated virtues such as commitment to disinterested inquiry'.[46]

If Posner is correct in his claim that pragmatism has no political valence, then it is puzzling how he can claim that concept 2 democracy is the 'democracy of the pragmatists'. It is difficult to imagine how an inherently apolitical pragmatic method can be linked to one theory of democracy over another. Posner thus must resort to a variety of unpragmatic contortions to free himself from this logical bind.

Although Posner contends that there is no connection between Deweyan democratic theory and pragmatism, he is mistaken. Of course, pragmatists have reached very different, sometimes mutually exclusive, political views. But the fact that pragmatists can arrive at different political conclusions does not imply that pragmatism is completely neutral as to which conclusions one might reach.

Pragmatism refuses to accept on face value claims about methods being 'neutral'. Rather, pragmatism recognizes that our critical investigations are infused with value commitments. No neutral determination is possible. Under this account, the point of philosophy is less a matter of securing objective truth and more a matter of facilitating effective growth in the face of particular problems. Pragmatism is not a method purified of experience. Pragmatism does not start out from some Archimedean point; it begins with commitments, which have certain valences. Pragmatism asks particular kinds of questions and suggests we abandon other types of questions. As Dewey argued:

> [T]he conviction persists – though history shows it to be hallucination – that all the questions that the human mind has asked are questions that can be answered in terms of the alternatives that the questions themselves present. But in fact intellectual progress usually occurs through sheer abandonment of questions together with both of the alternatives they assume – abandonment that results from their decreasing vitality and a change of urgent interest. We do not solve them: we get over them.[47]

Since all questions guide the focus of our intellectual attention, they lead us in particular directions.

For Dewey, pragmatism is not simply a tool external to democracy, and it would be a mistake to use pragmatism to determine the ideal democratic structure. This is not the type of question pragmatism suggests we investigate. For the pragmatist, there is no ideal democratic structure; rather, a democracy is a process whereby a community continually seeks to define itself as it moves into the future. A democracy is therefore not static, but continually evolving. Moreover, democracy is more than just a set of political structures; it is a way of making certain decisions about the future of the community. Dewey believed that democratic decisionmaking should be pragmatic. Pragmatists certainly agree that pragmatism is a more productive method of engaging our problems than other methods. To the extent that pragmatism is successful in this way, then not only individuals, but also entire communities, should engage in pragmatic inquiry. Under this view, pragmatic democracy is, like pragmatism, a commitment to a form of inquiry – the endorsement of experimental method on the social and political stage.

For Dewey, democracy is 'a way of life, social and individual'.[48] John Stuhr explains Dewey's conception of democracy as 'a form of *life* rather than a form of *government* alone'.[49] Under this view, democracy does not primarily consist of institutions or government structures: 'Democracy exists only on paper and in statute unless individuals enact it in their own transactions day by day and face-to-face in local communities. That is, a society of individuals can become a democracy only as those individuals act democratically.'[50] As Dewey observed, 'democracy is much broader than a special political form, a method of conducting government, of making laws and carrying on governmental administration by means of popular suffrage and elected officers.'[51]

Thus, even if our government has a democratic structure, we are not democratic unless we live our lives democratically. We should not see democracy as something that has been accomplished simply by the choice of an appropriate set of representative governmental structures that can be passed down from generation to generation. Instead, the meaning of democracy must change continually with changes in culture, and this reconstruction is democratic only to the extent means are found to fully involve all members of the community in this reconstruction.

While Posner's thin account of pragmatism seems insufficient for generating substantive ends, a thicker account of pragmatism recommends that a community pragmatically reconstruct its ends. On this thicker account, democracy and pragmatism go hand in hand.

Certain characteristics of democracy facilitate the community's engaging in pragmatic inquiry about the future shape of its democracy. Pragmatic inquiry enables a community to make itself more democratic. Pragmatism and democracy are thus mutually reinforcing.

PRAGMATISM'S POLITICAL VALENCE

As developed by classical pragmatists like Dewey, pragmatism is not neutral. Of course, this account of pragmatism does not imply a specific theory of political philosophy. But it does have valences. In order to ask *what political future does pragmatism recommend?*, we must also ask *in what political culture can pragmatic forms of inquiry about the political future best be carried out?* The answer to this latter question leads us in the direction of what we call a 'general democratic culture'.

First, pragmatism subjects existing institutions and the status quo to ongoing critique, since it recommends that we critically examine our ends. When one commits oneself to a thoroughgoing use of pragmatic method, certain conclusions are ruled out in advance, such as a politics informed by supernatural or transcendental ideals, or a politics that arbitrarily excludes particular viewpoints. Supernaturalism and absolutism conflict with the general approach of the pragmatic method, which is to subject our ideals, ends and conclusions to the test of experience. Indeed, it is this commitment that in part motivates Posner's rejection of philosophical theory, for much philosophical theory has traditionally harboured ideological commitments that were then foisted upon the unaware from the altar of theory. But the fear of ideology can lead to cures that are worse than the disease. Although Posner claims to adhere to a neutral pragmatic method without political valences, the results of his application of this method are deeply ensconced in ideology. Posner's pragmatism does have a particular political valence, one that favors the dominant ends of the status quo. The result is that while Posnerian pragmatism rejects supernaturalism and absolutism, it starts with an unquestioning acceptance of current institutions. Ironically, it winds up in a similar posture to supernaturalism and absolutism, for in each of these instances certain issues are insulated from critical scrutiny.

Second, under Deweyan pragmatism, democracy depends upon deliberation. Democratic deliberation is the way we establish shared meanings and determine the ends of a community. It is important to distinguish between individual and community ends. Individuals can readily choose their own ends, but for communities, the task is more difficult. This is because a community's ends depend on the identity of the community, which must be ascertained by examining the history of that community and soliciting input from across the community as a whole. Examining community identity leads us to ask: Who are we becoming? How are we growing? Do we want to continue in this fashion? Who do we want to become? There is no movement into the future that does not presuppose a judgement about the past and present. Pragmatists therefore need to encourage public deliberation about our identity since there is no way to determine what is better or worse without reference to that identity.

Since community rather than individual ends are at issue, dialogue becomes essential. Community ends are determined collectively, and doing so requires communication. This dialogue does not need to be an academically sophisticated discourse; rather, pragmatism merely requires that people participate in a discussion of the meaning of ends understood in the context of present circumstances. These are philosophical discussions not because they take place in universities, but because they ask about the good life under present social conditions. A pragmatic approach to democracy is one that understands itself as part of existing political conversations about the nature and ends of the community.

Third, since experience is social and meanings are constituted through communication, efforts to describe experience and formulate an account of social problems must seek contributions from a wide range of participants in social experience. Under Dewey's theory, participation is a highly valued end. For Posner, in contrast, participation has no value unless it can achieve results that benefit one's self-interest.

Beyond being valuable in and of itself, participation is valuable instrumentally as well. According to Dewey, self-government 'is educative', for it 'forces recognition that there are common interests'.[52] Thus, the purpose of democracy is not to take the people as they are. The value of democratic participation is to educate people, to enable them to realize common interests and see themselves as part of a community.

Dewey's experimental method does not simply consist of presenting hypotheses; rather, it requires testing proposals to resolve present problems by seeing how they work in experience. Interpreting the social meaning of a particular set of experiments requires recourse to the larger community. We increase our chances of finding effective solutions to social problems by looking to a broad range of contributors.

Therefore, in contrast to Posnerian pragmatism, the account of pragmatism we offer openly acknowledges that it is not completely neutral. Although pragmatism does not point to precise resolutions for our debates, it does send us in a particular direction based on the types of questions it recommends we investigate. It puts on the table for debate a wide range of issues, especially the identity of a community and its ends. It requires dialogue, for the task of determining a community's ends cannot be achieved without communication. And it relies on the participation of the community, not merely upon a group of elites who impose their own ends upon the community.

Since democracy depends upon the widespread participation of a community in a dialogue over its ends, the pragmatist pays special attention to questions concerning the conditions for effective community discussion. Posner rejects such questions as hopeless and doomed because it is not realistic to achieve complete community engagement. But these are precisely the ways in which a community pragmatically resolves the more specific political arrangements it shall adopt. Because this account of pragmatism suggests that we engage in a critical examination of the dominant ends of society, and that we must do so through dialogue and through broad community participation, it points us more toward concept 1 democracy than concept 2. This does not foreclose us from embracing some features of concept 2, but it certainly rejects the insular nature of concept 2, which leaves too few avenues for dialogue and community engagement.

Pragmatic democratic inquiry would lead us to ask: What are the pressing problems of the day? What are the relevant community ends? What means can we use to achieve these ends? The inquiry would also go deeper to ask: To what extent are the community ends contested? What is the pedigree of the prevailing community ends? How did these ends become the prevailing ones? For what purposes were these ends originally adopted? Do the reasons these ends were adopted still have currency today? To the extent that there are competing accounts of a community's ends, can common ground be discovered?

The pragmatist would also recognize that answering these questions pragmatically at the community level requires certain features of a democratic culture – ones that may need significant improvement. The quality of our pragmatic inquiry into the above questions depends upon the quality of our democratic culture. To improve our democratic culture, the pragmatist would explore ways to improve public deliberation and civic participation. For example, the pragmatist would look to improving education, which enables individuals to assess experience critically and share their assessments with others. The pragmatist might also examine how to promote new means of communication to enable democratic discussions to take place.

One might object that such projects are not pragmatic because they are often engineered by elites. Deweyan democracy, however, need not be antagonistic to elites so long as elites see their role as guiding and advising the public rather than running the show with minimal public involvement.

Posner would also respond that these projects are too utopian because too many people do not want to participate and are not educated enough to do anything but vote. But the pragmatist does not simply accept human nature as given. Democracy, for Dewey, is about the 'maturing and fruition of the potentialities of human nature'.[53] Institutions must be changed; further experimentation is needed in order to help enable society to become more democratic. In this way, Dewey was idealistic about democracy. He believed that a commitment to democracy makes 'claims upon our future conduct' and therefore it *'is an ideal'*.[54] Dewey would not view the charge that concept 1 is idealistic as troubling at all; he would say that this is precisely the point of democracy.

The normative goal of democracy for Dewey was the realization of people's full capacities.[55] For Dewey, then, unlike Posner, one cannot simply take human beings and social institutions as one finds them. In the end, Dewey was committed to using the power of intelligence to bring about a better society capable of facilitating the growth of individuals. He was convinced that the form and commitment to inquiry that had so decisively enabled us to increase our control over nature in the realm of science and technology might also be used to improve the political governance of society. But he knew that assessment of this claim would have to await the results of trying to put it into practice. From Dewey's point of view, it was far too early to pronounce pragmatic attempts at reconstruction as failures or successes, because by and large they simply had not been tried. This remains true today. Even as Posner recommends our acquiescence to the status quo, his claims that aspirations for a more deliberative society are too utopian seem driven more by his affirmation of the present than by any demonstration that improvement is not possible.

CONCLUSION

Many contemporary neo-pragmatists such as Posner view ideals as useless and philosophical theorizing as empty. Lacking any meaningful approach for scrutinizing social goals, pragmatism thus devolves into an efficiency exercise. The task of the pragmatist becomes merely finding the appropriate means to achieve our given ends. This thin theory of pragmatism, having eschewed attempts to evaluate ends critically and having effectively pronounced its agnosticism about community ends, leads naturally to a vision of democracy as principally an efficient mechanism for dispute resolution. This vision of democracy is conservative not only because it privileges the inherited demands of the present, but even more because it rules out as misguided the projects of reconstructing community identity through public deliberation.

In contrast, the pragmatism of the early pragmatists, especially Dewey, encourages us to approach our present problems more radically. We should subject both means and ends to critical inquiry and empower communities to engage in self-formation by reconstructing the settled habits and ideals that constitute the status quo. For Dewey, 'The end of democracy is a radical end. For it is an end that has not been adequately realized in any country at any time. It is radical because it requires great change in existing social institutions, economic, legal and cultural.'[56]

Far from being timorous, far from accepting our current practices and institutions as given realities, pragmatism subjects them to criticism and reconstruction. Pragmatism is anything but banal – it is radical.

NOTES

1   Grey, 1989, pp. 787, 814.
2   See Symposium, 1990; Symposium, 1996.
3   See Rorty, 1991a, p. 89 ('I think it is true that by now pragmatism is banal in its application to law').
4   Posner, 2003, pp. 1, 59, 73.
5   Posner, 2003, pp. 26, 84.
6   Rorty, 1991d, pp. 70, 75.
7   Rorty, 1991d, p. 3.
8   Rorty, 1991d, p. 60.
9   Rorty, 1991d, p. 77.
10 Rorty, 1991d, p. 50.
11 Smith, 1990, pp. 409, 411.
12 Dworkin, 1986, p. 161.
13 Posner, 2003, p. 71.
14 Of course, it is still no easy matter to determine whether or not a precedent applies along the formalist model. One has to determine that the present facts are similar in the relevant way to the facts of the past case, and there can be, therefore, great difficulties in predicting the action of the courts even if they maintain a staunch commitment to taking precedent seriously.
15 Posner, 2003, p. 6.
16 See Posner, 2003, pp. 105–6.
17 Posner, 2003, p. 55.
18 James, 1975b.
19 Tamanaha, 1996, pp. 315, 328.
20 Baker, 2002, pp. 697, 718.
21 Baker, 2002, p. 79.
22 Dewey, *Experience and Nature*, LW1: 3, 17.
23 Dewey, *The Quest for Certainty*, LW4: 3, 11–12.
24 Dewey, *Reconstruction in Philosophy*, LW14: 115, 117.
25 Dewey, 'The Need for a Recovery of Philosophy', MW10: 3, 36.
26 Dewey, 1958a, p. 7.

27 Dewey, *My Philosophy of Law*, LW14: 115.
28 Posner, 2003, p. 3.
29 Posner, 2003, pp. 3–4.
30 Pragmatists like John Lachs contend that academic insularity is created by institutional structures that reward and punish their behaviour. The best solution does not involve having the public ignore the academy, but having the academy stop ignoring the public. See Lachs, 2003, 8–9.
31 As Charles S. Peirce, has pointed out, to understand a concept is to understand the conceivable sensible effects of that concept. This does not mean one cannot use words such as 'justice', 'fairness' and 'equality', but that one must understand the meaning of the terms not by reference to Platonic forms, but by reference to the practical consequences they entail. Peirce, 'How to Make our Ideas Clear', EP1: 132.
32 Luban, 1994, 138.
33 Dewey, *Human Nature and Conduct*, MW14: 48, 121.
34 Dewey, MW14: 47.
35 Dewey, MW14: 43, 47, 90, 17–18.
36 Dewey, 'Evolution and Ethics', EW5: 34, 48.
37 See Farber, 1988, pp. 1331, 1350 ('For a pragmatist the analysis must start – but not finish – with an examination of our constitutional text, history, and traditions').
38 Dewey, *The Public and its Problems*, LW2: 235, 336.
39 Dewey, 'The Evolutionary Method as Applied to Morality', MW2: 3, 26.
40 Dewey, MW2: 26–7.
41 Posner, 2003, 106–7, 131.
42 Posner, 2003, pp. 130, 164, 154.
43 Posner, 2003, p. 143.
44 Posner, 2003, p. 98.
45 'The connection between the liberal-visionary and the pragmatic is purely historical and contingent': Posner, 2003, p. 46.
46 Posner, 2003, pp. 107–8.
47 Dewey, 'The Influence of Darwinism on Philosophy', MW4: 4.
48 Dewey, 'Democracy and Educational Administration', MW9: 217.
49 Stuhr, 2003.
50 Stuhr, 2003, p. 64.
51 Dewey, MW9: 217.
52 Dewey, LW2: 364.
53 Dewey, 'Freedom and Culture', MW2.
54 Stuhr, 2003, at 55.
55 Dewey, 1935, 41.
56 Dewey, 'Democracy Is Radical', LW11: 296–9.

BIBLIOGRAPHY

JOHN DEWEY

The standard critical edition of Dewey's works is *The Collected Works of John Dewey, 1882–53* (Carbondale, IL: Southern Illinois University Press, 1969–91) in 37 volumes, edited by Jo Ann Boydston. These are cited as EW, MW and LW, followed by the volume then the page number. The electronic edition of the same title is edited by Larry Hickman.

The Early Works of John Dewey, 1882–1898, 15 vols: (1969–72)
The Middle Works of John Dewey, 1899–1924, 5 vols (1976–88)
The Later Works of John Dewey, 1925–1953, 17 vols. (1981–91)

Individual works cited from this collected edition

'Analysis of Reflective Thinking', LW8: 196–210.
'Anti-Naturalism in Extremis', LW15: 46–63.
Art as Experience LW10:
'Context and Thought', LW6: 3–21.
'Contributions to *A Cyclopedia of Education*', MW7: 328.
'Creative Democracy: The Task before Us', MW14: 224–30.
Democracy and Education, MW9.
'Democracy and Educational Administration', MW9: 217.
'Democracy in Education', MW3: 229–339.
'Democracy Is Radical', LW11: 296–9.
'The Development of American Pragmatism', LW2: 3–21.
'Education as Growth', from *Democracy and Education*, MW9: 217.
'Ethical Principles underlying Education', EW5: 54–83.
'Evolution and Ethics', EW5: 34.
'The Evolutionary Method as Applied to Morality', MW2: 3.'

Experience and Nature, LW1: 3–17.
'Freedom and Culture', MW2
How we Think, MW6: 105–352.
Human Nature and Conduct, MW14: 48.
'The Influence of Darwinism on Philosophy', MW4: 4.
Logic: The Theory of Inquiry, LW12
'The Lost Individual', in *Individualism Old and New*, LW5
'My Philosophy of Law', LW14: 115, 117
'The Need for a Recovery of Philosophy', MW10, 3, 46.
'The New Psychology', EW1: 56.
'The Pattern of Inquiry' in *Logic: The Theory of Inquiry*, LW12.
The Public and its Problems, LW2: 235.
Psychology, EW2
The Quest for Certainty, LW4: 232.
Reality as Experience, EW3
Reconstruction in Philosophy, LW14: 115
'The Reflex Arc Concept in Psychology', EW5: 96–109.
'Search for the Great Community', in *The Public and its Problems*, LW2
'Some Stages of Logical Thought', MW1: 151–74.
Studies in Logical Theory, MW2

Other editions and cited works by Dewey

1898. 'Evolution and Ethics', *Monist*, p. 32.
1927. 'Half-Hearted Naturalism', *Journal of Philosophy* 24, pp. 57–64.
1929a. *Experience and Nature*. London: George Allen and Unwin.
1929b. *The Quest for Certainty: A Study of the Relation of Knowledge and Action*. London: Allen and Unwin.
1933. *The Quest for Certainty*. New York: Capricorn Books.
1934. *A Common Faith*. New Haven: Yale University Press.
1935. *Liberalism and Social Action*. New York: G. P. Putnam's Sons.
1938. *Logic: The Theory of Inquiry*. New York: Henry Holt.
1949. 'Experience and Existence: A Comment', *Philosophy and Phenomenological Research* 9, pp. 709–13.
1957. *Reconstruction in Philosophy*. Boston: Beacon Press.
1958a. *Experience and Nature*. Dover.
1958b. *Art as Experience*. New York: G. P. Putnam's Sons.
1965. *The Influence of Darwin on Philosophy and Other Essays in Contemporary Thought*. Bloomington: Indiana University Press.
1981. *The Philosophy of John Dewey*, ed. J. J. McDermott. University of Chicago Press.
1993. 'The Need for a Recovery of Philosophy', in Debra Morris and Ian Shapiro (eds.), *John Dewey: The Political Writings*. Hackett Publishing Company.

2002. *The Varieties of Religious Experience*. Centenary edn. London: Routledge.
2004a. 'The Development of American Pragmatism' in Malachowski, 2004a. vol. 1.
2004b. 'The Practical Character of Reality', in Malachowski, 2004a, vol. 1.
Dewey John (ed.), 1903. *Studies in Logical Theory*. University of Chicago Press.

Net resources

John Dewey johndewey.org/.
John Dewey Society doe.concordia.ca/jds/.
Center for Dewey Studies www.siuc.edu/~deweyctr/.

WILLIAM JAMES

For a comprehensive collection of William James's work see *The Works of William James*, edited Frederick H. Burkhardt, Fredson Bowers and Ignas K. Skrupselis, in eighteen volumes (Cambridge, MA: Harvard University Press, 1975–88).

OTHER EDITIONS CITED

1884. 'What is an Emotion?', *Mind* 9, pp. 188–205.
1897. *The Will to Believe*. New York: Longman's Green and Co.
1948. *Essays in Pragmatism*. London: Macmillan.
1950. *The Principles of Psychology*, 2 vols. New York: Dover.
1955. 'What Pragmatism Means', in *Pragmatism*, 1975b.
1971. 'Remarks on Spencer's Definition of Mind as Correspondence', in Bruce Wilshire (ed.), *William James: The Essential Writing*. Harper & Row.
1975a. *The Meaning of Truth*. Cambridge, MA: Harvard University Press.
1975b. *Pragmatism: A New Name for Some Old Ways of Thinking*. Cambridge, MA: Harvard University Press.
1976. *Essays in Radical Empiricism*, ed. F. Burkhardt. Cambridge, MA: Harvard University Press.
1977. *A Pluralistic Universe*. Cambridge MA: Harvard University Press.
1979. 'The Moral Philosopher and the Moral Life', in *The Works of William James: The Will to Believe*, ed. Frederick Burkhardt. Cambridge, MA: Harvard University Press.
1991. *Pragmatism*. New York: Prometheus Books.

1996a. *Essays in Radical Empiricism*. Lincoln and London: University of Nebraska Press.
1996b. 'The Thing and its Relations', in James, 1996a, pp. 92–122.
1996c. 'A World of Pure Experience', in James, 1996a, pp. 39–91.
1997. *The Meaning of Truth: A Sequel to Pragmatism*. New York: Prometheus Books.
1998. *Pragmatism and The Meaning of Truth*. Cambridge MA: Harvard University Press
2002. *The Varieties of Religious Experience*. Centenary Edition, London: Routledge.
2004a. 'The Practical Character of Reality', in Malachoswki, 2004a.
2004b. 'What Pragmatism Means by Practical', in Malachowski, 2004a.
2005. 'The Will to Believe', in J. M. Capps and D. Capps (eds.), *James and Dewey on Belief and Experience*, pp. 95–110. Carbondale: University of Illinois Press.

Net resources

William James Society w.w.w.wjsociety.org/.
William James Studies williamjamesstudies.org/.
William James Emory University w.w.w.edu/EDUCATION/mfp/james.html.

CHARLES PEIRCE

References to Peirce's work employ standard scholarly conventions for these writings. Material available in the *Writings of Charles Peirce: A Chronological Edition* (1931–60) is referred to as 'W' together with volume and page number (for example W3: 256). Material which is not available there but is in the *Collected Papers of Charles Sanders Peirce* (1931–60) is referred to by 'CP' together with the volume and numbered section or page number. When material is available in *The Essential Peirce* (1998) references are also given to that work as 'EP' plus volume and page number.

1931–60. *Collected Papers of Charles Sanders Peirce*, 8 vols., eds. C. Hartshorne, P. Weiss and A. Burks. Cambridge, MA: Harvard University Press.
1982–. *Writings of Charles S. Peirce: A Chronological Edition*, eds. M. Fisch, E. Moore, C. Kloesel, N. Houser et al. Bloomington, IN: Indiana University Press.
1998. *The Essential Peirce: Selected Philosophical Writings*, eds. Nathan Houser and Christian Kloesel, 2 vols. Indianapolis: Indiana University Press.

Works cited from these editions

'The Doctrine of Chances'. W3: ch. 62, EP1: 142–54 (ch. 9)
'The Fixation of Belief'. EP1: 109–23; W3: 242
'How to Make our Ideas Clear'. EP1: 124–41, W3.
'Issues of Pragmaticism'. EP2: 346 (ch. 25), CP5: 438.
Lectures on Pragmatism. EP2: 134, 135, CP5: 18, 19.
'Review of Dewey's *Studies in Logical Theory*'. CP8: 188–90.
'Some Consequence of Four Incapacities'. W3: 211–13, EP1: 28–9
What Pragmatism Is'. EP2: ch. 24.

Other works and editions

1877. 'The Fixation of Belief', *Popular Science Monthly* 12.
1878. 'How to Make our Ideas Clear', *Popular Science Monthly* 12, pp. 286–302 (http://www.cspeirce.com/menu/library/byscp/ideas/id-main.htm, accessed October 2009).
1955. 'Pragmatism in Retrospect: a Last Formulation', in Buchler, pp. 269–89. New York: Dover.
1972a. 'Issues of Pragmaticism', in *Charles S. Peirce: The Essential Writings*, ed. Edward Moore. New York: Harper, p. 281.
1972b. 'Question concerning Certain Faculties', *Charles S. Peirce: The Essential Writings*, ed. Edward Moore. New York: Harper, p. 86.
1987. 'Some Consequences of Four Incapacities', in John Stuhr (ed.), *Classical American Philosophy*. New York: Oxford University Press.
1997. *Pragmatism as a Principle and Method of Right Thinking*, ed. Patricia Turrisi. Albany: State University of New York Press.
2004. 'What Pragmatism Is', in Malachowski, 2004a

Net resources

The Charles Peirce Society w.w.w.peircesociety.org/.
Charles Peirce Studies w.w.w.peirce.org/.
The Peirce Edition Project w.w.w.ipui.edu~peirce/-United States.

HILARY PUTNAM

1988. 'After Metaphysics, What?', in Henrich and Horstmann, pp. 457–66.
1990. *Realism with a Human Face.* Cambridge, MA: Harvard University Press.
1992. *Renewing Philosophy.* Cambridge, MA: Harvard University Press.

1994a. *Words and Life*. Cambridge MA: Harvard University Press.
1994b. 'A Comparison of Something with Something Else', in Putnam, 1994a, pp. 334–50.
1995. *Pragmatism: An Open Question*. Oxford: Blackwell.
1999. *The Threefold Cord*. New York: Columbia University Press
2002. *The Collapse of the Fact/Value Dichotomy and Other Essays*. Cambridge, MA: Harvard University Press.
2004a. 'James's Theory of Truth', in Malachowski, 2004a, vol. II, pp. 124–39.
2004b. 'The Uniqueness of Pragmatism', *Think* 8, pp. 89–105.

W. V. O. QUINE

1953. *From a Logical Point of View*. Cambridge, MA: Harvard University Press.
1960. *Word and Object*. New York: MIT Press.
1969a. *Ontological Relativity and Other Essays*. New York: Columbia University Press
1969b. 'Epistemology Naturalized', in Quine, 1969a, pp. 69–90.
1969c. 'Ontological Relativity', in Quine, 1969a, pp. 26–68.
1970. *Philosophy of Logic*. New Jersey: Prentice-Hall
1981a. *Theories and Things*. Cambridge MA: Harvard University Press.
1981b. 'On the Nature of Moral Values', in Quine, 1981a, pp. 55–66.
1981c. 'On the Very Idea of a Third Dogma', in Quine, 1981a, pp. 38–42.
1985. *The Time of my Life: An Autobiography*. MIT Press.
1990. *Pursuit of Truth*. Cambridge MA: Harvard University Press.
2004a. 'Confessions of a Confirmed Extensionalist', in Roger F. Gibson (ed.), *Quintessence: Basic Readings from the Philosophy* Cambridge MA: Harvard University Press, pp. 329–37.
2004b. 'Truth by Convention', in Roger F. Gibson (ed.), *Quintessence: of W. V. Quine*, Cambridge MA: Harvard University Press, pp. 3–21.
2004c. 'Two Dogmas of Empiricism', in Malachowski, 2004a, pp. 3–20.

RICHARD RORTY

1961. 'Pragmatism, Categories, Language', *Philosophical Review* 70, pp. 197–223.
1980. *Philosophy and the Mirror of Nature*. Princeton University Press.
1982a. *Consequences of Pragmatism*. Minneapolis: University of Minnesota Press.
1982b. 'Dewey's Metaphysics', in Rorty 1982a, pp. 72–89.

1982c. 'Pragmatism, Relativism, and Irrationalism', in Rorty, 1982a, pp. 160–75.
1985. 'Solidarity or objectivity?' in J. Rajchman and C. West (eds.), *Post-analytic Philosophy*. Columbia University Press, pp. 3–19.
1989a. *Contingency, Irony, and Solidarity*. Cambridge University Press.
1989b. 'Education without Dogma', *Dissent* (spring), pp. 198–204.
1990. 'The Dangers of Over-Philosophication: Reply to Arcilla and Nicholson', *Educational Theory* 40(1), pp. 41–4.
1991a. 'The Banality of Pragmatism and the Poetry of Justice', in *Pragmatism in Law and Society*, ed. Michael Brint and William Weaver. Boulder, CO: Westview Press, pp. 89–97.
1991b. *Objectivity, Relativism and Truth: Philosophical Papers*, vol. I. Cambridge University Press.
1991c. *Essays on Heidegger and Other Philosophical Papers*, vol. II. Cambridge University Press.
1991d. 'The Professor and the Prophet', *Transition* 52.
1995. 'Response to Gouinlock', in Saatkamp, pp. 91–9.
1997a. Introduction to Sellars, 1997.
1997b. 'Religious Faith, Intellectual Responsibility, and Romance', in C. D. Hardwick and D. A. Crosby (eds.), *Pragmatism, Neo-Pragmatism and Religion: Conversations with Richard Rorty*. Peter Lang, pp. 3–24.
1998a. *Truth and Progress: Philosophical Papers*, vol. III. Cambridge University Press.
1998b. 'Dewey Between Hegel and Darwin', in Rorty 1998a, pp. 290–306.
1998c. 'Is Truth a Goal of Inquiry? Donald Davidson versus Crispin Wright', in Rorty 1998a, pp. 43–62.
1999a. *Philosophy and Social Hope*. New York: Penguin Books.
1999b. 'The Banality of Law and the Poetry of Justice', in Rorty, 1999a.
1999c. 'Relativism: Finding and Making', in Rorty, 1999a
2000. 'Universality and Truth', in Robert Brandom (ed.), *Rorty and His Critics*, Oxford: Blackwell, pp. 1–28.
2007a. *Philosophy as Cultural Politics: Philosophical Papers*, vol. IV. Cambridge University Press.
2007b. 'Holism and Historicism', in Rorty 2007a, pp. 176–83.
2007c. 'Philosophy as a Transitional Genre', in Rorty 2007a, pp. 89–104.
2007d. 'Wittgenstein and the Linguistic Turn', In Rorty 2007a, pp. 160–75.
2010a. 'Philosophy as Science, as Metaphor, and as Politics', in Voparil and Bernstein 2010, pp. 211–226.
2010b. 'From Philosophy to Post-Philosophy: An Interview with Richard Rorty', in Voparil and Bernstein, 2010. New York: Wiley-Blackwell, pp. 492–9.

Rorty, Richard (ed.), 1992. *The Linguistic Turn: Essays in Philosophical Method.* University of Chicago Press.

WORKS BY OTHER AUTHORS

Addams, Jane, 2002. *Democracy and Social Ethics.* Urbana and Chicago: University of Illinois Press.
Akins, Kathleen, 1996. 'Of Sensory Systems and the "Aboutness" of Mental States', *The Journal of Philosophy* 93(7), pp. 337–72.
Alexander, Thomas M., 1987. *John Dewey's Theory of Art, Experience, and Nature: The Horizons of Feeling.* Albany: State University of New York Press.
Anderson, Douglas, 2009a. 'Old Pragmatism, New Histories', *Journal of The History of Philosophy* 7(4).
  2009b. 'Peirce and Cartesian Rationalism', in Shook and Margolis, pp. 154–65.
Aristotle, *Poetics*, in *The Complete Works of Aristotle*, ed. J. Barnes, 1984, vol. II, Princeton University Press, pp. 2316–40.
  Metaphysics, trans. W. D. Ross, in *The Complete Works of Aristotle: The Revised Oxford Translation*, vol. II, book IX, chs. 6–9, pp. 1655–60.
  Nichomachoan Ethics, in *The complete works of Aristotle*, 4 ed. J. Barnes, 1984, vol. II.
Arnheim, R., 1965. *Art and Visual Perception.* Berkeley: University of California Press.
Auxier, Randall E. and Hahn, Lewis Edwin (eds.), 2010. *The Philosophy of Richard Rorty.* La Salle, IL: Open Court.
Ayer A. (ed.), 1959. *Logical Positivism.* New York: The Free Press.
Baker, Gordon (ed.), 2003. *The Voices of Wittgenstein: The Vienna Circle: Ludwig Wittgenstein and Friedrich Waismann*, trans. Gordon Baker, Michael Mackert, John Connolly and Vasilis Politis. London: Routledge.
Baker, G. P. and Hacker, P. M. S., 1985. *Rules, Grammar and Necessity.* Oxford: Blackwell.
Baker, Lynne A., 2002. 'Just Do It: Pragmatism and Progressive Social Change', in Malachowski, 2002b, vol. II, pp. 215–32.
Baldwin, T., 1990. *G. E. Moore.* London and New York: Routledge.
Barrett, Cyril (ed.), 1972. *Lectures and Conversations in Aesthetics, Psychology, and Religious Belief.* Berkeley, CA: University of California Press.
Barzun, J., 1983. *A Stroll with William James.* New York: Harper and Row.
Bergmann, Gustav, 1992. 'Logical Positivism, Language, and the Reconstruction of Metaphysics', in Rorty, pp. 63–71.
Bergström, L. and Føllesdal, D., 2000. 'Interview with Willard Van Orman Quine in November 1993', in D. Føllesdal, *Philosophy of Quine.* Vol. I:

General, Reviews, and Analytic/synthetic, New York: Garland Publishing, pp. 193–206.

Berleant, Arnold, 1991. *Art and Engagement*. Philadelphia, Temple University Press,

Bernstein, Richard J., 1964. 'Peirce's Theory of Perception', in E. C. Moore and R. Robins (eds.), *Studies in the Philosophy of Charles Sanders Peirce*, Second series. Amherst: University of Massachusetts Press, pp. 165–84.

1966. *John Dewey*. New York: Washington Square Press.

1971. *Praxis and Action*. Philadelphia: University of Pennsylvania Press.

1983. *Beyond Objectivism and Relativism*. Oxford: Basil Blackwell.

1988. 'Pragmatism, Pluralism, and the Healing of Wounds', APA Presidential Address.

1992. *The New Constellation: The Ethical-Political Horizons of Modernity/Postmodernity*. MIT Press.

1995a. 'American Pragmatism: The Conflict of Narratives', in Saatkamp, 1995, pp. 54–67.

1995b. 'Whatever Happened to Naturalism', *Proceedings and Addresses of the American Philosophical Association* 69(2), pp. 57–76.

2005. *The Abuse of Evil: The Corruption of Politics and Religion since 9/11*. Polity Press.

2010a. *The Pragmatic Turn*. Cambridge: Polity.

2010b. 'Charles S. Peirce's Critique of Cartesianism', in Bernstein, 2010a, pp. 32–52.

Boisvert, Raymond D., 1998. *John Dewey: Rethinking Our Time*. Albany: State University of New York Press.

Bouveresse, Jacques, 1996. *Wittgenstein Reads Freud*. Princeton University Press.

Brandom, Robert, 1994. *Making it Explicit*. Cambridge, MA: Harvard University Press.

1997. Study Guide in Sellars, 1997.

2000a. *Articulating Reasons: An Introduction to Inferentialism*. Cambridge, MA: Harvard University Press.

2010. *Between Saying and Doing: Towards an Analytic Pragmatism*. Oxford University Press.

Brandom, Robert (ed.), 2000b. *Rorty and his Critics*. Oxford: Blackwell.

Brodsky, Gary, 2004. 'Rorty's Pragmatism', in Malachowski, pp. 175–94.

Browning, Douglas, 1998. 'Dewey and Ortega on the Starting Point', *Transactions of The Charles S. Peirce Society* 34(1), pp. 69–92.

1999. 'Understanding Dewey: Starting at the Starting Point' (invited paper), *XIV Congreso Interamericano de Filosofía*, Puebla, Mexico.

2007. *Introduction* to Larry A Hickman (ed.), *The Influence of Darwin on Philosophy and Other Essays in Contemporary Thought*, pp. ix–xxxii. Southern Illinois University Press.
Buchler, Justus (ed.), 1955. *Philosophical Writings of Peirce*. New York: Dover.
Burger, A. J. (ed.), 2001. *The Ethics of Belief: Essays by William Kingdon Clifford, William James and A. J. Burger*. Roseville, CA: Dry Bones Press.
Burke, T. 1994. *Dewey's New Logic: A Reply to Russell*. University of Chicago Press.
Bush, G. W., 1999. *A Charge to Keep*. New York: William Morrow.
Cahn, S. M., 1977. *New Studies in the Philosophy of John Dewey*. Hanover: The University Press of New England.
Campbell, James, 1995. *Understanding John Dewey: Nature and Co-operative Intelligence*. La Salle, IL: Open Court.
Cartwright, N., 1999. *The Dappled World: A Study of the Boundaries of Science*. Cambridge University Press.
Cavell, Stanley, 1988a. *In Quest of the Ordinary: Lines of Skepticism and Romanticism*. University of Chicago Press.
  1988b. *Themes out of School: Effects and Causes*. Chicago University Press.
  1998c. 'The Fact of Television', in Cavell, 1998b, pp. 235–68.
  1990. *Conditions Handsome and Unhandsome: The Constitution of Emersonian Perfectionism*. Chicago University Press.
  1995. 'Notes and Afterthoughts on the Opening of Wittgenstein's Investigations', in *Philosophical Passages: Wittgenstein, Emerson, Austin, Derrida*. Oxford: Blackwell, pp. 125–86.
Chomsky, N., 2000. 'The Ethic of Belief', in D. Macedo (ed.), *Chomsky on Miseducation*. Rowman and Littlefield.
Clifford, W. A., 2001. 'The Ethics of Belief', in Burger, pp. 9–40.
Crary, Alice (ed.), 2000. *The New Wittgenstein*, London: Routledge.
Csikszentmihalyi, M., 1991. *Flow: The Psychology of Optimal Experience*. New York: Harper Perennial.
Curren, R., 2009. 'Pragmatist Philosophy of Education', in H. Siegel (ed.), *Oxford Handbook of Philosophy of Education*. Oxford University Press.
Damasio, Antonio R., 1995. *Descartes' Error: Reason and the Human Brain*. New York: Harper Perennial.
Danto, Arthur Coleman, 1981. *The Transfiguration of the Commonplace: A Philosophy of Art*. Cambridge, MA: Harvard University Press.
  1986. *The Philosophical Disenfranchisement of Art*. New York: Columbia University Press.
  1997. *After the End of Art: Contemporary Art and the Pale of History*. Princeton University Press.

Darwin, Charles, 1872. *The Expression of the Emotions in Man and Animals*. London: John Murray.
Davidson, Donald, 1980. 'Mental Events', in D. Davidson, *Essays on Actions and Events*, Oxford: Clarendon Press, pp. 207–25.
  1984. 'On the Very Idea of a Conceptual Scheme', in D. Davidson, *Inquiries into Truth and Interpretation*, Oxford: Clarendon Press, pp. 183–98.
  1990. 'Afterthoughts, 1987', in Malachowski, pp. 120–38.
  2006a. *The Essential Davidson*. Oxford University Press.
  2006b. 'A Nice Derangement of Epitaphs', in Davidson, 2006a, pp. 251–65.
  2006c. 'What Metaphors Meant', in Davidson, 2006a, pp. 209–24.
DeWaal, C., 2005. *On Pragmatism*. Belmont, CA: Wadsworth.
Dickie, G., Sclafani, R. J. and Roblin R. (eds.), 1989. *Aesthetics: A Critical Anthology*, 2nd edn, New York: St. Martin's Press, pp. 223–41.
Diggins, J. P., 1994. *The Promise of Pragmatism: Modernism and the Crisis of Knowledge and Authority*. University of Chicago Press.
Dobson, Andrew, 2000. *Green Political Thought*. London: Routledge.
Donovan, Rickard, 1995. 'Rorty's Pragmatism and the Linguistic Turn', in Hollinger and Depew, pp. 208–23.
Dworkin, Ronald, 1986. *Law's Empire*. Farber.
Dykhuizen, George, 1973. *The Life and Mind of John Dewey*. Southern Illinois University Press.
Edwards, James C., 1985. *Ethics without Philosophy: Wittgenstein and the Moral Life*. Tampa, FL: University Presss of Florida.
Edwards, Paul, 1967. *The Encyclopedia of Philosophy*. New York: Macmillan.
Ekman, P. 1972. *Emotions in the Human Face*. New York: Pergamon Press.
Eldridge, Michael, 1998. *Transforming Experience: John Dewey's Cultural Instrumentalism*. Nashville, TN: Vanderbilt University Press.
Etzioni, Amitai. 1993. *The Spirit of Community Rights, Responsibilities and the Communitarian Agenda*. New York: Crown.
Euripides, 1955. *The Medea*, trans. R. Warner, in *The Complete Greek Tragedies*, ed. D. Grene and R. Lattimore, vol. 1, Chicago University Press, pp. 56–108.
Farber, Daniel A. 1988. 'Legal Pragmatism and the Constitution', *Minnesota Law Review* 72, p. 1331.
Fesmire, Steven, 2003. *John Dewey and Moral Imagination: Pragmatism in Ethics*. Bloomington: Indiana University Press.
Fitzgerald, John J., 1966. *Peirce's Theory of Signs as Foundation for Pragmatism*. The Hague: Mouton.
Freeman, C., 2003. *The Closing of the Western Mind*. London: Pimlico.
Friedman, Michael and Creath, Richard (eds.), 2007. *The Cambridge Companion to Carnap*. Cambridge University Press.

Gardner, M., 1983. *The Whys of a Philosophical Scrivener*. New York: St Martin's.
Garrison, Jim, 1997. *Dewey and Eros: Wisdom and Desire in the Art of Teaching*. New York: Teachers College Press.
Gascoigne, Neil, 2008. *Rorty*. Cambridge: Polity.
Gilbert, K. E. and Kuhn, H., 1956. *A History of Esthetics*. London: Thames and Hudson.
Godfrey-Smith, P., 2006. 'Theories and Models in Metaphysics', *Harvard Review of Philosophy* 14, pp. 4–19.
Goldie, Peter, 2000. *The Emotions: A Philosophical Exploration*. Oxford University Press.
    2003. 'Emotion, Feeling and Knowledge of the World', in Solomon, 2003c.
Goodman, Nelson, 1978. *Ways of Worldmaking*. Indianapolis: Hackett.
Goodman, Russell, 2002. *Wittgenstein and William James*. Cambridge University Press.
Gouinlock, James, 1972. *John Dewey's Philosophy of Value*. New York: Humanities Press.
    1995. 'What Is the Legacy of Instrumentalism? Rorty's Interpretation of Dewey' in Saatkamp, pp. 72–90.
Greenspan, P. S., 1988. *Emotions and Reasons*. London: Routledge.
    1995. *Practical Guilt: Moral Dilemmas, Emotions and Social Norms*. Oxford University Press.
    2004. 'Emotions, Rationality and Mind/Body', in Solomon, pp. 125–34.
Grey, Thomas, 1989, 'Holmes and Legal Pragmatism', *Stanford Legal Review* 41, pp. 787–870.
Griffiths, Paul E., 1997. *What Emotions Really Are: The Problem of Psychological Categories*. Chicago University Press.
Groopman, J., 2007. *How Doctors Think*. Boston, MA: Houghton Mifflin.
Gunn, G., 1998. 'Religion and the Recent Revival of Pragmatism', in M. Dickstein (ed.), *The Revival of Pragmatism: New Essays on Social Thought, Law and Culture*, Durham, NC and London: Duke University Press, pp. 405–17.
Haack, Susan and Lane, Robert Edwin, 2006. *Pragmatism, Old and New*. New York: Prometheus Books.
Habermas, J., 1976. *Communication and the Evolution of Society*. London: Heinemann.
Haddock Seigfried, Charlene, 1996. *Pragmatism and Feminism: Reweaving the Social Fabric*. University of Chicago Press.
Hagberg, Garry, 1991. 'The Aesthetics of Indiscernibles', in N. Bryson, M. Holly and K. Moxey (eds.), *Visual Theory*, New York: HarperCollins, Icon Eds, pp. 221–30.

1994. *Meaning and Interpretation: Wittgenstein, Henry James, and Literary Knowledge*. Ithaca: Cornell University Press.
1995a. 'Apollo's Revenge: Music and Nietzsche's Twilight of the Idols', *Historical Reflections/Réflexions Historiques* 21(3), pp. 437–49.
1995b. *Art as Language: Wittgenstein, Meaning, and Aesthetic Theory*. Ithaca: Cornell University Press.
1996a. Review, *Journal of Aesthetics and Art Criticism* 54(3), pp. 295–7.
1996b. Review of Ridley, *Music, Value and the Passions, Philosophy of Music Education Review* 4(2), pp. 128–33.
Harris, William T., 1867. 'The Speculative', *Journal of Speculative Philosophy* 1, pp. 6–22.
Haskins, Casey and Seiple, David I. (eds.), 1999. *Dewey Reconfigured: Essays on Deweyan Pragmatism*. Albany: State Univesity of New York Press.
Hatzimoysis, Anthony (ed.), 2003. *Philosophy and the Emotions*. Cambridge University Press.
Hayes, C., 2008. 'The Pragmatist', *The Nation*, 29 December.
Heidegger, Martin, 1962. *Being and Time*, trans. John Macquarrie and Edward Robinson. New York: Harper & Row.
  1982. *The Basic Problems of Phenomenology*, trans. Albert Hofstadter. Bloomington: Indiana University Press.
  1992.*History of the Concept of Time*, trans. Theodore Kisiel. Bloomington: Indiana University Press.
Henrich, D. and Horstmann, R.-P. (eds.), 1988. *Metaphysik nach Kant?* Stuttgart: Klett-Cotta.
Hertz, R., 1971. 'James and Moore: Two Perspectives on Truth', *Journal of the History of Philosophy* 9, pp. 213–21.
Hickman, Larry A., 1990. *John Dewey's Pragmatic Technology*. Indiana University Press.
  1998. *Reading Dewey: Interpretations for a Postmodern Generation*. Indiana University Press.
Hildebrand, David L., 1999. 'Pragmatism and Literary Criticism: The Practical Starting Point', in *REAL: Yearbook of Research in English and American Literature 15*, ed. Winfried Fluck (de Gruyter), pp. 303–22.
  2003. *Beyond Realism and Antirealism: John Dewey and the Neopragmatists*. Nashville, TN: Vanderbilt University Press.
  2008. *Dewey: A Beginner's Guide*. London: Oneworld Press.
Hogarth, W., 1772. *The Analysis of Beauty*. London.
Hollinger, Robert and Depew, David J., 1995. *Pragmatism: From Progressivism to Postmodernism*. Westport: Praeger Publishers.
Hookway, Christopher, 2000. *Truth, Rationality, and Pragmatism: Themes from Peirce*. Oxford: Clarendon Press.

2004a. 'The Principle of Pragmatism: Peirce's Formulations and Examples', *Midwest Studies in Philosophy* 28(1), pp. 119–36.
2004b. 'Truth, Reality and Convergence', in Misak (ed.), *The Cambridge Companion to Peirce*. Cambridge University Press, pp. 127–50.
2005. 'The Pragmatist Maxim and the Proof of Pragmatism', *Cognitio* 5, pp. 25–42.
2007. 'Fallibilism and the Aim of Inquiry', *Proceedings of the Aristotelian Society*, supp. vol. 81, pp. 1–23.
2008. 'Peirce and Scepticism', in John Greco (ed.), *The Oxford Handbook to Scepticism*. Oxford University Press, pp. 310–29.
Hutcheson, Francis, 1725. *An Inquiry into the Origin of Our Ideas of Beauty and Virtue*. London.
Hutchinson, Phil, 2008a. 'Emotions–Philosophy–Science', in Ylva Gustafsson, Camilla Kronqvist and Michael McEachrane (eds.), *Emotions and Understanding: Wittgensteinian Perspectives*. London: Palgrave Macmillan.
2008b. *Shame and Philosophy*. Basingstoke: Palgrave Macmillan.
Hutchinson, Phil and Read, Rupert, 2005. 'Whose Wittgenstein?', in *Philosophy* 80(313), pp. 432–55.
2008. 'Towards a Perspicuous Presentation of "Perspicuous presentation"', *Philosophical Investigations* 31(2), pp. 141–60.
2010. 'Therapy', in Kelley Dean Jolley (ed.), *Wittgenstein: Key Concepts*. London: Acumen Press.
(forthcoming). *Wittgenstein on Meaning*.
Hutchinson, Phil, Read, Rupert and Sharrock, Wes, 2008. *There is No Such Thing as a Social Science: In Defence of Peter Winch*. London: Ashgate.
Jackson, F., 1994. *From Metaphysics to Ethics*. Oxford University Press.
Jackson, Philip W., 2000. *John Dewey and the Lessons of Art*. New Haven: Yale University Press.
Jordan, J., 1997. 'Pragmatic Arguments', in P. L. Quinn and C. Taliaferro (eds.), *A Companion to Philosophy of Religion*. Oxford: Blackwell, pp. 352–9.
Kant, Immanuel, 1987. *Critique of Judgment*, trans. Werner Pluhor. Indianapolis: Hackett Publishing.
1998. *Critique of Pure Reason*, trans. Paul Guyer and Allen Wood. Cambridge University Press, 232; A. 106.
1929. *Critique of Pure Reason*, trans. N. Kemp-Smith, London: Macmillan.
Katz, Jerry, 1990. *The Metaphysics of Meaning*. Cambridge, MA: MIT Press.
Kenny, Anthony (ed.), 2003. *Action, Emotion and Will*. London: Routledge.
Kermode, Frank, *The Sense of an Ending; Studies in the Theory of Fiction* (London: Oxford University Press, 1968).

Koskinen, H. J. and Pihlström, S., 2006 'Quine and Pragmatism', *Transactions of the Charles S. Peirce Society* 42.(3): pp. 309–346.

Krieger, Murray, *Arts on the Level: The Fall of the Elite Object*. Knoxville: University of Tennessee Press, 1981.

Lachs, John, 2003. *A Community of Individuals*. London: Routledge.

Lehrer, J., 2009. *How We Decide*. Boston, MA: Houghton Mifflin.

Leonard, George, 1994. *Into the Light of Things: The Art of the Commonplace from Wordsworth to John Cage*. Chicago University Press.

Levi, Isaac. 1999. 'Pragmatism and Change of View', in Misak (ed.), *Pragmatism, Canadian Journal of Philosophy*, supp. vol. 24, pp. 177–202.

Light, Andrew and Katz, Eric (eds.), 1996. *Environmental Pragmatism*. London: Routledge.

Lorde, Audre. 1984. 'The Master's Tools Will Never Dismantle the Master's House', *Sister Outsider: Essays and Speeches*. Freedom, CA: The Crossing Press.

Lovejoy, Arthur O., 1965. *The Thirteen Pargamatisms*. Baltimore.

Luban, David, 1994. *Legal Modernism*. University of Michigan Press.

Macarthur, David, and Price, Huw, 2009. 'Pragmatism, Quasi-realism, and the Global Challenge', in Misak, pp. 91–121.

Magee, B. 1973. *Popper*. London: Fontana/Collins.

Malachowski, Alan 2002a. *Richard Rorty*. Durham: Acumen/Princeton University Press.

    2004b. 'Pragmatism in its own Right', in Malachowski, 2004a, pp. 337–42.

    2010. *The New Pragmatism*. Durham NC: Acumen.

    2011. 'Putting Pragmatism into Better Shape', *Pragmatism Today* 2(1), pp. 51–5.

    2014b. 'Life is no Argument: Nietzsche and Pragmatism', in Malachowski, 2014a, vol. III.

Malachowski, Alan (ed.), 1990. *Reading Rorty*. Oxford: Basil Blackwell.

    2002b. *Richard Rorty*. 4 vols. London: Sage Publications.

    2004a. *Pragmatism*. 3 vols. London: Sage Publications.

    2014a. *A History of Pragmatism*. 4 vols. Durham, NC: Acumen.

McDowell, John, 1996. *Mind and World*. Cambridge, MA: Harvard University Press.

Mead, G. H., 1934. *Mind, Self, and Society: From the Standpoint of a Social Behaviorist*, ed. C. Morris. University of Chicago Press.

Menand, L., 2001. *The Metaphysical Club: A Story of Ideas in America*. New York: Farrar, Strauss and Giroux.

Millikan, Ruth, 1984. *Language, Thought, and Other Biological Categories*. Cambridge, MA: MIT Press.

Misak, Cheryl, 2004. *Truth and the End of Inquiry.* 2nd edn. Oxford University Press.
    2010b. 'The Reception of Early American Pragmatism', in Misak, 2010a, pp. 197–223.
    2010c. 'Rorty's Place in the Pragmatist Pantheon', in Auxier and Hahn, 2010, pp.
Misak, Cheryl (ed.), 2009. *New Pragmatists.* Oxford University Press.
    2010a. *The Oxford Handbook of American Philosophy.* Oxford: Oxford University Press.
Moore, E. C. and R. Robins (eds.), 1964. *Studies in the Philosophy of Charles Sanders Peirce.* Second Series. Amherst: University of Massachusetts Press.
Mounce, H. O., 1997. *The Two Pragmatisms.* London: Routledge.
Mulhall, Stephen, 1994. *Stanley Cavell: Philosophy's Recounting of the Ordinary.* Oxford University Press.
Mulhall, Stephen (ed.) 1996. *The Cavell Reader.* Oxford: Basil Blackwell.
Murphy, John, 1990. *Pragmatism: From Peirce to Davidson.* Boulder, CO: Westview.
Myers, William T., 2001. 'Dewey and Whitehead on the Starting Point and Method', *Transactions of The Charles S. Peirce Society* 37(2), pp. 243–55.
Myers, William T. and Pappas, Gregory F., 2004. 'Dewey's Metaphysics: A Response to Richard Gale', *Transactions of The Charles S. Peirce Society* 40(4), pp. 679–700.
Nagl, Ludwig and Mouffe, Chantal (eds.), 2001. *The Legacy of Wittgenstein: Pragmatism or Deconstruction.* Berlin: Peter Lang.
Nash, R. A., 1989. 'Cognitive Theories of Emotion', *Nous* 32, pp. 481–504.
Nevo, Isaac, 1995a. 'Richard Rorty's Romantic Pragmatism', in Hollinger and Depew, pp. 284–97.
    1995b. 'James, Quine, and Analytic Pragmatism', in Hollinger and Depew, pp. 153–69.
Nicholson, C., 2004. 'Elegance and Grass Roots: The Neglected Philosophy of Frederick Law Olmsted', *Transactions of The Charles S. Peirce Society* 40(2), pp. 335–48.
Noe, Alva, 2009. *Out of Our Heads.* New York: Hill and Wang.
Norberg-Hodge, Helena, 2000. *Ancient Futures: Learning from Ladakh.* London: Rider.
Nussbaum, Martha, 2003. *Upheavals of Thought: The Intelligence of Emotions.* Cambridge University Press.
Obama, B., 2006. *The Audacity of Hope: Thoughts on Reclaiming the American Dream.* Vintage Books.
Okrent, Mark, 1988. *Heidegger's Pragmatism: Understanding, Being and the Critique of Metaphysics.* Ithaca: Cornell University Press.

2007. *Rational Animals: The Teleological Roots of Intentionality*. Athens: Ohio University Press.
Ortega y Gasset, José, 1969. *Some Lessons in Metaphysics*, trans. Mildred Adams. New York: W.W. Norton.
Packer, G., 2008. 'The New Liberalism', *The New Yorker*, 17 November.
Palmer, F., 1992. *Literature and Moral Understanding*. Oxford University Press.
Papini, G., 1907. 'What Pragmatism is Like', *Popular Science Monthly* 71(10).
Pappas, Gregory F., 2008. *John Dewey's Ethics: Democracy as Experience*. Indiana University Press.
  2009. Review of Shook and Margolis. *Contemporary Pragmatism* 4(2), pp. 141–7.
Paulson, R., 1975. *Emblem and Expression: Meaning in English Art of the Eighteenth Century*. Cambridge, MA: Harvard University Press.
Perry, Ralph Barton, 1935. *The Thought and Character of William James*. New York: Little Brown & Co.
Peters, Michael, A. and Ghiraldelli, Jr. (eds), 2001. *Richard Rorty: Education, Philosophy, and Politics*. Boston: Rowman and Littlefield.
Phillips, D., 1984. 'Was William James Telling the Truth After All?', *Monist* 67(3), pp. 419–34.
Pippin, R. B., 2008. *Hegel's Practical Philosophy: Rational Agency and Ethical Life*. Cambridge University Press.
Plato, 1961. *Ion*, in *The Collected Dialogues of Plato*, ed. E. Hamilton and H. Cairns. Princeton University Press, pp. 215–28.
Popper, K. R. 1947. *The Open Society and its Enemies*, 2 vols. Routledge.
  1957. *The Poverty of Historicism*. London: Routledge.
Posner, Richard A., 2003. *Law, Pragmatism, and Democracy*. Cambridge, MA: Harvard University Press.
Pratt, S. 2002. *Native Pragmatism: Rethinking the Roots of American Philosophy*. Indiana University Press.
Price, Huw, 2010. 'One Cheer for Representationalism' in Auxier and Hahn, pp. 269–89.
  2011. *Naturalism without Mirrors*. Oxford University Press.
Prinz, Jesse, 2003a. 'Emotions, Psychosemantics, and Embodied Appraisals', in Hatzymoysis, 2003.
  2003b. *Gut Reactions: A Perceptual Theory of Emotion*. Oxford University Press.
  2003c. 'Embodied Emotions', in Solomon
Ramberg, Bjorn, 1989. *Donald Davidson's Philosophy of Language*. Oxford: Blackwell.
  2000. 'Post-ontological Philosophy of Mind: Rorty versus Davidson', in Brandom, 2000a, pp. 351–70.

Read, Rupert, 2002, 'Marx and Wittgenstein on vampires and parasites', in G. Kitching and N. Pleasants (eds.), *Marx and Wittgenstein*. London: Routledge, pp. 279–81.
  2004. 'Nature, Culture, Ecosystem (or, Why Nature can't be naturalised)', in Malachowski, pp. 368–88.
  2007a. Review of Denis McManus, *The Enchantment of Words*, *Philosophy* 82, pp. 657–61.
  2007b. *Philosophy for Life*. London: Continuum.
Rescher, Nicholas, 2000. *Realistic Pragmatism: An Introduction to Pragmatic Philosophy*. Albany: State University of New York Press.
Richardson, Alan, 2007. 'Carnapian Pragmatism', in Friedman and Creath, pp. 295–315.
Ridley, A., 1995. *Music, Value, and the Passions*. Ithaca: Cornell University Press.
Robin, Richard, 1967. *Annotated Catalogue of the Papers of Charles S. Peirce*. University of Massachusetts Press.
Robinson, Jenefer, 1995. 'Startle', *Journal of Philosophy* 92(2), pp. 53–74.
Rogers, M. L., 2009. *The Undiscovered Dewey: Religion, Morality and the Ethos of Democracy*. Columbia University Press.
Rorty, A. O. (ed.), 1998. *Philosophers on Education: New Historical Perspectives*. London: Routledge.
Rosen, C., 1988. *Sonata Forms*. New York: Norton.
Rosenthal, D. (ed.), 1991. *The Nature of Mind*. New York: Oxford University Press.
Royce, Josiah, 1959. *The World and the Individual*. New York: Dover.
Russell, B., 1946. *The History of Western Philosophy*. London: Routledge.
  2004. 'Dewey's New Logic', in Malachowski, 2004a, vol. III, pp. 49–62.
Ryan, A., 1998. 'Deweyan Pragmatism and American Education', in Rorty.
  1995. *John Dewey and the High Tide of American Liberalism*. New York: W.W. Norton.
Rybczynski, W., 1999. *A Clearing in the Distance: Frederick Law Olmsted and America in the Nineteenth Century*. New York: Scribner.
Saatkamp, Herman J. (ed.), 1995. *Rorty and Pragmatism: The Philosopher Responds to His Critics*. Nashville, TN: Vanderbilt University Press.
Santayana, G. 1955. *Scepticism and Animal Faith*. New York: Dover.
Sellars, Wilfrid, 1963. *Science, Perception and Reality*. London: Routledge.
  1997. *Empiricism and the Philosophy of Mind*, ed. R. Brandom. Cambridge, MA: Harvard University Press.
Shook, John R. and Margolis, Joseph (eds.), 2009. *A Companion to Pragmatism*. Oxford: Wiley-Blackwell.
Short, T. L., 2007. *Peirce's Theory of Signs*. Cambridge University Press.

Shusterman, Richard, 1992. *Pragmatist Aesthetics: Living Beauty, Rethinking Art*. Oxford: Blackwell.
  1999. 'Dewey on Experience: Foundation or Reconstruction?' in Haskins and Seiple, pp. 193–219.
  2011. *Pragmatism Today*.
Shusterman, Richard (ed.), 2004. *The Range of Pragmatism and the Limits of Philosophy*. Oxford: Blackwell.
Singer, P., 2004. *The President of Good and Evil: The Ethics of George W. Bush*. New York: Dutton.
Sleeper, Ralph W., 1986. *The Necessity of Pragmatism: John Dewey's Conception of Philosophy*. New Haven: Yale University Press.
  1992. 'What is Metaphysics?', *Transactions of the Charles S. Peirce Society* 28(2), p. 184.
  2002. 'Rorty's Pragmatism: Afloat in Neyrath's Boat, But Why Adrift?' in Malachowski, 2002b, vol. II, pp. 151–9.
Smith, John, 1970. 'Radical Empiricism,' in J. Smith, *Themes in American Philosophy: Purpose, Experience, and Community*, pp. 26–41. New York: Harper and Row.
  1992. 'The Pragmatic Theory of Truth: The Typical Objection', in John Smith, *America's Philosophical Vision*. University of Chicago Press, pp. 37–52.
Smith, N. H., 2005. 'Rorty on Religion and Hope', *Inquiry* 48(1), pp. 76–98.
Smith, Stephen D., 1990. 'The Pursuit of Pragmatism', *Yale Law Journal* 100, p. 409.
Solomon, Robert C., 1976. *The Passions*. Garden City, NY: Anchor/Doubleday.
  2003a. *Not Passion's Slave*. Oxford University Press.
  2003b. 'What is a "Cognitive Theory" of the Emotions?', in Hatzimoysis, 2003.
Solomon, Robert C. (ed.), 2003c. *What is an Emotion? Classic and Contemporary Readings*. New York: Oxford University Press.
  2004. *Thinking about Feeling: Contemporary Philosophers on Emotions*. Oxford University Press.
Sparshott, Frances, 1982. 'Cold and Remote Art', *Journal of Aesthetics and Art Criticism* 41(2), pp. 127–36.
Sprigge, T. L. S., 2004. 'James, Aboutness, and his British Critics', in Malachowski, vol. III, pp. 93–108.
  2009. 'James, Empiricism, and Absolute Idealism', in John R. Shook and Joseph Margolis (eds,), *A Companion to Pragmatism*. Malden, MA: Wiley-Blackwell, pp. 166–76.
Stephen, Mulhall, 1994. *Stanley Cavell: Philosophy's Recounting of the Ordinary*. Oxford University Press.

Stephens, Piers G., 2009. 'Towards a Jamesian Environmental Philosophy', *Environmental Ethics* 31(3), pp. 227–44.
Stern, Michael 2004. *Wittgensteins 'Philosophical Investigation': An Introduction*. Cambridge University Press.
Stocker, Michael, 1987. 'Emotional Thoughts', *American Philosophical Quarterly* 24(1), pp. 59–69.
Stocker, Michael with Hegeman, Elizabeth, 1999. *Valuing Emotions*. Cambridge University Press.
Stout, Jeffrey, 2009. 'On Our Interest in Getting Things Right: Pragmatism without Narcissism', in Misak, pp. 7–31.
Strawson, P., 1959. Introduction, in P. Strawson, *Individuals*. London: Methuen.
Stroll, Avrum, 1994. *Moore and Wittgenstein on Certainty*. Oxford University Press.
Stuhr, John, 2003. *Pragmatism, Postmodernism and the Future of Philosophy*. London: Routledge.
Stuhr, John (ed.), 1987. *Classical American Philosophy*. New York: Oxford University Press.
Suckiel, Ellen Kappy, 2009. 'William James', in Shook and Margolis, pp. 30–43.
Symposium, 1990. *The Renaissance of Pragmatism in American Legal Thought. Southern California Law Review* 63, p. 1569.
 1996. *The Revival of Pragmatism. Cardozo Law Review* 1.
Talisse, Robert, 2010. 'Pragmatism and the Cold War' in Misak, 2010a, pp. 254–68.
Talisse, Robert and Aiken, Scott H., 2008. *Pragmatism: A Guide for the Perplexed*. London: Continuum.
Tamanaha, Brian Z. 1996. 'Pragmatism in US Legal Theory: Its Application to Nominative Jurisprudence, Sociolegal Studies and the Fact–Value Distinction', *American Journal of Jurisprudence* 41, p. 315.
Tartaglia, James, 2007. *Rorty and the Mirror of Nature*, London: Routledge.
Taylor, Gabriele, 1985. *Pride, Shame, and Guilt: Emotions of Self-Assessment*. Oxford University Press.
Thayer, H. S., 1967. 'Pragmatism', in Edwards, vol. VI, pp. 430–5.
 1981. *Meaning and Action: A Critical History of Pragmatism*, 2nd edn. Indianapolis: Hackett Publishing Company.
Tiles, J. E., 1988. *Dewey*. London: Routledge.
Trainer, Ted, 1995. *The Conserver Society*. London: Zed Press.
Turrisi, P. A., 1997. Introduction and commentary to Peirce, pp. 1–20, 21–105.
Van Niekerk, A. A., 2005. 'Contingency and Universality in the Habermas–Rorty Debate', *Acta Academica Supplementum* 2, pp. 21–41.
Voparil, Christopher, 2005. *Richard Rorty: Politics and Vision*. Maryland: Rowman and Littlefield.

Voparil, Christopher and Bernstein, Richard (eds.), 2010. *The Rorty Reader.* New York: Wiley-Blackwell.
Wallace, David Foster, 2011. *The Broom of the System.* Abacus: London.
Walton, K. 1989. 'Categories of Art', in Dickie *et al.*, pp. 394–414.
Warnock, M., 1962. 'Final Discussion', in D. Pears (ed.), *The Nature of Metaphysics*, pp. 142–62. London: Macmillan.
Weiss, Penny and Friedman, Marilyn (eds.), 1995. *Feminism and Community.* Philadelphia, PA: Temple University Press.
Welchman, Jennifer, 1995. *Dewey's Ethical Thought.* Cornell University Press.
Wenley, R. M., 1917. *The Life of George Sylvester Morris.* New York: Macmillan.
Wernham, James C. S., 1986. 'Alexander Bain on Belief', *Philosophy* 61(236), pp. 262–6.
West, C., 1989. *The American Evasion of Philosophy: A Genealogy of Pragmatism.* University of Wisconsin Press.
Westbrook, Robert B., 1991. *John Dewey and American Democracy.* Cornell University Press.
  2005. *Democratic Hope: Pragmatism and the Meaning of Truth.* Cornell University Press.
  2010. 'The Pragmatist Family Romance', in Misak, 2010a, pp. 185–96.
Whipps, J., 2008. 'Pragmatist Feminism', in *The Stanford Encyclopedia of Philosophy*, ed. Edward N. Zalta, http://plato.stanford.edu/archives/fall2008/entries/femapproachpragmatism.
White, M., 1950. 'The Analytic and the Synthetic: An Untenable Dualism', in S. Hook (ed.), *John Dewey, Philosopher of Science and Freedom: A Symposium, Dial*, pp. 316–30.
Whitehead, A. N., 1997. *Science and the Modern World.* New York: Free Press.
Wiener, P. P. (ed.), 1973. *The Dictionary of the History of Ideas: Studies of Selected Pivotal Ideas*, vol. III. New York: Charles Scribner's Sons.
Wiggins, David, 2004. 'Reflections on Inquiry and Truth Arising from Peirce's Method for the Fixation of Belief', in C. Misak (ed.), *The Cambridge Companion to Peirce.* Cambridge University Press, pp. 87–126.
Williams, Bernard, 1985. *Ethics and the Limits of Philosophy.* Cambridge, MA: Harvard University Press.
Williams, Jerry and Parkman, Shaun (2003). 'On Humans and Environment: The Role of Consciousness in Environmental Problems', *Human Studies* 26, pp. 449–60.
Williams, R., 1983. *Keywords: A Vocabulary of Culture and Society*, rev. edn. Oxford University Press.

Wittgenstein, L., 1953. *Philosophical Investigations*. London: Macmillan.
  1967. *Zettel*. Berkeley: University of California Press.
  1969a. *The Blue and Brown Books*. Oxford: Blackwell.
  1969b. *On Certainty*, ed. G. E. M. Anscombe and G. H. von Wright. Oxford: Basil Blackwell/New York: Harper.
  1972. *Lectures and Conversations in Aesthetics, Psychology, and Religious Belief*, ed. Cyril Barrett. Berkeley: University of California Press.
  1975. *Wittgenstein's Lectures on the Foundations of Mathematics*, ed. Cora Diamond. Chicago University Press.
  1979. *Remarks on Frazer's 'Golden Bough'*, R. Rhees (ed.). Atlantic Highlands, NJ: Humanities Press.
  1980. *Culture and Value*. University of Chicago Press.
Wollheim, R., 1974. 'The Art Lesson', in *On Art and the Mind*. Cambridge, MA: Harvard University Press.
  1980. 'Criticism as Retrieval', in R. Wollheim, *Art and Its Objects*. 2nd edn. Cambridge University Press, pp. 185–204.

Net resources

Pragmatism Cybrary w.w.w.pragmatism.org/
Nordic Pragmatism Network w.w.w. Nordprag.org/
Pragmatism: Stanford Encyclopedia of Philosophy plato.stanford.edu.entries/pragmatism/
Contemporary Pragmatism: A Philosophical Journal contemporary.pragmatism.org/
European Journal of Pragmatism and American Philosophy lnx.journalofpragmatism.eu/
Pragmatism Today: The Journal of Central-European Pragmatist Forum www.pragmatismtoday.eu/

INDEX

a priori method 253
abduction 31
Absolute of German Idealism 194
absolute idealism 37, 41–3, 105–6,
　108–10, 115–16
absolute and perspectival knowledge 199
absolute truth 28
absolutism 105, 338
absolutist moral theory 38
abstract theorizing 327–38
Addams, Jane 131, 232, 240, 242–3
adverbial interpretation of pragmatism
　251, 257, 268
aesthetic edification 274
aesthetic emotion 292
aesthetic experience 272–93
aesthetic expression 292
aesthetic perception 284
aesthetic sensibility 277
aesthetic theory 11–12, 272–3
agent-centred thinking 176
AGW (anthropogenic global warming)
　178–80
Aiken, Scott H. 4–5
Akins, Kathleen 134–5
Alexander, Thomas 63
all-embracing mind 42
alternative conceptual schemes 92
American Constitution 258–61
Analysis of Reflective Thinking 68
analytic metaphysics 202
analytic philosophy 3–5, 189–90, 210
analytic statements 94
analytic/synthetic distinction 90, 92,
　100
ANS (autonomic nervous system) 179

anthropogenic global warming (AGW)
　178–80
anti-abstraction strategy 315
anti-epistemology 208
anti-representationalism 131, 133
anti-scepticism 21–2, 189
anti-scientistic considerations 214
appearance and reality (metaphysics) 192
appearance/reality division 218–19
Arnold, Matthew 314
art
　in human experience 273–80
　and morality 276
　spontaneity in 290–1
　structural coherence in 288
Art as Experience 74–5, 272
art/aesthetic theory, Dewey on 272–93
Articulating Reasons 114
artistic creativity 283–93
artistic expression, role of medium 287,
　289
assertibility conditions 125
attitude of orientation 1
autonomic nervous system (ANS) 179

Bain, Alexander 2
Baker, Lynn 327
bald naturalism 118
Barzun, Jacques 256, 264
Begriff (concept) 116
behavioural outcomes 223
behaviourism 164, 215–16, 286
Being of Dasein 124, 126, 143–55
Being and Time 126
being-in 139–40
being-in-the-world 124, 139, 146, 151–3

belief acquisition 44–6
belief and human needs 307
belief/valuation duality 101
beliefs 20, 31–2, 302, 312
believing truth 305
Bellarmine–Galileo controversy 306
Bergman, Gustav 2
Bergson, Henri 87–8, 251
Bernstein, Richard xv, 2, 8–10, 76, 213, 223–4, 254–5, 269, 300
Bildung (nature) 181
biological commonplaces 274
biological normativity 149, 153
biological pragmatists 136
biological-naturalist pragmatism 134–5
Blackwell Companion to Pragmatism 249
Blondel, Maurice 251
Boutroux, Emile 251
Brandom, Robert 7, 9–10, 112, 114, 119–20, 150, 312
Brodsky, Gary 215–16
The Broom of the System 220
Browning, Douglas 59
Bush, George W. 258–61

capitalist growthism 171
Carnap, Rudolf 3, 83–4
Cartesian distinctness 23
Cartesian dualism 285–6, 290
Cartesian duality 274
Cartesian scepticism 40–1
Cartesianism 108–9
certainty
  quest for 169
  rejection of 308
choices in life 260
Chomsky, Noam 265
clarity
  grades of 23
  and logic 22–4
classic pragmatism 211
Clifford, W. A. 304–6, 312
climate change 178–80
Clinton, Hillary 264
cognition
  as human activity 95
  and practice 85–7
cognitive activities, and inference/argument 31
cognitive processes 84

cognitivism 178–9, 181–3, 199
coherence theory of truth 41
collective social experience 333
A Common Faith 308–9, 311
communication and democracy 74
communitarianism 241–2
communities, distortions of power in 246
community
  democratic 233–47
  diversity/pluralism in 241–2
community action 236–8
community life, as moral 238–9
concept
  of democracy 335
  notion of 128–9
  of an object 126
conceptual content 125–6
conceptual scheme/empirical content distinction 92–3
confirmation 89
conjunctive relations 43
conservatism
  constraints of 44–6
  in prejudices 218
contemporary communitarianism 241–2
contested narratives 2
contextualized sensory experience 275–8
continuous action, between total organism and objects 284
continuous learning 71–2
Contributions to a Cyclopedia of Education 65
conventionalism, in logic 94
correspondence 85–6
correspondence theory of truth 301–2
creation 283–93
Creative Democracy: The Task Before Us 73–4
creative process and emotional development 288–9
creative role of spectator 283–93
Critique of Judgement 118
CRM (cockpit resource management) training 266
cultural change 216
cultural commonsense 183
cultural naturalists 173
cultural politics 313
cultural prerequisites 182
Curren, Randall 268

Index

das Man (the One) 147
Dasein's world 124, 126, 143–55
Davidson, Donald 38, 48–9, 92–3, 150, 210, 213, 219
deduction 31
deed (pragma) 174
deflationary naturalists 173
deliberation and democracy 339
deliberative democracy 335
deliberative harmony 239
democracy 70–1, 244–7, 334–8
  and communication 74
  conservative vision of 342
  constitutional 326
  and deliberation 339
  and education 72–4
  elite 335, 341
  and human capacity 341–2
  and participation 340
  of the pragmatists 336
  two concepts of 335
  types of 335
Democracy and Education 70–2
democratic communication 236–8
democratic community 233–47
democratic culture 341
democratic deliberation 339
democratic participation 339–40
Denken (thought) 116
dependence, religious sense of 319
descriptive metaphysics 204
design in nature 39
The Development of American Pragmatism 17
Dewey, John
  on art/aesthetic theory 272–93
  A Common Faith 308–9, 311
  on community life 238–9
  death of 3
  on democracy 336–7
  early Hegelianism 106–8
  on education 250, 256
  on equality 239–40
  on experience 279–82
  four facets of thought 60
  on freedom 238
  functionalism 60
  on habit 331
  James's influence on 62–3
  live creature 273–9
  and metaphysics 195–8, 201–2
  Morris's influence on 106
  personal acievements 55
  on philosophy 85, 328, 331
  philosophy of education 256
  pragmatism of 55–77
  as pragmatist 58–9
  Psychology 60–2
  The Public and its Problems 74, 134
  Religion and our Schools 308
  religion and the religious 307–11
  therapeutic/socially reconstructive aims 190
  and Wittgenstein 173
dialogue 339
dichotomies, philosophical 86
Diggins, John Patrick 250
direct experience 43
discursive judgements 143
disenchanted concept of nature 117
diversity in community 241–2
The Doctrine of Chances 24
doubt 20, 22
Du Bois, W. E. B. 252
dualism 290
Duhen, Pierre 251
Dworkin, Ronald 326–7
dying, engagement with 153

ecological damage 171
ecological problems 172
education 70–1
  continuous learning 71–2
  and democracy 72–4
  general theory of 71
  philosophy of 65, 256
  and pragmatic temperament 249–70
Edwards, James C. 159
effective environmentalism 174–5
egotist models of redemption 315–16
emergent naturalism 118
Emerson, Ralph Waldo 252, 258–61
emotional development, and creative process 288–9
emotional experience, specificity of 287
emotional meaning, and expressive art 286
emotional security, and religion 319–20

emotions
    discharging/expressing 285
    as gross and undefined 289
    as world-taking 181
emotive content, and linguistic meaning 291
empirical confirmation 90–1
empirical lowlands 329
empirical significance 95
empirical underdetermination doctrine 95–9
empiricism
    and classical rationalism 66–8
    of Hume and Locke 281
    physicalist version 84
    and pragmatism 88–9
    removal of 93
Empiricism and the Philosophy of the Mind 112, 120
empiricist attitudes 193
empiricist naturalism 93
empiricist tradition 217
engaged acknowledgement of problem 182
engagement
    as structure of 127–34
    with death 152
    with dying 153
    with the merely possible 152
    with self 152–4
entity, relations with 127
environmentalism 172–4
epistemic authority 215
epistemological behaviourism 92, 215–16
epistemological instrumentalism 63
epistemology
    anti-representationalist critique of 209
    of ethics 101
    and fallibilism 189
    foundationalism in 38, 86–7
    repudiation of 66–8
equality in communities 239–40, 244–7
Essays in Philosophical Criticism 106
essence of belief 25
Ethics Without Philosophy 159
everyday practicalities 217
evidential holism 42
evolution 65, 240
Evolutionary Love 256

experience 212–14, 275–8
    and art 280
    collective social 333
    developing underlying quality of 281
    Dewey on 59, 107–8, 279–82
    emotional, specificity of 287
    as inchoate 280
    integrated quality 280
    lived 284
    as method 57
    and participation 339–40
    as social 339–40
    structures and forms 292
    as stuff 57
Experience and Education 71–2
Experience and Nature 74–6
experiential approach, to aesthetics 59–60
experiential depth 279–82
experiential enquiry 332
experimentalism 58, 195
explanatory power 135
explicit theory/metaphysics, emphasis on 174
expressive art and emotional meaning 286
extensional language 90
extensionalism 102–3
extensionality theory (Quine) 89, 95
extentional contexts 89
extra-linguistic fact 91

Fach (Rorty) 304
fact–value dualism 189
fact/value distinction 88, 99–103
fallacy of misplaced concreteness 256
fallibilism 19, 21–2, 86, 89, 97–8, 114, 189
falsehoods, preponderance of 48
family communities 131
fear 182
feminism and pragmatism 231–47
final truth 320
Firstness, Secondness and Thirdness (Peirce) 108–9, 114
The Fixation of Belief 8, 12, 18–20, 253
flesh and spirit 277–8
flexible intellectual interest 254
flexible/firm temperaments 258–61
flight from intention 89–91
for-the-sake-of 154

Index

Forms, Plato's separation of 256
foundationalist epistemology 38, 93
Franklin, Benjamin 252
free will problem 39
freedom 238
Fregean notion of Sinn 129
Freud, Sigmund 159–60
functional psychology 60–2
functionalism 60, 70–1
funded experience 209

Gardner, Martin 263–4
Geist (mind) 115–16
general democratic culture 338
general theory of education 71
German idealism 105
Gestalt psychology 281, 288, 290–1
the given 210
global atomism 43
God's existence 302–3
Goodman, Nelson 189–90
grades of clarity 23
grammatical nexus 166
grasping fear 182
Green, Thomas Hill 106
Grey, Thomas 324
Griffiths, Paul E. 162
Groopman, Jerome 266
growth 60
Gunn, Giles 300, 302

habit 25, 331
   of action 302, 304, 312
   and intelligence 73
Haddock Seigfried, Charlene 231, 252
Hagberg, Garry 11–12
Hall, G. Stanley 60
Harris, W. T. 105
Hebraist tradition 314
Hegel, Georg Wilhelm Friedrich 9–10, 105
   renewed interest in 111–12
Hegelian historicism 255
Heidegger, Martin 9, 124–55
Heidegger's Pragmatism: Understanding, Being and the Critique of Metaphysics 9–10, 126
historic intellectualism 196
historical empiricism 281
historicism 215

holism
   and biological pragmatism 136–7
   and idealism 41–3
   of William James 36–50, 63
   of Quine 83, 91–9, 101
holistic practical competence 141
holistic trade-offs 45–6
Holmes, Oliver Wendell 17
Hook, Sidney 252
How Doctors Think 266
'How to Make our Ideas Clear' 2, 8, 18–20, 22–6, 31, 302
How We Decide 266
Hull House community 242–3, 252
human beings
   as creators of knowledge and truth 40–1
   dualistic representations of 40
   as holistically embedded creatures 40
human capacity, and democracy 341–2
human cognition 84–5
human engagement, *as* structure 127–34, 139
human experience 272–93
human happiness, and truth 319–20
human need, and religion 317
human reasoning 279
human thinking, independence of 46
humanism 3, 58, 105–6
Huntington, Samuel 269
hushed reverberations from the past 276
Hutchinson, Phil 10
hypothetico-deductive method of induction 100

idealism
   absolute 37, 42, 105–6, 194
   and holism 41–3
   and pragmatic realism 292
idealist metaphysics 41
ideas and ideology 254–5
ideas and impressions 281
identity theory of truth 182
ideology, fear of 338
imagination
   in metaphysics 200–1
   and objectivity 219–20
   role of 219–20
   and Romantic philosophy 221
   and truth 216–25

imaginative self-creation 316
immanence doctrine of truth 96–9
imperialism, and empiricism 163
impressions, and ideas 281
induction 31
  hypothetico-deductive method 100
inductive reasoning 22
inferential semantics 119–20
inquiry 20, 58, 60, 68–70, 189
instrumental enquiry 60
instrumental epistemology 59–60
instrumentalism 3, 58, 60, 65–6, 68–70
integrated quality of experience 280
intellectual hospitality 254
intellectual metaphysics 193
intellectual standards and pragmatism 44
intellectualism 195–6
intelligence, and habit 73
intensional agents engagement 132–3
intensional engagement 131, 134, 143
intensionality 141, 154–5
intention 90–1
intentional claims 89
intentional directedness 127
intentional engagement 142
intentionality 127, 141, 150, 154–5, 189–90
interpretative involvement 149
introspectionism 60–2
irrationalism 43–4, 47
irrealism 189–90
irreducibility 90
irritation of doubt 20
Issues of Pragmaticism 32–3
itself *as* itself 150

Jackson, Frank 192
James, William
  on absolute idealism 42
  characterizations of pragmatism 1
  early critics of 36–7
  God's existence 302–3
  habits of action 302
  on Hegel 109–11
  holism of 36–50, 63
  influence on Dewey 57
  knower as actor 85
  and metaphysics 193–5, 198
  overriding epistemic moral 46–7
  Pascal's wager 302–4

pluralism of 37
pragmatic theory of truth 256
and pragmatism 43–7
on psychology 161–2
radical empiricism of 42–3, 49–50, 161–2, 304
and the reflex arc 62–3
on religion 301–7, 300–1
and shift in philosophy 44
on types of temperament 256–7
Varieties of Religious Experience 307, 318
The Will to Believe 176, 260, 304–7, 318
and Wittgenstein 160–4
Journal of Speculative Philosophy 105, 113
justice, language of 330

Kant, Immanuel, influence on Peirce 18, 66–8, 118–19, 128–9, 251, 314
knowing 58–9
knowledge 68–70
  non-representational account of 224

language
  and causal sensitivity 221
  Davidsonian concept of 219
  of justice 330
  and meaning 221
  and metaphor 221–3
  non-representational account of 224, 255
Le Roy, Edouard 251
Lectures on Pragmatism 25, 30–1, 33
legal pragmatism 324, 328–9
Lehrer, Jonah 266
Lewis, C. I. 83–4
liberal individualism 171
liberty 238
linguistic assertions 143
linguistic evidence/practice 284
linguistic idealism 220
linguistic meaning 125–6
  and emotive content 291
linguistic reframing 176
linguistic turn 76, 223
live creature 273–9, 281, 291
lived experience 284, 329
Logic: The Theory of Inquiry 29, 74–5

Index

logic
   and clarity 22–4
   conventionalism in 94
   proving 29–30
   and science 21
   transcendental 66
logical positivism 33–4, 86, 190–1, 196
Lord, Audre 131
love of truth 317
Lovejoy, Arthur O. 249
Luban, David 330

Macarthur, David 6, 8
McDermott, John 300
McDowell, John 9–10, 112, 114
MacIntyre, Alasdair 111–12
Making it Explicit 114
map/territory split 218–19
materialism and theism 194
materialist attitudes 162
mathematical exactitude in philosophy 18
mathematical proof of pragmatism 19
maxim of pragmatism *see* pragmatist maxim
Mead, G. H. 72, 286
meaning 165–6
The Meaning of Truth 36, 193
meaning/fact distinction 102
means and ends 143, 331–4
medium, role in artistic expression 287
meliorism 59–60
   and role of philosophy 75
Menand, Louis 254–5
metaphilosophical attitude/stance 58
metaphor in language 221–3
metaphorical meanings 223
metaphysics 41, 189–204
Metaphysical Club 2, 17, 250
metaphysical disputes 194
metaphysical dualisms 65
metaphysical extensionalism 102–3
metaphysical fantasy 190
metaphysical realism 190, 199, 201–2, 224
metaphysical speculation 200
metaphysical systems 191, 200
metaphysical thinking 200
method
   of authority 253
   and pragmatism 253
   of tenacity 253
Mill, John Stuart 18, 317, 313
Miller, Marjorie 11
Millikan, Ruth 189–90
Mills, C. Wright 252
mind 60
Mind and World 114–16
mind-independent reality 21, 218
Mirror of Nature 159
Mitchell, Lucy Sprague 232, 240
modernization, of pragmatism 6
monistic idealism 110
monistic pluralism 109
monotheism, Hebraist tradition 314
Moore, G. E. 3, 36–8, 105
moral function, of metaphysics 196
moral right, and democracy 334
moral scepticism 306
moral sentiment 279
morality and art 276
morality touched by emotion 309–10
Morris, G. S. 106–7
Mounce, H. O. 165–7
multiple communities 237
My Pedagogic Creed 71–2
Myth of the Given 113, 115–16

NASA study 266
natural embeddedness 212
natural realism 199
naturalism 58, 68, 118
naturalist pragmatism 134–5, 139, 143, 154–5
naturalist-extentionalist perspective 94
nature
   concept of 118
   disenchanted concept of 117
   and spontaneity 117
nature/culture divide 115
neopragmatism 76
neutrality of pragmatism 325, 327, 338
Nevo, Isaac 9, 37
New Pragmatism 7
The New Psychology 60–2
Nicholson, Carol 11
Nicomachean Ethics 282
Niebuhr, Reinhold 252
nihilism 87
No Child Left Behind policy 265

Noe, Alva 135, 145
nominalism 27, 32–3
nominalist conception of reality 28
non-cognitivism 199
non-cognitivist ethics 87
non-contradiction 94
non-intentional agents 131
non-linguistic stratagems 176
non-reductive emergent naturalism 118
nonaesthetic, twin poles of 281–2
normativity 147–8
noumenal world 218

Obama, Barack 258–61
Ode 279
Okrent, Mark 9–10
Olmstead, Frederick Law 252
On Humans and Environment: The Role of Consciousness in Environmental Problems 170–7
ontological metaphysics 18
operationalism 58
opportunism 265
organisms-in-environments 60–2
outside observer *see* spectator
over-belief 307
Owl of Minerva 173

Papini, Giovanni 249, 251, 253, 258
Parkman, Shaun 10, 170–7
participation, democratic 339–40
Pascal's wager 302–4
Pater, Walter 279
pathological social problems 236
patriarchal prejudices 239–40
Peirce, Charles Sanders
    agent's conception of an object 124–5
    ambivalence to Hegel 108–9
    anti-Cartesian message 57
    doubt, enquiry and method of science 12
    Evolutionary Love 256
    first rule of logic 265
    Firstness, Secondness and Thirdness 108–9
    and *The Fixation of Belief* 8, 12
    habits of action 302, 304
    and *How to Make our Ideas Clear* 2, 8, 18–20, 22–6, 31, 302
    logic of 23
    as originator of pragmatism 12
    on pragmatic temperament 261–2
    and pragmatist maxim 22–6, 29–32
    on realism and pragmatism 32–4
    on religion 300–1
    on truth and reality 26–9, 256
    and Wittgenstein 159, 164–9
Peirce–Wittgenstein nexus 168
perception 63–4
perceptual experience 64
perceptual integration 281
phenomenological access, to the world 138
phenomenological methodology 138–9
Phenomenology of Spirit 110, 113–14
Philosophical Conceptions and Practical Results 1–2
philosophical dichotomies 86
Philosophical Investigations 165–7
philosophical naturalism 73
philosophical theorizing 325
philosophy
    as criticism 74–5
    and living 74–6
    melioristic role of 75
Philosophy as Cultural Politics 316
Philosophy and the Mirror of Nature 10, 210, 215–16, 311
phyrrhonistic scepticism 305
physiological psychology 60–2
pictures and metaphysics 201
Pittsburgh Hegelians 114
Platonic epistemology 38, 93
Plato's Forms 200
pluralism 105–6
    in community 241–2
A Pluralistic Universe 109
Poincaré, Henri 251
political valence, of pragmatism 325, 335, 338–42
polytheism 317–18
populist democracy 335
positivism 162
Posner, Richard 12, 324–43
poststructuralist theory 284
potentiality-for-Being 153
practical consequences 39, 43, 45
practical difference 39, 43
practical relevance and utility 209
practical starting point 59–60

Index

practice and pragmatism 11
practice-superior reality 46–7
practice-transcendent reality 46
pragmatic adjudication 324–6
pragmatic aesthetics 272–93
pragmatic realism and idealism 292
Pragmatic Sanction of Bourges 263
pragmatic temperament 249–70
pragmatic verification 136, 138
pragmaticism 3, 19
Pragmatism 36, 38, 44, 193, 251
pragmatism
   adverbial interpretation 251, 257, 268
   alternative terms for 3, 58, 250–1, 263–5
   as attitude 334
   British 251
   and dogmatism 264
   early American beginnings 250
   early criticism of 3
   first use of term 1–2
   French 251
   as happy harmonizer 256–7
   as humanism 57
   as instrument of cultural change 216
   Italian 251
   and method 253
   nature of 84–91
   as neutral 325, 327, 338
   as philosophical school 256
   and philosophical theorizing 325
   political valence of 325, 335, 338–42
   Posner's account of 327–38
   radical 324–43
   and relativism 263
   use of term 263–5
Pragmatism, Categories and Language 10
Pragmatism and Feminism: Reweaving the Social Fabric 231
Pragmatist Feminism 231
pragmatist maxim 18, 22–34
pragmatist method 1, 39
Pragmatist Philosophy of Education 268
pragmatist tradition, Rorty on 208–11
pragmatist verificationism 126
pragmatist-holist perspective 94
Pratt, Scott L. 252
Praxis and Action 111
precautionary principle 179

precedent 326
prefiguration 278
Prezzolini, Giuseppe 251
Price, Huw 7
principle of Peirce 17–18
principle of practicalism 1–2
The Principles of Psychology 62
private language 165
privileged representations 92
probability concept 24
problem of substance 39
prope-Hegelianism 120
prophetic pragmatist 258–61
psychic entities 62
Psychology 60–2
psychophysical dualism 63–4
The Public and its Problems 74, 134
pure cognitivists 178–9
Putnam, Hilary 5–8, 10, 37–8, 98–100, 102, 159, 162, 170, 189–204
   and metaphysics 198–204

The Quest for Certainty 59, 74–5
Quine, W. V. O. 3, 9, 38, 48, 83–103, 159, 203, 210

radical empiricism 3, 42–3, 49–50, 58, 75, 161–2, 193
radical pragmatism 324–43
rational argumentation 217
rationalism, and classical empiricism 66–8
rationalist metaphysics 193
rationalist pragmatism 119–20
rationality 215, 312
   results oriented 222
Read, Rupert 10, 173
realism 199
realism and pragmatism 32–4
realist concept of reality 27
reality 24, 26–9, 84
   and truth 26–9
reason as slave of passions 313
reasoning, human 279
reception theory 284
reconstructing psychology 62
Reconstruction in Philosophy 59
recontextualization of human life 292
redemption from egotism 315–16
reflection and sensation 281

reflex arc 62–4
The Reflex Arc Concept in Psychology 62, 71
regulative ideals 332
reification 255–6
relations with an entity 127
relativism 43, 97–8, 263, 300
religion
　attitudes to 309–10
　and fear of dark powers 310
　perspective on 310
　and pragmatism 320
　and the religious 307–11
　and romantic polytheism 317
　and science 310–11
Religion as Conversation-Stopper 312
Religion and our Schools 308
religious faith 310–11
religious fundamentalism 317
religious impulse 318
religious naturalism 308–9
religious toleration 315
Renewing Philosophy 189–90
representation 85, 128–9
representationalists 130, 133
Rescher, Richard 9
results oriented rationality 222
revision 94
reward/penalty axis 100
romantic polytheism 317–18
Rorty, Richard 5–8, 10, 12, 38, 41, 44, 49–50, 76, 87–8, 92, 99, 111–13, 120, 159, 162, 207–25, 250, 255, 269, 300–1, 304, 317
Royce, Josiah 42, 105–6, 109
Russell, Bertrand 3, 36–8, 105, 265, 300

Santayana, G. 276
scepticism 86
　of authority 308
　Cartesian 40–1
　moral 306
　phyrrhonistic 305
scheme/content distinction 218–19
Schiller, F. C. S. 32, 249, 251
scholastic doctrine of realism 32–4
The School and Society 71–2
Schumpeter, Joseph 335
Schutzian phenomenology 170
science and logic 21

science/ethics distinction 101
scientific method 212–14
scientific theory, empirical underdetermination of 95–9
self
　of child 72
　engagement with 152–4
　and known objects 65
self-constitutive interaction 274–5
self-creation 316
self-directed intentionality 150
self-examination 138
self-formation 342
self-government 339
self-integration 277, 289
self-interpretation 138
self-knowledge 289
self-reliance 308, 318
self-responsibility 318
selfhood 131
Sellars, Wilfrid 9–10, 92, 112–15, 150, 204, 210
semantic doctrine of truth 96, 98
semantic holists 136
semantic significance 138
sensation and reflection 281
sensational empiricism 65
Sense Certainty 114
sensori-motor coordinations 62
sensory experience 275–8
Shusterman, Richard 213
signs and representation theory 32
Sinn (sense or meaning) 129
skepticism *see* scepticism
Smith, John E. 300
Smith, Nicholas 312–16, 319
Smith, Steven 325
social customs, and habit 331–2
social embeddedness 212
sociocultural matrix 70
Solove, Daniel J. 12
Some Consequences of Four Incapacities 21
Some Stages of Logical Thought 65–6
Sorel, Georges 251
soul, religious notions of 40
specific intellectual 176
spectator, creative role of 283–93
spectator model of knowing 64
spectator theory of knowledge 209

Index

spiritual sentiment 279
spontaneity 113, 117–18
   in art 290–1
spontaneity/receptivity distinction 88
Sprigge, Timothy 37, 42
standard meanings 223
Stout, Jeffrey 224
Strawson, P. 204
stream of consciousness 62
structural coherence, in art 288
Studies in Logical Theory 66
Stuhr, John 337
subject/object dichotomy 91, 163
subject/object dualism 218–19
subjectivism 43, 64, 300
substance 39
Suckiel, Ellen Kappy 42
Sullivan, Michael 12
super-empirical reason 67
supernaturalism 338

Taft, Jessie 232
Talisse, Robert 4–5
Tamanaha, Brian 327
Tarski, on truth 96, 98–9
Taylor, Charles 111–12
teleological context 131
teleological function 140
teleological significance 140
teleological structure 143–55
teleology
   of action 134
   and harmonic resolution 275
temperament
   mixtures 257–8
   types of 256–61
Thayer, H. S. 210
theism *see* monotheism, polytheism, religion
theoretical starting points 75
theory and practice 327–38
theory/given distinction 92
thick moral concepts 102
Thielman, Greg 259
third dogma of empiricism 92–3
traditional epistemology 196
traditional metaphysics 86, 192–3
traditional philosophical problems 223
transcendence 98–9
translation 89

Trilling, Lionel 252
truth 68–70, 86, 88–9, 305
   coherence theory of 41
   correspondence theory of 101, 301–2
   final 320
   in general 91
   and human happiness 319–20
   identity theory of 182
   and imagination 216–25
   immanence doctrine of 96–9
   James's theory of 256
   logical 94
   loving 317
   non-immanent 92–3
   practical outcome of 28
   Quine on 95–9
   and reality 26–9
   and utility 209
Two Dogmas of Empiricism 83, 94

ultimate reality 90–1
uncertainty 266
unconditional interpretants 32
Understanding of Being 151
unit of empirical significance 95
universals and reality 27
utilitarianism 313

valuation, bipartite nature of 101
value commitments 332
Van Niekerk, Anton 12
Varieties of Religious Experience 307, 318
verification 125–6, 219–20
Verstand (understanding) 113
virtue 281–2

Wallace, David Foster 220
web image 41
web metaphor 221
West, Cornel 252, 258–61
Westbrook, Robert 2, 250
Whipp, Judy 231
White, Morton 86
Whitehead, Alfred North 256
wider self 307
The Will to Believe 176, 260, 304–7, 318
Williams, Bernard 189–90
Williams, Jerry 10, 170–7
Williams, Roger 252
wisdom 60, 74–6

Wittgenstein, Ludwig 9–10, 159–83
   and Freud 159–60
   and James 160–4
   on metaphysics 191
   and Peirce 164–9
Wittgenstein-pragmatism nexus 10, 159, 169–71, 191
words as tools 222

world-taking cognitivism 181–3
would-be knowers, laws for 305
Wright, Chauncey 17
Wundt, Wilhelm 60

X (Socratic question) 203

Young, Ella Flagg 232, 240